Violet Oaklander, Ph.D.

Windows to Our Children

A GESTALT THERAPY APPROACH
TO CHILDREN AND ADOLESCENTS

A Publication of the Gestalt Journal Press

This book was originally published by Real People Press in 1978.

Cover artwork by Kevin R. Sweeney.

Copyright © 2015 The Gestalt Journal Press

Published by:

The Gestalt Journal Press
P.O. Box 278
Gouldsboro, Maine 04607

Printed in the United States of America. All rights reserved. This book or parts thereof may not be reproduced in any form without the written permission of the publisher.

ISBN: 978-1-938304-02-6

*This book is dedicated to the memory of my son
Michael*

Contents

Introduction to the 2015 Edition	ix
Foreword	xiii
Introduction to *The Gestalt Journal* Edition	xv

1. *Fantasy* — 1

2. *Drawing and Fantasy* — 21
- Your World — 21
- Family Drawings — 27
- The Rosebush — 34
- The Scribble — 39
- Anger Pictures — 45
- My Week, My Day, My Life — 48
- The Squiggle — 48
- Colors, Curves, Lines and Shapes — 49
- Group Drawing — 50
- Free Drawing — 51
- Painting — 52
- Finger Painting — 54
- Foot Painting — 55

3. *My Working Model* — 57
- More Ideas for Fantasy and Drawing — 68

4. *Making Things* — 73
- Clay — 73
- Other Exercises with Clay — 82
- Plastic Modeling Clay — 83
- Dough — 84
- Water — 85
- Sculpture and Constructions — 85
- Wood and Tools — 87
- Collage — 87
- Pictures — 90
- Tarot Cards — 91

5. Storytelling, Poetry and Puppets	93
Storytelling	93
Books	99
Writing	103
Poetry	106
Puppets	113
Puppet Shows	115
6. Sensory Experience	119
Touch	120
Sight	121
Sound	124
Music	125
Taste	130
Smell	130
Intuition	131
Feelings	133
Relaxation	135
Meditation	137
Body Movement	138
7. Enactment	149
Creative Dramatics	149
Touch	152
Sight	152
Sound	153
Smell	153
Taste	153
The Body	154
Pantomiming Situations	154
Characterization	155
Improvisations with Words	155
Dreams	158
The Empty Chair	164
Polarities	171

8. *Play Therapy*	173
The Sand Tray	180
Games	186
Projective Tests as Therapeutic Technique	189
9. *The Therapy Process*	195
The Child Comes into Therapy	195
The First Session	199
What My Office is Like	206
The Process of Therapy	207
Resistance	210
Termination	214
10. *Specific Problem Behaviors*	221
Aggression	222
Anger	225
The Hyperactive Child	238
The Withdrawn Child	248
Fears	255
Specific Stress Situations or Traumatic Experiences	265
Physical Symptoms	271
Insecurity, Hanging on, Excessive Pleasing	279
The Loner	284
Loneliness	287
The Child Who is In and Out of Reality	290
Autism	293
Guilt	296
Self-esteem, Self-concept, Self-image	300
11. *Other Considerations*	307
Groups	307
Adolescents	313
Adults	321
The Older Adult	322
Siblings	323
Very Young Children	324
The Family	327
Schools, Teachers, and Training	334
Sexism	340

12. Interview with Violet Oaklander, Ph.D.	343
A Personal Note	399
About the Author	405
Bibliography	407
Index	417

Introduction to the 2015 Edition

This year marks the thirty-fifth anniversary of the publication of *Windows to Our Children* by Real People Press. In 1978, when this book first appeared, there were only two or three English language books available that described what actually happens in a therapy session with a child.

While earning her Masters in Special Education in 1971, Violet Oaklander read the available child psychotherapy books. She was fascinated, especially with *Dibs in Search of Self* by Virginia Axline and with Clark Moustakas's work, but found that the books did not teach what to do in therapy with children. She was also looking for an effective way to provide children more timely relief from the symptoms they were experiencing. The transient military and low-income families of the children she was working with couldn't support the lengthy psychoanalytic approach.

In 1973, drawing on ideas she had developed during her years as a camp counselor, teacher, special education teacher, her experiences with Gestalt therapy, and with her own children, Violet wrote a very long paper describing how to work with children. That paper, written as she was interning for her Masters in Psychological Counseling and teaching a class at Chapman College, eventually came to be the outline for *Windows to Our Children*.

It was, however, the ever present question, "What do you *do* with the kid?" that was asked as Violet gave workshops through the Gestalt Therapy Institute of Los Angeles and the repeated requests from therapists and counselors for additional written materials that prompted Violet to begin writing this book.

Windows to Our Children describes a Gestalt therapy approach to children and adolescents. It isn't easy to give a brief description of the Gestalt therapy theory upon which Violet's approach is based. In the interview that appears at the end of this edition, Violet identifies places where she has written more about the theoretical underpinnings of this work. A good place to begin to find that material is in her article in *The Gestalt Journal*, Volume 5, No. 1. In essence, the work of Gestalt therapy is to enhance awareness of the phenomenological field through experiential work and attention to the contact functions seeing, hearing, smelling, tasting, touching, moving, and sensing all done in the context of an I-Thou relationship which is authentic, honest, clear and respectful.

Applying Gestalt therapy theory to work with children and adolescents results in a creative and experiential approach that enhances the child's sense of self through awareness, and replaces interruptions of contact with presence. Violet says, "I don't fix kids." Inherent in this remark is her adherence to an authentic approach which respects and values children's experience. Violet's approach carves out space for self-discovery. Her tools allow children to find their emergent self and their own unique path and to bring those qualities into life effectively. As you read through these chapters, you'll discover that the therapeutic setting Violet describes here is rich and vibrant with a multitude of materials to facilitate experiential work, including such varied and diverse media as puppets, paints, pastels, paper, clay, musical instruments, games, books, writings, batakas, sand tray, water, toys and dolls.

The material in this book predates the writings of neurobiologist Daniel Siegel and others who have recently highlighted the importance of an approach to human well-being that integrates mindfulness and attachment. The exercises in this book are the exact processes that allow for a deepened development of one's sensory awareness. And they do that in the context of relational work. They facilitate growth and change, emerging from awareness and the use of the contact functions. You will see, evidenced in the stories she shares here, how Violet's presence with children is characterized by her delight and joy in their process.

Introduction to the 2015 Edition

As soon as the first edition of this book was published, Violet began receiving stacks of fan mail from counselors, therapists and teachers who were using *Windows to Our Children* in their work. There was no book tour, but Violet received invitations to speak about her work and to train therapists in her approach, which now has become known as "The Oaklander Model." She traveled throughout the U.S. and to Ireland, Germany, Israel, Australia, Canada, Mexico, Brazil, South Africa, Italy and Spain. For many years Violet traveled to some far away city once or twice every month to teach.

In 1982, Violet offered the first of her annual two-week summer residential training programs based on the material in *Windows to Our Children*. For twenty-six years, those trainings attracted therapists and counselors from the U.S., Canada, Mexico, Finland, Sweden, Norway, Turkey, Ireland, Scotland, England, Belgium, Germany, Switzerland, Czech Republic, Yugoslavia, Italy, Saudi Arabia, Israel, Jordan, South Africa, Brazil, Argentina, El Salvador, Guatemala, New Zealand, Australia, China, Taiwan, Okinawa, South Korea, Mexico, Chile, and Cyprus. For the two dozen or more participants, each training provided tools for enriching their work with children and adolescents, as well as opportunities to build deep connections within the group and to reconnect with their own childhood experiences.

"*Windows*," as this book has come to be known by those around Violet, has provided the answer to that "What-do-you-do-with-the-kid?" question for thousands of therapists and counselors world-wide. Since its initial publication, *Windows to Our Children* has been published in fourteen other languages: German, Portuguese, Hebrew, Croatian, Serbo-Croatian, Korean, Japanese, Spanish, Russian, Chinese, Czech, Italian, and Lithuanian, and soon to be published in French and Georgian. The English language edition is used widely as a text in the U.S., Canada, New Zealand, Australia, the United Kingdom, and South Africa. Her second book *Hidden Treasure* has been translated into German, Russian, Lithuanian, Czech, Korean and Spanish.

In 2003 the Violet Solomon Oaklander Foundation (www.vsof.org) was formed to continue to further Violet's work. Trainers from VSOF now are teaching her approach in Lithuania, Kyrgyzstan, Russia, Brazil,

France and Italy. The foundation continues to receive requests for training worldwide.

Violet's level of productivity has been astounding. Her thorough research of child psychotherapy exemplifies her dedication to the field. In addition to teaching throughout the world, she has written, written and written — chapters for books, articles for journals, scripts for audiotapes.

There now are additional books available on the subject of what you actually *do* with the child in psychotherapy. Several of those are based on Violet's model such as Rinda Blom's *Handbook of Gestalt Play Therapy*, published in 2006, and anthologies such as Charles Schaefer's *Foundations of Play Therapy*, which include chapters written by Violet.

Violet has been recognized by the Association for Play Therapy and was featured as one of the "State of the Art" faculty at *The Evolution of Psychotherapy Conference* in 2009. In the spring of 2012 the Reiss-David Child Study Center and Institute honored Violet as the Eighth Edna Reiss-Sophie Greenberg Chair. She is one of the featured therapists in the Psychotherapy.net video series "Child Therapy with the Experts Series."

Violet is a master clinician and trainer of child psychotherapy. This is timeless material and I welcome you to the discoveries ahead.

— *Christiane Elsbree*
November 26, 2012

Foreword

When I read the manuscript of this book I thought, "Everyone must be interested in it — everyone who has anything to do with children."

I didn't notice that my "everyone" left someone out.

When the galley proofs were being read aloud to check them against the manuscript, Summer, age seven, came in. She started drawing crayon designs. She didn't fuss or fidget; she didn't ask her mother when she was going home. She was exquisitely quiet, listening to this book being read aloud. Later, she said that she liked it.

A substantial part of this book is children speaking of themselves, with the honesty that Violet Oaklander makes possible for them. Who should be more interested in this than another child? Yet when I thought of people who would be interested, I saw only grownups: therapists, teachers, parents. I did not include the people the book is about. Violet shows that this is a prime cause of many of the difficulties that children get into. We adults often exclude them from information and expression, leaving them in confusion.

Pause for a moment to recall your own childhood, and your struggles to understand the grown-up world . . .

Violet remembers clearly, and this is an important part of her knowledge and understanding of children. She has all the official credentials, but her experiences with children and her memories of her own childhood are far more important. This is what she relies on for her unique understanding of "how they have lost themselves."

WINDOWS TO OUR CHILDREN

Some grownups have never found themselves. For them, this book can be a beginning of self-discovery: a refinding of parts of themselves that were left behind in childhood.

Violet says that she didn't originate any of the methods she uses. But the way that she uses them is highly original and creative, a flexible living gestalt: "I go where my observation and intuition direct, feeling free to change direction at any time." The full range of her senses is involved as she moves with the children in the rediscovery of their own experiencing. She is at ease with her mistakes, mentions them in passing, and says, "I believe there is no way you can make a mistake if you have good will and refrain from interpretation and judgements." (Most of us have the good will; few of us refrain from judgements, or even notice that we are interpreting.)

Violet talks with children in a simple, direct way — a way that most of us would like to be talked to all the time, but seldom experience, even with close friends and intimates.

"I launch into a big explanation . . . and then finally I say, 'Debby, as a matter of fact I really don't know for sure.'"

"We talked about her loneliness for a while, and then I told her something about my own loneliness."

This book can be a window to the child within you, as well as to the children you are with.

—*Barry Stevens*
June 1978

Introduction
To
The Gestalt Journal Edition

Debby (age nine): "How do you make people feel better?"
"What do you mean?" (Obviously I'm stalling.)
Debby: "Well, when people see you they feel better. What do you do to make that happen? Is it hard to do?"
"It sounds like maybe you feel better."
Debby: (nodding vigorously) "Yes! Now I feel better. How come?"

I launch into a big explanation of getting people to tell about their feelings, how I do this, how I did it with her, and finally I say, "Debby, as a matter of fact I really don't know for sure."

* * *

I wrote the above paragraphs more than ten years ago and since that time I've spent great amounts of time trying to answer Debby's question. I can't honestly say today that I don't know what makes people feel better since I'm much closer to the answer than I was then. I have a much clearer idea about the therapeutic process with children and how, with the right kind of experiences, the organism pushes its way toward healthful life and growth.

In these ten years I've been in contact with literally hundreds of children and families and probably thousands of people who work with children all over the world. All of these people have been my teachers and have helped me come closer to the answer to Debby's question. This book has traveled even further than I have and from the thousands of letters I have received, some of the most heartfelt letters I have ever read, I know that this book has served the purpose that I had hoped it would.

I feel privileged to have found effective ways of helping children ease through some difficult passages in their lives. The world has not been kind to children in these last ten years. What I do find encouraging is the increased awareness for the needs of children. I have written this book to share my experiences with those of you who know these needs and are looking for ways to help children grow strong in spite of the traumas of their lives.

A decade is a long time. When I read through this book, I am still deeply attuned to what I wrote those ten years earlier. Yet I am acutely aware of wanting to say more at every page. I have been enriched by many, many more children, have had incredible experiences with them; I have expanded on many of the techniques described here and have developed some wonderful new ones. I have been excited about new concepts and reorganized some old ones. I have found many new resources to help me, and those I teach, in our work. All of this is to be expected. I revel in the fact that as I get older, I continue to stretch my own boundaries. Perhaps there will be time some day to come to include these new learnings in a new book. Meanwhile, I hope that this good old one will continue to reach out and inspire.

— Violet Oaklander
Santa Barbara, California

1

Fantasy

"In a minute I'm going to ask all of you in the group to close your eyes and I will take you on an imaginary fantasy trip. When we are finished, you will open your eyes and draw something that will be at the end of this trip. Now, I'd like you to get as comfortable as you can, close your eyes, and go into your space. When you close your eyes, there's a space that you find yourself in. It's what I call your space. You take up that space in this room and wherever you are, but you don't usually notice it. With your eyes closed, you can get a sense of that space — where your body is, and the air that's around you. It's a nice place to be, because it's your place, it's your space. Notice what's going on in your body. Notice if you're tense anywhere. Don't try to relax these places where you might be tight and tense. Just notice them. Run down your body from your head to your toes and take notice. How are you breathing? Are you taking deep breaths or are you breathing with small, quick breaths? I would like you to take a couple of very deep breaths now. Let the air out with some sound. Haaaaaaah. OK. I'm going to tell you a little story now, and take you on a make-believe trip. See if you can follow along. Imagine what I tell you, and see how you feel while you're doing it. Notice if you like going on this little trip, or if you don't. When you come to parts you don't like, you don't have to go there. Just listen to my voice, follow along if you want to, and let's just see what happens.

"I want you to imagine that you're walking through the woods. There are trees all around and there are birds singing. The sun is coming through the trees, and it's shady. It feels very nice walking through these woods. There are little flowers, wild flowers, along the side. You're walking along the path. There are rocks along the sides of the path and every now and then you see a small animal scurrying away, a little rabbit maybe. You're walking along, and soon you notice the path is rising and you're going uphill. Now you know you are climbing a mountain. When you reach the top of the mountain, you sit on a large rock to rest. You look around. The sun is shining; birds are flying around. Across the way, with a valley in between, is another mountain. You can see that on the mountain there is a cave, and you wish you could be on that mountain. You notice that the birds are flying over there easily, and you wish you were a bird. Suddenly, because this is a fantasy and anything can happen, you realize that you have turned into a bird! You test your wings, and sure enough you can fly. So you take off and easily fly to the other side. (Pause to give time for flying.)

"On the other side you land on a rock and instantly turn back into yourself. You climb around the rocks looking for an entrance to the cave, and you see a small door. You crouch down and open it and enter the cave. When you are inside there's plenty of room to stand up. You walk around examining the walls of the cave and suddenly you notice a walkway — a corridor. You walk down this corridor and soon you notice there are rows and rows of doors, each with a name written on it. All of a sudden you come to a door with your name on it. You stand there in front of your door, thinking about it. You know that you will open it soon and go to the other side of that door. You know that it will be your place. It might be a place you remember, a place you know now, a place you dream about, a place you don't even like, a place you never saw, an inside place or an outside place. You won't know until you open the door. But whatever it is, it will be your place.

"So you turn the knob and step through. Look around at your place! Are you surprised? Take a good look at it. If you don't see one, make one up right now. See what's there, where it is, whether it is inside or out. Who is there? Are there people, people you know or don't know? Are there animals? Or is no one there? How do you feel in this place. Notice how you feel. Do you feel good or not so good? Look around, walk around your place. (Pause.)

Fantasy

"When you are ready, you will open your eyes and find yourself back in this room. When you open your eyes, I would like you to get some paper and crayons, or felt pens or pastels, and draw your place. Please do not talk while you do this. If you must say something, please whisper. If you don't have the right colors for your place, feet free to come quietly and get what you need, or borrow from someone else. Draw your place as best you can. Or if you want to, you can draw your feelings about the place, using colors, shapes, and lines. Decide whether you will put yourself in this place and where and how — as a shape or color or symbol. I don't have to know what your place is all about by looking at your picture; you will be able to explain it to me. Trust what you saw when you opened the door, even if you don't like it. You will have about ten minutes. Whenever you feel ready, you can begin."

A fantasy such as this needs to be told in a fantasy voice. It is told slowly with many pauses to give children a change to "do" the things I tell them to do. I often close my eyes and go through the fantasy myself as I tell it. I have done this kind of fantasy-drawing with individual children as well as in group settings, and with a variety of ages from about seven on up to adulthood. Here are some examples of the children's "places" and how I work with them.[*]

Linda, age thirteen, drew a picture of a bedroom which included a bed, a table, a chair, three dogs standing on the floor, and a picture of a dog on the wall. The picture was very neat and had many blank spaces. Linda described her picture. Since she was in a group, the other children asked questions such as, "What's that for?" and she answered them.

I asked Linda to choose something in the picture she would like to pretend to be. She chose the dog who was a picture on the wall. I asked her to talk as that dog picture and say what she looked like and what she was doing. She described herself: "I'm a picture up here on the wall." I asked her how it felt to be up there on the wall.

Linda: I feel — all alone. I don't like watching those dogs play.

Talk to those dogs down there and tell them that.

---

[*] The children's drawings appearing here are the original drawings. The major features of some have been enhanced with a felt pen or crayon for clearer reproduction.

WINDOWS TO OUR CHILDREN

Linda: I don't like being up here watching you play. I'd like to come off the wall and join in with you on the floor.

Do you, Linda the girl, ever feel that way, like the dog in the picture?

Linda: Yes! That dog is really me. I'm always on the outside.

I'd like to know if you feel that way here too now.

Linda: Yes, I feel that way here too. But maybe not so much now.

What are you doing here that makes it not so much, now?

Linda: (Very thoughtful voice) Well, I'm doing something. I'm not just sitting here doing nothing but looking like that dog on the wall.

I asked Linda to give me a sentence to write on her picture that would best sum it up. "I'd like to come off my wall and join in."

I often ask children to tell me a sentence to write on the picture, and their statements often sum up in a very succinct manner where they are in their lives. Providing Linda with a channel for becoming more aware of her stance in life, to be able to own it, is my goal for her. With increased awareness comes the opportunity for change. In this piece of work she not only gave voice to her feelings of loneliness and isolation, but she allowed herself to experience something different, a joining in. Moreover, I think it sank in that she could take responsibility for her life, that she could do something about her loneliness.

Fantasy

Tommy, age eight, drew a picture of the baby Jesus, Mary, and the wise men bearing gifts. (It was close to Christmastime.)

After he described his picture, I asked him to lie down on some pillows and be the baby. With much giggling he did. I said that the other children would be the wise men and I would be the Mother. We all acted out a little scene of bringing gifts and talking about this wonderful baby. My own enthusiastic hamming it up provided a good model for the other children to follow. Tommy became very quiet. As he lounged on the pillows, his relaxed body and his serene smiling face evidenced complete enjoyment of the moment. I asked him how he liked being a baby. He said he liked it very much because he got so much attention.

You really like to get attention.
Tommy: Yes!
You would like to get more than you do.
Tommy: That's right!

Tommy asked me to write on his picture as his statement, "I like to be the middle of attention and get presents and then I'm happy."

In previous sessions, Tommy had to choose between staying in the group and waiting in another room because of his very disruptive activity.

WINDOWS TO OUR CHILDREN

He often made the choice of going into the other room, since he felt he "could not control himself." For the rest of this session Tommy participated and listened to the other children, and was not disruptive in any way. He remained calm and relaxed (this child had been diagnosed as "hyperactive"), and his questions and comments to the others about their pictures were sensitive and perceptive. Somehow Tommy had always managed to get attention through his disruptive behavior. The kind of experience he had in this particular session was a very important one for him; his disruptive behavior decreased markedly from that time on, and he got attention for himself through the beautiful wisdom he was able to display in our group.

In an individual session with me, twelve-year-old Jeff drew a picture of a castle with the faces of Donald Duck and Mickey Mouse peering through windows. He labeled this place Disneyland. He described it to me, telling me how much he loved Disneyland. I asked him for a sentence that I could write on his picture to sum up his place and his feelings about it. He dictated, "My place is Disneyland because I have FUN and I like the characters. Everything is happy there." My attention focused on his emphasis on the word fun, and his words "everything is happy there."

Fantasy

We talked a while about Disneyland and its characters, and then I asked him to tell me about the part of his life that was not so much fun. He did this easily, contrary to his prior resistance to getting into any unpleasant areas of his life.

Thirteen-year-old Lisa drew a desert scene, a typical theme of hers in drawing and sand tray work. Lisa was in a foster home, was classified as "pre-delinquent" by law enforcement authorities, was highly disruptive in school, had no friends, did not get along with the other children in her foster home, and generally characterized herself in speech, manner, and dress as "tough." Nothing bothered her. In this session she drew her desert, a snake and a hole. After she described her picture I asked her to be the snake, give it a voice as if it were a puppet, and describe her existence as a snake.

Lisa: I'm a snake, I'm long and dark, I live here in the desert, I look for food and then I go back into my hole.

Is that all you do? What do you do for fun?

Lisa: Nothing. There's no one around here to play with.

How does that feel?

Lisa: Very lonely.

Lisa, do you ever feel like that snake?

Lisa: Yes, I'm lonely.

WINDOWS TO OUR CHILDREN

Lisa then lost her tough-guy stance and began to weep. We talked about her loneliness for a while and I told her something about my own loneliness.

A fourteen-year-old boy, Glenn, drew a musical rock group called "The People." His statement: "A fantasy I've given up temporarily, sort of." This was the first time in several weeks of therapy that he was able or willing to admit to being interested in anything at all. His words, "temporarily, sort of" told me that something inside of him was opening up to the possibility that he might do something in life after all. Previously our sessions were involved with his despair; now we began to explore his hope.

Often children will draw places that are in direct opposition to their feelings of the present. Fantasy scenes with castles and princesses, knights and beautiful mountain retreats are common. Helping children tell about the feelings represented by these pictures opens the door to expression of their opposite feelings. I will sometimes ask a child to "draw a place you remember from your childhood as nice, or a place you know that is nice, either real or make-believe." Again, as with the cave fantasy exercise, I will ask them to close their eyes and go into their spaces, as I did in describing the first fantasy.

Fantasy

One boy, age thirteen, drew a scene from when he was seven. I wrote on his picture as he dictated, "This was when I was seven. We lived in Ohio. My Dad just got back from Vietnam. I was happy. But then he started making me tell him everything I do. My mother let me do anything when he was away. He bothers me. My brothers are climbing the tree. I wish they'd fall down and break their arms. I liked Ohio." Then in a very soft voice he began talking about his wanting to be free "just for little things." This child fidgeted constantly, and was considered hyperactive. He truly could not sit in one place for very long, and moved often in the group meetings. But when he finished talking, he lay down and fell fast asleep. In further sessions we looked at his picture and his statements — which I had written just as he had dictated — and talked about some of his ambivalent feelings, his shuttling between the then of his memory in Ohio and the now of his present life.

Most of what I write about in this book involves the use of fantasy. To anyone not convinced of the immense value of fantasy in the growth and development of children, I recommend highly Singer's very comprehensive book about children and fantasy, *The Child's World of Make-Believe*.[*] He and others have conducted numerous studies which show statistically that children who are able to be imaginative have higher IQs and are able to cope better, and that encouraging a child to be imaginative improves his or her ability to cope and learn.

Through fantasy we can have fun with the child and we can also find out what a child's process is. Usually her fantasy process (how she does things and moves around in her fantasy world) is the same as her life process. We can look into the inner realms of the child's being through fantasy. We can bring out what is kept hidden or avoided and we can also find out what's going on in the child's life from her perspective. For these reasons we encourage fantasy and use it as a therapeutic tool.

As I think about the value of fantasy for children, I remember a time in my own life when fantasy served me greatly. When I was five years old, I

---

[*] All books and other sources mentioned are in a bibliography at the end of this book, listed alphabetically by title.

was badly burned and had to be hospitalized for several months. Since that was before the days of penicillin, I was not allowed to have toys of any kind to play with for fear of infection. (I know this now; no one told me then.) Furthermore, visiting hours were quite limited, and I spent hour upon hour flat in bed with no one to talk to and nothing to play with. I survived this ordeal by immersing myself in fantasy. I told myself endless stories as I lay there, often getting very involved in the scenarios.

Some parents have asked me to distinguish between fantasy and lying. Others are worried that their children seem to get lost in a fantasy world. Lying is a symptom of something that is not right for the child. It is a mode of behavior rather than a fantasy, though sometimes the two become fused. Children lie because they are afraid to take a stand about themselves, to face reality as it is. They are often immersed in fear, self-doubt, a poor self-image, or guilt. They are unable to cope with the real world around them, and so they resort to defensive behavior, acting oppositely from how they really feel.

Often children are forced to lie by their parents. Parents may be too harsh or inconsistent, may have expectations too difficult for the child to meet, or may not be able to accept the child for who he is. The child is then forced to lie as a form of a self-preservation.

When a child lies, he often believes himself. He weaves a fantasy around the behavior that is acceptable to him. Fantasy becomes a means of expressing those things that he has trouble admitting as reality.

I take a child's fantasies seriously, as expressions of his feelings. Because other people generally do not hear, understand, or accept his feelings, neither does he. He does not accept himself. He must resort to a fantasy and subsequently to a lie. So here again it is necessary to begin to tune into the child's feelings rather than to his behavior. To begin to know him, to hear him, to understand him and accept him. The child's feelings are his very core. By reflecting his feelings to him, he too will begin to know and accept them. Only then can the lying be seen realistically for what it is: a behavior that the child makes use of for survival.

Children manufacture a fantasy world because they find their real world difficult to live in. When I work with such a child I may encourage

Fantasy

him to tell me about, and even elaborate, his fantasy images and notions, so that I can understand the child's inner world.

Children have a lot of fantasies of things that never really happened. Nevertheless, they are very real to these children and are often held inside, causing them to behave in sometimes inexplicable ways. These imagined-real fantasies often stir up feelings of fear and anxiety; they need to be brought out into the open to be dealt with and finished.

There are many different kinds of fantasy material. Children's imaginative play is a form of fantasy that can be extended into improvisational dramatics with older children. Another form of fantasy is storytelling in all its forms: talking, writing, puppetry, the flannel board. Poetry is fantasy as well as imagery and symbolism. There are long guided fantasies and short open-ended ones. Guided fantasies are generally done with eyes closed, but there are also eyes-open fantasies. Sometimes we express fantasy through a drawing or with clay.

Sometimes children resist closing their eyes. Some are frightened by the loss of control they feel with their eyes closed. If they protest, I will usually say, "Try it, and feel free to peek whenever you need to." Usually kids will close their eyes after a while, when they've found, after a couple of tries, that nothing terrible has happened. Asking them to lie on their stomachs as I tell the fantasy sometimes helps, too.

Some children just can't or won't let go into fantasy when directed to. Some are unwilling. Others are tight and constricted. Some at first think it's silly.

For those children who have trouble "getting into" a fantasy, it is helpful to begin with one in which the eyes are kept open.

Put Your Mother on the Ceiling, by Richard de Mille, has some excellent, irresistible, eyes-open fantasies. For example:

> This game is called Animals. We are going to start with one little mouse, and see what we can do. Let us imagine that there is a little mouse somewhere in the room. Where would you like to put him?/ All right, have him sit up and wave to you./ Have him turn green./ Change his color again./ Change it

> again./ Have him stand on his hands./ Have him run over to the wall./ Have him run up the wall./ Have him sit upside down on the ceiling./ Turn him right side up and put him in a corner up there./ Put another mouse in another corner up there./ Put another mouse in each of the other two corners up there./ Put other mice in the four corners down below./ Are they all there?/ Turn them all yellow./ Have them all say "Hello" at the same time./ Have them all say "How are you?"/ Have them all promise to stay in their corners and watch the rest of the game. (pp.56-58)

After doing this with a group of eleven and twelve-year-olds, one girl remarked, "I can never come into this room without checking my mice."

Another helpful opener for fantasies is to ask children to close their eyes and imagine they are standing in their living rooms (or any room). Have them look around. If they are able to do this, I tell them that they will have no trouble with fantasies. The Scribble technique, described later, is another helpful method for helping children to free themselves for fantasy work.

After children have had some experience with eyes-open fantasies, I like to start all further fantasies with an eye-closed, meditative exercise, as described in the beginning of the cave fantasy. Guided fantasies can be very brief. Ariel Malek, a colleague of mine, makes up her own. She has a series of excellent short guided fantasies. With her permission, here is one that I have used:

> Pretend that you notice something funny on your back. All of a sudden you notice that you are growing wings! How do these wings feel on your back? ... Try moving your wings and see how that feels ... Now look in the mirror and flap your wings ... Now, imagine you are walking up a hill with these new wings on your back. When you reach the top you open your new wings and soar through the air ... What can you see as you fly? How does it feel to be able to fly through the air?

Fantasy

Do you see other animals or people? Now imagine that you are going to land. When you land your wings will vanish and you'll be back in this room.

Six-year-old John drew himself heading straight for a black rock. He said, "I made something. I made a sun and a rock. I have a crash helmet. Then I put my head like this so my head will crash on the rock. I'll feel nausea. Go Superman!"
Do you wish you could fly?
John: Oh no, no, no.
Do you feel like you crash a lot in your life?
John: Yes!

WINDOWS TO OUR CHILDREN

His sister (present in the room): He always gets into trouble.
John: Yeah.
Tell me some of the ways you get into trouble. (John began to tell me very specifically about his troubles.)
Six-year-old Jill said of her picture, "I have an ugly person. I'm walking up the mountain. I've made my feet like birds'. I am just starting to fly off the mountain. I wish in my dreams that I was a huge bird and I could take the whole school on a trip. We have 150 kids in the school. My name is Jill. When the wind comes, it blows up my feathers."

Do you ever feel like an ugly person, Jill?
Jill: Yes! Some boys don't like me because they think I'm ugly. That makes me feel bad.
Do you wish sometimes that you could do something wonderful for everyone in your school and then all the kids would like you?
Jill: Yeah, like I wished in my story.
Then we talked some about Jill's feelings of being outside and rejected by the children at school. She had no friends and previous to this would never acknowledge this fact.

Fantasy

Eight-year-old Cindy said of her picture, "I flew off the mountain and I'm looking at the flowers and the nice green grass and my wings are silver. My name is Cindy. I wish I was a good witch and then I could fly home instead of walk."

Tell me about witches.

Cindy: Well, there are good witches and bad witches. Bad witches do bad things. Good witches are nice, and of course witches can fly on broomsticks.

Are you ever a bad witch?

Cindy: Well, my mother thinks I am!

Is your life always full of flowers and nice things?

Cindy: No! Only sometimes.

Cindy and I then talked some about her thinking that her mother thought of her as bad.

Twelve-year-old Karen drew a gorgeous butterfly. She said, "My wings are very lovely. I fly over water and mountains with the birds to a bright new green planet." In the distance was drawn a small green circle with yellow lines around it that gave the effect of energy coming from the planet.

Tell me some more about your new planet.

Karen: It's a beautiful place. Everything is new and green and there are no bad people there.

Are there bad people here in your life?

Karen: It seems like the world is full of bad people.

Indeed in Karen's life it seemed so to her. We continued to compare this world with her planet, with Karen expressing much feeling.

An excellent source for fantasy ideas is *Making It Strange*. This is a series of four 8 x 11 paperback books designed as creative writing workbooks. The fantasy ideas in these books are wonderful. Instead of using them for creative writing, I have adapted them for fantasy work. One that is a special favorite of mine is called *Fighting Back*:

> Write a story about a small boat in a big storm. The wind is wild, and the waves knock about the small boat. Try to imagine that you are the small boat and explain how you feel. Use

comparisons in your story to tell how it feels to BE a small boat in a big storm.

The wind shrieks and whines as it tries to sink the tiny boat. The boat fights back. Think of some kind of struggle in the animal world that is like the boat-storm situation. Write it here:

Describe why this animal struggle is like the boat-storm situation.

Imagine that you are the tiny boat. Tell what the different parts of your body must do to fight the storm.

How do the different parts of your body tell you whether you are winning or losing the fight?

Suddenly the wind makes one last attack on the little boat; then the wind dies. The boat has won! What real-life experiences have you had that are like the wind dying and the little boat winning the fight?

Imagine that you are the little boat who has just beaten the storm. How do you feel toward the storm?

Imagine that you are the great storm who can't even sink a tiny boat. How do you feel toward the boat? (Book 4, pp. 37-43)

Fantasy

There are many ways to use this fantasy. The most effective way for me is merely to ask the child (after a meditative breathing exercise) to imagine with eyes closed that he is a small boat in a big storm. I say something about the waves and the wind and the struggle. I ask the child to be the boat, to be aware of how he feels as this boat, what's happening now, what happens next. Then I will ask him to draw a picture of himself as this boat in a storm. Much material invariably comes forth about this child's place in his world and how he copes with outside forces.

Another exercise deals with a spider. A beautiful full-page photograph of a web is accompanied by instructions about being a spider trying to spin a web on a rainy, stormy day. In a children's group I used this idea to begin a continuation story. I started by saying, "Once upon a time there was a spider who was trying to build a web on a rainy, stormy day. Then . . ." And each child in turn added something to the story. After the story was finished, I asked the children to draw their thoughts of the spider building a web.

One boy, age nine, dictated to me as I wrote on the back of his picture, "My name is Irving. I have a web with a bunch of holes in it because of the rain and the rain made it different colors. Because people put chalk on top of it, and on the house. It turns blue. The fence turns all different colors. I feel nice and good at the people because they made my web different colors." In the course of our work together on this picture, he told us that he has been feeling very happy lately; things were going well for him.

In contrast, an eleven-year-old girl dictated, "I feel very mad. I can't make my web because of this gloomy and wet weather.

I feel like I just can't succeed my goal. I feel like a complete failure. No matter how hard I try, I can't build my web. But I'm determined and I won't give up." She very readily owned her feelings of failure and poured them out to us in the group. Each picture and story was different, revealing, and moving. Some had touches of humor, as one boy, age ten, said, "If this rain doesn't stop in a few minutes I'm gonna pick up my webs and start home."

In another group I asked the children to imagine, with eyes closed, that each was a spider, and to share out loud their experiences of being a spider building a web in the rain.

"I'm a spider. I don't live anywhere. I like to wander around. I have lots of friends but I wanted to be alone today and not be around anyone."

"I'm a spider. I like climbing up flowers. I like seeing flowers and birds. I feel kind of bad in this rain."

"I'm a black widow biting a boy."

"I was taking a walk. I tried to climb a flower but didn't make it to the top. I fell down."

In an exercise about a balloon that floats away (Book 3, p. 38) one girl drew a picture of a balloon floating over a city and said, "I like it out here; it's fun." She then added, "My Mommy always picks on me but I don't want to be free like a balloon." Another girl drew a similar picture saying, "I'm far away from my home and that's OK with me."

Ideas for fantasies abound. In the bibliography are many books where fantasy material can be found. Along with the new interest in humanistic education, the teaching of values in the schools, and stimulating the right hemisphere of the brain, there is a proliferation of books related to these subjects and containing many wonderful ideas. In the book, *Toward Humanistic Education*, there are several good fantasies presented that are especially suitable for teenagers.

Here is a fantasy I like. "You have been walking a very long time. You are very, very tired. You lie down to rest and you fall asleep. When you wake up you find yourself trapped. How are you trapped? Where are you trapped? What do you do?" Dr. Herbert Otto in his book, *Fantasy Encoun-*

Fantasy

ter Games, offers numerous fantasies similar to this one that can be modified to suit a variety of ages.

I have asked children to fantasize that they are an animal and, depending on the age of the child, to move and sound like one. I ask each child to be this animal, tell about herself, perhaps tell a story about herself.

I have a large old key I sometimes use in fantasy play to pretend to wind a child up to do a variety of things, and he can do the same to me. A magic wand works well, too.

Many art techniques lend themselves to fantasy use after the fact. String painting and butterfly pictures are interesting ink-blot-like forms. I have asked children to give these pictures titles, to tell me what they see in the pictures, to make up a story of the shape or object they see in one. Directions for making these pictures along with other good ideas can be found in books for preschool children's activities. It's too bad that many of us stop doing creative things at that level.

One of the most successful art-fantasy experiences I have had is drip painting with car paint, which can be purchased in auto supply stores and paint stores. This is how we manage it. First, it must be done in an area where messes are OK. It's best to cover the area well with newspaper. A couple of spoonfuls of white paint are dripped over a 5 x 7 inch, or larger, piece of Masonite to coat it white. Over this white surface the child drips a little of another color and moves the board around, allowing it to run in its own pattern. Then another color is used, and so on. Car paint dries to a tacky finish very fast — an advantage in this kind of painting. The colors do not mix as water colors do, and the results are brilliant and beautiful and pure.

We set them up and step back to look at them. Children give their wonderful creations names, and easily tell marvelous fantasy stories about them. One picture looked like a brilliantly colored cave. I asked the creator to go into her cave and tell us what she saw, what it was like, what happened. This activity is so satisfying that even the children who are most hyperactive or "uncontrollable" do it without any problems. Most have never before in their lives created such beauty, and felt such satisfaction.

2

Drawing and Fantasy

Your World, in Colors, Shapes and Lines

At other times I ask the children to create their own world on paper, just using shapes, lines, curves, colors — but nothing real. I might say, "Close your eyes and go into your space. See your world — what is it like for you? How would you show your world on paper just using curves and lines and shapes? Think about the colors in your world. How much space would each thing take on your paper? Where will you put yourself in the picture?"

Susan, age thirteen, took up only half the sheet with her drawing, leaving the other half blank. She used pastels of many colors, interspersed with dark figures. Her designs consisted of round figures with sun like rays, all touching, with a heavy black and red triangle made by a felt pen in the center of her rays. In the group, Susan described her picture by saying that she was in the center of her designs, which represented her worries, her disappointments, her fun things, and her happy feelings. Her worries and disappointments were in dark colors.

> Child: Could you tell us some of those disappointments?
> Susan: No, I'd rather not right now, but I know what they are.

WINDOWS TO OUR CHILDREN

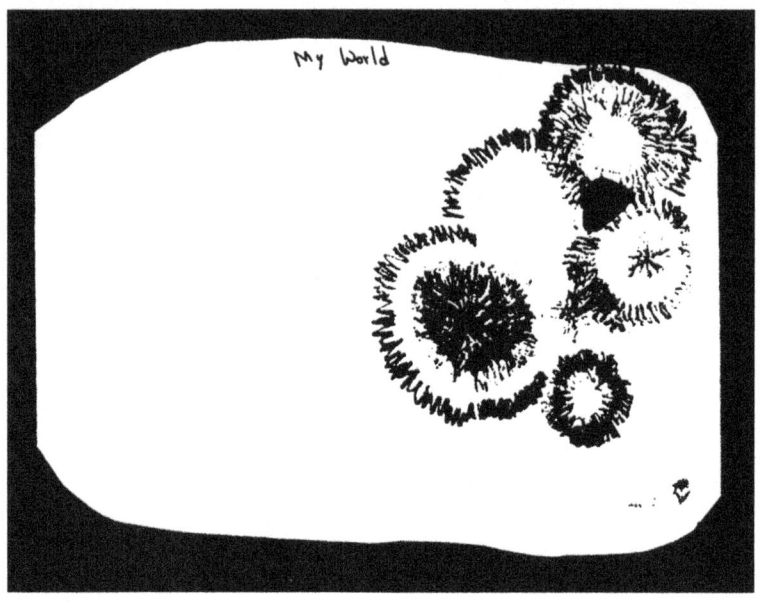

Child: Are you disappointed with any of us?

Susan: Well . . . yes. (Susan then began to talk about an annoyance she had with one of the boys in the group — something he had said that had been bothering her but that she had kept to herself. They discussed this for a while — she and the boy — and then seemed finished with it.)

Would you be willing to give the black and red triangle, you, a voice, and talk to your other parts?

Susan: Sure. I'm Susan and I'm here in the middle of all of you. Sometimes I'm in the middle of worries and disappointments and I feel terrible, and sometimes I'm in the middle of fun and happy things and I feel good.

What can you say to your worries and disappointments?

Susan: I don't like you when you're around. I don't want to talk about you. I wish you never came around. But you're there sometimes and I can't keep you from coming. But I don't have to talk about you if I don't want to!

I know you feel terrible about your worries and disappointments, Susan. It's OK with me if you don't talk about them now if you don't want

Drawing and Fantasy

to. I feel glad that you told Jimmy about your disappointment with him. Which one was it on your paper?

Susan: This one. (She crosses one out with a big black X. One less worry now.)

Are you willing to be another worry or disappointment and give it a voice now?

Susan: No.

OK. What can you say to your fun things and happy feelings?

Susan: I really like you. I like feeling good and I like to have fun. (Feeling good and having fun were new experiences for Susan.)

I see you have a lot of those in your world.

Susan: Yes! I used to feel miserable all the time. But now I really have a lot of fun and feel good a lot.

Will you be some of your happy things and feelings? (Susan readily tells about some of the things she enjoys doing and how they make her feel.)

Are there any people here (pointing to her picture) in your happy world?

Susan: Sure. This is my best friend. And this is a teacher I like a lot this year. And this is my mother who doesn't yell at me so much anymore, and this is my father (an alcoholic) who's really trying hard to work things out like I am, and this is my sister who really isn't such a brat (here she gave a big wink at sister, who was in the group), and this is all the group and this is you!

Will you tell us about the blank part of your paper? (Her picture was crowded all to one side.)

Susan: That's for my life that I will grow up into. I don't know what it will be, so I didn't put anything there.

There's a lot of room there for all kinds of things.

Susan: Right!

This strikes me as a good example of the importance of not doing interpretations as such. In viewing Susan's drawing I might have said to myself, on observing that her drawing was squeezed into one side of the paper and that she had left a large expanse of white, "Aha — this child is obviously constrained and constricted. She is fearful and keeps herself tightly closed, or she is unbalanced in some way." Any of those statements, and others, might have been true. Perhaps Susan did feel closed and constricted when she made her world. Maybe she felt that her world was tight and restricted and confined. I can't be certain about that; but I do know that after Susan's experience of visualizing and drawing her world, and then sharing and elaborating on her drawing with us, she was able to look at the white expanse and offer the possibility that there was more to come in her life. I felt that her statement, along with her voice and face as she said it, showed optimism, hope, an opening, a reaching out to life.

Another note about this work with Susan: As I read this over, I can see that I might have stayed a bit longer with Susan's "triangle" self, delve further into herself, her experience of self. I might have said, "Be that part, that triangle, and describe yourself." I would like to have asked her to be the dark border around the triangle. "Be that border and say what you do." Perhaps she might have talked about how she protects herself in her world (an interpretation). I would like to have asked her to be the very core of herself, the center, which looked so fiery and full of energy to me. I might have explored the points of the triangle. In retrospect, there is no telling how useful this would have been. It seems now that Susan's sense of self might have been strengthened if I had done this.

Tommy, age nine, colored in a series of curves that looked like hills and made an enormous, smiling sun coming out from behind the hills. He told us that he was a little dot behind a dark hill at the very bottom. Some of the hills were brightly colored and some were dark. He had used felt pen, pastels, crayons, and colored pencils for different effects. He said, "I'm way at the bottom of the hills and I have to climb them. It's not easy to do. Some of the hills are nice and some are hard. I can rest on some of the hills and play, too. I'm trying to get to the top where the sun is. It will take a long time."

I asked him to be the sun and talk to the little dot.

Drawing and Fantasy

Tommy (as sun): I see you down there. You have a long way to go. You'll make it though. I'm always here.

Tommy (as dot): I'm trying. It feels like a long way. I see you there and you make me feel warm. I'll keep trying.

This kind of expression contains the seeds for much productive work. The drawing itself tells much about what goes on inside of Tommy. In working with this drawing, I might ask him to elaborate about each of his hills, how he experiences himself as a small dot behind a hill, what it's like to be the sun. I am forever moved by the depths of feeling and insight that young children express. As I write about this event, which happened about five years ago, I shiver just as I did when I first listened to Tommy's inner wisdom.

Three months after that session the same group, including Tommy, was working with clay. I instructed the children to make some kind of abstract creation that could be their world today and to place themselves, as a symbol, in this world. Tommy made a tall triangular shape with a little ball resting at the top. He described his clay world, his feelings as he worked with the clay, and ended by saying, "And this little ball at the top is me." Immediately one of the children remembered his previous world drawing and reminded him of it. Tommy's face was shining as he said, "Wow! I guess it didn't take me so long to get to the top, after all!" This impressed me as a strong statement of Tommy's increasingly good feelings about his own self worth. This is the same boy who, in the cave fantasy described earlier, drew the Christmas scene about getting attention.

In an individual session with a fourteen-year-old boy, I asked him to close his eyes and imagine his world in colors, lines, and shapes. Then I asked him to draw what he had envisioned: "Don't draw anything real, but see what shapes you'll use, what kinds of lines fit for your world, what colors. Will you use dark colors, light colors? What is your world like?" He drew a large blue box with heavy lines of various colors in the box.

Jim: My picture has a big box and lots of colored curvy lines inside. I don't know what it means. I just drew it.

That's OK. I'd like you to be this dark blue line that makes the box and talk to the stuff in the box.

Jim: I'm a big box around you and I'm going to keep you in there.

Now have these lines talk back — what are they like? What do they say to the box?

Jim: Oh, we're a bunch of light curvy lines. We're really happy and we like to run around, but we can't get past you because you won't let us.

What is this heavy line? What could this be in your life? Is there anything in your life that keeps you from doing the things you want to do?

Jim: Well, yeah, my parents won't let me. And my father won't let me do a lot of things. (He then began to talk about some things he wanted

Drawing and Fantasy

to do, pointing to the area outside the box in his picture.) He's keeping me from getting into these places up here that are kind of scary.

Imagine that your father is sitting over here and tell him that. He's this pillow.

Jim: Well, I'm kind of glad you won't let me get out. I'm kind of scared. (He was still talking as the lines inside the box. He also had a very surprised look on his face.)

Be the stuff outside of the box and say what you are.

Jim: (Drawing in some lines in the space outside the box.) I'm a bunch of lines out here, out of the dark line. Jim thinks he wants to do what I am, but he's really scared. I'm a bunch of stuff that the kids at school want him to do, but his father won't let him, and it's a good thing. He could get hurt or in trouble. (Then he added, looking at me in astonishment) I guess I'm glad that I have this boundary around me. My lines inside are happy! I like this boundary.

Family Drawings

A very effective exercise is to have children draw their families as symbols or animals. "Close your eyes and go into your space. Now think of each member of your family. If you were to draw them on a piece of paper as something they remind you of, rather than real people, what would that be? If someone in your family reminded you of a butterfly because they flit around a lot, is that what you would draw them as? Or maybe someone reminds you of a circle because they're always around you. Start with the one that you think of first. If you get stuck, close your eyes and go back into your space. You can use blobs of color, shapes, objects and things, animals and whatever else you can come up with."

One boy, age eleven, drew a variety of symbols for his family. This is what he said (the comments in parentheses are mine):

WINDOWS TO OUR CHILDREN

"I'm in a cage, caught in the middle (a green starfish in a boxlike structure). My brother (age sixteen) thinks he's number one (a large purple circle with a huge number one in the middle). My sister (age twelve) thinks she's so great — she fools everybody but me (a blue circle with a red heart in the middle and claws coming out of the heart all around it). My Mom is nice (a flower). I made Dad as a brain because he thinks he knows everything. Donna (age eight) is nice: she doesn't call me names (a blue and pink butterfly). My brother (age ten) tells on me. He does things and just smiles all the time and people don't know, so he gets away with it (a vacant, smiling face). I'm closest to Mom. Everybody tells me what to do, picks on me, tells on me. I'm caught in the middle."

A fifteen-year-old girl stated about her picture,

"I'm closer to my mother (a heart with an arrow through it); she's sometimes too nice. She gives in too easy. I think she favors me. She takes me shopping and buys me things. I don't know how the other kids feel (a brother eleven, and sister thirteen). My brother is a bowling ball because that's all he talks about lately. My sister is candy and gum around her. She eats too much. My father is a light bulb — he's full of ideas. I'm waves because I love to swim. My father hears me out but we always get into an argument — he never seems to understand what I'm really trying to say."

Her drawing was done in a family session in which the whole family participated, doing these drawings and sharing themselves as they had never done before.

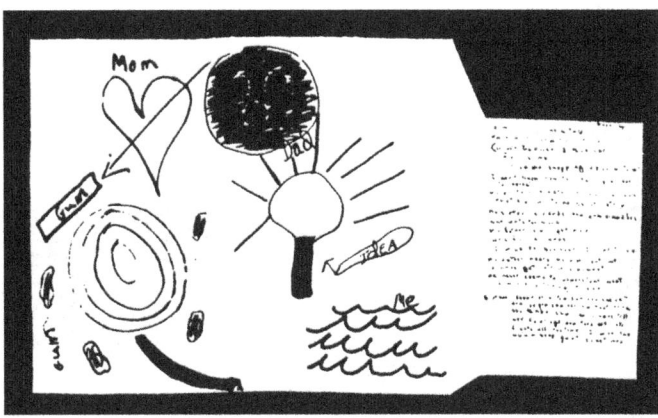

To this girl's last statement her eleven-year-old brother said, "Yeah, she once told Dad how she felt and he praised her for that, so now she thinks she can always tell her feelings and they get into fights all the time. I wish she would keep quiet sometimes." The brother, who consistently dislikes conflict, said of his drawing,

"I'm a bumblebee on my favorite flower. My sisters are butterflies. My parents are birds. Everything is moving — I like things that move. Everything is happy, bright, flowing along. (His picture included many colorful flowing lines.) The sun smokes a pipe like Dad. He says, 'I like your family down there!' Things are nice now that Dad's not drinking. We're all getting along better. We didn't have *one* fight between us kids this week. I stopped stealing four months ago. I decided it just wasn't worth it. I still get into trouble, but for little things. I like to keep peace, to have things peaceful. I don't like arguments."

For this exercise I often vary the instructions in working with the completed picture. After a general description by the child, I might ask her to make one statement about each person, if that seems missing in the description; or to say something to each person in the picture or have each person say something to her; or I may be more specific about what I want said — "Say something you like and something you don't like to each, or from each." I might have her conduct a dialogue between any two symbols.

WINDOWS TO OUR CHILDREN

So much material comes out through this exercise that it sometimes overwhelms me. Talking through pictures is so much safer and easier than talking to each other in a family session, or to me in an individual session. This same exercise (or any other exercise in this book) can be done each month with new feelings and material expressed each time. It is fun and interesting, too, to go back and look at the old pictures and talk to the child about what is still true and what has changed.

A thirteen-year-old girl: "Dad is nicest — I like him best. I'm con-

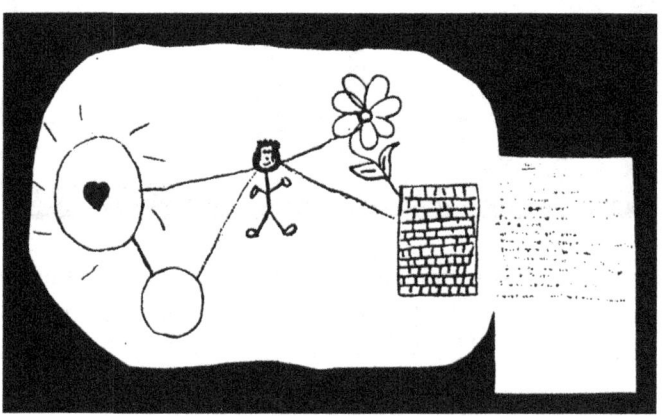

nected to him (round yellow circle with heart in the middle) I'm round, to be like him (she is a round circle with a line connecting her to her father) and also because I think I'm fat. Mom is super sweet (a pink flower). My brother is in the middle connected to everyone. He tries to get along with everyone. Mom is closer to my sister — they're connected. My sister is a brick wall (picture of a brick wall) because I can't get to her. I made her a blue wall because that's her favorite color and I wanted to be nice to her. I wish we could be closer."

Often we will move, in a family session, from the picture to the person. I asked this girl to tell her sister directly that she wanted to be closer. Her sister's answer: "We don't have much in common." This was the beginning. In a later session in which this family drew similar pictures, the thirteen-year-old drew a wall with a hole in it and stated, "I'm beginning to get through."

An eleven-year-old girl drew her family merely as blobs of colors with a color code in the corner. Each color meant something to her — her

Drawing and Fantasy

favorite color, a sad color, etc. This was her own idea and one I've used since with other children. Others have used shapes — squares, circles, etc. — instead of colors.

Although most children do not understand the word "symbol," they have amazing abilities to understand and use the meaning of the word. I use the word "symbol" in my instructions and then give several examples of what I mean.

I might also ask them to draw their ideal family in symbols, as well. A thirteen-year-old girl used nothing but groups of circles, triangles, dots, and stars for her family. "My Dad is the orange triangle. I'm closest to him even though he doesn't live with us. I like to do things with him. He's nicer since he doesn't live with my Mom. I fight a lot with my sister and my Mom. There's a lot of arguing, bickering all the time. We're always on top of one another — too much involved with each other. I'd like to get away sometimes. My ideal family is this flower here. I'm the orange dot in the middle." All this information came out as she explained the shapes in the picture, and she pointed to them as she talked. It was matter-of-factly presented — "This is the way it is."

Younger children, generally below eight, prefer to draw real people when asked to draw their families (although they sometimes will agree to draw animals). Asking the child to draw her family is a traditional diagnostic technique, and certainly much can be learned about the child by such a drawing. Using the information to relate and work with the child makes this task much more meaningful and useful.

A seven-year-old girl, when asked to draw her family, continually did the "wrong thing" in her own opinion. She drew her mother taller than her father, saying, "Oh, I made a mistake, my mother is shorter than my father." Then she wrote names over the figures and started to write "Mom" over her Dad. She crossed it out and said, "Oh, Dad." She first made her father's arms both held behind his back. Then she changed one arm so that he was reaching out for the mother's arm (which was held behind her back), saying, "I should make my father holding my mother's arm. That's the way it should be." By this time it was obvious to me that something was going on about her feelings toward her father, and I could focus some of my following sessions on getting her to express what these feelings were. Then she drew the baby, a seven-month old boy, at some distance from herself, mother, and father, who were now standing close together all touching each other. The baby was all by himself and his mouth was round, as if open. She and her mother were smiling, while her father's mouth was rather grim. I said, "Is the baby crying?" Laura answered, "Yeah."

Why is the baby crying?

Laura: Well, he's not holding hands with me.

She then drew a house around the whole family, including the baby.

Are you glad the baby is there in the house?

Laura: Oh, yes. I really like the baby. He likes me.

Are you sometimes glad the baby isn't there? (This seems to be a peculiar question as I now write it, but Laura seemed to understand its meaning.)

Laura: Sometimes I wish he wasn't born!

Then she began to tell me about how her mother lets her hold the baby and take care of him, but that he is a pain in the neck. She became more and more open about her feelings, and more and more comfortable with the idea that she could have both positive and negative feelings about the baby.

A similar incident occurred with a five-year-old boy. I asked him to be the baby in his picture.

Jimmy: Wah, Wah!
When does that happen?
Jimmy: At night, and I can't sleep.
Yeah, that must really make you mad.
Jimmy: Yeah, I can't sleep, and I'm tired.
Does your mother know about it?
Jimmy: No, my mother doesn't know about it.

He then began to express his anger at his mother who, he felt, was unaware of how the baby was interfering with his life. The mother had told me, "Oh, he loves the baby. There's no jealousy whatsoever." He *does* like the baby, but the baby also takes up his mother's time and wakes him at night and makes him angry. Somehow he was unable or unwilling to express his feelings directly to his mother. He expressed them in other ways: wetting his bed, and acting disruptive in school. I asked him to talk to his

Drawing and Fantasy

mother and the baby in the picture, and after he expressed his feelings he began to talk to me about his pride: he was going to teach this baby a lot; after all, he's the baby's big brother!

An eight-year-old boy, a fire-setter, drew a picture of his family with his mother, father, and sister all together but with himself far over at another end.

In looking at such a picture I may deduce what is going on. Even if I'm correct, writing this up in a report does nothing for a child. But if I can get the child to express his feelings about what is going on, then we are on the way to resolving the situation. After Lance described his picture, telling me who each person was, I asked him to tell me about each person — what each did all day, and what each liked to do. I then said, "You seem very far away from the rest of your family in your picture."

He answered, "Well, I didn't have any room for me on that side."

"Oh," I said, "I thought maybe that's how you might feel sometimes with your family — far away from them."

"Well, yes, I do sometimes. I think they give more attention to my sister than they do to me. They're always yelling at me for everything, so it doesn't really matter what I do."

This was the beginning of a lot of communication between us about his feelings. Later, when I worked with the entire family, I brought this up (with Lance's permission), and this was the first inkling they had of these feelings. He previously was unable to talk seriously about what he was feeling in their presence. In fact, he may not even have been aware of what he was feeling. We hear the expression often from adults, "I need to sort out my feelings." Children, too, get muddled and confused.

The Rosebush

In the book, *Awareness: Exploring, Experimenting, Experiencing*, there are some wonderful fantasies that can be used in conjunction with drawing. One I have used often is the rosebush fantasy. I will ask the children to close their eyes and go into their space and imagine that they are rosebushes. When I do this kind of fantasy with children, I do a lot of prompting — I give a lot of suggestions and possibilities. I find that children, especially children who are defensive and often constricted, need these suggestions to open themselves up to creative association. They will pick that suggestion which most fits for them, or will realize that they can think of many other possibilities.

So I might say, "What kind of rosebush are you? Are you very small? Are you large? Are you fat? Are you tall? Do you have flowers? If so, what kind? (They don't have to be roses.) What color are your flowers? Do you have many or just a few? Are you in full bloom or do you only have buds? Do you have leaves? What kind? What are your stems and branches like? What are your roots like? . . . Or maybe you don't have any. If you do, are they long and straight? Are they twisted? Are they deep? Do you have thorns? Where are you? In a yard? In a park? In the desert? In the city? In the country? In the middle of the ocean? Are you in a pot or growing in the ground or through cement, or even inside somewhere? What's around you? Are there other flowers or are you alone? Are there trees? Animals? People? Birds? Do you look like a rosebush or something else? Is there anything around you, like a fence? If so, what is it like? Or are you just in an open place? What's it like to be a rosebush? How do you survive? Does someone take care of you? What's the weather like for you right now?"

Then I will ask the children to open their eyes when they are ready, and draw their rosebushes. I generally add, "Don't worry about the drawing; you will be able to explain it to me." Later, as the child explains the drawing to me, I write the description down. I ask her to describe the rose-

Drawing and Fantasy

bush in the present tense, as if she were the rosebush. I sometimes ask questions such as, "Who takes care of you?" After the description I will go back and read each statement, asking the child if what she said as a rosebush fits in any way with her own life.

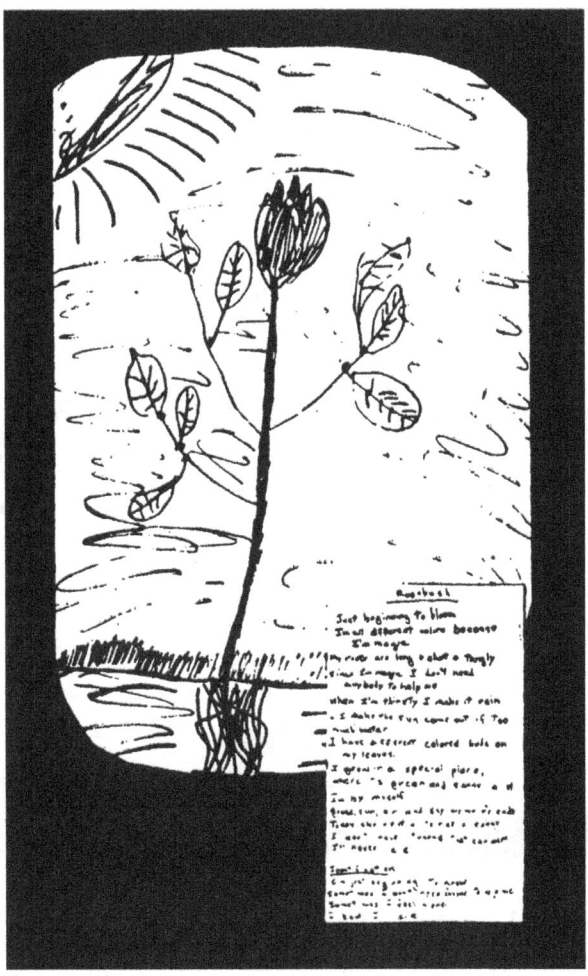

Carol, age ten, said of her rosebush, "I'm just beginning to bloom. I'm all different colors because I'm magic. My roots are long and short and tangly. Since I'm magic, I don't need anybody to help me. When I'm thirsty, I make it rain and I make the sun come out if there's too much water. I have different colored buds on my leaves. I grow in a special place where it's green and sunny a lot. I'm by myself; grass, sun, air, wind, sky are my friends. Today the sky is blue and it's nice and sunny. I don't have thorns that can hurt. I'll never die."

When I read each statement back to her, Carol said of herself, "I'm just beginning to grow. Sometimes I don't need anyone to help me. Sometimes I feel alone. I know I'll die." Much of what Carol said as a rosebush seemed extremely significant to me, knowing her as well as I did. We talked about what was most important to her. I might have gently led her into talking about some other areas if I had felt a need to, areas such as her feelings about being magic or wishing she were magic. She may not have wanted to talk about that at all, and that would have been fine. She was very willing to talk about the things she chose to talk about.

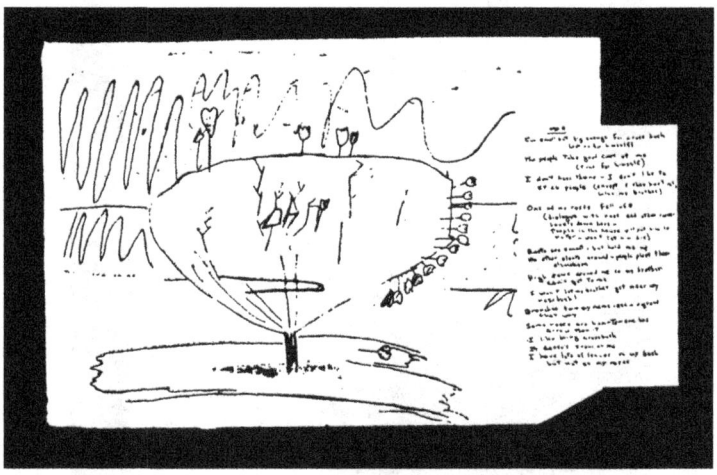

Nine-year-old David said, as a rosebush, "I'm small, but big enough for a rosebush. The people take good care of me and give me lots of water. I don't have thorns; I don't like to stick people unless they hurt me, like my brother. One of my roses fell off. My roots are small but hold me up. There are no other plants around; people plant them somewhere else. There's a high fence around me so my brother can't get to me; I won't let my brother get near the rosebush! Branches form my name and grew that way. Some roses are hearts; one has an arrow through it. I like being a rosebush. It doesn't snow on me. I have lots of leaves on my bush, but not on my roses."

David applied much of what he said to his own life. He had a lot of angry feelings toward his brother which came out in much of what he did with me. He had many complaints toward his parents too, and now as a rosebush he was able to feel that "the people (his parents) take good care of me. " I asked him to have a dialogue between the rose that fell off and the rosebush. As the rose he said, "I am very lonely on the ground but the people in the house will put me in water and won't let me die." He had often expressed feelings of being "thrown out," left, ignored. This was a new feeling he was having about himself — that his parents did love him, and cared for him.

Eight-year-old Gina said, "I have red roses, no thorns or leaves, and no roots. The soil helps me. I'm in Disneyland because I like to be happy. I'm protected — not like my life; the keeper takes care of me and waters me once a day. It's a sunny day. I'm pretty. Sometimes I'm lonely. I'm going to see my Daddy tonight. I'm small and bushy. I wish I were small — I'm too tall. It never rains. I don't like rain. Sometimes it snows — I miss snow here. I can see people. I'm surrounded by grass. I can grow easier if I don't have roots; if they want to replant me it will be easier. I always have buds."

WINDOWS TO OUR CHILDREN

Sometimes children identify easily with the rosebush, as Gina did. Gina is adopted and her parents have separated; since the separation she has had many uneasy feelings about her situation — much anxiety about what would happen to her. Her identification as a rosebush made it easier for us to begin to deal with her worries.

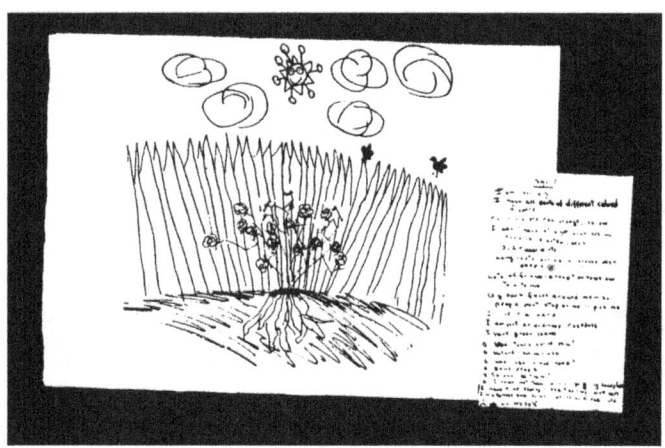

Ten-year-old Cheryl has lived in several foster homes since her mother abandoned her when she was about five. Because of legalities, she was unable to be permanently adopted until recently. She is a very bright, attractive youngster who has been in therapy because of sleepwalking and severe nightmares. She said of her rosebush, "I am very big. I have all sorts of different color flowers. I don't have straight branches; they're slanted, curvy. I'm in soft dirt and I have long roots buried in the ground very deeply. I have lots of friends — birds sit on the fence and talk to me. There's a big black fence around me so people won't step on me or pick me. I live in a yard. I'm just an ordinary rosebush. I have green leaves."

> I asked, Who takes care of you?
> Nature takes care of me — the rain and sun and soil.
> Who lives in the house?
> Some people.
> Do you like them?
> I never meet them; they're always going some place. I'm by myself.

Drawing and Fantasy

Out of this experience, we were able to deal openly with some issues that were held very deeply within Cheryl. One was her "big black fence," which protected her. She talked about her need for protection so she wouldn't be hurt. She was an aloof child, often called "snobby" by other children. We talked about her rosebush's people and her own relationship with the people who take care of her. This led to her feelings about her mother and the issue of adoption. Although it had been obvious that these things had been bothering her, Cheryl would not talk about them until now. Her rosebush drawing and some other similar activities freed something inside her. She truly felt by herself as her rosebush did, but she had never told anyone of this feeling. At the end of this session she said, "Oh yes, one more thing. Add 'I'm a famous bush by my colors.'"

The Scribble

In *Art As Therapy With Children*, Edith Kramer describes the use (and misuse) of the scribble technique with pre-adolescents. I find the scribble to be a very unthreatening method to help children express outwardly something of their inner selves. The original procedure consists of first having the child use her whole body to make a drawing in the air with wide rhythmic movements. Then the child, with eyes closed, draws these movements on a large piece of paper. I like the idea of having the child pretend there is a giant piece of paper standing in front of her as wide as her arms will reach and as high as her arms will stretch. I will ask her to imagine she is holding a crayon in each hand and to scribble on this imaginary paper, making sure every corner and every part of the paper is touched. This body exercise seems to have the effect of loosening and freeing the child to do a less constricted scribble on the real paper.

I then ask the child to draw the real one, sometimes with eyes closed, sometimes with eyes open. The next step consists of examining the scribble from all sides, finding forms that suggest a picture, and then completing the picture, obliterating lines as desired. Sometimes children will find several small pictures; others will outline and color in a large picture of a cohesive scene. Talking about the forms they see, and sometimes becoming those forms are fun like looking at clouds and being them. Children tell me stories about their pictures. Sometimes, if a child can find only one small picture, I will suggest that she create a scene of her own that will incorporate this little picture.

Melinda, age eight, drew a large head of a girl. I asked her to be the girl and tell about herself. She dictated a little story which I wrote down as she spoke. "I'm a girl with messy hair and I just now woke up. My name is Melinda. It feels like a shaggy dog. I don't look pretty. I might if my hair was combed. My hair has different colors. I went in the swimming pool and my hair is long and I didn't put a cap on, so it gets different colors. It happened to my friend — her hair turned green. I wish I had long hair and I'm going to have it. I like long hair." Melinda's story flowed easily into talking about her self-image, her feelings about how she looked and how she viewed herself as a person.

Cindy, age eight, found many hats in her scribble. This is her story:

Drawing and Fantasy

"The Story of the Hats. These hats have problems. One hat has a problem because he has buttons on him. Another hat has a problem because he got stained in the wash and nobody wants to wear him. One hat has a problem because he got all polka-dotted on him, and the two headed hat has a problem because they have holes in them with patches and no one wants to wear him, and one hat is happy because he's nice and purple and he has someone wearing him. One hat is sad because he's all striped and no one wants to buy him. The purple hat is magic and you can't hear shouting. I'm wearing it."

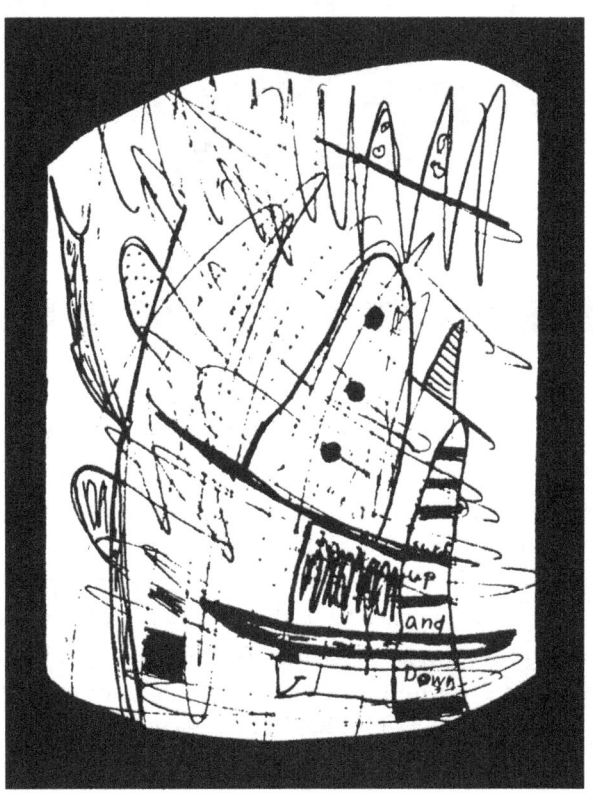

WINDOWS TO OUR CHILDREN

It is interesting to note that all Cindy's hats are masculine. I didn't mention this to her, though now — as I write this I wish I had found out what she might have said about that. I did ask her to imagine she was wearing her purple hat that was magic and tell me more about the shouting she did not hear.

Carol, age eleven, drew a large duck in water. Her story: "I'm a little duckling. I have wings but I can't fly yet. When I was born, I was all wet but I got feathers and now I'm fluffy. I live in the water and I follow my Mom around and we live — it's a park and there's a lake. When people come, they sometimes feed us bread crumbs. I have legs that help me to go through the water and the toes have skin in the middle." I asked Carol to compare herself to her duck. She said, "I've changed a lot since I was born too, but I still need my Mom. I'm not old enough yet to be on my own." Carol was a child who was left on her own a great deal.

An eight-year-old boy drew a figure of a boy sitting squarely in the middle of his scribble.

Drawing and Fantasy

He drew a comic strip balloon coming from his mouth with the word, "Ha!" printed in it nine times. I asked him to be the boy and say what he was laughing about. He said, "I'm laughing because this scribble is keeping everybody from getting at me. It's like a fence around me. I can see them, but they can't get at me." You can guess where we went from there.

Greg, age thirteen, had much trouble finding pictures in his scribbles. He looked at the first one he did, turned it over and over, and finally said there was no picture there. I said, "OK, here's another piece of paper; try again." He did a scribble and then, after careful scrutiny, could not find a picture. So I asked him to do another one. This time he found one very small face. He did a fourth, this time drawing several fish, one being hooked, an octopus with an arrow going through it, and one fish swimming along. He said, "I am a purple and yellow fish. Everybody is getting taken away but I am swimming along safe." I asked him to do a simple haiku-like poem from his picture:

WINDOWS TO OUR CHILDREN

fish
purple yellow
swimming along safely
coming at right time
fish

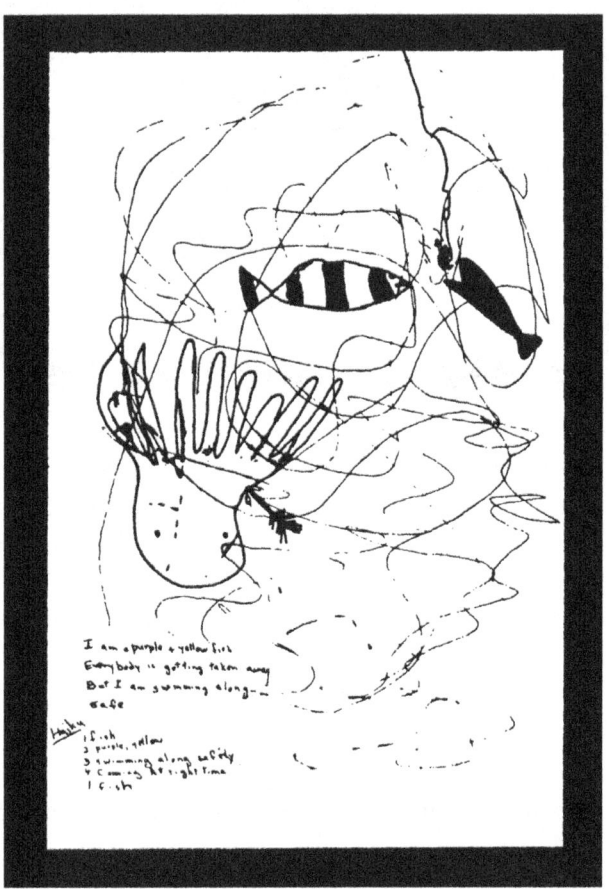

He wanted very much to do another scribble. Again he made fish. He said, "A big monster is trying to get this fish. The fish's friend, sort of an animal wearing a cap, is pulling the fish by a rope to save him, I'm the fish being saved." When asked if what he had said had anything to do with his own life, he said of the first fish picture, "I manage to keep out of trouble," and of the second, "I guess I get saved from getting into trouble, but I don't know how." Greg suffered psychosomatic physical symptoms (including bed wetting), and this was a good opening for me to move into his use of these symptoms to protect himself. Greg was very easygoing and quiet, never showing anger nor admitting to anything wrong in his life. He asked me why he couldn't see any pictures in his first scribbles, and I suggested that perhaps he was only now beginning to let his eyes "go" (freeing his eyes). He agreed and immediately took his very first scribble and drew a hand gripping a wall. He said that a man was trying to get over a wall but he didn't have a very good hold and was having trouble. He looked at me then, and said, "Maybe that's me trying to get a grip on things."

Anger Pictures

Now and then a child will express intense anger in the course of our session, and I can use the occasion to show the child how drawing feelings can be very relieving. An eleven-year-old boy became furiously angry as he talked about his brother. I asked him to draw his feelings at the moment. He grabbed a thick black crayon and scribbled and scribbled and scribbled feverishly on the paper. When he was through, he appeared relaxed and calm.

A thirteen-year-old girl did the same thing with red and orange crayons, labeling her drawing "Burning Mad." She did not appear to be relaxed, however, and I noticed that her markings were not flowing, like the boy's mentioned above, but were separate and distinct, each enclosed in its own jagged box. I asked her to be one of those fiery red scribbles and she said, "I'm a very angry, mad color, and I'm closed in." She said that although she could feel her anger strongly it was true that she did not know how to express it. We were then able to talk about what she was doing to herself and about appropriate ways for her to let those feelings out.

WINDOWS TO OUR CHILDREN

"Burning Mad."

A drawing made by another thirteen-year-old girl, after I asked her to draw a picture of her anger, showed some light, bright colors surrounded by a very thick border of black. When I asked her to tell me about the drawing she said, "The anger surrounds me and squeezes in the good feelings and they can't get out." Her statement accurately described her behavior.

Drawing and Fantasy

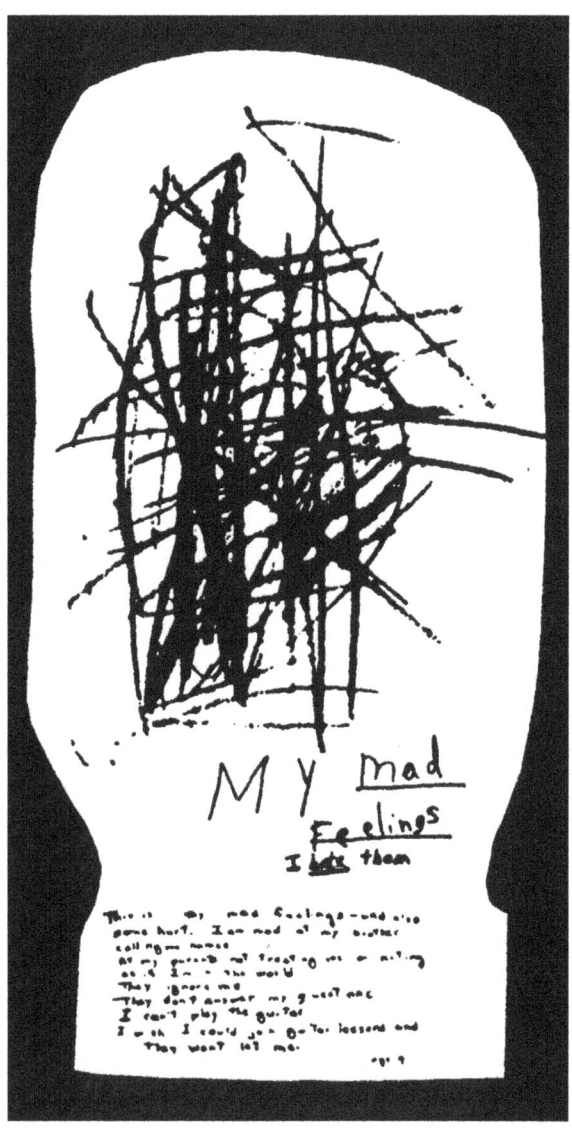

The people in her life rarely saw any of her good feelings; they only saw her depression and sullenness. This drawing was the first step in beginning to help this girl talk about her anger, about those things which made her angry, and to help her find some ways of expressing her angry feelings so her good feelings could emerge. Some of this we could do in my office with drawing and clay and using a Bataca, but she needed to learn how to take care of herself outside my office. She needed to learn to direct some of her resentments verbally toward the source. This is not an easy task for children who are constantly "shot down" for being straight and honest about what they are feeling — unless the feelings are liked by the adults in their lives. In this case I was able to bring the family in for some conjoint sessions. When I had tried that previously, this child sat in a corner and sulked; now she was able to hold her own, to call on her own strength and self support.

My Week, My Day, My Life

I can get an illuminating sense of the child's life by asking her to draw a picture of her week, or her day, or her life. The picture gives us an opening for talk. In one child's picture of her day she drew, among many other things, a large box labeled "school" with the word "YUCK" printed in big letters. She also drew a heart with an arrow going through it and a big initial on it — the initial of the boy she liked. Her feelings about school and her yearning for this boy took a great deal of energy from her. Some children draw very sparse pictures because that's the way they feel about their lives. Sometimes, without specific instruction to do so, children draw a fantasy picture of how they would like their day or week to be, and this gives me much to deal with.

The Squiggle

The squiggle is a term which describes making a random mark, usually black, on a piece of paper and asking the child to finish the picture. The child can then tell a story about the picture, be the picture, talk to the picture, etc.

There are adaptations of the squiggle in coloring book form. One is called The *Non-Coloring Book* and another is titled *The Un-Coloring Book*. Both employ a variety of doodles, rather than the one-stroke, very undefined squiggle, and the doodles can be finished as pictures. They are more suggestive of content than the squiggle.

In his book, *Therapeutic Consultation in Child Psychiatry*, D. W. Winnicott describes a method of making contact with children, using what he calls the Squiggle Game. His method is to sit down with a child at a table with two pencils and some paper before them. The therapist will shut his eyes and make a squiggle on the paper and ask the child to turn it into something, and the child will make one for the therapist to turn into something. As this procedure continues, they talk to each other about the pictures and any other material that comes up. It is obvious from his case studies that a great deal of communication results from this unique way of making use of an old game.

Colors, Curves, Lines and Shapes

I like to encourage older children, teenagers, and adults to draw their feelings and responses in colors, curves, lines and shapes. I encourage them to stay away from drawing real things and to go into the expression of feeling. One good method I have found is to ask a person or group to look at something I consider very beautiful for five minutes, and then to draw the feelings it aroused in only colors, lines, and shapes. Some objects I might use are: A flower, a leaf, a plant, a shell, a sunset if it's available, or a painting. Actually, any object will do to bring out some kind of feeling — a kitchen utensil, a toy, some household item. Or I might have them listen to a beautiful piece of music.

Sometimes people need a kind of training for allowing themselves to loosen up, to trust their own feelings and the expression of those feelings. I might ask children, "Draw a picture of how you feel every day at a certain time you pick. Bring them all in at your next session with me and we'll look at them." I would probably have them practice this with me first. "Close your eyes and be aware of how you feel, how your body feels. Your moods change. Your bodily feelings change. See how it is for you now. Then express this on paper just using colors, lines, and shapes." I often do this myself to give the children some idea of what I am asking for.

WINDOWS TO OUR CHILDREN

Group Drawing

I sometimes have a family, or two children, or just one child and myself draw a picture together on the same sheet. "Just draw a bunch of lines and circles and other shapes and colors on a piece of paper. See how you feel doing this." Sometimes there is a fight over space on the paper, and it's interesting to see how this problem is solved. Does one give way to the other? Is there an agreement? Does one invade the other's territory? Older children can be instructed to do this as a silent exercise, whereas younger children need to talk. I will watch what happens and then afterwards we will all talk about the experience. I might ask, "What did it feel like for you to be pushed out of your space? Do you ever feel that way in life? Do you feel that way at home?" A child's process in a specific exercise is often quite indicative of her process in life.

I've asked a large group of children to draw a picture together. There are several ways of doing this, the mural being the most common. In a group of eight children I will give each a piece of paper and ask each to start a drawing. Then at a signal, all drawing stops and each paper is passed to the next person, who adds something to it. The cycle is repeated until at the end you have eight pictures to look at and talk about. Children enjoy this experience. They have fun talking about how the pictures look to them and sharing their own feelings about adding their mark to a group picture.

Another way of making a group picture is to have only one piece of paper; all but one must wait while one child at a time adds to it. As in a group story, the child may talk about what she is doing while the others watch or listen. Sometimes I begin the picture myself with a particular theme. Or I begin by drawing a line or shape or blob of color and begin a story about it. The next person continues the story while adding to my design, and so on. Again, what is interesting here is each child's process. I might start, "Once upon a time there was a small red circle who lived in a big field of space. One day...." The next child might then say, "One day a purple square came along and said to the circle, 'would you like to play with me?' The circle said, 'yes' and they started to play." The next child might say, "Then a big black triangle came along and started pushing the circle and square" (black lines coming out of the triangle toward the circle and square to represent pushing), and so on. When the drawing is finished, I

Drawing and Fantasy

might ask the child who drew the circle how his circle felt being pushed. After a while I might ask if he ever pushes others in his life. If specific material like this does not come out of the group drawing, it doesn't matter. What matters is what does happen: the group cooperation (or lack of it), the patience or impatience of a particular child, and so forth. The fun that is almost guaranteed to be part of the experience ought not to be minimized either. Many children with emotional problems need more joyful experiences to sustain their zest for living.

Free Drawing

Children often would rather draw or paint whatever they want to, rather than to be told what to do. This does not detract from the therapeutic process; the importance lies in what is foreground for the child.

Allen, age nine, drew a very large green dinosaur eating the top of a tree. At first it was easier for him to talk to the dinosaur. Then he became the dinosaur and talked about his great power and magnitude, in direct contrast to the helplessness he felt in his life.

Six-year-old Phillip drew a house with a bus next to it. He told a very elaborate story of where the bus took him.

Todd, age five, drew a large flower next to a tree.

WINDOWS TO OUR CHILDREN

I asked him to have them talk to each other. He said, "Hi, tree and flower. I want to talk to them. Hi, tree and flower. I like you. You grow big and tall. Do you think I'll grow big and tall some day?" I wrote this down on his picture as he talked, and read it over to him when he completed it. We discussed his feelings about growing up, and then he asked me to add to the writing, in answer to his own question, "Yes."

Carl, age five, drew several shapes. He looked at his finished product and dictated, "This is a baby pool, and that is for Dads and Moms and big people. I'm going into the big pool because I'm big." This led to a discussion of what it might have been like when he was a baby. "I lived with my Mom and Dad." (He presently lived in a foster home.) At a subsequent session he stated about another picture, "This is a big giant pool. A giant is swimming in it. That's all." He delighted in becoming this giant. Of still another picture he said, "This is a potato bug with no eyes. This is the crab. This is the King Kong. This is the black widow. He will get some people and the baby bites him. He doesn't want to get killed by a monster." Through his own process, Carl was beginning to allow and experience his angry feelings and to regain some of his own strengths.

Painting

Painting has its own special therapeutic value. As paint flows, often so does emotion. Children enjoy painting, especially those past the age of nursery school and kindergarten. They often don't have the experience of painting again after those ages except perhaps from small tins of water colors. Children love the streaming quality and the brilliance of paint colors. They like the experience of painting, and I often suggest that they paint just anything, and I will wait and see what happens.

Seven-year-old Nancy painted a sky with clouds and a large airplane in flight. When she was finished, we talked about her painting and about flying. She picked up the brush and painted a dot at one of the windows. "That's my mother," she said. I asked her to talk more about that: where was her mother going? "My mother is on the plane. She's going somewhere. I don't know where." I asked her to say something to her mother on the plane. "I don't want you to go away and leave me." I asked her if she talked to her mother about that sometimes. (She and her mother live together —

Drawing and Fantasy

just the two of them.) And then came an outpouring of secret fears of abandonment. "No, I haven't told my mother; I did once and she said that was silly." These fears, based on a divorce, long-distance moving, and separation from her father and other close family members had much to do with Nancy's whining, clinging attitude toward her mother. Getting this out in the open and allowing her to have her feelings taken seriously had an enormous effect on Nancy. I spent several sessions letting her focus on those feelings — telling stories, asking her to draw pictures or act out scenes about being left, how that would feel for this little doll, what she might do, and so forth.

Since the tone, color, and fluidity of painting lends itself so well to states of feeling, I might ask a child to paint a picture of how she is feeling right now, or how she feels when she is sad and how she feels when she is happy. Children seem to represent feelings with paint easier than with other art media. When they get crayons or felt pens in their hands, they tend to be more graphic and representational.

I asked Candy, aged nine, to paint how she felt when she was happy and how she felt when she was sad.

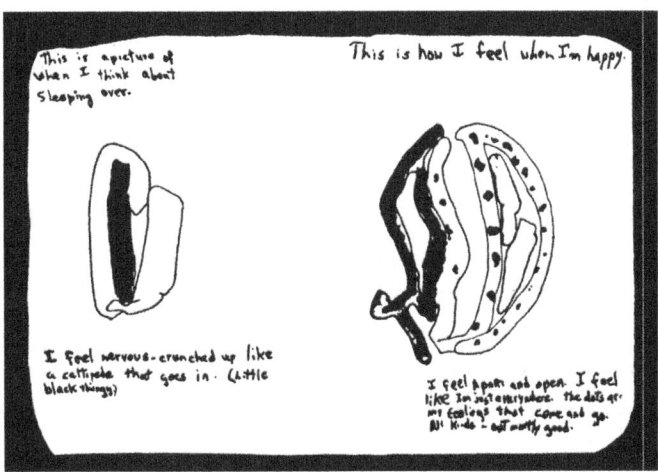

On one side of the paper she painted an abstract design for which she later said, "I feel apart and open. I feel like I'm just everywhere. The dots are my feelings that come and go, all kinds, but mostly good." On the other

53

WINDOWS TO OUR CHILDREN

side she said of her lines and colors, "I feel nervous, crunched up like a little black bug, a centipede, that goes in. This is a picture of when I think about sleeping over."

A thirteen-year-old boy painted a very large picture of how it felt to wet his bed. The painting consisted of large blue and black and gray areas. Prior to this I had asked him how it felt and he had merely shrugged and said, "I don't know."

Young children like to paint without instruction. They will become very absorbed in spreading and mixing color. Later they will describe what they see as a sort of fantasy story. Six-year-old John said of his painting, "That's a machine and some stuff comes out. There are pipes with oil coming out. It goes in there. It's hot oil and you can't touch it." I asked him to be this machine and tell me again about his oil. He did with energy. I said, "You sound like a machine that's mad." "Yeah," he said, "and I'm going to spit my oil all over everybody that bothers me." Then he actually got up and walked around the room in a crouched position, arms bent out, grimacing and spitting and shouting angry words such as "I'm gonna get you! Watch out!" Finally he sat down on the floor next to me and we talked a little about his own angry feelings.

In a session with another six-year-old boy, I had a similar experience. He painted mostly with black. Off to the side was a little ring of bright colors. He said, "This is oil and water. Some dirt's coming in here. There's some ocean water coming in" (pointing to the ring of color). I asked him to have a conversation between the oil and the ocean water. He said, as the oil, "Don't come near me. I'll spoil you. You'll get all dirty." When I asked later if the oil or water were anything like his feelings, he said, "This oil is when I'm mad! Don't come near me when I'm mad!" This boy had sores all over his body where he had scratched and gouged himself — his only way (up to now) of doing something with his anger. We had many sessions with paint and other media to help him express his anger in ways other than self-destruction.

Finger Painting

Finger painting and clay have similar tactile and kinesthetic qualities. Finger painting is one of those activities that, sadly, is usually restricted to

Drawing and Fantasy

the preschool set. It has so many fine qualities. Finger painting is soothing, flowing. The painter can make trial designs and pictures and quickly erase them. He doesn't experience failure and doesn't need much skill. He can tell a story about a painting he decides is finished or he can talk about something the picture reminds him of. I make my own finger paints by using powdered poster paint sprinkled on a dab of liquid laundry starch. Have you ever tried finger painting using Vaseline, cold cream, or chocolate pudding?

Phillip, age ten, finger-painted often in our sessions. He was a restless child who found it difficult to sit still in school. He hit other children often, argued with everyone, had much difficulty in his motor coordination. But whenever he finger painted he became absorbed, appeared calm and content, and breathed deeply. For many finger painting sessions he did not complete any one picture. He did, however, begin to talk to me about his life, his bad feelings about himself, and his angry feelings toward his parents and teachers.

Finally one day, Phillip completed his finger painting experience with a picture. He seemed ready to commit himself strong enough to make his mark. This picture was the face of a clown. I asked him to tell me a story about his clown. "My clown makes people laugh. He looks funny to everyone. But inside he is a very sad clown. He has to paint his face and dress funny to make people laugh or they might cry because if he showed what he really looked like, everyone would feel very sorry for him." Phillip was able now, for the first time, to talk about the despair that he felt.

Foot Painting

Foot painting? Yes, foot painting! The feet are very sensitive, and they are mostly locked up in shoes, where they can't feet anything. Lynn Pelsinger, a marriage, family, child counselor and special education teacher, uses foot painting with groups of children in special classes in the public schools. She will ask the children to take off their shoes and socks — not encouraged in the schools very often, unfortunately — and describe how their feet feel now that they are free. She tells them they will paint with their feet. After this idea sinks in, she asks them to tell about what they can imagine their feet will be able to do. Then she places butcher paper on the floor and small trays of paint. She directs them to see how much paint they can get with their toes and what happens when the paint is released. The children will experiment with this for a while and then go on to painting with all parts of the feet, walking on the paper to make a variety of prints, painting with various toes, painting with the heel, the sides of the foot, trying each foot to notice any differences.

Sometimes Pelsinger continually directs awareness to the feet; at other times the children freely experiment without direction. A bucket of water is close at hand for washing the feet, and towels for drying.

When the session is over, they will sit together and talk about the experience. They have just experienced one of the most relaxing, pleasurable, sensual experiences of their young lives. In all of her experience, Pelsinger states, the activity has never gotten out of hand (or foot). There is a feeling of calmness and joy, a knowledge that they are engaging in an activity that is special and privileged in a school setting.

There are various ways of using foot painting. Children can do individual paintings, group paintings, and murals. The process in the group interaction is fruitful for later discussion. Pelsinger tells about her awareness of kids' feet and shoes after first introducing foot painting and listening to what the children had to say about their feet, about shoes, about socks, about walking and running. She began to look at the way children walked. Some with torn socks looked as if they were walking on glass. Children with bad fitting shoes or socks have grouchy, bad temperaments — wouldn't you? She noticed that after a rain, these children went out of their way to get their feet wet on the way to school, knowing that she would let them take their shoes off.

When the children are through with foot painting and have washed their feet, Pelsinger helps dry them off with a towel and encourages them to do this for each other. Massaging the feet in this way is delightful and soothing, and the children love it. (She noticed that after a rain, they were also eager to have her dry their heads with a towel, rubbing the scalp.)

3

My Working Model

Specific techniques for helping children express feelings through the use of drawing and painting are endless. Regardless of what the child and I choose to do at any session, my basic purpose is the same. My goal is to help the child become aware of herself and her existence in her world. Each therapist will find his or her own style in achieving that delicate balance between directing and guiding the session on the one hand, and going with and following the child's lead on the other. The suggestions presented here are intended merely to show you the endless possibilities and to free your own creative process. They are not meant to be followed mechanically. The process of work with the child is a gentle, flowing one — an organic event. What goes on inside you, the therapist, and what goes on inside the child in any one session is a gentle merging.

Pictures can be used in endless ways, for a variety of purposes and at different levels. The very act of drawing, with no therapist intervention whatsoever, is a powerful expression of self that helps establish one's self-identity and provides a way of expressing feelings. From this as a starting place, the therapeutic process might evolve as follows:

1) Having the child share the *experience* of drawing — her feelings about approaching and doing the task, how she approached and continued the task, her process. This is a sharing of self.

2) Having the child share the drawing itself, describing the picture in her own way. This is a further sharing of self.

3) On a deeper level, promoting the child's further self-discovery by asking her to elaborate on the parts of the picture; making parts clearer, more obvious; describing the shapes, forms, colors, representations, objects, people.

4) Asking the child to describe the picture as if it were the child, using the word "I": "I am this picture; I have red lines all over me and a blue square in my middle."

5) Picking specific things in the picture for the child to identify with: "Be the blue square and describe yourself further — what you look like, what your function is, etc."

6) Asking the child questions, if necessary, to aid the process: "What do you do?" "Who uses you?" "Who are you closest to?" These questions will come out of your ability to "get into" the drawing along with the child, and to open yourself up to the many possible ways to exist, function, and relate.

7) Further focusing the child's attention, and sharpening her awareness by emphasis and exaggeration of a part or parts of a picture. Encouraging the child to go as far as she can with a specific part, especially if there is some energy and excitement within you or within the child, or if there is an exceptional lack of energy and excitement. Questions often help. "Where is she going?" "What is this circle thinking?" "What is she going to do?" "What will happen to it?" And on and on. If the child says, "I don't know," don't give up; move on to another part of the picture, ask another question, give your own answer and ask the child if that's right or not.

8) Having the child dialogue between two parts in her picture or two contact points or opposing points (such as the road and the car, or the line around the square, or the happy side and the sad side).

9) Encouraging the child to pay attention to colors. In giving suggestions for a drawing while the child's eyes are closed, I often say, "Think about the colors you're going to use. What do bright colors mean to you? What do dark colors mean to you? Will you use bright colors or dull colors, light colors or dark colors?" One child drew her troubles as dark colors, and she drew her happy things with bright, light colors, and there was even

a difference in how hard she pushed with her crayon when she used different colors. I might say, "This looks darker than these," to encourage expression, or "It looks as if you pressed hard on this." I want the child to be as aware as she can of what she did, even if she's not willing to talk about it.

10) Watching for cues in the child's voice tone, body posture, facial and body expression, breathing, silence. Silence can mean censoring, thinking, remembering, repression, anxiety, fear, or awareness of something. Use these cues to promote flow in your work. Here's an example of how watching a body cue was the most important single factor in clearing up a difficult situation.

Cindy, age five, was brought in to see me because she was having trouble sleeping. At our first session I asked her to draw her family, and she drew herself, her sister, and her mother willingly. I knew that her mother and father were divorced and that she saw her father regularly. I gave her another paper and said, "I know your Daddy doesn't live with you but he's still your family, so would you draw him here?" For an instant, panic crossed her face and just as quickly disappeared. But I caught her fleeting expression and I gently said, "You are afraid about something when I ask you to do that." She very, very softly replied, "Well, Jill lives there, too." So I said, "Oh — well, how about drawing your Dad and Jill on this other paper." She smiled happily and went to work. (It was almost as if she needed my permission.) She liked Jill (a fact that came out in her dialogues with the family pictures), but her mother didn't. This five-year-old child had been feeling responsible for her mother's feelings and because of this was afraid to include Jill in her first picture. When I said, "I guess your mother doesn't like Jill too much," she nodded and looked at me shyly and knowingly.

With Cindy's permission, I asked her mother to join us from the waiting room, I wanted to tell her that because of her own negative feelings toward Jill, Cindy did not feel entitled to enjoy the positive feelings she had toward Jill and that she needed to help Cindy know that each could have her own feelings, that it was all right for Cindy to like Jill, even if she didn't. With this new awareness, Cindy's mother was able to discontinue imposing her own feelings on her daughter, and I did not have to see Cindy again. A rapid closure, based on a small body cue.

11) Working on identification, helping the child to "own" what has been said about the picture or parts of the picture. I may ask, "Do you ever feel that way?" "Do you ever do that?" "Does that fit with your life in any way?" "Is there anything you said as a rose bush that you could say for you as a person?" and so on. Questions like this can be phrased in many ways. I will ask them carefully and very gently.

Children do not always have to "own" things. Sometimes children will pull in and are very frightened to do so. Sometimes they are not ready. Sometimes it just seems to be enough that they've gotten something out in the open through the picture even if they don't own it for themselves. They can tell that I've heard what they had to say. They've expressed what they needed to or wanted to at the time, in their own way.

12) Leaving the drawing and working on the child's life situations and unfinished business that come out of the drawing. Sometimes this is precipitated directly from the question, "Does this fit with your life?" and sometimes a child will associate to something in her life spontaneously. Sometimes the child will suddenly be very silent, or a look will cross her face. I might say, "What just happened?" and the child will usually begin to talk about something in her life now or in the past that relates in some way to her present life situation. (And sometimes the child answers, "Nothing.")

13) Watching for the missing parts or empty spaces in the pictures and attending to that.

14) Staying with the child's foreground flow, or attending to my own foreground — where I find interest, excitement, and energy. Sometimes I go with what is there and sometimes I go with the opposite of what is there. The boy who drew Disneyland in the cave fantasy stressed the pleasure and fun of the place. Going with the opposite of his foreground, I said, "I guess your own life doesn't have so much pleasure and fun in it."

I usually work with what's easy or comfortable for the child first, before going into the harder, uncomfortable places. I find that if we talk about the easier things with children, they are then more open to talking about the harder things. In a picture where I have asked them to paint sad feelings on one side and happy feelings on the other, they will often find it difficult to share the sad feelings until they have shared the safer happy feelings. This is not always true though. Sometimes children who are holding in much anger will need to let this out before the good feelings can come through.

I may choose to deal with my own foreground. As I am with the child, I may feel sadness or discomfort of some kind. Or I may be struck by the child's body posture as she talks, and focus on that.

When I see children who show disturbance in some way, I know that there is some malfunction in the natural balance and flow of the total organism, the person. Doing therapy can be described as going back to locate and restore the misplaced function.

The normal development and growth of a child is an essential part of my working model. The infant is very much in touch with her senses: she delights in her new awareness of smell and sound and light and colors and faces and taste and touch. She revels in her sensuousness and thrives on it. Soon the baby becomes aware of her body and learns that she can do the touching, reaching, grabbing, dropping. She moves her legs and arms and body and discovers control and mastery. As her senses and body are reaching new heights of awareness, so are her feelings. She makes no effort to hide her feelings; she expresses them fully. When a young child is angry, we know it. When she is happy, we know it. We know when she is hurt or frightened or peaceful or delighted. She has already found out that those sounds she had heard and then made herself had meaning and that she could begin to communicate with others verbally to make her needs known: first through sounds, then words, then sentences. As her intellect develops she begins to express curiosity, thoughts, ideas. All this time, her senses and body feelings are arriving at more and more sophisticated levels of development. The baby has no problems with self-esteem as yet; she simply is. She is in every sense an existential being.

The healthy, uninterrupted development of a child's senses, body, feelings, and intellect is the underlying base of the child's sense of self. A strong sense of self makes for good contact with one's environment and people in the environment.

Children soon learn that life isn't perfect and that we live in a very chaotic world, a world of contradiction and dichotomy. Furthermore, parents who are raising children have their own personal difficulties to contend with. Children learn to cope and compensate. Many do quite well in their living and growing and learning. Many don't.

I find that most children who are singled out as needing help have one thing in common: some impairment in their contact functions. The tools of contact are looking, talking, touching, listening, moving, smelling and tasting. Children in trouble are unable to make good use of one or more of their contact functions in relating to the adults in their lives, to other children, or to their environment in general. How we make use of our contact functions is evidence of the relative strength or weakness we feel. Since a strong sense of self predisposes good contact, it is no wonder that almost every child I see in therapy does not think too well of herself, though she may do everything she can to keep this fact hidden. Young children do not place blame for their problems upon their parents or the world outside. They imagine that they themselves are bad, that they have done something wrong and that they are not pretty enough or smart enough. And yet on some level there is a very strong will to survive, to make it through. There is still something of the original natural infant that has not been squelched.

Children protect themselves in some way. Some withdraw to keep from getting hurt. Some conjure up fantasies to entertain themselves and to make their lives easier and more livable. Some play-work-learn (for it is all connected) as if nothing were the matter, shutting out what is painful. Some protect themselves by striking out in some way; these children get the most attention, which often tends to reinforce the very behavior most hated by adults.

Children do what they can to get through, to survive. The thrust of children is toward growth. In the face of lacks and interruptions of natural functioning, they will pick some behavior that seems to serve to get them through. They may act aggressive, hostile, angry, hyperactive. They may withdraw into worlds of their own making. They may talk as little as possible or perhaps not at all. They may become fearful of everybody or everything or some particular thing that affects their own life and everyone involved with them in some way. They may become exceptionally overly pleasing and "good." They may obnoxiously hang on to the adults in their lives. They may wet the bed, shit in their pants, have asthma, allergies, tics, stomachaches, headaches, accidents. There is no limit to what a child will do in the attempt to take care of her needs.

As the child becomes a teenager these behaviors may become more exaggerated, or change into new ones such as seductiveness and promiscuity, or excessive use of alcohol and other drugs. Beneath these attempts to cope there are always unmet needs that result in a lost sense of self.

Sometimes the child functions in her life on ideas that do not belong to her, are not rightfully hers. Children often grow up believing what they hear about themselves, swallowing whole faulty information about themselves. For example, a child may believe she is stupid because her father, while angry, called her stupid out of his own frustration. She may pick up an underlying, unspoken message that she is clumsy because her parents laugh at her when she drops things or are continually impatient with her labored attempts at making things. Children will often take on and act out the characteristics and descriptions that they have taken in from others. My task, then, as a therapist, is to help the child separate herself from these outside evaluations and erroneous self-concepts, and help her to rediscover her own being.

So whenever I work with a child, adolescent, or for that matter, an adult, I know that we will need to go back and remember, regain, renew, and strengthen something that she once had as a baby but now seems lost. As her senses awaken, as she begins to know her body again, she can recognize, accept, and express her lost feelings. She learns that she can make choices and verbalize her wants and needs and thoughts and ideas. As she learns who she is and accepts who she is in her differentness from you, then she will contact you, and you will know it. She can do this whether she is three or eighty-three years old.

I work to build the child's sense of self, to strengthen the contact functions, and to renew her own contact with her senses, body, feelings and use of her intellect. As I do this, the behaviors and symptoms that she has used for her misdirected expression and growth often drop away without her being fully aware that her behaviors are changing. Her awareness is redirected to the healthy mindfulness of her own contact functions, her own organism, and thus toward more satisfying behaviors.

The baby develops through experiencing. Awareness is so tied in with experiencing that they are one and the same. Similarly, as the child in therapy *experiences* her senses, her body, her feelings, and the use she can make of her intellect, she regains a healthy stance toward life.

So I give the child as much experience as I can in the areas where she needs it the most. And when I can, I encourage her to be aware of her process of experiencing. When I ask a child to give me a sentence to write on her drawing which sums up her position, this is a statement of her awareness. When I say, "Do you ever feel that way?" in response to a rose that has fallen off the bush and is dying, or "Does that fit with you in your life?" in response to a story about a bear that is looking for her real mother bear, I am reaching for explicit awareness. Such awareness does facilitate change. As the child's awareness develops, we can begin to examine the options and choices available, experiment with some new ways of being, or deal with the fears that the child has hidden to prevent herself from making new choices that would improve her life.

In a couple of anecdotes in this book I say, "I don't really know what happened." I do know that the child experienced something with me and then felt better — often without any explicit statement of understanding or awareness. With one child I made a baby out of a piece of clay, told her it was she, and made believe I was giving it a bath. The child felt happy and satisfied, and that evening she suggested to her mother that she begin to take showers. (She had previously refused to take baths or showers.)

If this child had said, "I'm aware that I miss being treated like a little baby again now that my baby brother is on the scene, and I won't take a bath until someone recognizes this," I would probably "understand what happened." All I really know is that I was able to give the child an experience that was satisfying to her and that allowed her to feel secure enough to easily take another small step toward growing up.

If you have followed me in this discussion you might be saying, "OK, I'm willing to give this a try. What do I do next?" It is the how that is important. How do we build a child's sense of self, strengthen her contact functions, renew her own contact with her senses, body, feelings, and mind? How do we help the child *experience* her senses, body, feelings, the use of her intellect?

My Working Model

The answer to these questions can come out sounding very simplistic, but I must warn you that this book is not meant to be used as a repair manual. I am reminded of my work in the schools to help children overcome their learning disabilities. Some fine work has been done by researchers in delineating the problems many of these children have with areas of perception. Some children have trouble with figure-ground differentiation and are unable to pick out a letter or a word from a sea of letters and words. Some children have visual directional problems that make b's and d's or "was" and "saw" look the same. People have invented wonderful games and exercises to help correct these deficiencies, and strengthen areas where children are weak. So we spend hours with the child, helping him pick out red blocks from a variety of colors, and squares from among triangles and circles, to improve his figure-ground skills. The child becomes quite adept at this after much practice, but often he still can't read. It's just not that simple.

When I give suggestions for improving the senses I do not mean to imply that as soon as the child is able to tell the difference between soft things and rough things, or high notes and low notes, that he will suddenly feel better about himself and change his behavior. Children are complicated creatures, and many things happen simultaneously. For example, a child is offered finger paint to experience and strengthen his tactile sense. The flow of the paint and the sensuous feel of it, as well as the sheer enjoyment of the activity, open the child up to sharing some deep feelings, and this leads to his talking about some problem in his life, which in turn leads to a discussion of his options in resolving that problem. Or none of this may happen. He may finger paint in silence for the whole session. Or he may reject the whole idea of finger painting as childish. The therapist must be closely attuned to the child as he responds to the activity in order to recognize the ebb and flow of the child's process. The therapist must move closely with the child in order to know when to speak and when to remain silent.

Elsewhere in this book I give many examples of techniques for giving the children sensory, body, feeling, intellectual, and verbal experiences. These ideas ought to open the therapist's imagination to endless creative possibilities. While working with a particular child, it is not very difficult for me to decide which technique is needed. As I get to know the child, everything falls into place. The child is often the one who shows what he needs by the very activity he chooses. And sometimes he shows precisely what he needs by his insistent resistance to an activity!

I must say that I am sometimes worried about the role of therapeutic intervention with children. Am I working to get them to behave in a way that is often contradictory to their own cultural milieu and expectations? Or am I subduing their own joyful growth and self-determination to help them adjust to an inhuman situation, sweeping problems under the rug? I must remind myself that my task is to help children feel strong within themselves, to help them see the world around them as it really is. I want them to know that they have choices about how they will live in their world, how they will react to it, how they will manipulate it. I cannot presumptuously make this choice for them. I can only do my part to give them the strength to make those choices they want to make, and to know when choices are impossible to make. I need to help them know that they cannot take responsibility for those choices that don't exist for them. As they grow older and stronger and they can see themselves in relation to the world more clearly, then they can make determinations, perhaps, to change the social structures that keep them from making the kind of choices they need to make.

There are certain basic foundations anyone who works with kids needs. Liking kids, establishing an accepting, trusting relationship, knowing something about the way kids develop and grow and learn, and understanding the important issues that correspond with particular age levels. One ought to be familiar with the kinds of learning disabilities that affect children, not only getting in the way of their learning, but often causing emotional side effects. I think one ought to have an ability to be direct without being intrusive, to be soft and gentle without being too undirective and passive.

I think one who works with children needs to know something about the workings of family systems and to have an awareness of the environmental influences of the child — home, school, other institutions with which the child may be involved. I think one ought to be familiar with the cultural expectations placed on the child. One ought to believe firmly that each child is a unique, worthwhile person entitled to human rights. One

My Working Model

ought to be comfortable with using good basic counseling techniques such as reflective listening, and communication and problem solving techniques. I believe it's essential to be open and honest with the child. And one needs to have a sense of humor, to allow the playful, expressive child which rests in all of us to come through.

I would like to appeal to all therapists who are reluctant to work with children. Children need allies, and I hope that more and more therapists who are interested in humanism and equality will begin to see that when they refuse children as clients, they are perpetrating a separatism that furthers the oppression of young people. Children deserve better.

The approach I present is self-monitoring. I believe that there is no way you can make a mistake if you have good will and refrain from interpretations and judgements — if you accept the child with respect and regard. If you do this, you can make contact with any child, and be effective in helping him. Within these broad limits you cannot fail. Children will open themselves to you only to the extent that they feel safe to do so.

Parents can use the techniques described here to find out what their children are all about, and to help the kids find out what their parents are all about. Teachers have reported astonishing results after trying out some of these techniques. One can stay in shallow waters or venture into deeper places, depending on one's training and skill.

At almost every class I have taught, someone brings up the subject of contraindications, or what things you would not do with a child.

Aside from the more obvious don'ts which are the direct opposite of the do's (don't be judgmental, etc.) I have very little to say on this subject. I can't think of one across-the-board generality that fits all children. I won't say "Don't use finger painting with hyperactive children," because I do, with excellent results. True, there may be some hyperactive children who won't respond to this activity. But children generally will let you know if something is not good for them. One must tune in to the child's needs, respect his defenses, move in gently.

Some have said, "Well, you wouldn't use fantasy with a child who is living only in a fantasy world," Yes, I would use fantasy with such a child. I begin with him wherever he is. I want to make with him and maybe I need to do it through the safety of fantasy. There will come a time when I will gently pull him back to reality, and if he is ready he will follow me. If he isn't, he won't.

I never force a child to do or say something he absolutely does not want to do or say. I try to avoid interpretations, so I check out my guesses and hunches with the child. If he's not interested in responding, that's fine. I don't insist that he "own" anything if he needs to keep things safely protected.

I also try not to do anything I am uncomfortable with or dislike doing. If I really don't feel like playing checkers, I will suggest an alternative more to my liking.

More Ideas for Fantasy and Drawing

The following list contains many of the inspirations, motivations, directions, and techniques I use to bring out children's emotions via the medium of drawing and fantasy. Many of these also lend themselves to painting, clay, writing, body movement, and other media. This by no means exhausts all possibilities, rather it is intended to convey a general idea of the types of things I have done with children, done myself, read somewhere, heard about, thought about, or plan to use. The scope of ideas is as wide as the imagination. Some of these ideas are described elsewhere in this book in more detail.

Present the child with a variety of material to choose from — all sizes of paper (newsprint is fine), felt pens, crayons, pastels, colored pencils, fat felt pens, a pencil. Children also enjoy gadgets. Use a kitchen timer at times, a stop watch, egg timer, counters such as a golf counter, market price counter, beads, etc. You might say, "We're going to look at this flower for one minute. I will call time by my stop watch and then ask you to draw — not the flower, but how you felt looking at it or how you felt when I called time."

Visualize your world in colors, lines, shapes, symbols. Visualize how you would like your world to be.

Do some breathing exercises. Draw how you feel now.

Draw: What you do when you're angry. How you would like to be. What makes you angry. A scary place. Something scary. The last time you cried. A place that makes you happy. How you feel this minute.

My Working Model

Draw yourself: as you are (think you are), how you wish you looked, when you're older, when you're old, when you were younger (specific age or not).

Go back to a time or scene: A time you felt most alive. A time you remember. The first thing that pops into your head. A family scene. Your favorite dinner. A time in childhood. A dream.

Draw: Where you wish you could be: an ideal place. A favorite place or a place you dislike. A favorite time or a time you dislike. The worst thing you can think of.

Look at this (use flower, leaf, shell, painting, anything) for two minutes. Draw your feelings. (Set timer. Also use a piece of music.)

Draw: Your family now. Your family in symbols, as animals, as dabs of colors. Your family with each person doing something. The part of you you like best, least. Your inner self, your outer self. How you see yourself. How others see you (you imagine). How you wish they would see you. A person you like, hate, admire, are jealous of. Your monster. Your demon.

Draw: How you get attention. How you get what you want from different people. What you do when you feel depressed, sad, hurt, jealous, lonely, etc. Your loneliness; a lonely feeling; when you feel or felt lonely. An imaginary animal. Something that bugs you about someone here, someone close to you, yourself, the world around you. Your day, your week, your life now, your past, your present, your future.

Draw: Happy lines, tender lines, sad, angry, afraid, etc. (Make sounds, body movement, with the drawing.) Left or right-handed.

As you work with someone, ask him to draw sequential pages illustrating how he feels now, that feeling exaggerated, this part of the drawing, etc.

Draw what you're describing or having trouble describing, in colors, shapes, lines.

Draw in response to: a story, a fantasy, a poem, a piece of music.

Draw polarities: weak/strong; happy/sad; like/don't like; good/bad; positive/negative; angry/calm; responsible/crazy; serious/silly; good feelings/bad feelings; when you're outgoing/when you feel withdrawn; love/hate; joy/misery; trust/suspicion; separate/together; open/closed; alone/not alone; brave/afraid; best part of yourself/ worst part of yourself, etc.

WINDOWS TO OUR CHILDREN

Draw: When you were a child, a teenager, as an adult. (For adults, three images of yourself). A make-believe place. Your most pressing problem. A physical pain — your headache, your backache, feeling tired.

Make a scribble — find a picture. Make a squiggle — complete a picture.

Preschool art: string painting, butterfly painting, finger painting. Car paint (automobile enamel dries fast and can drip for beautiful fantasy pictures; good on Masonite boards).

You draw the child, and have him comment on the drawing.

In a group, pair off and each draw the other. Draw something with a partner. Agree on a theme: being laughed at, ridiculed, picked last, teased, etc.

Draw a road map of your life: show good places, bumpy spots, barriers. Make the map show where you have been, and where you want to go. Draw specific situations and experiences (what it feels like to wet the bed).

A group, family, or a group that is role-playing a family, can decide on a theme and draw together (Be in touch with the process and interaction). Where I am now in my life. Where I come from. Where I used to be. Where I want to go. What's keeping me from getting there (blocks, obstacles); what I need to get there. "I used to be . . . but now . . ." Do a round-robin drawing, with each person adding something in turn.

Draw: How you felt yesterday, today, now, how you will feel tomorrow. Being selfish, stupid, crazy, ugly, mean. Something you want. How you get what you want. A secret. Being alone. Being with others; being serious, being silly.

Draw a picture of yourself exaggerating how you think you look.

Just allow your hand to move over the paper and do whatever it wants to.

Throw out a word and have people draw quickly to represent the word: love, hate, beauty, anxiety, freedom, charity, etc. How you feel as a woman/ man/ child/ adult/ boy/girl. How you imagine you would feel if you were the opposite sex.

Outline the child on a large piece of paper; have the child talk to the outline of himself. Draw your body image in colors, shapes, lines. With eyes closed imagine yourself in front of you.

My Working Model

Draw: yourself as an animal, and a setting to put it in. An image of your mother/father in colors, lines, shapes.

Think back to when you were very little and draw something that made you very happy, excited, made you feel good, something you had, something you did, somebody you knew, something that made you sad, etc. Draw it as if you were that age.

Draw something you wished would happen when you were little.

As the child talks and something comes up, ask her to draw that thing: a physical pain, an incident, a feeling, etc.

Draw an imaginary animal, as in the Dr. Seuss book *If I Ran the Zoo*. Be it — what could he do? In a group have two of the animals encounter each other. Draw an animal, or two animals, and write (or dictate) three words to describe each animal. Now be the animal and tell about yourself.

Draw something you don't like about what I do, and I will too. Draw something you're worried about. Draw three wishes. Have the child tell you what to draw, as you draw it.

Touch your face, then draw it.

Imagine that you have the power today to do anything you want in this world. Draw what you would do. If you were magic, where would you like to be?

Draw a present you would like to get, to give. Who would give it to you? Who would you give it to?

Draw: something you wish you didn't do. Something you feel guilty about. Or the feeling of guilt. Your power. Something you need to let go of.

Many other kinds of things can be used as themes for drawings. Many fantasies, stories, sounds, movements, and sights lend themselves to drawing. You can also combine poetry and writing with any of these.

Have the children use colors, lines, shapes, curves — light strokes, heavy strokes, long and short strokes; bright colors, light colors, dark and dull colors; symbols, stick figures.

Have people work quickly. If you notice a pattern, have them experiment with the opposite of what they usually do.

4

Making Things

Clay

Of all the materials I use with children, clay is definitely my favorite. I usually work with the clay right along with the children and this leaves me feeling good and relaxed. Clay's flexibility and malleability suit it to a variety of needs. Consider its attributes: It is wonderful because it is messy, mushy, soft, and sensuous, appealing to every age. It promotes the working through of the most primal of internal processes. It affords an opportunity for flow between itself and the user unequaled by any other material. It is easy to become one with the clay. It offers both tactile and kinesthetic experience. Many children with perceptual and motor problems need this kind of experience. It brings people closer to their feelings. Perhaps because of the flowing quality, a union occurs between the medium and the user. It often seems to penetrate the protective armor, the barriers in a child. People who are very out of touch with their feelings and who continually block their expression are usually out of touch with their senses. The sensuousness of clay often gives them a bridge between their senses and their feelings. The aggressive child can use clay to punch and pound. Children who are angry can vent their anger through clay in numerous ways.

Those who are insecure and fearful can feel a sense of control and mastery through clay. It is a medium that can be "erased" and that has no clear-cut, specific rules for its use. It's very difficult to make a "mistake" with clay. Children who need strengthening of self-esteem experience a unique sense of self through its use. It is the most graphic of all media in allowing the therapist to observe the child's process. The therapist can actually see what's going on with the child by watching how he works with the clay. It's a good link to verbal expression for nonverbal children. It affords the highly verbal, including those that parents and teachers accuse of talking too much, a means of expression leaning away from lots of words. It helps children cultivate and satisfy their curiosity about sex and body parts and functions. A child can enjoy the use of clay as a solitary activity, and clay work can also be a very social activity. Children have wonderful conversations among themselves during undirected activity. They often interact with each other on a new level, sharing thoughts, ideas, feelings, and experiences.

Some people are put off by the messiness of clay. Actually, it is the cleanest of all the art materials, second to water. It dries to fine dust and is easily washed, brushed, vacuumed, or sponged off hands, clothing, rugs, floors, tables. Clay has healing properties. Sculptors and potters have observed that cuts heal faster if left uncovered as they work with clay.

Most children readily take to clay, but one occasionally sees a child who is fearful of the wet, "messy" mass the clay represents to him. This in itself tells the therapist a great deal about the child and a useful direction to pursue in the therapy. Certainly there is a direct link between his cleanliness compulsion and his emotional problems, and this may not become obvious with any of the other materials presented to the child. I will work gently, gradually introducing clay again after the initial resistance to it. Such a child is often fascinated as well as repelled, and begins to move in cautiously.

When I work with children who withhold bowel movements or mess their pants, I use clay. One nine-year-old boy loved to make the clay as wet and mushy as possible, pouring water with delight over it and into cavities he would make. Then suddenly, without warning it seemed, something would happen inside him, and he would suddenly jerk away, tense up, and announce to me that he was finished playing with clay. For a long time he was unable to openly communicate what thoughts, feelings, or memories occurred at that instant of pulling away. Then one day he spoke of his fascination with his own feces. He told me that once when he was about

Making Things

four he remembered wanting to feel the consistency of this material he himself had manufactured, reaching into the toilet and being yanked back with great force by his mother, who gave him a very severe lecture. After that he made other attempts to touch the stuff but was so consumed with shame and guilt that he stopped this forbidden activity. This incident alone may or may not have brought about his bowel problems, but it was certainly an important factor. After this sharing of his memory (which may have surfaced only as a result of his contact with the clay) he became much more comfortable with the clay and more relaxed generally. This relaxation helped him to work toward opening himself to other expressions, and eventually he gained normal bowel control.

I find that children often have a narrow repertoire of what to do with clay. Give a child a lump of clay and he will inevitably make an ashtray or a bowl or perhaps a snake. The more experience a child has with the amazing flexibility and versatility of this medium, the greater the opportunity for expression. I find that it helps to provide a box of "tools" to use with clay: a rubber mallet (essential), a cheese cutter, a putty knife, a garlic press, a scraper or food chopper (hand style), a pencil for poking, a potato masher, etc. I'm always on the lookout for other interesting items from the kitchen, tool chest, anywhere. The more unlikely the item (that is, not specifically designed to be used with clay), the better.

Where we work does not matter. Sometimes the child sits at a table, using the clay on a thick piece of board (like a cutting board). Sometimes we move the board and sit on the floor. Sitting outside somewhere is delightful. When I use clay with groups we usually sit around in a circle on the floor and I give each child an extra heavy paper plate (which lasts through many uses) on a newspaper. I provide paper towels and pre-moistened towelettes to ease any mess anxiety. Little pans of water are important for wetting the clay, smoothing areas, and simply to pour over it.

I often do the following exercise to give children experience in the many things one can do with clay:

"Close your eyes as we do this. Notice that with your eyes closed, your fingers and hands are more sensitive to the clay and can feel it better. When your eyes are open, they can get in the way of your feeling the clay. Try this both ways to check this out. If you need to peek once in a while, that's fine; then just close your eyes again. Sit for a moment with your hands on your lump of clay. Take a couple of deep breaths. (I work right along with some clay as I instruct, in order to have a sense of timing.) Now follow my directions.

"Feel the lump of clay as it is now — make friends with it. Is it smooth? Rough? Hard? Soft? Bumpy? Cold? Warm? Wet? Dry? Pick it up and hold it. Is it light? Heavy? . . . . Now I want you to put it down and pinch it. Use both hands. Pinch it slowly. . . . Now faster. . . . Take big pinches and small pinches. Do this a while. . . .

"Squeeze your clay. . . . Now smooth it. Use your thumbs, fingers, palms, back of hands. After you smooth it, feel the places you have smoothed. . . . Bunch it up together in a ball. . . . Punch it. . . . If it gets flat, bunch it and punch again. Try your other hand too. . . . Bunch it up and stroke it. . . . Pat it. . . . Slap it. . . . Feel the smooth place that you made after slapping it. . . .

"Bunch it up. Tear it. Tear little pieces and tear big pieces. . . . Bunch it up. Pick it up and throw it down. You may have to peek for this. . . . Do it again. Do it harder. Make a loud noise with it. Don't be afraid to hit HARD. . . .

"Now bunch it up again. . . . Poke at it with your fingers. . . . Take a finger and bore a hole in the clay. . . . Bore a few more holes. . . . Bore one right through to the other side. Feel the sides of the hole you made. . . . Bunch it up and try making lines of bumps and little holes with your fingers and fingernails and feel those things you make. . . . Try your knuckles, the heel of your hand, the palm — different parts of your hand. See what you can make. You might want to even try your elbows. . . .

"Now tear a piece off and make a snake. It gets thinner and longer as you roll it. Wrap it around your other hand or a finger. Now take a piece and roll it between the palms of your hands and make a little ball. Feel that ball. . . . Now bunch it all up again. Sit for a moment again with both hands on your piece of clay. You know it pretty well now."

As the children first begin this exercise in a group there is often giggling and talking. I speak softly, almost continuously giving directions, and soon the children are very quiet, concentrating on listening to me, very involved and being with the clay.

Making Things

Afterwards we talk about the experience. "What did you like best? What did you hate doing?" Sometimes I explore further what they liked or didn't like. A boy responds, "I loved pinching the clay. I didn't want to stop." I say, "Do this now — pinch it. What does it make you think of as you do this? Do you get a flash of memory, or does it remind you of something, or how does it make you feel?" The boy says, "I'm pinching my sister. I'd like to pinch her and pinch her. She'd hate it. I'm not allowed to hit her. My father once hit me with a strap because I hit her. He says I'm not allowed to hit her because she's a girl. So she teases me and makes me mad and pinches me sometimes, and I'd like to kill her, but she knows I can't touch her!" He smiles at all of us as we nod and listen.

And then he says, "She's really not so bad all the time — I have this game I taught her how to play and it's kind of fun playing it with her at night when we can't go out." Perhaps another time we will deal with some of the other parts of his statements such as his father's hitting him with a strap, and the attitudes building up inside him about girls.

Another child says, "I like smoothing it." I ask her to do this again. She says, "It's like petting my cat. I like to pet my cat." She continues to smooth. "I remember crawling in bed sometimes with my mother and she would hug me." (Her mother had died the year before.) "You must miss her very much," I say. "Yes," she says, "I do a lot. I used to think I couldn't live without my mother. How would I live without a mother to take care of me? But we're doing OK. I can do lots of things to help. We've worked it out in our family. But I sure miss her a lot sometimes. But sometimes I forget about it!"

It's fun sometimes to play music while children explore with the clay on their own. Or I might beat a drum in various rhythms as they poke and pinch and slap in time to my cadence.

I often work with clay in the same way I work with art. "Close your eyes and go into your space. Feel your clay with both hands for a few seconds. Take a couple of deep breaths. Now I would like you to make something with your clay, keeping your eyes closed. Just let your fingers move. See if the clay seems to want to go its own way. Or perhaps you want it to go your way. Make a form, a shape. If you have something in mind you want to make, do it with your eyes closed and see what happens. Or just move the clay around. Let yourself be surprised. You will have only a few minutes to do this. When you're finished, open your eyes and look at what you've made. You can add finishing touches, but don't change it. Look at it. Turn it and see it from different sides and angles."

Here are some examples of the results of the last exercise, taken from a group session. The children were asked to describe their object of clay as if it were themselves: "Be this piece of clay — you are the clay."

Jimmy, age eleven: I am an ashtray, I have a smooth bottom and a ledge all around me. I have two places on each side to hold cigarettes. I have some rough places and scratches on me,

Jimmy, who uses you?

Jimmy: my father.

Well, how does he use you?

Jimmy: He drops ashes in me and then he smashes the cigarettes into me to put them out. (Jimmy becomes silent as he stares at his piece of clay.)

(Very softly.) Does this fit into your life as Jimmy in any way?

Jimmy: (Looks at me, voice rising.) Yes! That's what he does to me. He smashes me. He grinds me like a cigarette.

Would you like to share more about that with us?

Jimmy nods and begins, for the first time in the group, to tell us about his relationship with his father and his feelings of not being understood. He begins to cry. The other children gently enter into the discussion, sharing some of their own experiences, indicating genuine understanding of what Jimmy is experiencing. At a certain point, when I think it's a good time to end our focus on Jimmy, I thank him for sharing his feelings with us and I know by the calm look on his face that he has come another step toward wholeness and maturity. This session with the clay opened the door to later sessions in which Jimmy was able to express much of his anger towards his father, talk about how he handled his anger, examine some of the ways he actually manipulated his father into anger, what he wanted from his father, and so forth.

Sheila, age eleven: I am a sun. I am flat. I have two eyes and marks all over my face. I like the sun because it is warm and makes things shine.

Can you say "me" instead of "sun" and say that again?

Making Things

Sheila: I like me because I am warm and make things shine, and I have a smiling face on me.

Does any of what you said as a sun have anything to do with you — Sheila?

Sheila: Well, yes, sometimes I can make things — people — feel warm. Sometimes I feel shiny and warm. I'm smiling now and I feel good. (Broad smile. Suddenly Sheila hunches, looks away from me and others, loses her smile.) I don't always smile! Most of the time I never feel like smiling.

One of the other children asks Sheila what kinds of things make her feel like not smiling. She tells about some of the conflicts in her life with friends, teachers, siblings, and parents. Everyone listens intently. I then ask her what some of the things are that make her smile like her sun. She looks around at us, bringing herself back into the room and back into her good feelings, and smiles broadly again. "I feel happy when I'm the sun," she giggles.

Sheila has many conflicts in her life. She worries a great deal about everything, always expecting the worst, since the worst is not unfamiliar to her. She is learning now to allow herself to enjoy the good things in her life rather than ruin those good feelings with gloomy forecasts. She is learning to cope with her very real conflicts. She is finding out that in her existence she is not a helpless victim. She is discovering the concept of polarities of life and self, that if she sometimes feels angry or sad, she can accept and experience these feelings with the knowledge that at other times she feels calm and happy. She is letting herself experience her joyful moments as well as her miserable ones, without fear.

Joe, age twelve: I didn't make anything.

I see that you have something here — your clay. I would like you to describe it, just as it is.

Joe: (staring at his piece of clay for a moment.) I'm a lump of nothing. And that's the way *I* feel most of the time — like a lump of nothing.

And now?

Joe: And now I feel like a lump of nothing.

You feel like you're not worth much.

Joe: That's right, I'm not.

WINDOWS TO OUR CHILDREN

Thank you for sharing your feeling with us, Joe. I feel very appreciative of you for doing that.

Joe: (slight smile.) That's OK.

What is evident here is Joe's low self-esteem, which he openly shared with us. In doing so, in telling us about his existence in life as he perceived it, I believe Joe made a giant step toward renewed selfhood. The fact that I experience him as a neat kid makes little difference at this point; I must accept him just as he is to himself. Arguing with him about his own perceptions would weaken, not strengthen, his self-esteem.

In an individual session, a nine-year-old boy said, "I'm a piece of clay. What else do you want me to say?"

Just tell me what you look like. Are you bumpy?

Doug: Well, I've got a lot of bumps on me and I've got cracks. I have a seat. I look like a chair without legs.

What happened to your legs?

Doug: Well, the family that had me didn't use me right. They jumped up and down on me, and they broke my legs.

Then what happened?

Doug: They gave me away.

Where are you now?

Doug: I'm out in the dump. They didn't give me to Goodwill or anything. They just threw me out in the dump.

What's it like out there in the dump? Do you like being there?

Doug: No. (His voice begins to change — becomes lower, softer.) No, I don't like it here.

Doug, is there anything you said about you as this clay chair that fits for you in your own life?

Doug: Yeah. They might as well throw me out in the dump.

Who's the "they?"

Doug: My mom and dad. They never listen to me, they never think anything I say is good. They don't care anything about me. They like the other kids better. They're always picking on me. I'd be better off in a dump.

The quality of Doug's expression in this session was quite different from previous times when he voiced complaints. Instead of his usual whiny or rebellious tone, he spoke from a place of deep feeling. In truth he had

Making Things

taken onto himself much of what he perceived as coming from his parents. In our later sessions he said that he actually felt, believed, that he was "not good, no good." He felt so lost, so insignificant in his life that he admitted feelings of wanting to be dead (a not so uncommon wish among young children). He reacted to these feelings with nervous behavior, poor performance in school, angry outbursts at home as the result of fairly minor occurrences, and severe headaches. It was only when his deepest feelings of despair began to emerge that we could begin to work on helping Doug feel a sense of his own worth and entitlement. Some of the subsequent sessions with his whole family became effective and dynamic when these dark feelings became visible.

Over and over again, I am impressed with the exceptional power of clay. It is as if the sense of touch and movement of muscles with and against the resistive yet yielding movement of the clay provides an access, an opening into one's deepest places. Whether the session is directed or undirected (whether I introduce a specific exercise, or the child just plays as we talk), something new seems to come through where the child and I can see it and examine it.

It is with clay that the child's process seems most evident. As he works with it or shares his experience with it, I watch him closely; I watch for grimaces, gestures, and changes in tone or posture. The body seems to communicate through the clay; when I receive these messages, I know something is going on within the child that is important to him. At these moments I may decide to say, "Do you ever feel this way?" Or "Does that ever happen in your life?" Sometimes these moments pass so quickly that unless the therapist becomes attuned to catching them, the fertile moment is gone.

Other questions you can ask are: How are you used? How could you be used? Are you of any use at all? Are you nice to look at? What happened to you? What happened next? Are you good? Are you bad? Do you like yourself as a piece of clay? Do others like you as this piece of clay? Does this fit in any way into your own life? Does this remind you of anything in your life? Did anything you said as this clay fit for you as a person? Where are you? And on and on.

WINDOWS TO OUR CHILDREN

Other Exercises with Clay

With eyes closed, make a form, a shape — let the clay lead. Make an imaginary animal, bird, fish. Make a real animal, bird, fish. Make something imaginary. Make something real. Close your eyes and visualize your world, your life. Show this in clay. Make something special or nothing special. Make something from another planet. Make something you'd like to be. Make something from a dream. Make a story, a scene with your clay.

Make your family as people or objects or animals or symbols. Make your problem. Make your ideal family — how you wish it were. Make a symbolic image of yourself. Keep your eyes closed, and make an image of yourself when you were a baby, or very young. Have two people work with a lump of clay together. Have two people work with their own pieces, but make things that fit together with the other person's things. Have a group make a cooperative panorama together. Let it happen spontaneously, or discuss the theme in advance.

A three-minute time limit with any of the themes above eliminates perfectionism and often provides a more interesting result than a longer time.

Younger children much prefer to work with clay with their eyes open. Very young ones (ages four, five, and maybe six) like to play with clay and talk, often resisting too much direction — though they do enjoy the exercise of pinching, poking, hitting, etc.

In a small group of children, ages six, seven, and eight, we all did a family sculpture. I asked the children each to join me in making figures representing our families. As we talked about each person, some of the children told little stories about a family situation. Gail told about her father's picking her up for their visit together. She moved the figures as she talked, to the great interest of the others who were all children of divorce. Some of them had asked if they should make their fathers! When I said yes, Gail responded with "Good!" and proceeded to make and remake him about eight times, showing much anxiety in her process. After her story, I said, "You had trouble making your father figure. You seem worried about him in some way." She began to cry and said that her father hardly ever came to see her.

Making Things

I asked the children in turn to say something they liked and something they didn't like to each figure. At my turn after I had made my "I like" statement to my former husband, Tim said, "I expected you to be mad! How can you be nice if you're divorced?" They listened in fascination as I explained my initial pain and grief and my present caring and friendly relationship with Harold.

At another session the children each made an object and shared themselves beginning with "I am." Tim: "I'm a duck that plays baseball. (to me:) I play good baseball." Gail: "I'm a candle. I'm warm and bright and pretty." (Big grin following this statement.)

Plastic Modeling Clay

This kind of clay, sometimes called Plasticine, never dries out or hardens, nor is it fired in a kiln. It is difficult to use when cold and requires "working" with the hand to make it soft and pliable. Because it doesn't need the care that real clay requires (wet rag to keep it from hardening, etc.), it is very useful for carrying around and available for spontaneous use. It is not as clean as real clay; it tends to stick to the hands and to furniture, and is harder to wash off.

As I talk with a child, I may fiddle with a piece of this kind of clay, giving the child a lump to fiddle with, too. If a child talks about his brother, I may fashion a very quick clay brother and say, "Here he is. Tell *him* what you are saying." In this way I can bring the situation into present experience to be dealt with in a much more fruitful way than if he continued to talk "about" the situation. Talking "about" tends to lead nowhere, often skirting the real feelings involved.

When Julie, age seven, came in for her session, her mother remarked, "See if you can find out why Julie won't take a bath. She just won't do it!" So Julie and I talked about her bath-taking problem. She wouldn't say much about her aversion to bathing, but did begin to talk about her baby brother and how she helped her mother bathe him. My hunch was that Julie was jealous about her baby brother's bath time. This prompted me to find a way to give her a vicarious experience of being a baby getting a bath, so as she talked, I quickly fashioned a crude baby and tub. I announced that the baby was Julie and I began to "bathe" her, using all the expressions generally murmured to a little baby during a bath. ("Now I'm going to wash your cute little feet," etc.) Julie smiled broadly as she watched, sometimes responding as the baby, giggling, cooing. I went through the whole procedure. Then Julie became very busy making a figure of her own with the clay. She announced that the figure was herself, and sat it on a larger lump of clay which she said was a bean bag chair. "My Daddy has a bean bag chair, but he never lets me sit in it. He says I'll break it. This is me sitting in it and I'm reading." I ask the clay figure to describe how it felt to be in the chair. Julie, speaking for the clay, responded that it was comfortable. We continued a dialogue for a while, and finally, just as our session ended, Julie announced, "I think I'll tell my mother I'm old enough to take a shower." (She had previously ignored this helpful suggestion from her mother.)

I'm not sure what happened in this session, although I could certainly give several interpretive guesses. I do know that Julie *experienced* something for herself which helped her to grow as an individual.

In a group situation, children can pair off and make objects that must fit or go together in some way. When the group reassembles, the children, as their objects, share themselves. "I'm a tree." "I'm a flower growing under the tree." They can dialogue with each other as flower and tree, creating a spontaneous interaction. They can also later talk about the process: how it felt to work together in this way, who made most of the decisions, and so forth.

Dough

You can buy play-dough or make your own. Here is the recipe: 4 cups flour, 2 cups salt, 1 cup water, 2 tbsp. oil, 1 tbsp. food coloring of your choice. Mix the salt and flour. Mix the water, oil and coloring separately. Gradually add the liquid to the rest of mixture until you achieve the desired consistency. It keeps for some time in an airtight plastic bag.

This material provides a different kind of sensation to the touch, but it does not replace clay. It is especially fun for older children who have outgrown its use at home. Figures can be made which harden and can be painted. Fooling with it, molding it, using all kinds of tools and baking equipment provide good tactile and sensory experiences. Finger painting with play-dough provides another kind of experience. Add water until the dough has a loose, pudding like consistency and move it around on paper, table or tray with fingers just as you would finger paints.

Water

There's something about water that's very soothing. Most of us are familiar with the relaxing effects of a bath. It has the same effect on children. When my own children were preschoolers, they would stand for hours on a stool at the kitchen sink, apron-clad, washing and pouring, pouring and washing.

I will sometimes offer a child a basin of water and a variety of plastic pouring items. The child and I have much good conversation as he engages in this kind of water play. I have a doctor set which includes some miniature vessels. Children as old as twelve have enjoyed pouring water into and out of these. Some children, especially younger ones, will not begin to express themselves verbally or through other expressive media until they have practically saturated themselves with water play. I describe working with water in conjunction with sand more fully in a later discussion of sand.

Sculpture and Constructions

There are many ways of doing simple sculpture. Useful materials include clay, plaster, wax, soap, wood, wire, metal, paper, pipe cleaners, boxes, and many more. Art books written for young children give some good ideas for sculptures that are easy to do with children. Many of the suggestions given for art, clay, and collage can be adapted for sculpture. However, I don't think one always needs to give direction; some children go off easily on their own, and I can work effectively with whatever they come up with, or merely with their process as they work.

Flexible wire such as armature wire, picture wire, or any other wire found at a hardware store, makes interesting pieces. Using pliers and wire cutters as well as paper towel rolls, pencils, or small boxes to loop the wire around gives one mastery over the wire. A wire sculpture is much like a three-dimensional scribble drawing. The finished piece can be stapled onto a block of wood or set into clay or plaster of paris. Plaster of paris can also be poured over parts of the sculpture to give it new effects.

WINDOWS TO OUR CHILDREN

After a nine-year-old girl absorbed herself for some time in making a bird, she told me this story: "This bird was once a free bird. One day it flew into a yard with lots of big bushes that needed cutting. It got stuck in the bushes and didn't know how to get out. It pulled and pushed and broke its leg. She cried and cried for help but no one came. Time went by and she was stuck there forever like this." When I asked her if there was anything in her story that fit for her own life she answered, after much thought, "Sometimes I feel as if I'm crying for help inside of me and no one comes to help." A child is often helped to reveal the secret places of her heart through creative absorption.

Plastic modeling clay makes a fine non-hardening base for sculpture. A variety of materials can go into this base to form an interesting, abstract creation.

One of the most successful sculpturing activities I ever experienced with children was what we called "junk sculpture." When I worked with emotionally disturbed children in the schools, this was second in effectiveness only to woodworking. The children and I collected all the junk we could think of from our garages, houses, classroom. Nothing that had possibilities was thrown away. The children each selected what they wanted from a communal box. On individual blocks of wood they nailed, glued, stapled, taped, and nailed some more, until each had a fantastic original creation. We then sprayed the pieces with gold or silver paint, and they shone as true works of art. The pride they had (not to mention their fun in making the pieces) was immensely therapeutic to these children, who were often considered clumsy, awkward, uncoordinated. Sometimes we (myself included) would make up fantastic stories about the pieces — they almost cried out to be taken into fantasy — and sometimes we would have fun analyzing the particular items in our creations. "I am a clothespin. I pinch. I can pinch hard!" "I am a bolt with a nut on me. My nut goes up and down but it can't get out. Yeah! I can't get out either. I'm stuck in this school!" "I'm a Styrofoam ball. It's easy to stick things in me. I have things stuck all over me. That's me all right." "I'm just a piece of junk made up of lots of junk that was going to be thrown away. Jim thinks I'm pretty nice. I am pretty nice. It's a good thing I wasn't thrown away. (Low whisper:) Sometimes I think if she could, my mother would throw me out with the garbage."

Making Things

Wood and Tools

Given scraps of wood, saws, hammers, hand drills, nails, and a sawhorse, children can make all sorts of interesting objects. If at all possible, opportunities for using tools with wood should be made available to all children. I have had tremendous success in using woodwork with even the most hyperactive, poorly coordinated children. Rules and limitations need to be made clear and strictly adhered to, since tools can be quite dangerous. In my experience, however, I have never had a child misuse tools. Most children, especially those with problems, aren't given much opportunity to use tools; they love it and are quite willing to be careful. When I worked in the schools, this was the favorite activity, and once I've offered wood and tools to children in individual therapy, I have a problem in getting them to do anything else. As soon as they know this experience is available, that is what they want to do every time. This tells me that here is an activity children love but never get enough of.

During the vogue of behavior modification I was criticized by the local university, which placed student teachers in special education in my class, for not using woodworking as a reward for good behavior or work completed. In my classroom, "building," as the children called it, was an every-morning activity. The school of thought was that anything that kids enjoy so much ought to be held out almost beyond their reach, as an incentive to do better and be better. Nothing makes my hair stand on end more than hearing this kind of pronouncement. These kids were entitled to build! I could rationalize the activity by saying that it was a good learning experience that promoted problem solving, camaraderie, and sharing. True as that may be, it is beside the point. The children deserved it and had the right to it, not because it was good for them but simply because they liked doing it.

Collage

Coming from the French word that means a pasting or a paper hanging, a collage is any design or picture made by pasting or attaching materials of any variety to a flat backing such as cloth or paper. Sometimes a collage is made in conjunction with drawing, painting, or some kind of writing.

WINDOWS TO OUR CHILDREN

Working on a collage is a familiar activity in nursery school, where pieces of cut or torn paper, and sometimes other materials as well, are pasted onto a larger sheet of paper to form a design. I have found the collage to be an exciting medium of expression for all ages.

Some of the materials that can be used for collage are: *Paper* — of all kinds: tissue paper, construction paper, gift-wrapping paper, old greeting cards, newspaper, paper sacks, corrugated paper, doilies, wallpaper. *Various textures of cloth* — cotton, wool, burlap, flannel, silk, lace. *Soft things* — feathers, cotton, furry pieces. *Rough things* — steel wool, sandpaper, sponge. *Other things* — yarn, string, buttons, aluminum foil, cellophane, mosquito netting, orange sacks, egg cartons, plastics, bottle caps, leaves, shells, ribbons, seeds of all kinds, noodles and macaroni, chicken wire, driftwood, pebbles, tongue depressors, cotton swabs, cork. *Anything* that's lightweight and can be attached, pasted, or fastened to a flat surface in some way.

Good collage work can be done merely with magazine pictures, a pair of scissors, glue, and some kind of backing. The most important things to have for a collage are pictures — old magazines (or new ones), calendars and date books with pictures on them, anything with pictures or photographs. Words cut out of magazines and newspapers appeal to some. Coloring books, children's activity books, and old storybooks are good to have on hand, too.

The backing can be poster board, drawing paper, butcher paper, heavy cloth (such as burlap), newspaper, one side of a cardboard carton, glass, wood, or plastic. Scissors, a stapler, paper fasteners, scotch tape, masking tape, glue, paste, a hole punch, string — are all useful. All the ideas and themes at the end of Chapter 3 can be used as a basis for a collage.

A collage can be worked with in many ways, similarly to a drawing or sand tray creation. Sometimes the child will just share her view of her own collage: "This picture of an airplane is because I wish I could go on one." Or "This sandpaper is for the rough time I'm having in school." Or "This clock is because I'm always having to worry about what time it is." Sometimes the child will tell a longer story about the collage.

A twelve-year-old boy cut out a variety of pictures and pasted them on a poster board. When he was through, he said that he had just cut pictures that appealed to him, that they had no meaning for him. So I asked him to tell me a story about each picture. "Once there was a racing car...." Much material to work with came from this exercise.

A fourteen-year-old girl also said she just chose pictures she liked. I asked her to *be* each item in her pictures. Of a picture of breakfast cereal, she said, "I am cereal. Kids like me. I like being liked. My brother likes me — not really me, but the cereal." This paved the way to talk about her own feelings of wanting to be liked.

Sometimes the *process* of making the collage or later telling about the collage is most significant. A thirteen-year-old boy told some short stories about his pictures and after each one said, "This doesn't make sense!" or "That's a dumb one." When he was through, I pointed this out to him and mentioned that I thought he was hard on himself. His response, "Yeah! At school when I make three mistakes I go crazy!"

Sometimes nothing comes through to work with, but the child has at least had a chance to express himself, to make a statement about himself. If nothing else, collage is fun to do and helps free the imagination.

Collage can be used as a sensory experience as well as an emotional expression. In the book, *Art for the Family*, by Victor D'Amico, Frances Wilson and Moreen Maser, collage is referred to as "feeling and seeing pictures."

> Do you know that you can see with your fingers? Of course you can see with your eyes, but your fingers tell you much that your eyes can't. They tell you that things are warm or cold, rough or smooth, hard or soft. We all love to touch things. It helps us to find out about the world and how we feel about it. We may find that we like to touch things that other people don't. That's because everybody is different. Your art tells what you feel, see and know. You can make a picture of what you feel. (p. 11)

This book gives some wonderful suggestions for individual and group collage:

WINDOWS TO OUR CHILDREN

> Make a feeling and seeing portrait of a person you know, like your mother; someone you have seen, like a girl dressed for a party; or someone you imagine, like a princess or a beggar. Choose the kinds of materials that seem to tell about the person you have in mind. Cut them in the sizes and shapes that tell more about the person, and arrange them on a background to make a design that is interesting to look at and to touch. (p. 15)

> Choose the materials that tell how you feel inside. Happiness, sadness, excitement, shyness, loneliness, and other feelings can be expressed through the colors, textures and patterns you choose and the way you cut and arrange them. (p. 16)

Sometimes I ask children to give the collage a title after it is done (since it might stray from the original thematic instruction), such as "Me" or "My Worries" or whatever they come up with.

Collage is a comfortable activity whether done with partners, in a group, or with a family. I sometimes do one along with an individual child, because I find this to be a very helpful way to motivate the child to do one freely.

Pictures

In writing about collage and stories based on collage, I have mentioned using pictures from magazines or wherever. I recently heard about a technique for using pictures that I have tried with success.

I have made a collection of pictures that I have found interesting — pictures that catch my eye in a newspaper or magazine. To this collection I have added some picture postcards, some illustrations from worn-out children's books, some smaller art prints, tarot cards, cards with various words written on them such as love, hate, quiet, and noisy, and pictures from calendar notebooks. These pictures are not "childish" pictures, though there are many pictures of children and children doing things. Besides the pictures that just appeal to me, I have tried to gather a representative assortment based on the images in Jung's *Man and His Symbols* and those so carefully delineated in Assagioli's *Psychosynthesis*. Assagioli divides symbols into categories: nature symbols, animal symbols, human symbols, man-made symbols, religious and mythological symbols, abstract symbols (numbers and shapes), and individual or spontaneous symbols such as emerge in dreams and daydreams.

The child is asked to select some pictures — perhaps ten — and to lay them out on the floor or table or on a large sheet of paper (not glued down, since I keep the pictures). I might ask the child to select them at random — whatever is appealing — or I might request that the selection be in line with some title or theme. Much is revealed through the selection of pictures. The mood displayed by the set chosen can say something about what the child is feeling at the moment or in her life in general. We work with these pictures in the same way as discussed previously.

Tarot Cards

A deck of tarot cards is a very fertile identification device, and the Rider deck has the most detail. I have an inexpensive deck that I use with children of all ages. Young children can select a card that appeals to them and weave a fantasy story around it. With older children I will ask them to choose two or three cards that have some kind of impact — good or bad — upon them and to identify with the illustrations selected.

"I am the empress. I tell everybody what to do. I am very wise and people come to me for advice," said one thirteen-year-old girl.

Is that how it is for you in your life? I asked.

No, but I sure wish I had some answers to some things!

Like what? (Said gently) Imagine that you can ask your empress on this card whatever you want to ask. Pick one thing to ask her now.

She proceeded to have a dialogue with herself about some pressing problems in her life, and to her surprise, she found that she did indeed have an inner wisdom.

Sometimes we play the tarot game according to the directions, and this helps us to talk a lot about the child's life.

5

Storytelling, Poetry and Puppets

Storytelling

The use of stories in therapy involves making up my own stories to tell to children; the children's making up stories; reading stories from books; writing stories; dictating stories; using things to stimulate stories such as pictures, projective tests, puppets, the flannel board, the sand tray, drawings, open-ended fantasies; and using props and aids such as tape recorder, video tape, walkie-talkies, toy microphone, or an imaginary TV set (a large box).

Dr. Richard Gardner describes his mutual storytelling technique in much detail in his book, *Therapeutic Communication with Children*. Essentially, he first has the child tell a story; then Gardner tells his own story, using the same characters that the child has used but offering a better solution. Since the child's story is a projection, it will generally reflect something about the child's life situation. Each story is ended with a lesson or moral derived from the story situation. When using this technique it is important to know something about the child and his life, and to quickly understand the main theme of the child's story.

I have used Gardner's technique, adding some of my own variations at times, and find it to be very effective for some children. Using video tape or a tape recorder is essential; a mock radio or TV station is set up to create the proper atmosphere for the storytelling session.

Although Dr. Gardner asks the children to make up a story rather than use ideas from TV or movies or books, I have found that it doesn't matter if they do. They choose whatever appeals to them for some reason, and they always change it into their own version.

The following example shows how I used this technique with a six-year-old boy. Bobby was brought in to see me for problems involving bed-wetting, overeating, walking in his sleep, and nightmares. He was a chubby, easygoing, amiable child. As his symptomatic behavior improved, he began to act in very aggressive ways such as shouting and screaming when he was angry, throwing eggs at other children when he was mad at them, hitting other children. He was beginning to lose many friends. Here was our session:

Into tape recorder microphone — my recorder has a built-in microphone but I find that attaching a regular one that the child can hold is more appealing. "Hello Ladies and Gentlemen, Boys and Girls. This is Station KOAK and welcome to Story Hour. We have as our guest Bobby ———. (I turn to Bobby.) We're glad to have you on the program. Will you tell us how old you are?"

Bobby: Six years old.

Let's get right down to our program. Here are the rules, radio audience. Bobby will tell us a story. It must have a beginning, middle, and end. When he is through I will tell a story using the same characters in my story as in his. Each story will have some kind of lesson or moral to it. Go ahead, Bobby.

Bobby: (long pause, then whispers) I don't know what to say.

I'll help you. "Once upon a time there was a. . . ." (a suggestion offered by Gardner to help kids get started.)

Bobby: "A shark."

"And this shark . . ."

Bobby: "Liked to eat people."

What happened?

Bobby: "He went around the ocean eating people. That's all."

That's only the beginning. We need the middle and the end.

Bobby: "Well, he saw some fishermen and scared them. They fell out of their boat and the shark swam up and ate them up. Then he swam out to sea, far out where it was very deep. That's where he lived. The end."

Thank you very much for your fine story. What is the lesson?

Bobby: I don't know.

Storytelling, Poetry and Puppets

OK. Now it's my turn. "Once upon a time there was a shark who went around eating people. He ate everyone in sight. Some fishermen came along and got so scared they rowed away as fast as they could to get away from the shark. Everyone was afraid of him. Even the other fish and even the other sharks were afraid because sometimes he tried to eat them, too. Pretty soon he got bored with all of it. He wanted to play but no one would play with him. Everyone ran away from him."

Bobby: So what happened?

"Well, he didn't know what to do. Finally he went to the king of the sharks in a big deep cave way out in the ocean and asked him what he should do. The king of the sharks said, 'You have to find someone who will not be afraid of you, who will trust you, so everyone will see you really want to be friendly. Someone who's not afraid of you might play with you — someone who doesn't know how you've been eating people and scaring people.' And the shark said, 'Where will I find such a person?' The king of sharks said he'd have to figure that out himself."

Bobby: (In a loud whisper to me, avoiding the microphone) I know! A newborn baby!

"So the shark swam off to find someone who would trust him. Soon he came to a big boat and there was a family with a newborn baby. When the people saw the shark, they all ran to hide in the cabin, forgetting the baby in their rush. The shark began to do tricks for the baby. The baby laughed and cooed. When his parents saw this, they came back up and made friends with the shark, realizing he wanted to be friendly and wouldn't hurt them. So they became friends and the shark was very happy. The End. The lesson of my story is if you want to be friends with people you have to act friendly."

Bobby: Can we listen to that again?

I rewind the tape and we listen to both stories. Mine is pretty long compared to his, but he listens with great absorption. When it's through, we begin to talk about his own problem with friends these days, and some things he could do when he's angry that wouldn't drive them away. Bobby asked to hear my story four or five times following that session, asking his mother to come in and listen as well.

Susie, age seven: "Once there was a lion. This lion had lots of hair. One day the mother lion told the lion to comb its hair and the lion wouldn't. They had a big fight. The lion just wouldn't comb her — I mean its — hair. So the mother lion wouldn't let her go out to play."

What happened at the end?

Susie: "The lion had to go to its room. It was very sad."

Did the lion get to go out to play at all?

Susie: No. "The End. The lesson is if the lion doesn't comb its hair, it goes to its room."

Thank you very much, Susie. Now for my story. "Once upon a time there was a lion that had lots of hair. One day she wanted to go out to play but her mother wanted her to comb her hair first because it was all tangly and she looked messy. This mother lion was afraid that all the neighbors would think she was a bad mother if they saw her child all messy. She wanted them to think she was a good mother who kept her child's hair nice. The lion wouldn't do it. She *hated* to comb her hair. She thought she looked all right. And she was anxious to get out to play. Her friends were out there having fun. But her mother wouldn't let her go. The lion was going to lie on the floor and scream, but the mother started to tell her how important it was to her to have the neighbors think she was a good mother. Since the lion kind of liked her mother and didn't want the neighbors to think her mother was bad (though she didn't understand what hair had to do with it) she combed it. Her mother was very happy. The lion went out to play with her friends and had a good time until it was time to come in for supper. The lesson of my story is that sometimes it's easier to do what your mother says because then you get to go out to play."

Susie: That's a good story!

Thank you very much! Do you ever have that happen to you? Do you ever have to do things your mother wants you to even if you don't, and you go to your room if you don't do them?

Susie: Yeah! (nodding vigorously)

We talked about this a while and then she asked me if we could play Blockhead. (Susie and her mother were engaged in a great power struggle which we were beginning to sort out.)

These two examples are not carefully selected to give you a sample of my successes. They are typical of most of the storytelling sessions I have had. It is an effective, attractive technique. Occasionally I will find that a child does not want to tell a story in this way, so we will move to some other kind of activity.

I often use the *Children's Apperception Test* (*CAT*) pictures for story telling. These pictures show animals in human-like situations. In a therapy group I was doing I brought the pictures in one day with the idea that each child would select a different picture for a story. Each child wanted to tell a short story about each picture, and every story was different! I have not had the problem of children copying each other's stories. If I did, I might say, "Oh, your story starts out the same as his. Now what happens to *your* bear?" In this group all the stories were taped (I did not tell any), and at the next session I replayed some of them to give us a chance to talk about the experiences and feelings expressed. One picture shows three bears playing tug-of-war. At one end is the largest bear, and at the other end the baby bear and probably the mother bear.

Here is Donald's (age twelve) story: "There's three bears, Papa, Mama, and the little baby bear, and they're fighting over a jar of honey! So they're tugging, Papa loses. So Papa bear, he cheats the little bear and cuts the rope and they all fall down the hill."

Which one are you? Be one of them.

Donald: I guess the baby bear.

Talk to your Papa bear — tell him how you feel about being cheated.

We continue along this vein until I finally ask Donald if he has ever felt cheated by his father. Lots of feelings come out for us to look at.

A ten-year-old adopted girl told a story about a little bear looking for her real parents when she was concentrating on the *CAT* picture of two large bears asleep in a cave as a little bear lies there, eyes open. "When the bears were finally asleep, the little bear ran out." She had lots of feelings she had been unable to express to her adoptive parents.

Sometimes in a group after such stories, I might ask the children to act out one of them, adding their own interpretations. Or the child who told the story might play out the different parts. Some interest is added if the child who told the story selects the various actors for the script.

I have a special box of pictures to motivate story telling. School supply stores, sometimes called educational suppliers, offer some fine sets of

WINDOWS TO OUR CHILDREN

pictures geared for therapeutic work. *Moods and Emotions* and *Just Imagine* are excellent. The set of *Thematic Apperception Test* (*TAT*) pictures is especially suitable when working with teenagers. The pictures in *The Family of Man* are also excellent.

Another interesting story telling technique that appeals to children of all ages is the *Make a Picture Story* test (*MAPS*). This set provides small black-and-white cardboard figure cutouts and quite a few large cards with black-and-white scenes of everything from a graveyard to a schoolroom. The child selects figures and positions them on the card she selects. Then she tells a story or enacts a play. She can move the figures and add new ones in the course of the story. Generally the stories are fairly short, and some children like to do more than one card. With a sequence of stories, themes and patterns often become clear. In the following example, Allen, age eleven, did five scenes. I wrote his stories down on a large pad as he told them.

1) Street scene: "A robber tries to rob a woman. A boy tries to help — he knows karate, but it doesn't work. Superman flies down, helps her, kisses her, they go off together." (When asked which one he was, he chose Superman.)

2) Raft: "There's a shipwreck, a man is dying, and another man is there and a boy and a dog. They are hungry. (He holds his stomach as he relates this.) Boy's parents were in shipwreck but they die. On the raft the dying man dies, but the rest get saved. The boy gets new parents after he's in a foster home. He's happy." (He identifies with the boy.)

3) Cave: "A snake bites woman. She's trapped. There's no way out. Two men come and chase snake, find a way out, all is OK."

4) Doctor's office: "Man comes in. He's hurt a leg in an accident. (The figure is on crutches.) Doctor calls another doctor and they fix leg. Just as they are leaving, they open the door and a bleeding man falls in. They call an ambulance. 'You need more help, we're just doctors in an office' the doctors tell the man, and he's OK."

5) Schoolroom: "Picture of a ghost is on blackboard. It's Halloween. Teacher tells class that a policeman will lecture class on being safe on Halloween. A boy is a bully and disruptive. He leaves. Teacher doesn't know

what to do with him. Boy has problems. He's unhappy." (Allen wouldn't identify with anything in the last three pictures.)

Each of these stories is full of material that could be used for therapeutic exploration. In this case I chose to look at the pattern of all five. At the beginning of this session Allen had voiced the idea that he could begin to phase out of therapy — he felt his life was going fine now. We talked about the scenes. In each case there is some kind of catastrophe or problem, and except for the last one, there is help that arrives. Allen's life has been filled with catastrophe. We focus on the last story and the boy who has problems. Allen says, "He comes to see you and then he's OK." We talk about some of the happenings in his own life and his feelings about them now.

The flannel board (a board covered with a piece of flannel) is an aid to storytelling. A child can make up many stories or scenes and manipulate them on the flannel board as she talks. Flannel, felt, sandpaper, and Pellon (an inner facing found in fabric stores) will stick to a flannel board. Gluing small pieces of any of these to the backs of cutouts from coloring books or handmade figures is all that needs to be done to get them to stick. Or items can be made directly from flannel, felt, or Pellon and outlined (or not) with a felt pen. Commercial packets for flannel boards are available in school supply stores. Items such as family members, animals, folklore stories, fantasy figures, neighborhood and city buildings, trees, and so forth lend themselves to interesting work.

Books

I make use of many different kinds of books in my work with children. I find that children like to be read to, even when they seem past the age for this. (Is anyone ever past the age for this?) Books lend themselves by their subject matter to different themes for sessions. I look for interesting books in libraries and book stores and have a small collection of special books to work with. *The Temper Tantrum Book* is very successful; it is asked for over and over by my younger children. *Where the Wild Things Are*, about monsters, appeals to children and gets us in the mood for talking about scary things. *There's a Nightmare in my Closet* never fails to bring recollections of dreams from children. A book called *Go Away, Dog* lends itself to talking about rejection, and *A Frog and Toad are Friends* and *I'll Build My Friend a Mountain* lead into talking about relating to other kids. A book for very young children called *Is This You?* lends itself to talking about the child, his family, his house, and so forth.

Sylvester and the Magic Pebble and *The Magic Hat* (about a little girl who, when she puts on a magic hat, can do anything a boy can do) lead into exploring the child's wishes and fantasies. I mention here only a smattering of books that I have used, to give the reader some idea of how books can be used. One begins to develop an eye for book possibilities. I find that children don't respond as well to books written specifically for getting at feelings as they do to books that have been written not for that purpose but merely to tell a story and to entertain the child. Children are bored by "corny" books — they see through them immediately.

The *Story of Ferdinand* is about a bull who's different, and many children feel just that. *Leo the Late Bloomer* is about an animal who couldn't do much of anything until one magic day. *Spectacles* is a charming book about a little girl who has to wear glasses. *Nobody Listens to Andrew* hits home with many children, and a book called *Not THIS Bear* lends itself to talking about similarities and differences. *Fish is Fish* is a charming book about a fish who tries to live out of water like a person or a bird or a frog or a cow. He learns just in time that a fish out of water dies; a fish is a fish and can't be what he isn't.

Some of the finest books for children are found in feminist book stores, for they are usually carefully selected. Such books as *Grownups Cry Too*, *My Body Feels Good*, and *Some Things You Just Can't Do by Yourself* are wonderful books that I have rarely seen anyplace else.

What is a Boy? What is a Girl? deserves special mention. This excellent book, with its superior photographs, talks about body differences between boys and girls, men and women. *The Sensible Book* is good to use in talking about seeing, touching, tasting, smelling, and hearing, and *Feelings, Inside You and Our Loud Too* is another fine book.

Fairy tales and folk tales offer a wealth of material for working with children, and I find that children still love stories from them as much as we did when I was a child. The story of "The Little Blue Spruce" in a little book, *Famous Folk Tales to Read Aloud*, tells about a little tree in a forest who, though a very fine spruce tree, wants to be like the other kinds of trees in the forest. The age-old story about Hansel and Gretel (in *Treasure Book of Fairy Tales*) leads directly into talking about one's own family conditions.

Much psychological meaning has been assigned to fairy tales. Whether one agrees with these interpretations or not, tales have great appeal and value for children. Fairy tales and folk tales, like folk music, spring from the depths of humanity and involve all the struggles, conflicts, sorrows, and joys that people have faced through the ages. Sometimes these stories are not pleasant. Bruno Bettelheim writes in *The Uses of Enchantment — the Meaning and Importance of Fairy Tales*:

> The dominant culture wishes to pretend, particularly where children are concerned, that the dark side of man does not exist, and professes a belief in an optimistic meliorism . . .
>
> This is exactly the message that fairy tales get across to the child in manifold form: that a struggle against severe difficulties in life is unavoidable, is an intrinsic part of human existence — but that if one does not shy away, but steadfastly meets unexpected and often unjust hardships, one masters all obstacles and at the end emerges victorious.
>
> Modern stories written for young children mainly avoid these existential problems, although they are crucial issues for all of us. The child needs most particularly to be given suggestions in symbolic form about how he may deal with these issues and grow safely into maturity. "Safe" stories mention neither death nor aging, the limits to our existence, nor the wish for eternal life. The fairy tale, by contrast, confronts the child squarely with the basic human predicaments. (pp. 7-8)

Fairy tales are unique, not only as a form of literature, but as works of art which are fully comprehensible to the child, as no other form of art is. As with all great art, the fairy tale's deepest meaning will be different for each person, and different for the same person at various moments in his life. The child will extract different meaning from the same fairy tale, depending on his interests and needs of the moment. When given the chance, he will return to the same tale when he is ready to enlarge on old meanings, or replace them with new ones. (p. 12)

Fairy tales do indeed hit squarely on the basic universal emotions: love, hate, fear, rage, loneliness, and feelings of isolation, worthlessness, and deprivation.

I agree with Dr. Bettelheim that if it were not for the fact that the classic fairy tale is, above all, a work of art, it would not have the impact that it does. There is something rhythmic and magical about the way a fairy tale reads, providing a flow into and out of the listener's heart and mind. Even though these tales often use vocabulary far beyond the child's understanding, the child listens enraptured, absorbed, listening with all of him, taking it all in.

Some educators and parents have voiced concern about the fact that fairy tales set forth a world that is unreal — a world that offers a perfect and magical solution for everything. Moreover, many of these tales are very sexist: women are valued for their beauty alone, while men are shown as gallant heroes. Despite these drawbacks there is much in classic fairy tales and folk tales that children can readily identify with. As an antidote for the drawbacks, Dr. Richard Gardner has written several books for children: *Dr. Gardner's Fairy Tales for Today's Children*, *Dr. Gardner's Modern Fairy Tales*, and *Dr. Gardner's Stories about the Real World*.

When I'm using these stories in my work with children, I have found it very useful to explicitly compare the fantasies and magical solutions presented in fairy tales, as well as any sexist bias, with the child's own life. Further, I agree with Dr. Bettelheim, who says that stories ending with "and they lived happily ever after" do not fool children for a minute. I am inclined to think that the general quest in our culture for eternal happiness, our thirst for the latest in electrical appliances, or the sportiest looking car is what causes much of the confusion about life among the young. It is the contradictory values of those who control children's real-life activities that disconcert them, not what they read in books. The values set forth in fairy tales are clear and simple, black-and-white.

Storytelling, Poetry and Puppets

There are numerous variations on story telling, some leading into other areas such as working with puppets, acting out stories, or writing stories. Sometimes it's fun to start a story in a group and have each child add whatever she wants to, forming a story collage.

Sometimes I begin a story and ask the child to end it, or she might begin it and I might end it. Sometimes we decide to make up a different ending to one we have read together.

In *Psychotherapeutic Approaches to the Resistant Child*, Dr. Gardner describes several games he invented to enhance the story telling technique. Some of these involve picking a toy or object out of a bag and telling a story about it, telling a story about a word chosen from a bag of words, or telling a story upon completion of a word in the game, *Scrabble for Juniors*.

Writing

I rarely ask children to do their own writing, not because I see no value in it, but because most children have not had good experiences with writing. I am sorry that most children are reluctant to write, for I think writing is one of the most satisfying, valuable, effective tools there is for self-expression and self-discovery.

Over and over I make some attempts to encourage children to write, but because of their resistance and the lack of time for me to begin to help children discover the excitement of writing, I move on to other techniques.

However, since writing is merely another form of the same words we use for talking, I can begin to give children the sense that they are *already* writers. When a child tells a story into the tape recorder, I can type her story and present it to her in written form. Or I can write or type the story as she dictates it to me.

Because I believe that a direct verbal statement by the child has great power in enhancing inner strength, I will often ask the child to make some kind of statement about a drawing which she has made during the course of a piece of therapeutic work between us. As she makes her statement, I will write it directly on the drawing, to be read back to her as further reinforcement. Sometimes I encourage children to write a few words as a beginning to more fluent writing. "Write any words you want to, that you think of, that might go with your angry picture." An eleven-year-old boy wrote across his picture, "Mr. and Mrs. Motherfucker," after such an instruction. If you want children to express themselves fully, you can't censor them!

I think children are often reluctant to write because the schools put primary emphasis on spelling, form, sentence structure, and even penmanship, thus stifling and choking off the child's creative flow. It seems to me that grammar and spelling ought to be separated from real writing, taught separately or perhaps later, after writing has become a familiar activity for the child. Imagine what would happen if we should insist that a baby formulate her sentences perfectly correctly before we allow her to say any words! Babies learn to talk correctly by imitating the talk of the adults around them. If we would let children alone and not frighten them about writing, they would learn to write in the same way that they learn to talk.

I give every child I work with a small spiral notebook in which to write. I may ask her to use the notebook to record bed-wetting episodes, or to write "things that make you mad this week," or to put down her dreams. Here are the notations of one boy, age nine, about things that made him mad. 1) Mr. S. wouldn't let the boys play softball. 2) I had to clean the bathroom and bath ring out, wash clothes and hang up the towels. 3) I have to go to bed at 8:30 and wake up at 7:30 in the morning. And I have to eat, comb my hair, get dressed and leave the house at 8:30. On this same theme, a ten-year-old girl wrote: My mother wouldn't let me tell a girl something. She made me take a bath when I wanted to tell my friend something.

Sometimes we will make little booklets complete with covers, with titles like "Complainings," "Mads," "Happies," "Braggings," "Things I Hate," "Things I Like," "My Wishes," "If I Were the President," "If I Were My Mother," and so forth. One booklet was titled "Something About Me." One boy, age eight, wrote, "Eyes Brown. Plain Boy." Another drew an elaborate picture of himself and wrote, "I got brown and black hair. I have green eyes. I am wearing blue dungarees. I am wearing black shoes. I am wearing a yellow and light blue shirt. I am wearing white socks. I have two arms. I have two legs. I have two green eyes. I have ten fingers on both of my hands. I am ten years old. I am four feet, ten inches high. I am sorta skinny. I have two ears." Another, age nine, merely wrote, "I am ugly." And one boy, age ten, wrote, "I had a dog win I was one and two. He was bigger

Storytelling, Poetry and Puppets

than me — a way lot bigger. He used to play with me all the time." He drew a small sketch of a little boy playing ball with a dog bigger than him.

A six-year-old child brought in a book he had made in school with the title, "Feelings." Each page started with a phrase the teacher had written on the board for the children to copy and then complete with their own ideas. His went like this:

Love is . . . when a person says I love you and everyone doesn't fight and that makes everybody feel bad. So be nice. (The teacher had written "Do over" because she was not happy with the printing!)

I feel afraid when . . . I get in a fight. And get lost in the middle of no where (small picture of a boy standing in the middle of a desert).

Other sentences were: It isn't fair when . . . I feel happy when . . . I feel sad when . . . I feel lonely when . . . I feel like singing when . . . My best friend is . . . What I like about myself . . . Three important things that have happened in my life are . . . The best thing I can do are . . . Three wishes I pick would be . . . The happiest day of my life was when . . . The funniest thing that ever happened to me was . . . The most beautiful thing in the world is . . . If I were the teacher . . . If I were the President of the U.S. . . . My parents are happy when . . . If I were a father I would . . . If I were a principal . . .

Completing unfinished sentences is an excellent way to encourage children to make declarative statements about themselves, to get in touch with their wishes, wants, needs, disappointments, thoughts, ideas, and feelings. Incomplete sentence tests offer more ideas for such sentences.

Since I like to encourage children to be aware of the polarities of human feeling and personality, I will often pair opposing statements, such as, I'm happy when . . . and I'm mad when . . . , It's easy for me to . . . and It's hard for me to . . . , One thing I like about you is . . . and One thing I don't like about you is . . .

Sometimes I will ask children to write a whole page of sentences beginning with "I am" or "I want." A twelve-year-old boy wrote, "I am a boy. I am happy. I am funny. I am cold. I am warm. I am getting very bored doing this." And on the other side of his paper he wrote a list of "I am nots" (his own idea). "I am not dumb. I am not a girl." Etc.

For children who are willing to begin to do some writing, I might give the following instructions: Imagine you have the power today to do anything you want to do in the world. Write about what you would do. Or: Write a letter to some part of your body, such as, "Dear Stomach: There's something I would like to say to you."

In a group, a colleague of mine asked the children to each write a secret but not sign the paper, fold it, and place it in a pile in the middle of the room. Each child in turn then picked one and read it to the group as if it were that child's own secret. The session was exciting and moving.

Herbert Kohl, in his book, *Math, Writing and Games in the Open Classroom*, talks about the problem of getting kids to write. He contends that at least in the schools, children will not write if they are afraid to talk. Children will write if they can write about the things they know best, the things that are important to them. If they can't talk about these things freely, how can we expect them to write? In describing his experiences with children and writing, he gives many excellent suggestions for encouraging children to express themselves through writing.

Two valuable publications, which include a variety of articles on writing with children, are *The Whole Word Catalogue 1 and 2*.

Poetry

Ask a child to write a poem and she automatically struggles to make the words rhyme. I'm not saying that a poem ought not to rhyme, but rhyming is a separate skill in itself. Rhyming poetry is not the most useful for free-flowing expression.

Poetry comes from the heart. One can say things in the form of a poem that might be difficult to share in ordinary talking and writing. In poetry one can let go freely, even crazily.

There are some good books available that deal with children's poetry writing. Among the best is *Wishes, Lies, and Dreams*, by Kenneth Koch. He suggests various ways of freeing children to write poetry and includes many poems written by children which, at first glance, may seem to bear little relationship to the feelings of the children who wrote them. In a section called "Lies," one poem by an eleven-year-old, for example, reads:

> I fly to school at 12:00 midnight
> I run to lunch at 9:00
> I go underground to go home at 11:00
> My name is Clownaround James Jumpingbean
>   Diego Spinaround Jimmy and Flipflop Tom
> My head was born in Saturn my arms were born
>   in the moon
> My legs in Pluto and rest of me was born on the earth
> My friend the bee zoomed me home. (p. 196)

Like the scribble, like *Put Your Mother on the Ceiling* fantasies, a poem like this can be the first step toward allowing oneself the freedom and flow of revealing what is in one's heart and soul. Consider this poem by a twelve-year-old in a section called "Noises":

> The wind coming out of your mouth
> Is like the wind in a dark alley
> When you hear older people talking
> You hear groaning
> Hitting a chair with a ruler
> Is like hearing a machine-gun fire
> Hearing a dog whine
> Is like a fire truck's siren
> Seeing two boxers connect with a punch
> Is like a bullet hitting a tin can. (p. 124)

I find that one of the most effective ways of getting children interested in writing poetry is to read other children's poems to them. The poems in *Wishes, Lies, and Dreams, My Sister Looks Like a Pear, Me the Flunkie, The Me Nobody Knows, Somebody Turned on a Tap in These Kids, The Whole Word Catalogue 1 and 2, Begin Sweet World, Miracles,* and *I Never Saw Another Butterfly*, are powerful, wonderful, honest. My favorite one is *Have You Seen a Comet?* This book, produced by the United States Committee for UNICEF, includes art and writing from children all over the world.

WINDOWS TO OUR CHILDREN

When I read a poem I will ask the child to close her eyes and allow the poem to go through her. When I am through reading, I request that she draw a picture of her feelings about the poem and what she became aware of through the poem. Or I ask that she draw a picture of something the poem reminded her of — perhaps one word or one sentence struck some chord within her.

The poem "There Is a Knot" in *Have You Seen a Comet?* never falls to bring forth some feelings usually kept hidden. This is a translation of a poem by an eight-year-old Turkish child:

There is a knot inside of me
A knot which cannot be untied
Strong
It hurts
As if they have put a stone
Inside of me

I always remember the old days
Playing at our summer home
Going to grandmother
Staying at grandmother's

I want those days to return
Perhaps the knot will be untied when they return
But there is a knot inside of me
So strong
And it hurts
As if it is a stone inside of me (p. 32)

After hearing this poem, a ten-year-old girl drew a figure standing on top of a hill, a black dot in her middle, arms outstretched, with the words, "I hate you, I hate you" written around the figure. She dictated to me: "My knot is anger inside of me." Prior to this she had defensively denied feelings of anger, in spite of her rebellious behavior at school and at home.

Another child, age nine, drew a picture of her grandmother's house and a figure of a girl standing some distance from the house. This girl, too, had a black dot on her abdomen. The dot represented "a lie I told my mother." She felt guilty about this lie and felt she could not tell her mother about it because her mother would be very angry. (She did tell me about it at this point.) Her grandmother had died recently, and she was the only person this child felt truly loved her, the only one to whom she might have revealed what she had done without severe punishment. From this picture we were able to deal with the child's worries as well as her grief.

It's fun to make up a group poem. Each child writes a line, perhaps about a wish. I then collect the lines and read them back to the group as a lovely poem. The children are quite impressed with their poetic abilities. Sometimes I will ask children each to be an animal or a season or a vegetable of their choice and to write some lines about themselves. I will generally read their poems aloud to them — their words always seem to sound better when someone else reads them.

Poems can be written in conjunction with art. I asked one group to draw, in colors, how they felt at the moment. When they finished I asked them to write words, phrases, or sentences to describe the feelings they had as they looked at the drawing. One child wrote, "The colors wash over me and gently sooth and comfort me — first lightly, then with strength."

Sometimes, before beginning a poetry session, we might talk about words that can describe feelings, words that evoke pictures, words that one likes, words that sound harsh. Experimenting with words and expanding one's awareness of words helps in writing poetry.

I often use a simple haiku-like form with children. A haiku is a Japanese poem with three lines of five, seven, and five syllables each. I use a simplified five-line form consisting of one word, then two words that say something about the first word, then three words that say something more about the first word, then four words that say something further about the first word, and the fifth line repeating the first word.

Here are some examples dictated to me by children:

Girls
Love you
I love girls
Like girls very much

WINDOWS TO OUR CHILDREN

Girls
   (eight-year-old boy)

Dinosaurs
I wish
They were alive
I'd rather ride their backs
Dinosaurs
   (seven-year-old boy)

Rockets
Black, pretty
Blow fire out
Blows from the bottom
Rockets
   (eight-year-old boy)

Rockets
Have window
Go in space
Men float in space
Rockets
   (nine-year-old boy)

Boys
Stupid brats
Fight with girls
Ugly faces, ugly hair
Boys
   (nine-year-old girl)

Girls
Pretty, good
Have pretty hair
They always are good
Girls
   (ten-year-old boy)

School
Run away
Beat up someone
Don't like to read
School
   (eight-year-old boy)

Boys
Love girls
Beat me up
I like some boys
Boys
   (eight-year-old boy)

Nothing
That's all
Won't say nothing
Not going t'say nothing
Nothing
   (ten-year-old boy)

Women
Big, pretty
Have pretty hair
Lovely, I love them
Women
   (nine-year-old girl)

These little poems tell a great deal about children's internal thoughts and feelings. They are another little window opening into the child's secret rooms, a crack in the door, making it possible for it to be opened wider and wider.

WINDOWS TO OUR CHILDREN

Poems written for children by adults often appeal more to adults than to children. It is not easy to write in ways that the child can connect with. Sometimes I will come across a book that I enjoy and feel sure a child will enjoy as much, only to discover that I am wrong. A book that does reach children is *Where the Sidewalk Ends*, poems and drawings by Shel Silverstein. Cindy Herbert's *I See a Child* was written for adults who work and live with children, but I have found that children are touched by some of her poems such as this one:

> I'm Sorry
> When something is missing
> When something is broken
> I get the blame
> It seems as if I'm always blamed
> So I
> Apologize —
> Feeling angry
> And humiliated
> But not a bit
> Sorry.

Great poetry can touch the heart, but most children back away from it, again, perhaps, because of the manner in which they are subjected to poetry in school. In his book, *Rose, Where Did You Get That Red?*, Kenneth Koch describes how he introduced poets like Blake, Shakespeare, Whitman, and others to elementary school children. He encouraged the children to imitate the styles of classic poets in their own poetry writing, thus creating much interest in the variety of poets and poems presented. For example, "The Tyger," a poem by William Blake, begins:

> Tyger! Tyger! burning bright
> In the forests of the night
> What immortal hand or eye
> Could frame thy fearful symmetry? (p. 33)

In this poem Blake questions a tiger, and Koch asked his students similarly to question some mysterious and beautiful creature. The poetry that resulted is beautiful:

Oh butterfly oh butterfly
Where did you get your burning red wings? . . . (p. 43)

Oh little ant that lives in a hole
How do you feel today?
The roses are in bloom and the purple sunlight is shining
How do you feel when dirt bombs are thrown? . . . (p. 53)

Why are you so small little bug?
You will get trampled on, little bug . . . (p. 55)

Songs, too, are poems. Never before our time has our culture encouraged so much original writing of song lyrics. The words to much of today's contemporary music are powerful, moving poems. Children have always been connoisseurs of the music of the day, and generally have favorite songs that appeal to their individual tastes. Many secretly write their own songs, I discovered. A twelve-year-old boy shared a song with me that he had written to a familiar rock tune. I was deeply moved by its content, which spoke of his longings and dreams. I remember a story a friend of mine told me about her 6-year-old daughter. She heard her at the piano one day banging away and in a sing-song voice saying something like, "I hate my teacher. She is mean. She wouldn't let me tell her what I wanted to. She is mean. No time, she said . . . ." She went on and on, making up her song of protest, finally finished it, then happily came to help her mother get ready for dinner.

Puppets

It is often easier for a child to talk through a puppet than it is to say directly what he finds difficult to express. The puppet provides distance, and the child feels safer to reveal some of his innermost thoughts this way.

WINDOWS TO OUR CHILDREN

I have used puppets in various ways — in direct exercises, spontaneously in the course of the therapy, and in puppet shows. Here are some of them:

Ask the child to pick a puppet to work with from the pile of puppets, and to be this puppet's voice — *be* the puppet. Say why you were chosen. (I might ask, "Puppet, why did John pick you?")

As the puppet, introduce yourself. Tell us something about yourself. (With younger children, I will ask the puppet questions like, "How old are you?" "Where do you live?")

As the puppet, introduce John (the child who picked it).

Pick one (or two) puppets who remind you of someone you know.

In any of these situations I (or the other children, if it's a group) can ask the puppet any number of different kinds of questions. There are also exercises with more interaction: While the rest of the group watches, the child and I, or two children, pick a puppet, and these two puppets interact nonverbally for a while. Then the two puppets talk to each other.

One child picks two puppets and they interact nonverbally, then verbally, as the rest of the group watches.

Puppets introduce other puppets or other children.

One learns much about a child through the puppet he picks. John picks the tiger puppet. "I am fierce. Everyone is afraid of me. I bite people who come near me." I may encourage more material by asking questions like "Who bothers you the most, tiger?" Or, "Do you have any friends — anyone that you don't bite?" Or, "What do you do that makes people so afraid of you, tiger?" At some point I might want to ask the child if anything he said about the tiger fits for him, John. "Do you ever do that? Do you ever feel that way? Are people afraid of you?" Or, "Are you afraid of someone who acts like a tiger?"

I might ask the puppet to say what he likes and doesn't like about the child who picked him, or I might ask the puppet to say something like that to other puppets or to other children in the group. I think it's important that I participate as much as possible with the child, so I will usually choose a puppet, and let it do the questioning, rather than me.

Sometimes in the course of a session in which other techniques are encountering resistance, a puppet can often come to the rescue. For example, Janice, age ten, had been living in a foster home for a year. Her mother

Storytelling, Poetry and Puppets

had abandoned the children, and they were put into foster homes. The children were "signed away." (There was no known father.) Finally, Janice, separated from her brother and sister, was placed in an adoptive home. Everything went well. At the time of legal adoption, Janice said to her social worker, "Do you have another home for me?" She refused adoption and would not discuss it.

In therapy, she would not discuss it with me, either. She would merely shrug and say, "I don't know."

I told her that I knew there must be a voice inside her that sometimes tells her things. I asked her to be the voice. She could not do this, so I asked her to pick out a puppet to be "her voice." She chose a funny floppy girl doll with a silly smile. As the voice of the doll, she told me she was afraid to be adopted. She was not sure what her fear was all about. I asked her to draw her fear. She drew a big black solid box. She said she had happiness too — a rectangular blue box that drifted up and somewhat brightened her fear. It was the puppet who described the drawing, and the puppet who suddenly said, "I'm afraid I'll never see my mother and brother and sister again." She preferred to stay in foster homes, rather than be "locked away." I turned to Janice and gently asked, "Is that how you feel Janice? Is the puppet right about how you feel?" Janice nodded, eyes filling with tears. We talked about the situation for a while. I knew we would need to work through Janice's anxieties, fears, and grief, and that now we could begin. At the end of the session, Janice said to me, "It's funny that I can talk to you better than I can to Mrs. L—" (her social worker with whom she had an excellent relationship). I answered, "Well, that's why Mrs. L— wanted you to come here."

With younger children I will sometimes pick up a puppet (my favorite is a little finger mouse) and talk to the child. The child in her delight responds much more quickly to the mouse than to me.

Puppet Shows

Children love to give puppet shows. A puppet theater is nice to have, though I use the back of a chair or sometimes the back of my large flannel board. The child gets behind the prop and uses the top of the chair or board for the stage. If we're having an individual session, I am the audience.

WINDOWS TO OUR CHILDREN

Sometimes two children will put on a show as a joint venture. And sometimes I give the show.

Puppet shows are much like storytelling — the child tells her story through the puppets. If I am doing the show, I might choose my own theme or I might ask the child for a story theme — "What should this show be about?" I might choose a theme based on some problematic situation in the child's life such as his method for getting attention. Or I might do a funny show just for the sake of entertainment.

When the child does the show, she often knows exactly what she wants to do, so I don't offer any suggestions unless the child has trouble beginning, or gets stuck in the middle of a story. Children's puppet shows are often characterized by two things: familiar stories and lots of hitting. I encourage the child to tell the story, whatever it is, and I patiently watch the fighting and hitting. I am often asked why children do this in their puppet shows. I can only guess at the answer. Perhaps they are influenced by Punch and Judy shows. Perhaps they need to safely play out aggressive feelings. Perhaps hitting is a reflection of their lives.

Some children never need suggestions. They know exactly what they want to do, selecting their puppets with care and acting out some grand theme, often closely related to their own lives, real or fantasy. But many children need some help in breaking through the persevering pattern of two puppets pounding each other. So I will suggest themes, and this often stimulates them to a better one of their own. The shows that I do for the children provide models for their own creations. They get ideas about the different possibilities by watching me.

Sometimes I do a kind of mutual storytelling technique with the puppets. After the child has done his show, I will take the same characters and do one of my own, sometimes something brand new, sometimes offering a better solution to the conflict presented. If there is time we might talk about the shows in terms of their own lives, just as I might do with any story situation.

I find that teenagers enjoy putting on shows, too. I will sometimes give them a situation to act out, something based on the problems in their own lives. Some young people enjoy experimenting with more involved situations. I have also used proverbs such as "When the cat's away the mice will play," as a kind of riddle to be unraveled. A show in which the children play out their interpretations of the proverb is fun, challenging, and revealing of the child as well. Or they might select a proverb from a list or pick one from a pile, leaving me or the rest of the group to guess what it is. (There are books of proverbs in any public library.)

I read about an interesting way of doing puppet shows in Adolf G. Woltmann's article "The Use of Puppetry in Therapy" in *Conflict in the Classroom*. Woltmann used his technique in a hospital setting with children. He selected one main character to be the hero of many shows, a boy named Casper, who wore a pointed cap and a multicolored costume. He wrote many stories around Casper that dealt with asocial behaviors, fantasy material, and moral and ethical values that concern children. In the middle of each story, he would have Casper come to the front of the stage and ask the children for their advice on what they would do or say next — how they would complete the drama.

In one story, the show opens with Casper's father leaving for work. The mother kisses the father good-bye, expressing a hope that Casper will follow in his father's footsteps some day. On stage alone, Casper tells the audience that he is sick and tired of going to school and plans to play hooky. He runs off without his books. Mother finds them and runs to school with them, believing that Casper forgot them. The second act shows Casper on a street alone. Hooky isn't as much fun as he expected. He doesn't have any money and he is lonely. The devil comes along, offers his services, and says he can be anything he wants. Casper chooses to be a king. In the third act he's dressed in king's robes and is in a castle. He has power to do what he wants with the world. He asks the audience to help him make decisions about schools, teachers, hospitals, parents, etc. A revolution breaks out when Casper's orders are carried out according to the children's suggestions, and his life is threatened. He is crying for help and the devil appears ready to take him to hell, but just at the right time, his parents rescue him.

The children who watch this show are very excited by it and very much involved. There are many different suggestions offered, and lots of arguments. It is a lively encounter. Although this kind of puppet show, with its costumes and settings, may be too ambitious for most of us, the idea is exciting and can easily be adapted to fit your own needs.

WINDOWS TO OUR CHILDREN

Although there are various kinds of puppets, I find hand puppets to be the easiest for children to use. I have a number of finger puppets which some children like, but many find them difficult to manipulate. I have used stick puppets (a drawing or cutout of a figure pasted or taped onto a ruler or stick), but I find that children become much more involved in a show with hand puppets, perhaps because more of themselves — their bodies — are involved.

I have a variety of puppets. Sometimes I don't have the right puppet for a particular story, but children adapt easily and fit the puppets to the characters they need. I have a man, a woman, a couple of boys, a couple of girls, a devil, a witch, a crocodile, a tiger, a baby, a king, a dog with long ears, and several small stuffed animals and doll figures I use as puppets. Helpful additions might be: a doctor, a police officer, a wolf, a snake, some grandparent figures, and a fairy godmother type. Children not only act out life situations through the different puppet characters, but they readily identify with various parts of themselves: the good, the bad, the fierce, the angelic, the angry, the baby, the wise. Sometimes through puppet play, they are able to resolve inner as well as outer conflicts and to balance and integrate the many aspects of themselves.

Children sometimes enjoy making puppets. Books are available in the children's section of the library that give suggestions and instructions. I have made several puppets myself out of felt, cutting out a back and a front to fit my hand like a mitten, sewing the two pieces together, and gluing on other pieces of felt to form the face and hair.

6

Sensory Experience

Throughout this book I write about giving the child experiences that will bring her back to herself, experiences that will renew and strengthen her awareness of those basic senses that an infant discovers and flourishes in: sight, sound, touch, taste, and smell. It is through these modalities that we experience ourselves and make contact with the world. Yet somewhere along the line many of us lose full awareness of our senses; they become hazy and blurred and seem to operate automatically and apart from ourselves. We come to operate in life almost as if our senses, bodies, and emotions don't exist — as if we are nothing but giant heads, thinking, analyzing, judging, figuring things out, admonishing, remembering, fantasizing, mind-reading, fortune telling, censoring. Certainly the intellect is an important part of who we are. It is through our intellect that we talk to people, make our needs known, voice our opinions and attitudes, state our choices. But our minds are only one part of our total organism that we own and need to take care of, cultivate, and use. Fritz Perls often said, "Lose your mind and come to your senses." We need to respect those other parts of ourselves that have so much power and wisdom for us.

It is not my intention here to describe all the kinds of exercises and experiments available for helping people heighten their sensory functions. Many books are available with hundreds of suggestions and ideas.

I will mention each of the senses briefly and give a few examples of how I focus on them. I find it interesting that many of these exercises can be found in books related to the dramatic arts, as well as in educational books on language arts. Practitioners in those two fields have long recognized the need to give children and adults many sensory experiences to improve their skills.

Touch

Clay, finger paint, sand, water, and foot painting provide good tactile experience. *What is Your Favorite Thing to Touch* is a book I have used often with children. This charming book talks about many feelings and textures that are pleasing to touch. Children are motivated by it to talk about their own favorite touching experiences. For touch experimentation, I have gathered a variety of surfaces: sandpaper, velvet, fur, ribbon, rubber, paper, wood, rock, shells, metal, etc. We touch and talk about how each thing feels, what it reminds us of in our lives.

I sometimes place the objects in a bag and ask a child to reach in and pull out something rough, or soft, or smooth. Then I take my turn, with the child telling me what to take out.

The ability to discriminate through tactile sensations is an important cognitive function. I put a pencil, a small car, a walnut, a paper clip, and a button in a bag, and ask the child to find a specific one without looking. Or I may say, "Find something that you write with," or "Find something that begins with *P*." Formed wood or plastic letters can be placed in a bag to help children discriminate letters. Tracing letters and words in sand is good, and making them out of clay or playdough is fun. Sometimes I will trace a letter or word or name or object on a child's back with my fingers to see if she can guess what it is.

We have done a sensory awareness exercise in which we write all the words we can think of that describe some touching sensation. We might draw pictures to represent some of the words (what colors are this word?) or something the words remind us of, or we might do some kind of body movement that would be fitting. Some words might be bumpy, fluffy, slippery, hard, soft, smooth, sticky, gooey, warm, cold, hot, freezing, rough, holey, prickly, tingly, feathery, rubbery, thin, spongy, mushy, silky, hairy.

We have taken off shoes and tried feeling a variety of textures with our feet. We have taken a walk barefoot indoors and out and talked about how our feet can feel. We've compared the feeling of our feet on cardboard, newspaper, fur, rugs, pillows, sand, grass, leaves, a towel, wood, rubber, velvet, sandpaper, cotton, beans, metal, cement, brick, dirt, felt, rice, water.

We have also talked about things that hurt our skin.

Two children can try out having a conversation with each other without words — just through gesture and touching.

Two children can touch each other's face and report how it felt to do the touching and how it felt to be touched. This can be done with eyes open or closed.

We can touch ourselves on the face, head, arms, legs, or anywhere on the body and describe or write the feelings.

We might play a game of blindman's buff, guessing who we touch while blindfolded.

We might take a child on a blind walk, blindfolding him and walking him around the house or outdoors.

I will often encourage parents to learn something about massage and to make a practice of massaging their children. Children can also enjoy massaging each other or themselves. In a group, children can pair off and follow instructions for massaging back, head, arms, legs, and feet.

Sight

Young children are not afraid to look. They see, observe, notice, examine, inspect everything, and often seem to stare. This is one of the important ways they have of learning about the world. Children who are blind do this same kind of thing with their other senses.

As we grow older we often "give our eyes away." We begin to see ourselves and our worlds through other people's eyes, like the populace in the story, "The Emperor's New Clothes." We adults encourage children to give their eyes away. We say, "Don't stare!" or "What will they think of us!" (referring to what others see us doing). We worry about how our children dress and appear to others.

Part of reowning one's eyes involves the awareness and strengthening of self, the ability to find comfort and familiarity with the self, trust one's self.

WINDOWS TO OUR CHILDREN

The ability to see the environment and the people around us is necessary for making good contact outside the self. To be able to see others clearly expands our horizons.

I remember a young girl who had to walk past a bus stop where people clustered waiting for a bus. Walking past this group of people made her extremely uncomfortable. She imagined that each person watched her with some kind of judgement. I asked her to walk very slowly the next time, as an experiment, and look at the people who were waiting for the bus. I asked her to see them as if she were a camera and to take a mental picture of two or three of the people so that she could report to me what she saw. The next time she came she reported initial embarrassment (a sure sign of giving your eyes away) but a disappearance of the embarrassment as she remembered my assignment. In fact, she said, she found the task extremely interesting once she got into it, and noticed that none of the people actually looked at her except for one little boy who smiled at her when he noticed her looking at him. She described some of the people, the color of their hair, their facial expressions, what they were wearing, how they were standing, She went on to talk about what she imagined they were thinking and feeling, what dramas might be taking place in their lives. We discussed the difference between what she could actually see and what she was imagining.

Seeing and imagining sometimes become intertwined. We can only see what is observable — we cannot see the inside workings of anyone's mind and heart. We can only imagine what a person is thinking and feeling — we cannot see these processes.

Many things get in the way of seeing besides imagining what people think and feel. One of these is jumping into the future rather than staying in the present. Often we spoil pleasurable sights and experiences by our worry about what might come next. We may look at a beautiful sunset, straining to catch every glimpse before it sinks into the horizon. That very straining, a sort of holding on, detracts from the pleasure of seeing the beauty of the moment. This kind of hanging on is universal. I enjoy taking pictures with my camera when I am traveling. I have found, however, that often the wish to capture the beautiful sight detracts from my enjoyment of that sight.

Sensory Experience

It seems important to me to give children many experiences with seeing, not just looking. As Frederick Franck says in his wonderful book, *The Zen of Seeing*:

> We do a lot of looking: We look through lenses, telescopes, television tubes.... Our looking is perfected every day — but we see less and less. Never has it been more urgent to speak of seeing. Ever more gadgets, from cameras to computers, from art books to videotapes, conspire to take over our thinking, our feeling, our experiencing, our seeing. Onlookers we are, spectators.... "Subjects" we are, that took at "objects." Quickly we stick labels on all that is, labels that stick once and for all. By these labels we recognize everything but we no longer SEE anything. We know the labels on all the bottles, but never taste the wine. Millions of people, unseeing, joyless, bluster through life in their half sleep, hitting, kicking, and killing what they have barely perceived. They have never learned to SEE, or they have forgotten that man has eyes to SEE, to experience. (pp. 3-4)

Although the exercises described in Franck's book focus on enhancing one's drawing ability through what he describes as "seeing/drawing as meditation," they are also excellent as experiences to get young people to enhance their seeing abilities. He talks about seeing/drawing as the art of unlearning about things:

> While drawing a rock I learn nothing "about" rocks, but let this particular rock reveal its rockyness. While drawing grasses I learn nothing "about" grass, but wake up to the wonder of this grass and its growing, to the wonder that there is grass at all. (p. 5)

So he suggests, for example, first sitting before a flower (or a branch, or a head of lettuce, or a leaf, or a tree) in a kind of meditative state, allowing oneself to be at one with the object, to see the object in all its wonder, and then allowing the hand to follow what the eye sees. By following this method, the eyes begin to see more than was ever thought possible.

When allowing the eyes to take everything in, the seeing becomes one with all of one's senses and feelings. I have asked children to pick out an object and to gaze at it for a period of time, perhaps three minutes, and then to draw their feelings or memories evoked through this meditative exercise, using only colors, lines, and shapes.

Other kinds of seeing exercises: Experiment with sensation and touch with eyes closed, then with eyes open. Look at things through glass, water, cellophane. Look at things from different perspectives close, far, upside down. The book, *Your Child's Sensory World*, gives some excellent exercises for helping a child increase her visual awareness.

Sound

Allowing sounds to enter our awareness is our first step toward contacting the world, the beginning of communication. We all know that many of us hear only what we want to hear, shutting out what we don't want to hear. Children do this openly and directly by holding their hands over their ears when they don't want to listen; adults often change the meaning of what they hear. The cry from many children is, "My father, mother just doesn't hear what I say!"

I doubt that there is such a condition as "tone deafness." Yet many children believe they are because someone has told them so, and on that basis alone they shut themselves off from some of the pleasures of sound, such as allowing their own voices to experiment with song. Helping children appreciate sound increases their sense of being in the world. Here are some exercises to increase children's awareness of the sounds around them.

Sit quietly with eyes closed and allow the sounds you hear to come to you. Notice your feelings as you take in each sound. Later we can share our impressions. This kind of exercise takes on completely new dimensions in various locations — indoors, in the city, at the beach, in the country.

Talk about sounds. Share which sounds feel harsh, soft, smooth, grating, pleasant, loud, gentle. *What is Your Favorite Thing to Hear?* is a good book to read to children as a prelude to this exercise.

Sensory Experience

Match sounds. I have taken some small jars and old medicine bottles and put a variety of objects — rice, beans, thumbtacks, buttons, washers, coins, anything that will fit — in pairs of bottles. I wrap the jars with masking tape or cover them in some way, so that the objects are hidden from sight. The child shakes each bottle and finds its match through the sound it makes.

Using a toy xylophone, hit various tones to give the child practice with tones that are the same, higher, lower, louder, softer. He can test you, too. This can be done with any instrument.

A game of sound recognition is fun. Behind the child's back, make a sound by some means, such as pouring water, tapping a pencil, crushing paper. Have him guess the sound. Always take your turn, with the child testing you as well.

Sounds and feelings go together. Talk about sad sounds, happy sounds, scary sounds, and sounds evoking other feelings. A harmonica or kazoo is a good instrument to experiment with in making such sounds. The tone of one's speaking voice, too, is indicative of feelings. Children can hear anger, for example, in the voice even when the adult is trying to hide it. Talk about this openly. Make voice sounds to indicate emotions.

Gibberish talk is fun. Attempt to communicate through sound and gibberish, using no real words. See if you can guess what is being expressed.

Drums and other rhythm instruments lend themselves to a variety of sound experiences and games. Have a child match your rhythm, or have him evoke an image from your rhythmic pattern.

Listen to some music and then talk about the sounds heard. Ask children to draw feelings, memories, images, after or while listening to music.

Music

In an article, "Music therapy" that appears in *Conflict in the Classroom* Rudolph Dreikurs; discusses the beneficial effects of music on several psychotic children:

> Using music brought results in cases where other approaches had failed. It seems that the pleasant experience with

> music, often merely in the background, stimulates participation, permits an increase in the child's attention span, and raises his frustration tolerance. External and internal tensions disappear, as reality becomes more pleasant and less threatening. The demands for participation are so subtle that they are not resented or defied. (pp. 201-202)

Melodic intonation has been used with aphasic children to help them learn to speak. Words are matched to familiar melodies, and with much repetition of the song, the child learns to say the words, first with and gradually without the tune. This is yet another example of the power of music.

Music and rhythmic beats are ancient forms of communication and expression. The use of this mode fits in nicely in therapeutic work with children.

Most of the music I use with children involves the kind I make myself with a comfortable old guitar. I find the guitar to be a powerful instrument in therapy with children. When I worked in the schools I played my guitar every day, and children of all ages eagerly looked forward to the musical interlude. The guitar seems to hold some particular kind of magic for children. I know it has nothing to do with musical talent, for I am at best a mediocre player; I just stick with simple chords, and strum to accompany the songs I sing with them.

When my daughter was in nursery school, every mother had to spend one day a week working with the children. As soon as the news leaked out that I could play the guitar, I was asked to spend part of my duty days playing for each group of children. The children, ranging from three to five, would sit enraptured for at least a half hour. Soon mothers were asking me to come to their children's birthday parties and were paying me $10 (good pay then!) for entertaining the tots for an hour. I never had to struggle for the children's attention. I think this had to do with the kinds of songs I considered appropriate, my ability to be very expressive with those songs, inviting participation whenever possible, and — most of all — the guitar itself. I have tried the Autoharp and have used drums and piano a bit, but I am convinced that the guitar has the most power of all, perhaps

Sensory Experience

because it gives the greatest opportunity for maintaining contact with the children as one plays.

When I taught nursery school I first began to experiment with using music as a way of getting the children to express themselves. I would sing a song like "Go Tell Aunt Rhody," about a goose who dies, and soon we would begin to talk about death and grief and sadness. Or after the music session a child would come up to tell me about his cat that died, or about his Grandpa who died, giving us an opportunity to talk about it. When I sang a song called "Simbaya Mamma's Baby," which describes violent reactions to a new baby in the family, many of the children could identify with that situation.

At times these songs had more power than storybooks. There is no end of wonderful folk songs that appeal to children and cover every emotion for every age level. For example: Love: "Sweety Little Baby" (Pete Seeger) "Magic Penny" (Malvina Reynolds). Recognition, belonging: "Mary Wore Her Red Dress" "Train Is a Comin'." Hostility, anger: "Simbaya" "Don't You Push Me" (Woody Guthrie) "Let Everyone Join in the Game" (using the word "no"). Sadness, sorrow, death: "Go Tell Aunt Rhody" "Three Caw" "I Had a Rooster" (using verse about a baby crying) "Mamma's Got a Baby" (Woody Guthrie).

There are songs that soothe, like "Hush Little Baby," and songs that appeal to a child's sense of humor, like "Jenny Jenkins." Many songs, like "I Wish I Were an Apple On a Tree," are open-ended, with verses to be made up.

There have been some very fine songs written for children in the folk song tradition and there are many songs in the archives of folk music to fit every need. There are songs about every feeling and life situation, nonsense songs, and songs that tell stories. Because such songs have lasted through time, they never appear contrived or "cute." They add vitality, beauty, and power to children's emotions, imaginations, and experiences. These songs are generally very flexible — they have gone through many changes and are adaptable to change. They were born in the hearts of people and have lasted because they were loved and shared.

Many of these songs can be found in folk music books and records. Songs for children that have great appeal have been written and sung by

WINDOWS TO OUR CHILDREN

Pete Seeger, Woody Guthrie, Ella Jenkins, Malvina Reynolds, Sam Hinton, Marcia Berman, Hap Palmer.

Music can be used in many ways. One can play music while children finger-paint or work with clay. The music can be in the background, or it can be the focus of the activity. I have asked children to draw shapes, lines, and symbols and use colors to music. Classical pieces are especially conducive for getting in touch with feelings and evoking moods and images. In his book, *Awareness,* John Stevens presents some excellent suggestions for combining fantasy with specific musical pieces. Here is an example (Gabor Szabo: Spellbinder, Side 1, Bands I and 2. Impulse AS9123):

> Lie down with space around you, and close your eyes. Imagine that you are inert matter on the bottom of a prehistoric sea. There is water all around you — sometimes gentle currents, and sometimes raging crushing waves of water. Feel the water flowing over your inert surface . . .
>
> Now as life develops, you become some kind of seaweed or underwater plant. Listen to the drumming and let the sound flow into your movements as the currents of the water move you . . .
>
> Now become a simple animal that crawls along the bottom of the sea. Let the drumming flow through your body and into your movements as this underwater animal . . .
>
> Now move slowly toward land . . . and when you reach land, grow four legs and begin crawling around on the land. Explore your existence, and how you move as this land animal . . .
>
> Now gradually become upright on two legs, and explore how you move and exist as a two-legged animal . . .
>
> Now continue your moving, and open your eyes and interact with the others through these movements . . . (pp. 266-267)

This kind of experience can be modified and adapted to the age of the children as well as to the space used. A sharing of feelings following this exercise is always revealing. You might ask the children to draw their feelings or the animal as they experienced it.

Sensory Experience

Children enjoy using colored chiffon scarves as they move to music, and they love to dance around to rock, boogie, and other contemporary rhythms.

Drums are very appealing to children — even those of us who have little skill can create an acceptable beat. You might say, "Show me what kind of drum beat you would make if you felt sad, or happy," or "Give us a drum beat and see if we can tell what feeling you're having."

Children love to use rhythm instruments. Tambourines, maracas, drums of all kinds, bells — in fact anything that can make sound — can be used for marching, dancing, keeping time while listening to music, or accompanying the guitar, and everything together can be a symphony in itself. I have recorded children's group efforts with an inexpensive cassette recorder and played them back, to their delight. They radiate with a sense of accomplishment when they hear themselves play, and they learn the feeling of group cooperation and synergism.

Making up lyrical stories about children or situations is fun. A student in a class told me she would make up different stories about the same person to her own guitar accompaniment and children would beg for more episodes. Children, too, can make up these stories.

I am continually amazed at the power of the guitar. I was once assigned as a student teacher in a fifth-grade class, and was put in charge of music immediately because the teacher disliked it. When I asked if I could use my guitar I was told no, it would stimulate the children too much (a common misconception). On my last day, she gave me permission to bring it. At the end of the session one little girl came up to me and very angrily asked me why I had never brought it before. She felt cheated, deprived, and I wished I had insisted at the beginning. I have never found music to be overstimulating. On the contrary, it usually has a tremendously soothing, calming effect. Parents report that children come home humming after some of my musical sessions.

Even the most hyperkinetic children become very soothed and involved with the music. In working with such children, I sometimes would sit down and without a word, pick up my guitar; the children would rush to sit down and would become very quiet in happy expectation.

Once I was teaching a group of fourth-grade children labeled as "culturally deprived." One day the principal walked in as we were having music. We were singing as I played on my guitar, "In the Woods There Was a Tree." This song, about a tree in a hole in the ground, requires repetition of a long list of words as we go along. Often I fumbled, but the children remembered every sequence. These were children who were having trouble learning and remembering, and the principal was flabbergasted. "Maybe we should teach math and everything this way," she said.

Taste

The tongue is an important part of our body, yet we usually take it for granted. The tongue is very sensitive; it tells us when things are sweet, sour, bitter, salty. The tongue is used for chewing, swallowing, and most of all, talking. I experiment with these functions with children so that they will become more conscious of what tongues do. Tongues help us to express emotions, too — sticking one's tongue out at someone is a satisfying expression of anger. (In some cultures, sticking one's tongue out is an expression of greeting!) The tongue is also a sensuous organ that sometimes provides erotic pleasure. All children are familiar with the pleasure of licking. I often provide an experiment in licking to enhance awareness of this pleasure (Ice cream in cones is good for this).

Talk about tastes. Discuss one's favorite and not-so-favorite tastes. Bring in sample things for children to taste. Compare taste and textures. The tongue cannot only discriminate between things that are sweet and sour, it can tell you if something is lumpy, hard, soft, coarse, hot, cold.

The teeth, lips, and cheeks are closely allied with the tongue. Be sure to include these in discussions and experiments.

Smell

Discuss the nose, nostrils, and breath. Experiment with breathing through the nose, mouth, each nostril. Feel the air with the palm of the hand as it comes out.

Talk about smells — favorite smells and unfavorite ones. Provide an experience with smell — flower, fruit, sweet, spicy. Put a variety of things with distinctive aromas in jars or containers — perfume, mustard, licorice,

Sensory Experience

banana, sage, witch hazel, apple slice, chocolate, vanilla, soap, flower petals, onion, pine cone, vinegar, coffee, orange peel, bath powder, lemon extract, celery, wood shavings, peppermint.

See if children can recognize the smell. Talk about likes and dislikes, and the memories evoked. Bring in other objects such as pine tree branches, soap, bark, leaves, and so forth.

How would your life change if you couldn't smell anything at all, like when you have a cold and your nose is all stuffed? Try naming ten things that have no odor at all. Take a walk through the house, or outdoors, and describe the smells.

Many sensory experiences actually involve a combination of senses. In fact, it is probably difficult to provide a single sensory experience that does not involve more than one of the senses.

Intuition

Many people are studying yet another ability that we know very little about, and this ability seems to involve something beyond the realm of what is clearly known.

I see this sixth sense as one that is basically intuitive, a knowing that rests somewhere in the body, rather than in the mind. Animals seem to have this sense, and so do young children. I am beginning to pay more attention to the truth that my body appears to know, before any words or thoughts are formed.

I have done an exercise with clients involving this kind of sense to give them more experience in trusting that inside place within themselves. I call it the yes-no exercise, or sometimes the true-false exercise. I will suggest a statement to the child such as, "I like string beans." I instruct the child to answer true or false from that part of the body that gives the answer, rather than from the head. For me, the source of the answer is sometimes in the chest and sometimes just above my navel. With practice, one can learn to tune in to those places that seem to embody intuitive truth.

I find it difficult to speak specifically about this sense, and yet I know that it is an important one that needs to be developed. This sense can be practiced and enhanced as can the other senses. We take sight and sound and taste and touch for granted, and yet we all have a much greater potential for their use than we have realized. The intuitive sense covers a wide range and can involve such processes as fantasy and imagery, creativity and imagination, body fields, and energy fields. Some feel that this sense is related to the spirit within us — that part of our very core that goes beyond the mind and the body.

I think that exercises involving fantasy and imagery experiences enhance one's intuitive sense. When I ask a child to allow a picture to form in his mind about something — for example, to imagine symbols for members of his family — I believe that he is allowing his intuitive sense to develop. Allowing mind pictures to form when listening to music is a good example of an exercise in opening up to new places within the self. In his book, *Go See the Movie in Your Head*, Joseph Shorr gives many techniques for enhancing one's imagery-making ability in order to promote self growth. Guided imagery is another process for helping people find new openings to places within themselves.

Making contact with the inner wisdom within the self is perhaps another form of employing the intuitive sense. Sometimes this knowing 'self,' the 'self that knows the answers to questions involving the dynamics of life, can be contacted through fantasy: the child can be instructed to meet a wise person on a mountain with whom he can talk and learn the answers to his questions.

Any fantasy can be used to contact the wise and creative aspect of a person. Josh, an eight-year-old boy who loved to use the toy telephones in my office, had lengthy conversations with me via the phones. One day he directed me to ask him a question that had to do with "one of the kids that come in here that has problems." So I said on the phone, "Josh, I have this kid who absolutely won't go to bed when his mother wants him to (this was a problem in Josh's family). What can I tell her to do?" He said, "Hang up and I'll call you back." He then dialed a number and yelled through the phone, "Hello Hello! Is this the 'Man from Mars'? Is it? Good. I need some advice." He then asked the 'Man from Mars' what to do about my problem boy, listened intently, hung up, and pretended to call me back. I picked up the phone, and he said. "Violet, tell this mother she needs to make a deal with him. He gets to watch TV for a half-hour after his sister goes to bed and then he'll go without any trouble."

We played this game often (at Josh's request), touching many of his own difficulties at home and within himself. In another session I said. "Josh, I have this boy who plays baseball on a Little League team, but because the coach won't let him pitch, he has violent temper tantrums and won't play his best, and yet he won't quit the team. He won't even let his mother talk to the coach about it and she's really upset over the whole thing." Josh said, after listening for some time to the Man from Mars, "The Man from Mars said the coach ought to give him more chances to pitch so he can learn. Once he did it and he wasn't too good, so now the coach only puts the best pitcher on, so how is this boy going to learn to pitch? He LOVES to pitch." Josh then put the telephone aside and said in a lowered voice, "If my mother talks to him, everybody will know, and think I'm a baby." He crumbled into sobs at that point. We talked about the various aspects of this situation for a while. Then Josh said, "Maybe I can find another way to practice pitching, and then I can tell the coach and he'll let me try again."

Feelings

Some children are not familiar with what feelings are. This seems like a strange statement, for children certainly feel. But I find that children have limited ability to communicate their feelings. They also tend to see things as black-and-white. I find that it is very helpful to give children experience with the vast variety of feelings and their nuances. There are games and exercises, too, that help children contact their own feelings.

Reading a book about feelings such as *Feelings Inside You and Outloud Too* or *Grownups Cry Too* is a good way to begin talking about what people feel. I think that talking about feelings is an important first step with children. They need to know what kinds of feelings there are, that everyone has feelings, that feelings can be expressed, shared, and talked about. They also need to learn that they can make choices about ways of expressing feelings. Children need familiarity with the many variations of feelings to help them get in touch with what they *are* feeling. Some of the feeling words that I have talked about with children are: happy, good, proud, angry, afraid, hurt, upset, disappointed, frustrated, pain, lonely, alone, love, like, jealous, envy, special, private, bad, joy, delight, sick, anxious, worried, glad, calm, nervous, silly, gloomy, blank, guilty, sorry, shame, disgust, cheerful, sure, strong, weak, pity, empathy, understanding, understood, admiration, grief, tired.

I talk with children about the relationship of the body to feelings, that all feelings are experienced through body sensation and expressed through body musculature. Our body posture and breathing patterns manifest what we are feeling. We experiment with exaggerating various movements and postures that might indicate certain emotions. When the child is feeling sad or fearful or angry or anxious while he is with me, I can help him tune into his body and become aware of what he is doing with his body at the moment to express the feeling.

Sometimes we work from the inside out. Tuning in to the body can tell you what you are feeling. We talk about how we avoid feelings, push them away, cloud them over, hide them, cover them. The body, however, stores the feeling, it doesn't dispel it. It is only when we acknowledge our feelings and experience them that we can release them and use our total organism for other things. Otherwise a part of us is continually harboring the feelings we ignore, leaving us with only part of ourselves for the process of living. So we learn how to listen to our bodies to get to our feelings.

A technique called the awareness continuum is an excellent method for helping us be more aware of our bodies. It consists of a game the child and I sometimes play in which we take turns reporting inside and outside awareness.

I am aware of your blue eyes. (outside) I am aware that my heart is pounding. (inside) I see the light shining through the window. My mouth feels dry. I notice your smile. I just realized my shoulders are hunched up.

It becomes apparent in the course of this game that nothing ever stays the same; our environment is always changing, and our body sensations are always changing.

I pay close attention to the child's body, his posture, his facial expression, and his gestures. I may sometimes call his attention to a particular gesture, asking him to exaggerate it. The child who was swinging her leg back and forth exaggerated this motion upon my request, and realized she wanted to kick the person she was talking about. Her kicking the pillow/person brought out her feelings of anger at that person — feelings that had been getting in her way and interrupting the healthy flow of her process.

The child who sits all hunched up as she talks to me finds, when I ask her to stay in that position, or to pull in even more, that she is very frightened of me and of what will happen in our sessions. As this comes out we can deal with it.

Relaxation

Children sometimes need as much help in learning how to relax as we adults do. Children tighten their muscles, become tense, suffer from headaches and stomach aches, feel fired or irritated. Physical and emotional tension is sometimes expressed through behavior that on the surface seems to be irrational. Helping children relax can ease their tension, and often help them express the source of the tension. Teachers find that providing many opportunities for children to relax in the classroom can benefit everyone.

Imagery is a helpful aid to relaxation. Young children will respond to an exercise. Such as these from *Talking Time*:

> Pretend you're a snowman. Some children made you and now they have left you to stand alone. You have a head, a body, two arms sticking out, and you stand on sturdy legs. The morning is lovely. The sun is shining. Soon the sun becomes so warm. You feel you are melting. First your head melts, then one arm melts, then the other. Gradually, little by little, your body begins to melt. Now only your feet are left and they begin to melt. Soon you are just a puddle lying on the ground.
>
> Let us pretend that we are candles on a cake. You may choose which color you like. First we stand up tall and straight. We look just like wooden soldiers. Our bodies are stiff like the

candles. Now the Sun is coming out very warm. You begin to melt. First your head droops . . . then your shoulders . . . then your arms . . . Your wax is melting slowly. Your legs droop . . . slowly . . . slowly . . . until you are all melted into a puddle of wax on the floor. Now a cold wind comes along and it blows "wh . . . wh . . . wh . . ." — as you stand up straight and tall again. (p.19)

Relaxation does not mean that children must lie down. Often bending and stretching the body does much more to help one relax. Yoga exercises are excellent. There are several yoga books for children on the market today. One that I have used is called *Let's Do Yoga*, by Ruth Richards and Joy Abrams. It has excellent illustrations and easy-to-follow instructions. *Yoga for Children* is another good one, as is *Be a Frog, a Bird, or a Tree*.

The Centering Book gives some of the best relaxation and breathing exercises for children that I have encountered:

> Let's close our eyes. Now tense every muscle in your body at the same time. Legs, arms, jaws, fists, face, shoulders, stomach. Hold them . . . tightly. Now relax and feel the tension pour out of your body. Let all the tension flow out of your body and your mind . . . replacing the tension with calm, peaceful energy . . . letting each breath you take bring calmness and relaxation into your body . . . (pp. 46-47)

Taking a child on a relaxing, pleasant, guided fantasy also works well. Sometimes I will ask the child to close his eyes and go somewhere very comfortable in his fantasy — a place he knows and likes, or a place he imagines that would be nice. After a while I ask the child to return to the room. This experience leaves him refreshed, relaxed, and much more present.

Sometimes at the beginning of a group I can feel the children's tension swirling around the room. I might ask them to close their eyes and take some deep breaths, letting the sounds out as they exhale, and to imagine that they are back in the situation they were in before they left for the group. I ask them to finish up, in their minds, whatever needs to be finished that seems to have been left untended, and then gradually to come back to the room, opening their eyes very slowly. We complete this exercise by inviting the children to look around the room, and make eye contact with others. This exercise never fails to reduce tension and bring everyone more into the present situation.

Meditation

Meditation is a fine way to learn to relax, and children make good meditators. *The Centering Book, The Second Centering Book,* and a book called *Meditating With Children* give good suggestions for helping children learn the art of meditation. Here is an example of one of the exercises from *Meditating With Children:*

> Close your eyes and feel that you are in an ocean of blue light; feel and believe that you are in a wave in that ocean and are floating up and down, gently up and down, just like a wave. Now feel yourself melt and disappear in that ocean just like the wave disappears into the ocean, ahhh, feel it relaxing you. You are now one with the ocean of blue light and there is no wave, no difference between you and the ocean. Now listen . . . very quietly within . . . hear the sound of the ocean inside your head, and feel yourself becoming one with that sound. Now the sound is fading away and the wave is starting to come back again, just like the wave in the ocean comes back after it has disappeared and forms into another wave and another and another until it washes into the shore and we open our eyes. (p. 66)

After this exercise the children can finger paint, or move to music like waves in the ocean.

I have used a small bell to help children meditate, instructing them to listen to the sound until it fades away. I continue this process for a little while — ringing the bell and following the sound into silence.

WINDOWS TO OUR CHILDREN

If you are unfamiliar with meditation, read a small book called *How to Meditate*, by Lawrence LeShan. This book discusses meditation clearly and thoroughly, giving an explanation of the varieties of meditation, as well as clear instructions on how to meditate.

Meditation and the concept of centering are very closely related. Meditation brings one back to the self, and this is the focus of the concept of centering.

Here is a variation of an aikido exercise that I have taught children to bring them back to themselves, to help them feel strong, calm, and centered. I, myself, do this exercise often, and it has an instant centering effect for me.

"Stand, sit, or lie down — position is not important. Close your eyes. Take two deep breaths, letting the air out each time with a sound. Now imagine that there is a ball of light suspended just above your head. It does not touch your head, but floats above it. It is round and glowing, full of light and energy. Now imagine that rays of light are coming out of this ball toward your body. These rays come continuously, for the ball of light has more than it needs and it is continually receiving new light energy from another source. These rays or beams of light enter your body through your head. They enter easily, effortlessly. As each ray enters, imagine it going to a special part of your body. Imagine one ray going through your head and into your left arm, down to your fingers, then coming out of your fingertips, entering the floor. Another ray goes down your right arm, and out. Another goes through your back torso, another your front, and others down your sides. One goes through your left leg and another your right. Continue to wash the inside of your body with these rays of light until you feel that you've had enough. They feel warm and good as they pass through all parts of your body. When you have had enough, slowly open your eyes."

Body Movement

In her book, *Your Child's Sensory World*, Lise Liepmann classifies movement as one of our. "Moving, or kinesthetic perception, is a kind of internalized touch sensation. It's what we feel as our muscles, tendons, and joints work."

Sensory Experience

The way we stand and move, how we use the body, how it feels, how we can improve it, is a subject so important that I would be presumptuous to think that in a few paragraphs I can do it justice. I can only give a few suggestions for doing body work with children and hope that the reader will read some of the books available in this area.

The baby makes full use of her body. Watch the absorption of the infant as she examines her hands and fingers, and later as she delights in newfound body skills — kicking, grabbing, rolling over, lifting the torso, dropping. As the young child grows, watch her absorption in picking up small objects with thumb and index finger as she discovers fine muscle control. Watch the child as she crawls and reaches and stretches and twists and turns and finally when she can pull up and walk and run and hop and jump and skip. The child seems to have unlimited energy, and she throws herself into each body activity with complete absorption. Sometimes there are difficulties, but she doesn't give up. She tries and tries again, practicing and practicing, until finally she delights in success.

But at some point in childhood something occurs that begins blocking this process. Perhaps it's illness, or the parent rushing in to help, or the child crying in frustration while the parent is confused about what to do, or a subtle or open disapproval of body enjoyment, or criticism for initial awkwardness or clumsiness. Many things happen to restrict one's body. Competition sets in, perpetuated by the school setting, and the child restricts herself further in her attempt to meet other's expectations. The child begins to contract her muscles in certain ways to hold back tears or anger or because she is frightened. She pulls in her shoulders and shortens her neck to fend off attacks or words or to hide her developing body.

As children become disconnected from their bodies, they lose a sense of self and a great deal of physical and emotional strength as well. So we need to provide methods for helping them regain their bodies, to help them know their bodies, be comfortable with them, and learn how to use them again.

Breathing is an important aspect of body awareness. Notice that when you are frightened or anxious, your breathing becomes quite shallow. We lose much of our body capability in this way. So exercises in breathing are important. We compare shallow breath with deep breath. We learn to feel the effects of deep breathing throughout various parts of our bodies and notice expansiveness and warming as we do this. We talk about the difference in feelings when we breathe deeply, and what we imagine we are doing when we hold back our breath. Holding back breath seems to be a protection, a shield, a holding back of self. But when we do this we are even more defenseless. We experiment with the contrast between what we can do when we hold back breath, and how much more we can do when we breathe fully.

Many young people I have worked with have made use of deep breathing in test-taking and have reported good results. One seventeen-year-old young man suffered from severe test-taking anxiety. He studied and knew the material, but he did poorly each time, due to his fear and anxiety. He told me that his mind would go blank, sometimes he shook so much he could barely hold his pen, and his heart beat so rapidly that he would feel faint. Besides dealing with his basic feelings of insecurity, his expectations, and so forth, we talked about breathing. He needed immediate tools to help himself. As he began to understand the workings of his body and what he was doing to himself by not letting himself breathe, he began to practice noticing his breath at such times. He experimented with some centering exercises that we practiced and he began to acquire the habit of breathing deeply, so that more oxygen would get to his feet and legs and especially to his brain. His composure during tests improved dramatically.

Children suffer from anxiety whenever they must enter new situations — moving to a new place, getting a new teacher, entering a new group, and so forth. Some children I have seen refuse to try any new situations and activities because of their intense anxiety.

There is a close relationship between oxygen, anxiety, and excitement. The more excitement a person feels, the more oxygen is needed to support the excitement. When we don't take in enough air, we feel anxious instead of the more pleasurable feeling of excitement. It can be exciting to go into something new. Anticipation and visualization of new situations often results in anxiety when they deserve excitement. Breathing deeply can dispel the anxiety and allow the pleasurable, exciting feelings to surge through our bodies, and give us the feeling of power and support we need at these times.

Sensory Experience

Children who are hyperkinetic are not feeling in control of their bodies, though they may make a lot of random body movement. Exercises in body control are essential and fun for them. A group of these children, all eleven years old, invented a game they wanted to play over and over. We stood in a circle of eight children and two adults in my very small office, creating a very small space inside the circle, where we placed several large pillows. Each child had a turn to go into the middle and do some kind of trick. The trick consisted generally of falling onto the pillows in some way. Because of the limited space, the falling had to be very controlled. Some fell backwards, others sideways, others forward, and so forth. They *loved* doing this, playing this game for a long time, patiently waiting their own turn, cheering each member enthusiastically as they invented new ways of falling. I thought about this experience and tried to figure out why they liked it so much. (Sometimes I find myself questioning, as I imagine many of you have, "This is therapy?") Finally I realized that these children, most of them classified as hyperkinetic by the schools, were enjoying a feeling of body control.

Children also enjoy using bean bags, Nerf balls, marbles, and such, in my office. There are a variety of games one can invent to help children experience muscle movement and control. One child used a Bataca as a bat and had a wonderful time slamming a Nerf ball to me.

An excellent resource for body movement exercises is the book *Movement Games for Children of All Ages*. Body movement is closely allied with the whole area of creative dramatics, since the best improvisations require a high degree of body involvement and control. Many useful ideas can be found in books devoted to drama, and in my discussion of improvisational dramatics, I can't help but talk about body movement. My discussion here, therefore, will be limited to experiences involving simply using the body.

It is now accepted that body movement and learning are interrelated. Children with learning disabilities characteristically also show a developmental lag in motor abilities. They will appear clumsy and awkward, and sometimes they have trouble learning to tie shoes, skip, ride a bicycle, and so forth. The resulting frustration and unhappiness aggravate the problem and cause the child to avoid the very activities he needs to engage in, further alienating the sense of self.

WINDOWS TO OUR CHILDREN

Recently I gave a talk to a group of teachers, counselors, and school psychologists at a high school, about how they could help improve the self-concept of their students. I talked about the need to recognize that children have feelings and are human beings — that how they feel, and what is going on in their lives, has a lot to do with how much they learn in the classroom. I believe that many schools are becoming more mechanistic and less humanistic, with harmful effects on the learning process. I believe that teachers need to begin to take time in their classrooms to contact their students as fellow human beings, and that schools and school administrations must allow time for this in order to facilitate better learning.

I talked particularly about physical education in the schools. Most of the junior high and high school students that I have worked with *hate* physical education. They may like specific sports, but even those somehow lose their appeal unless the child is a very good athlete. I talked about the sadness of this, since the physical education teacher is given the whole period to work with body movement and body awareness — both important aspects of the awareness of feeling. Unlike the math or science teacher, the physical education teacher is in a position to help a child express some feelings that may be blocking his attention to the lessons of the day, without having to "steal" time from the curriculum.

I was moved by the reaction of the physical education teachers. They spoke about the expectations placed upon them by their supervisors, and the curriculum demands they, too, need to meet. They just don't have time to pay attention to individual needs, and promote joy and self-awareness in the physical education program. They felt resigned to what they had to do, and hopelessness permeated the air as they talked. Other teachers expressed their needs to be treated as human beings, to be given an opportunity to express their feelings!

I had just finished looking through *The New Games Book* and George Leonard's *The Ultimate Athlete*. Both these books propose an entirely new dimension to the area of physical education, sports, games, and the use of the body — a dimension that stresses participation by all, joy in playing and experiencing the flow, movement, and energy of the body, and cooperation and harmonious interaction among players. I introduced these books to the teachers in hopes that somehow they might make some changes in physical education curricula. Certainly they were excited, though not optimistic about putting these ideas into practice.

How we play a game tells a lot about how we are in life. The more we learn about how we are in life, the more we can choose to try new ways of being if how we are isn't as satisfying as we'd like. A game I've used to pinpoint our game playing stance, and therefore our life stance, is called "back off." Two people stand facing each other a little less than arm's length, feet firmly on the ground about a foot apart. The object of the game is to throw the other person off balance — he loses if he lifts or moves a foot. The two people try to do this by palm-to-palm contact only. Each must keep palms open and each can hit out (with both hands together, or with one hand), bending, ducking, twisting, as long as both feet stay firmly on the ground without moving. It is interesting to try this game with a variety of partners: same sex, opposite sex, someone taller, someone shorter, someone older, etc. The strategy employed and the feelings we experience as we face each partner are shared when the game is over.

How we move our bodies correlates closely with our ability to be assertive, with our feelings of entitlement and self support. An experience which makes this correlation evident involves the use of haiku poetry. In a workshop on mime that I attended some time ago, I learned so much about myself through this exercise that I have been using it with other people ever since. The first line of the haiku is read aloud, and the person doing the exercise moves spontaneously in some way to express the words she has heard. Then the next line is read and another movement is made, and so forth. For example:

> Soft snow is melting (slowly dropping to the ground).
> Far in the misted mountains (gesturing with one arm in a wide sweeping motion, while waving the other arm around, the head coming to the knees; then rising with arms outstretched).
> A caw-cawing crow (taking on the position of a bird flying).

At first the movements might be stilted and awkward. With practice the movements become flowing, expansive, more spontaneous and diverse.

WINDOWS TO OUR CHILDREN

Children enjoy moving around to various kinds of music. I have used a drum beat with children, changing the rhythm every few moments. Or I might instruct children to walk stiffly, walk loosely, walk as if going through tall grass, walk as if going through quicksand or mud, walk through a body of water, walk on pebbles, walk as if the pavement were very hot, and so forth. Sometimes we pretend we're various animals, or one child moves like a particular animal and we have to guess what it is. Or we try out how it feels to twist, roll, squirm like a worm, crawl like a snake, twirl, and make other out-of-the-ordinary movements. Often we move with our eyes closed.

Sometimes I ask children to exaggerate or emphasize some gesture or movement, and I may ask them to share what that particular movement reminds them of, or how it makes them feel.

I have mentioned the use of the scribble in helping children become freer with their expressions in art. A movement therapist who took my class found that using the scribble before a movement session with her clients helped them to become freer in their movement expressions.

All emotion has a physical counterpart. Whether we are fearful or angry or joyous, our muscles will react in some way. Often we react in a constricting way, holding back the natural expression. Even in excitement and happiness we tend to prevent ourselves from the full natural response to run and dance and shout.

Children not only get in touch with what their muscles do when asked to move in specific ways to express emotions (for example, anger), they also discover ways of expressing outwardly, rather than inwardly. I find the best method for getting children to do this is to make up some kind of story in which, for example, something happens to a child, who becomes very angry as a result. "Be that child and move around the room to express your angry feelings. Make up an angry dance."

In *Movement Games for Children of All Ages*, Esther Nelson suggests this intriguing game:

> Untie an air-filled balloon, but hold it by the neck, throw it up in the air, and see what happens. It does a wild dance of its own, dipping, twisting, turning, shooting, as the air goes out. Experiment with several balloons — observe them. Each one

moves differently. Ask the children to describe the movements of the balloons in words. Talk about the shape and directions the movements take, and try to find vivid language — swoops and swerves, spurts and zooms and zips.

Then, when the children are actively involved, ask them to be balloons that lose their air . . . Remind the "balloons" that every part of them must move, that nothing can be left behind or just drag along. Keep using the descriptive words that the children have contributed. These will help to keep the movements fresh and lively. (p. 32)

The game of statues has always appealed to children. In this game one person swings another, and when one is let go he freezes into position. We then guess what he is. A variation is to have children move to a drum or music and when the music stops, freeze into position.

In an exercise I have used many times, I ask the children to close their eyes and remember a time when they felt most alive. I encourage them to relive this time in fantasy, to remember the feelings, what they were doing, and how their bodies felt. I have asked children to get up and move in any way they want to, to express the feelings they had at that time of aliveness. This exercise is particularly effective with teenagers who may need to contact that lost feeling of aliveness.

Sometimes after a drawing, I might ask the person to take a body pose or movement to further express that drawing. After drawing one's weak and strong sides, further hidden areas come through with body expression. One young woman, for example, lay flat on the floor to express her weakness. From this position came an outpouring of feelings. Movement can be an important means of further expression for any of the exercises in expression through sculpture, clay, collage, etc.

In *Left-Handed Teaching*, Gloria Castillo describes numerous activities involving the use of sheets. Each child has a double-bed sheet to use for a variety of purposes. The child's sheet becomes a special space all her own, a space she can lie on, use to protect her, roll in, create fantasies with, dance with. As the child lies on or under her private sheet, she enters into guided fantasies quickly and easily. Here is one of the exercises from that book:

WINDOWS TO OUR CHILDREN

Sit in a circle, not touching anyone.

Put your sheet over your head.

Now try to think of how you feel when no one wants you.

You know you are in a circle. When you feel like it, move away from the circle in slow-motion.

Find a place to stop.

You are all alone. No one is near. Only you, the sheet, and the floor. Be completely alone for a while. (Allow about three minutes.)

Now lie down on the floor — still covered with your sheet.

Roll yourself up in your sheet as tightly as you can. Be very still. Feel the sheet all around you.

Now begin to roll around. If you roll into someone, you may still wish to be alone. If so, move away. If you want to be close to someone, stay near whomever you touch.

Return to the circle.

Discuss what happened. How do you feel when you are alone?

Does this remind you of a time when you were really alone?

How did it feel to have other people touch you after you had been alone for a while? (p. 207)

In a movement workshop that I attended, the leader piled large pieces of cloth of many different colors in the middle of our circle. I eyed a lovely violet cloth (I have been partial to this color only in the last few years,

Sensory Experience

as I have learned to like my name), but chose to wait until the initial rush toward the cloth was over. The violet cloth remained for me, and I plucked it from the dwindling pile. The exercise involved using our cloth to wrap around us, or lie on, or curl up in, or twirl and twist in dance. We were instructed to become various characters as we moved around in various rhythms, and then to create a dance for ourselves to our own inner music. As I looked around I could see that each person was involved with his or her own drama, as I was. Finally I lay curled in my cloth experiencing my sensations, emotions, memories, and body — all these seemed wrapped up in my violet cloth. We afterwards wrote about the experience, in any form we wished. The group shared some moving experiences, some having to do with the color representation of the cloth, others with feelings that came through the body movements. I shared this poem I wrote:

I want violet
But I don't rush in
It lies there for me
I take it finally
I feel triumphant
I only want to wrap in it. It represents all moods to me
Joy, grief, sadness, gaiety
Most of all
Me

I feel close to my mother who gave me the name.
I feel close to my childhood which survived the name.
I feel close to the little girl who suffered pain.
I feel close to the little girl who laughed and rejoiced.
I feel close to all of me now.

7

Enactment

Creative Dramatics

It was Allen's turn. He reached into the pile of cards in the middle of the circle and picked one. Allen, nine years old, had trouble with reading, so he came over to me and asked me to help him. I whispered in his ear, "It says, 'You are walking along the sidewalk and see something on the sidewalk. You bend over and pick it up and look at it.' We have to guess what it is by what you do with it." He took a deep breath, straightened from his usual slouch and began to saunter around the room. Suddenly he stopped, looked down, opened his mouth and eyes wide and spread his arms out in a gesture of surprise. He bent over, picked up the imaginary object, and intently examined it. I thought it might be a coin — I could see by the way he touched it that it was round. He ran his fingers over it. No, it wasn't a coin. Now he was putting it up to his ear and shaking it. Now he was doing something else. I looked closer. He was making a twisting motion as if to unscrew something. It must be a small container. He looked in, shook it upside down. It was empty. He put his hand in his pocket, pulled out an imaginary something and put it in the container, screwed it back together, put it in his pocket, and with a big grin on his face, eyes glistening, he announced he was through. The children yelled wild guesses at him. Finally someone guessed it: a small round metal box into which he put a penny. I was delighted as Allen, smiling, sat down directly between two children on the floor with the rest of us. Could this be the same Allen who usually sat off by himself, hunched over, face tight and pinched?

WINDOWS TO OUR CHILDREN

Play acting helps children get closer to themselves by giving them permission to go out of themselves. This seemingly contradictory statement actually makes sense. In play acting children never in truth leave themselves; they use more of themselves in the improvisational experience. In the example above, Allen used his total self — mind, body, senses, feelings, spirit — to make his point. Usually he appeared to be a shy, withdrawn boy who sat off by himself, hunched over almost into a ball as though to contain himself. With the permission of the drama (and the trust he was experiencing within the group) he could call upon all of himself. And when he sat down, it was evident by his posture and facial expression that he had strengthened contact with himself and thus could make better contact with others.

Seven-year-old Carla came in for her first session after the Christmas holidays and plopped herself down on the floor against a big pillow. "I'm too tired to do anything," she said. I suggested we play a game, and I took down the *Talking, Feeling, and Doing Game*. In this game we roll dice and move a marker on a board the number of spaces indicated by the dice. If we land on a yellow square we pick a yellow card; white square, a white card; blue square, a blue card. Each card asks some question or gives some direction. Many of the cards have an improvisational dramatics flavor.

Carla landed on a white space. The card read: "You have just received a letter. What does it say?" I added some directions, "Pretend you go to your mailbox to get the mail. As you flip through the letters you see one for you. Act as you would if that really happened to you. Then open it and read it." Carla told me that she didn't feel like getting up but that she would imagine "in her head" that she was getting the mail. I agreed. Carla closed her eyes and sat quietly. Suddenly she opened her eyes, stood up, and told me she had the letter in her hand. I asked her to read the address to me. She held the "letter," turned it, brought it closer to her eyes, and said, "It's for me! It says CARLA," and she recited her address. "Who is it from?" I asked. Carla was now very excited. She yelled, "I know who it's from! It's from my Dad!" (Carla's had recently moved to another state.) "That's wonderful!" I said. "Hurry and open it! What does it say?" Carla slowly went through all the motions of opening a letter. She unfolded an imaginary sheet of large stationary and stared at it for some time without speaking. After a while I said softly, "What does it say, Carla?" I could sense that Carla was in a very private space and I didn't want to intrude clumsily. Carla finally answered, her words barely audible. "It says, 'Dear Carla, I wish I had been with you for Christmas. I sent you a present but maybe you didn't get it yet. Love daddy'" "You miss your Daddy a lot, don't you," I said. Carla looked at me and nodded. Then she whispered, "I just made that up about the letter." I nodded, and she began to cry.

Carla had cut herself off from herself to avoid her feelings. She felt tired, heavy, inert. Through the play-acting episode she allowed what was under the surface of her closing-off shell to emerge. Carla's whole manner changed in our session when she let herself cry. She was hurt and angry that she had not received a present from her father, yet she did not feel free to admit this feeling to her mother, who had doubled her own efforts during the holiday season, in an effort to compensate for the missing father.

In creative dramatics children can increase the self awareness at their disposal. They can develop a total awareness of self — the body, the imagination, the senses. The drama becomes a natural tool to help them find and give expression to lost and hidden parts of themselves, and to build strength and selfhood.

In creative dramatics, children are called upon to experience the world around them as well as their own selves. In order to interpret the world around them and to convey ideas, actions, feelings, and expressions, they call on all of the resources that they can muster within themselves: sight, sound, taste, touch, smell, facial expression, body movement, fantasy, imagination, intellect.

This is the enactment of our own lives, our own selves. We play out the parts in our dreams, we create the scenes, we rewrite as we go along. We don't just talk about the pain in our chests, we give voice to it, become it. We play out our mother, ourselves as children, our critical side, and so forth. We find that as we play these parts, we become more aware of ourselves, more involved, more real. We find ourselves, contact ourselves, experience ourselves in genuine, solid, authentic, clear ways. We can try out new ways of being in the realm of the theater. We can allow suppressed parts of ourselves to emerge. We can let ourselves experience absorption, excitement, and spontaneity that may be lacking in our day-to-day lives.

Pantomiming simple sensory images — using facial expressions and body movements without words — greatly enhances one's sensory awareness. On a more complex level, pantomime can involve expressing action and interaction through body movement, communicating feelings and moods, developing characterizations, playing out a story — all without words. On a still higher level we can introduce words into improvisations. Children who have already participated in many pantomime experiences will usually find it easy to add words to the dramatic pantomime.

What follows are a few examples for improvisational games, activities, and experiences.

Touch

Pass around an imaginary object to be handled, looked at, reacted to, and then passed along. This object can be a knife, a glass of water, a kitten, a dirty old wallet, an expensive bracelet, a hot baked potato, a book. The leader can announce the object, or the children can decide the object when it is their turn to pass it, or the same object can be passed around to the whole group before changing, or the group can try to guess what the object is.

Imagine that a table is covered with a variety of objects. Each person must go and pick out one thing, showing, by the way she handles it, what it is.

Go into a variety of different settings, looking for something you have lost, such as a sweater. The settings can be a very large room, a dark closet, your own room, a locker room.

Sight

You are watching a situation or a sports activity. Express the emotions that you feel as you watch. The group can try to guess what is being watched, or a story can be told by one person as another watches.

Enactment

Show how you would react to seeing a sunset, a child crying, an automobile accident, a skunk, a snake, a tiger loose in the streets, two lovers embracing, etc.

Imagine you see yourself in the mirror. Continue looking and reacting as you do this.

Sound

React to different sounds: an explosion, a small sound you are trying to identify, a military band coming down the street, a popular tune on the radio. Other sounds might be a baby crying, a prowler in the dark as you are sleeping, someone you know coming into the room, thunder, the door bell, etc.

You have just heard some bad news, good news, puzzling news, amazing news, etc.

Smell

Show how you would react as you smell a variety of odors: a flower, an onion, burnt rubber, etc.

Imagine a variety of situations involving smell: walking in the woods and smelling a campfire, smelling different perfumes on a counter, smelling something unpleasant and trying to decide what it is, smelling cookies baking as you come home.

Taste

Pantomime tasting a variety of things: ice cream, a lemon, etc.
Imagine eating something as the others try to guess what it is.
Eat an apple. Before eating, consider every aspect of the apple.
Eat it very slowly and silently and be aware of your jaw movement.
Eat something delicious, such as a piece of chocolate or creamy candy. Bite into a sour apple, or try something you have never tasted before.

Pantomime sucking through a straw, licking a lollipop, whistling, blowing a balloon in the air.

WINDOWS TO OUR CHILDREN

The Body

Although the body is, of course, used in the exercises just discussed, the following suggestions focus more on whole body awareness and movement.

A variation of "Simon Says" is suggested in *Theater in My Head*: "Simon says, 'Be a tightrope-walker, be a snail, be a monster, be a dog, be a ballet dancer . . .'" Children can take turns being the leader.

Pantomime walking: in a hurry, lazily, through a puddle, on grass, on a hot pavement barefoot, up a mountain, in snow, down a steep path, on pebbles in a creek, on hot sand, with a hurt foot, with shoes too big, too small.

Perform an action like setting a table, baking a cake, feeding the dog, getting dressed, doing homework. Actions can be assigned, picked from a card or folded papers in a pile, or thought up by each child to be guessed by the group.

Imagine you are in a very tiny box, a great big box; Imagine you are a chicken in an egg.

Do some "as if" experiments: Walk like a man in a hurry, a child late for school, a movie queen, a nearsighted person, a cowboy, a small child dragged off to bed, someone with a plaster cast, a giant.

Experiment with using fingers in different ways: sewing, cutting, wrapping a package, etc.

Play a game of tug-of-war with an imaginary rope. This can be done individually with different imaginary people, as with someone hostile, very strong, very weak. (or two people or a whole group can play)

Imagine playing with a ball that keeps changing. It can be a small rubber ball, a beach ball, a ping-pong ball, a basketball, a football, a tennis ball, a Nerf ball, etc. It changes size and weight and might even become a bean bag or a Frisbee.

Play jump rope with a group, using an imaginary rope.

Pantomiming Situations

Two people decide to do something, and the rest guess what it is: making a bed; playing ping-pong; playing chess; anything that two can do.

Enactment

You have just received a package. Open it. React.

You have been on a hike with friends. Suddenly you realize you are alone.

You are in an elevator. Suddenly it stops between floors. After a while it starts moving again.

Characterization

You are a group of people waiting for a bus. Each of you will be someone else (don't tell us), such as an elderly woman on her way to see her children, a businessman late for work, a girl on her way to high school, a blind man who needs help getting on the bus, etc.

You are a robber who is entering a house at night. While you are there, the people return unexpectedly. You listen and finally make your escape.

You go into a restaurant to order a meal. Do it as: 1) a teenage boy who is very hungry, 2) a middle age woman who has no appetite and can't find anything on the menu she wants, 3) a very poor old man who is hungry, but must limit his choice to what he can afford.

Have the children act out different occupations or kinds of people for the rest to guess. Writing some on a card to be picked at random is helpful to some children.

Have them act out an appliance or some machine for the group to guess, or be a color and see if we can guess what it is by what they do.

With very young children, I have used a "magic key" or a "magic wand." I wave the wand and say, "You are now a dog!" and the child becomes a dog for a few moments. Then I wave it and say, "You are now an old man!" and so forth.

Improvisations with Words

Any object can help a child or group of children act out an improvised story. In *Creative Dramatics in the Classroom*, McCaslin describes an elaborate story invented by a group of children with nothing but a whistle as a prop.

WINDOWS TO OUR CHILDREN

I have placed several items in a paper bag, items from around the house that seem to have no connection, such as a funnel, a hammer, a scarf, a pen, an old hat, a large spoon, and so forth. Four or five items are all that are needed in each bag. One small group can create a whole play from these items.

Give children varieties of situations to act out:

A salesman comes to the door. He insists on demonstrating a vacuum cleaner, although you tell him you have one. How do you handle the situation?

You are delivering papers. You throw one toward a house, but instead of landing on the porch, it breaks a window. Both the man and his wife come to see what has happened.

Children can also role-play situations that directly reflect episodes in their lives. Such situations can be true-to-life ones, or simulated ones. In these situations a conflict is presented to be worked through in the spontaneous dramatization. The children themselves usually come up with the best role-playing themes.

Children enjoy using hats, masks, and costumes in drama work. Provide a variety of hats and children will change characterizations as quickly as they change hats.

I have a large collection of Halloween masks, and many children enjoy using them. A mirror helps the child who is wearing a particular mask see the character he represents. The mask, like a puppet, gives the child permission to say things he would not say as himself.

A child in an individual session will sometimes look through all of the masks, choose one to wear, and talk to me as that monster, or devil, or witch, or princess. Sometimes I ask the child to wear each mask and make some kind of statement as that character.

In a paper about using costumes in play therapy, Irwin Marcus, in *Therapeutic Use of Child's Play*, advocates using costumes to stimulate spontaneous play patterns in older children and thus to help them play out fantasies, feelings, and traumatizing situations. He provided costumes which included those appropriate for a baby, mother, father, doctor, Superman, witch, devil, clown, skeleton, and ballerina, and included three large pieces of colored cloth to be used for a self-designed outfit. Each child was asked to make up a play using any of the costumes. Marcus found that the

Enactment

costume play brought out much valuable material involving not only content, but a great deal of the child's process.

Playmaking, whether with costumes, masks, hats, objects, puppets, or no props at all, is a kind of storytelling with a high degree of involvement on the part of the child. Here we have an opportunity to help the child make use of his total organism in a therapeutically visible situation. We can see clearly the child's holes — the areas in which his development lags and needs strengthening. We can see how he moves and uses his body; we can observe rigidity and constriction, or ease and flow of movement. We can pay attention to the organization of the play. We can work with the content that comes through the play as well as the process we may note within the play's content. Is there a lot of fighting? Does the main character lose? Perhaps no one listens to him. And we can also have a lot of fun.

Although the activities mentioned in this section seem to lend themselves to group work, I have been able to adapt many of them to individual therapy with ease. Often I am able to deal with material in more depth in the individual sessions.

A twelve-year-old boy put on a play for me without props or costumes. He assumed all parts, including that of the announcer. This boy was doing poorly in school, was accused of laziness and lassitude by his mother, and appeared sullen most of the time. In fact he was well organized; he could put on a highly complex play, could keep track of each character, and had a fantastic sense of humor.

I never know where any activity will lead. I remember playing a game with an eight-year-old boy in which each of us acted out some kind of animal for the other to guess. We were to wait until the other announced finishing before we made our guesses. This gave us the opportunity to play out a larger drama than merely the movement of the animal. Steven got on the floor and curled up in a little ball. Next he raised his head, moved it back and forth, moved his eyes as well, smiled, then hid his head back in his body ball. He did this several times. Suddenly he grimaced as though in pain, flailed his body around, turned over on his back, flung his arms out, and lay still — playing dead. At the conclusion, I guessed that he was a turtle and that something had happened and he was dead. Steven then told me that he once had a turtle and that his little brother had killed it. I suggested that he must have been very angry at his brother and very sad at the loss of the turtle. Steven reacted to my comment with violent rage. "I hate him! I'd like to kill him!" he hissed between his teeth.

In his real life, Steven was almost overly nice to his little brother, deflecting his angry feelings toward his mother. "At least he gets along well with his brother," she once told me. I guessed that he was terrified of his own rage and vengeful feelings toward his brother and found it safer to be angry at his mother. Because of this dramatic experience I could now give Steven some opportunity to express his repressed rage at his brother through clay, the Bataca, drawings. The turtle incident was not the only cause of his anger. Many small day-to-day irritants had been heaped onto this major one; Steven was fearful of letting himself be angry at his brother for anything.

Sometimes at the end of a creative dramatics experience we talk about what happened, what it was like for us, what we are feeling now, and so forth. I find, however, that the experience itself brings the movement and change, not the discussion. The girl who has played the part of an old man in a scenario has made contact with herself in a way that would be difficult for her to acknowledge in words. And it is not important that she convert her feelings into words. It is obvious to me and to everyone around her that the experience has left her more expansive in her nature and her expressions, that she acts surer and more confident than before.

Dreams

Fritz Perls, in "Four Lectures" (Chapter 2 of *Gestalt Therapy Now*), placed great emphasis on dream work as a way of contacting and experiencing the self.

> ... The dream is an existential message. It is more than an unfinished situation; it is more than an unfulfilled wish; it is more than a prophecy. It is a message of yourself to yourself, to whatever part of you is listening. The dream is possibly the most spontaneous expression of the human being, a piece of art that we chisel out of our lives. And every part, every situation in the dream is a creation of the dreamer himself. Of course, some of the pieces come from memory or reality, but

> the important question is what makes the dreamer pick out this specific piece? No choice in the dream is coincidental ... Every aspect of the dream is a part of the dreamer, but a part that to some extent is disowned and projected onto other objects. What does projection mean? That we have disowned, alienated, certain parts of ourselves and put them out into the world rather than having them available as our own potential. We have emptied a part of ourselves into the world, therefore we must be left with holes, with emptiness. If we want to own these parts of ourselves again we have to use special techniques by which we can reassimilate these experiences. (p. 27)

Children don't easily share their dreams for often the ones they remember are the very frightening ones. Or they may be so puzzling and bizarre to them that they attempt to put them out of their minds. I think that this is one reason children often have recurrent dreams. They try so hard to push them away that the dream keeps coming back as a reminder. It is not uncommon for adults to remember dreams from their childhood that still remain unfinished. They are unfinished because the conflict presented was not resolved, the disowned parts were too frightening to re-own. I remember two or three dreams that I seem to have dreamed over and over as a child. I recently worked on one of these dreams that I had so long ago and received a current existential message from this dream, I learned something about myself and what was going on in my life right now.

Sometimes I read a book involving dreams, to stimulate children to share their dreams. An excellent book is Mercer Mayer's *There's a Nightmare in My Closet*. Several years ago a colleague and I conducted a therapy group of children who had one common bond: all of their fathers were in a special alcoholic treatment program. My friend brought this book to one session and read it to the group. We asked the children if they ever had nightmares. Two of the children volunteered to work on their dreams after we told them that the dream would tell them something about their life.

Jimmy, age ten, recounted this dream: "My family and I were driving in a car on a freeway. Suddenly we came to a steep hill. My mother was driving and she can't brake the car. The brakes wouldn't work. I thought the car would go over the side of the road. I got really panicky and grabbed hold of the wheel. All of a sudden there was lots of water like a lake at the end. There was no way to turn off. We either had to turn and fall off the side or go right into the water. I woke up before it landed."

We asked Jimmy to retell the dream in the present tense. He did so and it seemed almost as if he were reliving (re-dreaming) the dream. In his work we asked Jimmy to play out all the parts of the dream, as if it were a play and he could speak for each person and thing. He played himself, his mother, his father, one of his sisters in the car, the car, the road, and the lake. In every situation he was panicked, and had no control. As the lake, he was large, deep, overwhelming. We asked him to imagine an ending to his dream. He said, "My father saves my mother, who can't swim. He remains calm and gets everyone out. I can't think of what to do but he gets me out, too." We asked Jimmy what he thought the message of his dream was, what the dream was telling him about where he was in his life right now. He said, "I know just what it's telling me! I'm afraid, so afraid my father might start drinking again! He's not drinking now and everything is really neat in our family. It was so bad when he was drinking! If he starts drinking it will be awful again, a disaster! I'm so afraid of that. Deep down I'm really afraid but I never say anything. I'm afraid to tell my parents I'm afraid. No one else seems afraid. If he does start drinking there'll be nothing I can do about it. I'm the youngest in the family. What can I do? I made up that ending — my father saves us. That's how I want it to be in our family."

Jimmy experienced great relief in sharing his fear. One of the other children, a nine-year-old boy, commented, "I have a road like that." When asked to say more about his road, he said, "I feel sometimes like I'm going down a steep road in a car that can't stop, too. I can't control anything."

Vicki, age thirteen, was eager to tell her dream. "In my dream everyone thinks I'm dead. I'm in a coffin. But I'm not dead! Everyone just thinks I am. A nice old lady is taking care of me and I sleep in the coffin. It's my bed. But people keep telling the lady, 'She's dead.' There's a thunderstorm going on, too."

I asked her to be the thunderstorm in her dream. Vicki thought for a while, then with a smile on her face got up and went around the room "zapping" people (explaining that she was lightning). She made a zapping motion with her arm at each person, yelling "Zap!" each time. She did this with great gusto, reporting her enjoyment to us. We then asked her to be the old lady in the dream. She became a kindly old lady talking to Vicki in a kindly way, putting her to bed in the coffin. Vicki told us that the old lady reminded her of her grandmother, who was very ill and dying. Her grandmother had always been kind to her and was one of the few people she liked a lot in her life.

At this point we faced a choice in her work — to ask her to leave the dream and work on her feelings about her dying grandmother or to stay with the dream. We decided to continue with the dream, and asked her to lie in a make-believe coffin and say what that was like and what was happening. Vicki lay down on the floor in a rigid position. "I'm lying here in this coffin. I'm supposed to be sleeping but everyone thinks I'm dead. No one pays any attention to the old lady who tells people I'm not dead."

What's it like in the coffin?

Vicki: It's not very comfortable. I can't move much.

(Taking our cue, the other children joined us in being the people looking at her. We said things like, "Oh, poor Vicki. She's so young to die. It's terrible. We feel terrible." We asked Vicki to talk back to the people.)

Vicki: Hey! I'm not dead. Don't cry. I'm alive. I can do things. I can do things.

What can you do?

Vicki: Lots of things. I can do lots of things.

We don't see you doing anything but lying there. Can you make a choice about doing something else, or do you want to lie there?

Vicki: (Getting up) I don't want to lie there and have everyone think I'm dead! See? See? (She stretches her arms and runs around the room.) I'm alive!

Make a statement that tells the message of your dream to you.

Vicki: (Thinks for a moment, then brightens and says) I'm alive and I can make choices! I can make lots of choices.

Like what? (a nine-year-old boy in group)

Vicki: (Looks at him, stumped for a moment.) Well, I can.

Boy: When?

Vicki, go around the room, pick out some people, and choose to do something with them.

Vicki stepped before each of us in the group and made her choices. "I choose to shake your hand . . . I choose to give you a hug . . . I choose to make a face at you." Vicki and the group enjoyed this exercise so much that each person in the group insisted on having a turn to go around the room and make choices.

I have worked with dreams in individual sessions with children as well. I give most of the children I see (except those who obviously hate to write) an inexpensive spiral notebook to keep. In this notebook I ask them to write various things, including dreams. Patricia, a twelve-year-old girl, made the following entry:

"Behind Disneyland. Opens when I'm in a big room without a roof and a big box of Disneyland balloons are next to me. And character costumes are hung up beside me. A tent is behind me. A man comes in so I hide. But then he leaves and I come out of hiding and put a costume on and blow up balloons and go outside and sell them."

She drew a small sketch of this dream at the end of the page. I gave her paper and asked her to draw a large-scale sketch, which she did with much more elaboration. She explained her picture to me as I wrote down the gist of her statements:

"Walls but no roof. I'm in the middle of the room. Man comes. I hide because I think he will punish me. I go into tent to hide. But he just gets balloons and leaves. He doesn't know I'm there or he would punish me. No one knows it's me but me, because of the costume I put on. Everyone thinks it's just a worker."

Patricia often drew pictures of Disneyland in our work together. After working on this dream (the first time she remembered actually *dreaming* about Disneyland), she was quick to formulate this message: "I'm afraid to be myself. I'd rather pretend I was something else, like a Disneyland character." Now we could at least begin to discover the Patricia that she was always covering up and hiding.

Soon after this, Patricia brought in another recorded dream. She introduced it by saying, "This is not the first time I dreamed this. I did when I was eight years old, and lots of times since, and last night again." Here is what she had written:

"A dark room with just one little light, a bed, and an ironing board, my Mom (real). I'm in bed right next to her. All of a sudden the lights go off and I hear a scream." At one corner of the page was a tiny sketch of this dream with the word DARK written across it.

I felt that this was a very significant dream. Patricia's natural mother had been the victim of a murder-suicide (the stepfather shot her and then himself) when she was about eight. It was Patricia who had discovered the bloody bodies as she wandered into their bedroom in the morning. I heard this story from her father, who brought her into therapy four years later, but until she revealed this dream to me, Patricia would only shrug whenever I brought the subject up, and say she couldn't remember. She worked on this dream and said, "My life went dark on me when my Mom went out like a light." This was the beginning of the grief work that, along with many other feelings, Patricia had never completed.

Even very young children can work on dreams. Six-year-old Todd often woke up in the night from his scary dreams. I asked him to tell me about one of them. He said that a monster always chased him, and sometimes it was a car that was chasing him. He resisted my suggestion to draw a picture of the monster, so I drew it for him as he described it to me. Working with my drawing, I asked him to tell the monster what he thought of it. He yelled, "Stop scaring me!" Then I asked him to imagine he could talk for the monster, as if it were a puppet. He said to himself, speaking as the monster, "You're a bad, bad boy! I have to scare you!" I asked him to continue to be the monster and tell himself why he was bad. "You're bad! You took some money out of your mother's purse and she doesn't even know it. You peed in your pants and she doesn't know it. You're bad, bad, bad." This boy was in therapy because of annoying behavior at school; the teacher had recommended to his mother that he get help. Through this dream we were able to begin to talk about his overwhelming guilt feelings and feelings of intense resentment and anger toward his mother, who had recently remarried. Though Todd liked his new stepfather, he was nevertheless jealous of a new person in the household. These mixed feelings confused him, and we needed to get them all out in the open to deal with. Instead of drawing, I might have asked Todd to select a monster figure (or car) and a boy figure, and to act out the chase in the sand tray, or on the floor.

In general, dreams serve a variety of functions for children. They may be expressions of anxiety — things that worry them. They may express feelings that children feel unable to express in real life. They may depict wishes, wants, needs, fantasies, questions and curiosities, attitudes. The dream can be an indication of a general stance or feeling about life. It may be a way of working through feelings and experiences — situations that children are unable to deal with directly and openly.

In working with a dream, I look for parts that are alien to the child, parts that he is fearful of owning. I watch for things that seem missing from the dream, such as a car without wheels, or a horse without legs. I look for the polarities and splits in the dream, such as the chaser and the chased, the flat place and the mountain. I watch for contact points such as a storm battering a house, or for points that prevent contact, such as a wall that separates two things. I may focus on a wish that comes through the dream, or on something which seems to be avoided. I may concentrate on the process of the dream — a dream of rushing around, or of nothing coming out right, or of feeling lost. I may look at the pattern of a series of dreams. The quality of the setting of the dream may be very important: a desert wasteland, a crowded street, a large house with many rooms. We may rewrite the dream, or add an ending. Sometimes I work with memories, daydreams, or fantasies in the same way as with a dream.

Whatever we choose to work with, I stay with the child closely. As he plays out the parts, or engages in a dialogue or describes the setting, I pay close attention to his breath, body posture, facial expressions, gestures, voice inflections. I may at any time choose to focus on what is going on with the child as he works on the dream, or to leave the dream for the purpose of working on content that comes out of the dream.

The goal is to help the child learn about himself and his life through his dream. I avoid analyzing and interpreting; only the child himself can become aware of what the dream may be trying to tell him. Children are fully capable of learning for themselves through dream work.

The Empty Chair

The empty chair technique was developed by Fritz Perls as a means of bringing greater awareness and clarity to therapeutic work. It is also used to bring unfinished situations into the here and now. For example, a person may have feelings and unsaid material held in toward a long-dead parent. When talking *about* this it is easier to avoid feelings and emotions. The experience of imagining the parent in the empty chair and saying what

Enactment

needs to be said to the parent rather than telling me *about* it is powerful, and often serves to close yet another unfinished gestalt in this person's life. When this happens, a feeling of calmness and relaxation is obvious in the person's body posture, and sometimes I will notice that he takes a very deep breath, close to a sigh. The empty chair technique helps convert past, unresolved situations into present, focused experience.

A mother began to tell me, in a high, complaining voice, about her exasperation with her fifteen-year-old son, who was not present in the room. I asked her to imagine that he was sitting in a nearby chair and to tell him what she was telling me. She looked at this chair, began softly to tell him, and then began to weep. When I asked her to tell him, in the chair, about her sadness, she related her feelings of guilt in regard to him, and our session went on to be much more productive than if I had allowed her to use me as an ear for her complaining.

Sometimes parts or symbols of one's self are put into the empty chair. A sixteen-year-old girl who was working on her overeating put her "overeater self" into the chair and was able to discover much more of what made her overeat — reasons her own "overeater self" expressed when she sat in the chair and talked back to the part of her that wanted to lose weight.

The empty chair technique is an aid in the clarification of one's splits and polarities, a clarification that is essential to the process of centering. Fritz Perls talks about the reconciliation of one's opposite parts so that they can be joined in productive combination and interplay, and will no longer use up energy in useless struggles with each other. The severest of these splits is between what Perls called topdog and underdog.

The voice of the topdog plagues and tortures the underdog with criticisms: "You should do this," "You should do that," "You should be better than you are." These "shoulds" are characterized mainly by bullying and an air of righteousness. The topdog always knows what the underdog should do.

The underdog is a counter force. He reacts to the topdog by acting helpless, tired, unsure, unable, sometimes rebellious, often devious, and always as a saboteur. His answers to the topdog's demands are, "I can't!" (in a whiny voice), "Yes, but —," "Maybe tomorrow," "I'll try," "I'm so tired" and so forth. These opposites live a life of mutual frustration and continued attempts to control each other. This deadlocked struggle produces a state of paralysis, exhaustion, and an inability to fully experience each moment with one's total organism in integrated harmony.

Teenagers are often plagued with topdog/underdog conflicts that keep them in a constant state of frustration. Sally, a sixteen-year-old girl, complained that it was difficult for her to study — she just couldn't concentrate. So she would drop her studies to be with her friends, and then could not enjoy herself because of her worries over her unfinished homework, papers coming due, and so forth.

I asked Sally to describe a specific situation. She told me that her favorite grandparents were visiting from the East, that the family was going to dinner that night, but that she had an essay due the next morning — one she had put off doing because of her lack of concentration. Sally was a good student and had high expectations of herself. She was nervous, anxious, and beginning to think she was "going crazy," as she put it. Sally played out the topdog and underdog parts of herself, using the empty chair.

Topdog: (harshly) Sally, you're disgusting! Don't even think about going out tonight. It's your fault for not doing this assignment before this. You *knew* Grandma and Grandpa would be here. You can't go tonight.

Underdog: (in a whiny voice) But I did try to do it before. I just can't keep my mind on what I'm doing. I'm tired of doing homework. I want to go tonight. Maybe I can ask the teacher if I can turn it in late.

Topdog: You know you won't have a good time if you go. You'll worry about the paper. I'll see to that!

This dialogue went on a while; finally Sally looked at me, smiled, and commented, "No wonder I never get anything done if that's what goes on inside of me all the time."

I explained to her that these two opposing forces used up energy, undoubtedly leaving her spent. The underdog always appears to win the battles since nothing gets done; but since the topdog doesn't give up, doing nothing is never very satisfying (Topdog makes sure of that!). Once the conflict is clear, it is useful to stand back and "observe," these two forces arguing within us. Then we can make our own free choice, perhaps negotiating a bit with each of these sides.

So Sally said to her topdog, "Look, I want to be with my grandparents. I don't see them often. Get off my back and let me do this. When I get

Enactment

home I'll stay up late and do the paper. And to her underdog she said, "I've decided to go out to dinner tonight; that ought to make you happy. So when I get home to do the paper, leave me alone and remember you had a chance to rest."

Sally later reported that she did go out to dinner and every now and then would feel the pull of her topdog, whereupon she would assert, "Get lost! I made this choice and I'll write the paper later. I can't do it now anyway." When she got home she stayed up until 2:00 A.M. and had no difficulty writing a terrific essay.

In some of our later sessions we explored the source of these two powerful forces. She began to learn how they were getting in the way of her life, and she became skillful at dealing with them.

In my work with emotionally disturbed children in the schools, we called the technique I've just described, the empty chair game. Two chairs always stood ready for use and were often used to help children clarify what they were doing in a situation, resolve conflicts, take responsibility for their own behavior, and find solutions to problems. A couple of examples will show the power of this:

Todd, age twelve: I need to use the chairs! (as he came in from a recess time on the playground)

Fine.

Todd: I hate you, Mr. Smith. (turning to me) He's always picking on me

Tell that to him.

Todd: I hate you! You're always picking on me! It's none of your business what I do with my own hands. (I now notice that Todd has black ink drawn all over his hands.)

Now change seats and be Mr. Smith and say what he might say or did say to you.

Todd: (in a sarcastic voice) Well, Todd, it just isn't a good idea to do that. Your mother will be angry and she'll blame the school and I don't know what the ink will do to your skin.

Todd: (changing seats again by himself, no more sarcasm in his voice) But you don't have to be so mean about it.

Todd: (as Mr. Smith) But, Todd, when I asked you to wash you hands off, you wouldn't do it. I just have to get tough with you.

WINDOWS TO OUR CHILDREN

Todd: (as himself, in a low voice) I guess I was pretty fresh. (Todd looks up at me expectantly.)

What do you want to do now?

Todd: I think I'll go and see if I can get this stuff off my hands. (Todd leaves the room walking straight, not hunched over as he usually is when he is defensive.)

Danny, age twelve: I'd like to work with the chairs. (He sits down in one.)

Who is in the other chair?

Danny: You.

Go ahead.

Danny: I don't want to do math now, Mrs. Oaklander. You can't make me.

Danny: (as me) But we're all going to do math now. That's what we usually do at this time.

Danny: But I want to finish that thing I was making last period. I just have a little bit to do.

Danny: (as me) But Danny, if I let you do it, everyone will want to.

Danny: But I just need to do something for five minutes and then I'll get busy on my math.

Danny: (as me) OK, Danny, that sounds cool.

Danny then gets up, goes to the back of the room, works on his project for a few minutes, comes back and sits down, and works harder on his math than he ever has before. During the whole episode, I say not one word. (Danny had actually made that same request prior to the above dialogue, and I said, "No.")

One might view this exercise of Danny's as manipulation; but in light of the math work Danny eventually did, I view it as a magnificent effort by a boy who was gaining self-support, learning to meet his own needs, taking responsibility for himself, and showing a teacher (through her own methods) how locked in she could become to a time schedule that she herself disliked — a schedule that sometimes seemed more important than a child's needs.

The following example illustrates how I use the empty chair technique with a much younger child. Gina, a girl of seven, was playing on the playground when a terrible fight erupted between her and another child.

Enactment

She came running to me in tears. We sat on the grass while she told me, through her sobs, a story of being pushed aside on the rings by the other child. I listened without comment. When she was through talking, I said, "I see that you're crying. You must feel hurt and angry at Terry." Gina continued to cry, nodding. As almost a demand, she asked, "Will you punish her?" I said, "First, I'd like you to do something for me. Pretend that Terry is sitting right here and tell her how angry and hurt you feel because of what she did to you."

Gina: You're mean! I hate you! You always want to be on the rings first! I don't like you to push me!

(I talk to an empty spot on the grass.) Terry, please tell Gina what you have to say to her. Gina, will you sit here and be Terry? (Gina moves over.)

Gina: (as Terry) Gina, I'm sorry.

Shall I call her over now and find out what happened between you two from her side?

Gina: No.

Do you want to tell the pretend Terry anything else?

Gina: Terry, I guess I kicked you, and I'm sorry too.

What do you want to do now?

Gina: (big smile) Go play.

She then ran off toward Terry and I watched them play with no more problems for the moment.

In another situation a little girl, age seven, was accused of stealing a coat. Someone said she had worn it home on the bus. She denied taking it. I asked to talk to her and we went off to a private corner of the room where no one could see us. I tried to get her to talk to me about the coat. She denied knowing anything about it. So I asked her to pretend that the other girl (who had lost the coat) was sitting next to her and to tell her she didn't know anything about the coat. She said, "I'm sorry you lost your coat and, um, I didn't take your coat and . . ." She began to cry. She told me that she did take the coat. I asked her to tell the other girl in the empty chair about the coat — how it felt to wear it. She said, "I like your coat. It feels nice and warm. I wish I had a coat like that." I asked her if she had anything else to say to her. "I'll bring it back tomorrow."

WINDOWS TO OUR CHILDREN

It seems to me that in this situation the child was caught in a situation where she was unable to admit taking the coat — she needed to be defensive and deny the act. How else could she react to an accusation? But bringing the situation into present experience with the nonthreatening empty chairs made it impossible for her to hide her feelings. The day she brought the coat back, I took her down to the lost-and-found section at school and we picked out an unclaimed coat for her.

Richard, age ten, provided another example of being able to save face with the empty chairs. Richard forgot to bring his library books back from home, and the librarian would not let him take any others. He cried bitterly. Then he began teasing another boy, Lee, and continued to do this all day. Lee carried a monkey puppet with him all the time and Richard grabbed it and threw it into the wastebasket every chance he got. Lee finally had enough and fought back, which precipitated an even harder crying spell for Richard. He began to scream and yell, and finally he threw his desk over onto the floor. Apparently he had gotten so far into this emotional place that he did not know how to get out of it. No matter what I said, he only screamed and cried harder. He refused to do any work and even refused to play during the free period. Finally, I said, Richard, come up to the chairs." He rushed up. The other children were noisily involved in free time activities.

Richard, put someone you're mad at in the chair.

Richard: It's Lee.

What would you like to tell him?

Richard: I'm not mad at you. I'm sorry I threw your monkey in the basket. It's not your fault.

Richard: (changes seats, as Lee) I'm sorry I choked you.

Richard: (as himself) I'm sorry I was mad at you.

Richard: (as Lee) OK.

Suddenly we both notice that the entire room is still. The other boys have been listening and watching. The real Lee calls out from the back of the room, "That's OK." They smile at each other. Richard then insists on putting the librarian in the chair.

Richard: I'm sorry I forgot my books. I'll try to remember to bring them.

Richard: (as librarian) Rules are rules. When you bring them in, you can take out some more books.

Richard now puts me in the chair, obviously thoroughly enjoying himself.

Richard: I'm sorry I threw the desk over and everything.

Richard: (as me) OK, Richard, that's good. (He leaves the room to go home in high spirits.)

Polarities

I want to emphasize the importance of working with polarities. The young person is frightened of the splits within her, as well as those she sees in the adults in her life. She is confused when she finds herself feeling angry and hateful toward someone she loves. She is bewildered when someone she sees as strong and protective feels weak and helpless.

She has trouble accepting those aspects of herself that she dislikes, or that her parents criticize. Her parents accuse her of gross hedonism because she would much rather enjoy herself than help with the housework, and she secretly wonders if indeed she may be selfish and lazy. As she despises and turns away from those parts of herself, she further broadens the gulf between her polar selves, causing increased fragmentation and self-alienation. An integration, reconciliation, or synthesis of one's opposing sides, positive and negative, is a prerequisite to a dynamic and healthy life process.

I provide children with a number of exercises and experiments to acquaint them with the concept of polarities in the self and to help them understand that polarities are an inherent aspect of everyone's personality.

We may discuss the opposite in feelings and personalities they know about: love/hate, sad/happy, suspicious/trusting, good/bad, sure/unsure, clear/confused, sick/well, weak/strong, and so forth. I may use any number of techniques to focus on these polarities:

Art: Draw a picture of something that makes you happy and something that makes you sad. Or draw how you feet when you're feeling relaxed and when you're feeling tense. Or draw how you see yourself when you're weak and when you're strong

WINDOWS TO OUR CHILDREN

Clay: Make an image of your inside self. Make another one of your outside self — how you present yourself to others.

Stories: "Once upon a time there was an elephant who was very silly; when he was with friends and very serious when he was at home. Now you be this elephant... you tell the rest."

Body movement: Portray various parts of self by means of charades to be guessed.

Collage : Make a representation of some opposing parts of yourself.

In the Psychosynthesis techniques we find a variety of methods for helping clients identify various parts of the self, called sub personalities. One such exercise involves repetitiously asking oneself the question "Who am I?" and writing down each answer as it comes. "I am a hard worker. I am lazy. I am afraid of heights. I am a good swimmer." Examining these answers provides information about one's various different parts.

Another exercise consists of drawing a pie with segments. In each segment is placed a word or sketch representing a part of one's self. One can then begin a dialogue with each of the parts to clarify the conflicts, demands, or aspects of each. With increased awareness, understanding, and acceptance of the parts of self comes greater self-strength and greater opportunity for choices and self-determination.

8

Play Therapy

Five-year-old Roger squirmed restlessly in his chair as his mother described his behavior at home and at school. He was, she said, hitting, kicking, grabbing, punching, jumping on other children so much that other parents were complaining about him. Roger appeared sullen and hostile with me, made no bones about his dislike of me, my office, and this waste of his time. But he examined all the toys carefully when we were finally alone together. I stood by quietly as he did this.

At the next session, he immediately took down the doctor set and ordered me to lie down. We spent the whole session playing doctor; I was the patient and he was the doctor. His whole manner changed when he played the doctor: he was kind and gentle to me, solemn, and he spoke quietly with great sympathy over my illness. I asked him if I would have to go to the hospital. He told me gravely that I was very sick and would have to go. He asked me if I had children. I said that I had one little boy and I was very worried about who would take care of him if I went to the hospital. I spoke about my concern over his welfare at home and at school, and the fact that he was so young he wouldn't understand and would worry too much about me. Roger listened intently. Finally, in the gentlest, kindest voice I have ever heard, he said, "Don't worry. I'll talk to him and explain that you'll get better. And I'll even take care of him for you when you're in the hospital." He patted my arm and smiled at me, and I thanked him for these wonderful things he would do for me.

WINDOWS TO OUR CHILDREN

Roger and I played doctor at least five sessions in a row, and each time, the drama became more elaborate and extensive under his direction. "Pretend you're at home and all of a sudden you feel sick and you call me."

Roger's gentle, sensitive manner carried over into school and at home following these sessions. At the first parent-child session, I had learned that the mother was quite ill at one time and had been in the hospital three times for extended periods. She was well now, however, and indicated that she did not believe that this past period of sickness could be a factor behind Roger's hostile behavior. His great interest in the doctor play, however, told me that his feelings about his mother's hospitalizations apparently needed expression in a way that had been difficult for him to do at home.

Play is the young child's form of improvisational dramatics. It is also more than that. Playing is how the child tries out his world and learns about his world, and it is therefore essential to his healthy development. For the child, play is serious, purposeful business through which he develops mentally, physically, and socially. Play is the child's form of self-therapy, through which confusions, anxieties, and conflicts are often worked through. Whereas Roger allowed himself to be gentle and thoughtful, other children play tough and aggressive. Through the safety of play every child can try out his own new ways of being. Play performs a vital function for the child. It is far more than just the frivolous, lighthearted, pleasurable activity that adults usually make of it.

Play also serves as a language for the child — a symbolism that substitutes for words. The child experiences much in life he cannot as yet express in language, and so he uses play to formulate and assimilate what he experiences.

Four-year-old Carly painstakingly placed the doll furniture in the various rooms of the doll house, moving and straightening pieces until she was satisfied. Then she placed the mother doll and the father doll in bed in one room and a child doll in bed in another room. "It's nighttime," she told me, and as I looked on, she manipulated the parent doll figures in a lovemaking scenario. Next she placed all the figures around the table in the kitchen and said to me, "It's morning."

I use play in therapy in much the same way that I might use a story, a drawing, a sand tray scene, a puppet show, or an improvised play. An outline of how I pace the technique follows, along with some comments on the play therapy process.

I observe the process of the child as she plays. How does she play, how does she approach the materials, what does she choose, what does she avoid? What is her general style? Is there difficulty in shifting from one thing to another? Is she disorganized or well organized? What is her play pattern? How she plays tells a lot about how she is in her life.

I watch the content of the play itself. Does she play out themes of loneliness? Aggression? Nurturance? Are there lots of accidents and crashes with planes and cars?

I watch for the child's contact skills. Do I feel in contact with her as she plays? Is she so absorbed in her play that I see she makes good contact with her play and herself as she plays? Is she continually at the edge of contact, unable to commit herself to anything?

What is the contact like within the play itself? Does she allow for contact between the objects of play? Do people or animals or cars contact each other, see each other, talk to each other?

I may take the opportunity to direct the child's awareness to her process and contact during the play. I may say, "You like to do that slowly." "You don't seem to like to use the animals — I notice you never touch them." "You get tired of things fast." "No one seems to like each other." "This plane is all alone."

I may choose to wait and direct the child's awareness to these things after the play. If the pattern repeats itself in the play, I direct my questions to her life. I may say, "Do you like things orderly at home?" "Do people mess up your room?" (One answer to this was a vehement "Yes!! My bratty sister!" — from a child who rarely spoke.)

I may simply direct the child's awareness to what she is doing: "You are burying the soldiers."

I may ask the child to stop at any point and repeat, emphasize, or exaggerate his action. For example, I noticed that a ten-year-old boy used a fire engine often in an elaborate situation he set up with cars, houses, and buildings — all done on the floor rather than in the sand tray. The fire engine came to the rescue in a variety of situations. I commented that I noticed that his fire engine did a lot of rescuing and asked him to do it once more for me to see. He did so and I asked him if it reminded him of anything in his life. His answer, "My mother expects me to help her with everything. Since my Dad's been away (in the Navy) she wants me to do *everything!*"

I may direct the child's awareness to emotions suggested through his play or the play's content. "You sound angry!" Or, "That father doll sure sounds mad at the boy." I watch his body, face, and gestures. I listen to his voice, cues, remarks. I may ask him to repeat something he says.

I may ask the child to identify with any of the people, animals, objects. "You be that fire engine. What does it say? Describe what it does in your story as if it were you." Or, "What might that snake say about itself?" "How is it to be that shark in the water?" Or, "Which one are you?"

I may ask the child to conduct an open dialogue between objects or people. "What would the fire engine say to this truck if it could talk?"

I bring the situation back to the child and his own life. "Do you ever feel like that monkey?" "Do you ever get in a fight like those two army men?" "Do you ever feel crowded?"

I am careful not to interrupt the flow, waiting for a pause before asking a question or commenting. When I stay very involved with what the child is doing, I know when it is the right time to speak or ask the child to do something. Often the child talks to me as he plays, and sometimes as a natural part of this contact with me I can direct his awareness in some way.

I never ask the child to identify, own, or discuss any of the play, process, or content if it does not feel right and appropriate to me, or if the child is reluctant. Very young children, especially, do not want to, or need to, verbalize their discoveries and awarenesses, or "own" what is expressed through the play. Just by bringing those feelings, situations, and anxieties into the open, a degree of integration occurs. Integration occurs both through the open expression, even though it may be symbolic rather than direct, and also through the child's experiencing the play situation in a safe, accepting atmosphere. Many parents report that the child leaves a session showing a sense of peacefulness and serenity.

Sometimes I set up a structured situation with the toys for the child to play out. I may select various items to fit some circumstance in the child's life or some mythical problem-solving dilemma, as in the roleplaying process. For example, I may select several doll house figures and ask the child to enact a scene with them. Or I might say (as I manipulate the dolls), "The girl is in the bedroom trying to go to sleep but she can hear her mother and father having a fight in the kitchen. What happens next?" Or, "Here is a family sitting around the table eating. The phone rings. It is the police saying that the son is at the police station because he was caught stealing. What happens?"

A nine-year-old girl was terrified of airplanes and did not want her parents to go on a trip they were planning. I set up a play airport, airplane, and doll figures representing herself and her parents. I asked her to play out her feelings in this pretend situation. In her play she managed to keep her parents from getting on the plane. (We had spent previous sessions going into her feelings surrounding her fear of planes and the impending disaster she expected, her fear of being abandoned, etc.) I set up the situation again, had the parents get on the plane after kissing her good-bye, and asked her to be the doll left at the airport and to describe her feelings. Much more material relating to her paralyzing fears came out in this enactment than ever before.

Sometimes when I am working with very young children (ages four or five) I will conduct a play session with the mother and the child. I may suggest they pick any of the toys to play with, or I may select some toys. A great deal of helpful information about the interaction between the mother and the child comes out this way. I was motivated to do this after reading *Are You Listening to Your Child?* by Arthur Kraft. Kraft writes about his experiences in teaching a group of parents how to conduct their own play therapy sessions with their children.

Brent, age five, and his mother sat on the floor in my office with some blocks, some farm animals, a few cars, a dump truck, and puppets. I suggested that they spend some time playing with any of the toys I had set out. The setting seemed artificial and strained to them at first, but soon the play began in earnest. Brent suggested that they each build a farm with the blocks and divide up the animals. He decided that he would be in charge of the animals and would put the ones he wanted to go to his mother in the truck and deliver them to her. She agreed to this. After a while Brent decided he needed more blocks and wanted to take some from the structure his mother had built. She would not go along with this, and Brent went through a sequence of arguing, whining, grabbing blocks, screaming, and then crying, huddled on the floor. His mother finally agreed to give him a few blocks. Suddenly Brent said he was tired of playing with the blocks and animals and announced he would do a puppet show for us. He looked each puppet over carefully and finally placed the alligator puppet in one hand and, with some difficulty, a lady puppet on his other hand. He then had the alligator puppet attack and gobble up the lady puppet as he shrieked with laughter and glee. I announced that it was time to stop, and we picked up the toys together.

I began a discussion with Brent and his mother about what happened during the play. Brent's mother said that what happened in my office was exactly what happened in almost every aspect of their life together. As long as he directed things, she said, everything seemed fine. But he would become more and more demanding. and when at some point he didn't get his way, he would have a tantrum. So she usually eventually gave him his way again, but everything was somehow spoiled and he wasn't happy. From the very graphic example of the play situation in my office, we could now deal with the evident power struggle that existed between Brent and his mother, and with his actual need for *her* to take the initial role of the strong director. She came to realize that a five-year-old typically becomes frustrated and rebellious when he is put in a position of setting too many of his own boundaries.

Older children also respond readily to play therapy. Jason, a ten-year-old boy, spent some time building with small blocks on the table. He described a structure as a jail to me as he built it. In the jail he placed a cowboy. As he played he told an elaborate story of the cowboy and his exploits. Finally he sat back and announced he was through. I asked a few questions about the various structures and people, and finally asked him to be the cowboy in the jail and describe what it was like to be there. I chose to do this because this is where I found my interest — a lone cowboy locked up in jail. He willingly complied and finally I asked, "Do you ever feel as if you're in jail like that cowboy?" This led Jason to share some very strong feelings about his life situation. Although there was not much we could do about his particular situation, it was still important for him to speak from his deepest places to me. Keeping these feelings inside only weakened him, and when the time came that the situation could be changed, feelings unspoken would have remained buried and stagnant, burdening him needlessly.

Play Therapy

Older children, though they have more language at their command, nevertheless often find it safer and easier to express themselves through play. It feels much less threatening to express hostility by having two animals attack each other, or by smashing clay, burying figures in the sand, and the like.

Sometimes I will ask a child to look around the room and pick out one specific toy. I will then ask him to imagine that he is this toy and to describe to me all the ways he is used, what he does, what he looks like, what he wants to do. Example: "I am a plane. I like to fly to new places. I feel free." "I am an elephant. I am clumsy and people think I'm silly." "I am a rock. I have a very rough side. But this side of me is very smooth and nice." In each instance, the person could "own" the statement, and this ownership led the way to opening up new areas of feeling. This type of exercise is useful for any age. I sometimes ask questions to bring out further material. Then I will say, "Does any of what you said fit for you? Would you like to do any of those things? Does any of what you said have anything to do with your life?"

One six-year-old girl chose a dump truck. She described herself picking up garbage, going around the streets. Soon she began to tell me that she had so much garbage to pick up she ran red lights all over the place. I asked her if she herself ever broke any rules. She grinned and nodded. We had an interesting session discussing this.

Although the child plays in an atmosphere of acceptance, this does not mean that limits are not set. In fact the limits become an important aspect of the therapy. Limits involve time (I generally see children in forty-five-minute sessions) and rules on abuse of equipment and the playroom, not removing equipment from the playroom, and no physical abuse to me or the child herself. The child needs to be given a little advance notice of the ending of the session: "We have only about five minutes left," or "We're going to have to stop soon." Of course, the child's desire to go beyond any of the limits needs to be accepted and acknowledged even though the limits are adhered to.

The playing done by children in the therapist's office is useful for purposes other than the direct process of therapy. Play is fun for the child and helps to promote the necessary rapport between the therapist and child. The initial fear and resistance on the part of the child is often dramatically reduced when he faces a roomful of attractive toys.

Play can be a good diagnostic tool. Often when I am asked to "evaluate" a child I will spend some time allowing him to play. I can observe a great deal about his maturity, intelligence, imagination and creativity, cognitive organization, reality orientation, style, attention span, problem-solving abilities, contact skills, and so forth. Of course I will avoid making snap judgments.

I think it's important to realize that a child can also use play to avoid expressing his feelings and thoughts. He may also get stuck in one kind of play, or resist getting significantly involved in any of the play. The therapist must recognize this obliqueness and deal with the situation directly and gently.

Sometimes when I talk to parents I find it helpful to advise them on the kinds of play materials their children would benefit most from at home. It is not unusual for children to express great interest in some, rather common materials that have not been available to them at home, such as clay or paints.

The Sand Tray

Sand is a marvelous medium for working with children of every age. Using it as a therapeutic medium is not new. Margaret Lowenfeld, in *Play in Childhood*, describes the values of sand play and briefly mentions the sand tray, a tray eighteen inches by twenty-seven inches, with a rim two inches deep, made of wood, with a waterproof liner.

> Sand and water lend themselves to the demonstration of a large variety of fantasies, as for example, tunnel-making, burying or drowning, land and seascapes. When wet, the sand may be molded, and when dry it is pleasant to feel, and many tactile experiments can be made with the gradual addition of moisture. Wet sand can be dried up again and reconverted to wet, or by adding further water it becomes "slosh," and finally water when the dry land has completely disappeared. (pp. 47-48)

Lowenfeld used the sand tray in conjunction with what she called "world" material: objects representative of real life.

Many Jungian therapists use the sand tray technique with adults as well as children. Many small objects and toys that lend themselves to particular symbolic meaning are used. The tray scene is viewed much as a dream sequence, and photographs are often taken of the sand tray work over a period of time in order to observe, through the photographs, progress in the therapy.

I purchased a bag of fine white sand at a toy store and use it in a plastic container somewhat less than 2 feet on each side, originally sold as a foot bath in a swimming pool supply store. My sand tray sits on a low plastic table with a plastic runner under it to catch any spillovers of sand. On shelves there are baskets containing many items (listed at the end of this section). Sometimes I ask the children to choose any items they wish for making a "scene" or a "picture" in the sand, and at other times *I* may choose the pieces in order to focus in on a particular situation. The advantages of this kind of activity are numerous. The figures are out in the open on the shelves, so the child does not have to create his own material as he does in a drawing. The sand makes a good base for the figures, holding them in place. It can be moved and shifted, to form hills, flat places, or lakes (the tray is blue). Figures can be buried in the sand, and they can be moved around to play out a situation. The sand feels wonderful to the fingers and hands, creating an ideal tactile and kinesthetic experience. The sand tray experience is not familiar to most children, and it sparks the child's interest. The child can create his own miniature world in the sand. He can say a great deal through this medium without needing to talk.

Mark, age nine, enacted many battle scenes in the sand. At different times he used army men, medieval knights, cowboys, and animals. At the end of each scene, one side was always left with a sole survivor who sadly buried his comrades while the other side celebrated its victory, perhaps burying one or two casualties. When asked which of the figures he was, Mark would always pick the captain or leader of the winning side. Mark wanted very much to be on the winning side of life. It took a number of sessions before he was able to "own" his need for friends and to identify with the lonely survivor of the losing team. (At least he still survived!) It was only then that we could face directly what got in the way of his making friends.

Debby, age seven, lived in a foster home and visited her mother on weekends about twice a month. She was referred to me because of her extremely aggressive behavior following each visit. Debby was unable to express her real feelings about her visits and would not communicate the cause of her bad feelings, if indeed she was even clearly aware of them. Her foster mother was becoming unwilling to have her visit her mother because of her subsequent behavior. At one session I asked Debby to enact in the sand her visits to her mother. She selected doll figures to represent her foster parents, the other children in the foster home, herself, her mother, her small sister who lived in yet another foster home, and even her mother's friend who picked up Debby and the sister for the visits. She built all of the houses with small blocks and even set up rooms using pieces of furniture. She then placed each figure in its appropriate place and, with her doll self, enacted the whole process, from being picked up to arriving back to where she lived. It was obvious to me as I watched, that the strain of these visits on Debby was tremendous, though her voice was detached, cool, flippant, and matter-of-fact as she told her story. As I watched the movements of her doll figure and the degree of emotional and cognitive "shifting of gears" involved, I myself felt exhausted. I voiced my own feelings of fatigue at just watching the whole business and of how I imagined that the doll, and perhaps Debby, herself, might feel. Debby looked into my eyes intently for a few seconds, and as I gazed back at her, her face crumbled, her body sagged, she broke into tears and crawled into my lap, where she sobbed for quite some time. With this new aspect of Debby's home visits out in the open, both to Debby herself and to the adults in her life, we were able to make some changes to ease the tension of the arrivals and departures.

Such enactments of real situations in a child's life can be done without the use of sand quite effectively. I find, however, that because the sand is so appealing to children, it lends itself to freer expression. I might add here that this episode is a good example of the importance of my paying attention to what is going on inside me. I have learned to trust and make use of my own feelings and body sensations when I work with adults. In working with children, this aspect of the work is even more important, for children are sensitive and very observant. If I pretend to be interested when

Play Therapy

I am bored, I rarely fool a child. When Debby looked into my eyes, she knew that I was telling her the truth about my own feelings and that she could trust me.

Lisa, age thirteen, also lived in a foster home but she never visited her real parents. Her behavior was characterized as "predelinquent." I asked Lisa to make any scene she liked in the sand. She worked intently, creating a desert with a few little bushes here and there, a rabbit, a snake going into a hole, and a girl standing on a hill. Lisa did not want to tell a story; she merely described her scene to me. She was, however, willing to identify with the scene, and with each figure. In every instance she described her existence as bleakness and desolation. When asked if anything she said fit in with anything in her own life, Lisa began to talk about her terrible loneliness. As Lisa was able to express these feelings in our sessions, her acting-out behavior gradually decreased.

Sometimes children will spontaneously move to the sand tray in a session, as thirteen-year-old Gregory did. He had drawn a large figure on the blackboard representing his mother, who, he said, was yelling. I asked him to be her and yell at himself. He began to scream, "Don't you do that! If you do that again you can't watch TV! No this, No that, No, No, No, No, No, NO! I will not talk to you, if you do that, for twenty-four, forty-eight or seventy-two hours!" As he spoke he began scribbling on the blackboard. Then suddenly he said he needed to work in the sand tray. He made a large house of Lego blocks and surrounded it with numerous animals in the sand including a large elephant, a giraffe, a snake, a donkey, a bird, a shark, a tiger, and a couple of other animals, as well as with some trees, bushes, and fences. A man lived in the house (he placed a figure of a man in the house), and the animals lived outside. When the man left for work in his car (he played this out) the animals played and wrecked the outside yard and the house as well. The elephant did most of the wrecking. This continued for a long time. Finally the man came back and held a meeting with the animals, telling them to clean things up, that he would listen to them and discuss their demands. The man left once more, and the animals, under the leadership of the elephant, rebuilt the house, straightened everything up, and added more bushes, fences, and a bridge. The man returned and expressed his approval. (Greg narrated to me as he moved the figures.)

WINDOWS TO OUR CHILDREN

When Gregory finished he sat back in the chair a while in silence. He needed to rest, he told me. Since our time was up, I asked him if he identified with the elephant. "Of course," he said. (Gregory was somewhat overweight, something that bothered him a lot and irritated his mother.) Gregory left smiling broadly. Before leaving, though, he grabbed a piece of paper, scribbled a note, and handed it to me as he went through the door. It said, "I like you."

Usually when I use the sand tray I will ask a child to build a scene in the sand using any items in any of the baskets. Younger children will often begin to play out something in the sand like a battle, while others will carefully and deliberately set items around the sand with no obvious plan. Older children seem to work out their scenes meticulously, choosing items with great care. The sand tray has no age limit. I may suggest that adolescents choose items from the shelves which appeal to them, without too much planning, or that they build their world as they see it and feel it. I might say, "Close your eyes and visualize, for a moment, your world. Now build a scene to represent what you saw in your mind's eye."

I work with the sand tray much as with a drawing or a dream. The children describe the scene to me, tell me a story about it, tell me what's happening, or what's going to happen. I may ask them to identify with various objects or have dialogues between objects. A child might say, "This tiger is going to eat everyone up," and I might ask him to make it happen. Sometimes something new happens when an action is carried out. For example, the tiger may eat everyone up except a small rabbit that he feels sorry for. Sometimes I look at the total picture and comment on the generalization I derive from it: "Your zoo looks very crowded. Do you feel crowded at home?" Or I may comment on the process: "You have a hard time selecting objects. Do you have trouble deciding things?"

Susan had gone through a terrifying experience: a man had entered the house, attacked her as she slept, and then set fire to the house. She spoke of the experience in a monotone, without feelings. Early in our work I asked her to do a sand tray scene, anything she wanted to make. Susan, now ten years old, rather nonchalantly took things off the shelf, put them back, tried new things. Finally she settled upon her scene, worked on it, then sat back and announced that she was finished. I asked her to describe it to me.

Susan: Well, it's a street. Here are the houses, and a couple of cars parked in front. And this big building at the end of the street is a museum. There's a lady walking home from work — she took a bus. She's a nurse. The museum has very expensive things in it, very valuable things. So this is a little guard house with two guards (toy soldiers) standing on either side. Anyone who comes into this street has to be checked by the guards because of the museum.

Are you anywhere around on this street? Where are you?

Susan: Oh, I'm in one of those houses.

How do the people feel who live on this street, how do you feel, having a guard house right on your street?

Susan: Oh, everyone likes it. I like it.

Why?

Susan: No strangers can come into this street without being checked. The people like that.

Susan, do you wish you lived on a street like that, a street with a guard house, after what happened to you?

Susan: Oh! Yeah! I can't get over how every time I do something in here we always get back to that same thing! I wasn't even thinking about it!

And then we were able to begin to deal with Susan's fear.

Recently I've added to my office a second sand tray in which I add water, standing beside the dry tray. The wet sand, just like that at the beach, can be shaped and molded. Wet sand is very popular with very young children; as soon as they discover that water is allowed in the sand, they want more water. A five-year-old boy asked if he could have more water in the tray, so I obligingly poured some in from a pitcher. He wanted still more. I added water until we reached the limit of the container, allowing some room for sloshing. Kenny moved the sand to form a beach and proceeded to play out a most interesting scene involving dinosaurs and an alligator in the water and on the beach, all in battle with army men which he positioned in the dry sand tray. The dinosaurs won. When we discussed this enactment Kenny told me the soldiers didn't stand a chance against dinosaurs and even an alligator. They were very big and strong, and the soldiers, well, they were just ordinary small people. I asked him whether he ever felt that way, small among giant people around him — not really giants, but sometimes seeming that way. He grinned and nodded, "That's right!"

These are the sand tray toys I have: *Vehicles:* Cars, trucks, boats, motorcycles, trains, army tanks and jeeps, planes, helicopters, an ambulance, a police car, fire engines. *Animals:* Domestic (cat, dog), farm, zoo, wild, dinosaurs, birds, numerous horses, snakes, alligators, crocodiles, numerous soft wiggly things, fishes, sharks. *Figures:* People — all kinds, cowboys, Indians, army men, knights, ballerina, bride, groom, Batman, Snow White and the seven dwarfs, Santa Claus, a devil, a witch, a large bear. *Scenic pieces:* Furniture, small blocks, buildings, trees, moss, bushes, stop signs, telephone poles, flags, bridges, totem pole, shells, pebbles, driftwood, plastic flowers, fences, Lego blocks (often used).

I continually add more, as I am always on the lookout for interesting, inexpensive items when I'm in a toy store, train store, aquarium, hobby shop, drug store, party shop, hardware store, dime store, garage sale. . . .

I keep the items fairly well organized in baskets of various sizes. Aluminum foil baking dishes make good containers, as do any small boxes, though they are not as attractive as baskets. It is helpful to have the objects sorted into categories and shelved in separate, open containers.

Games

In my work in the schools with disturbed children, games were a much-used tool for social learning. These children had trouble taking turns, playing without cheating, watching someone else be ahead of them on the board, and most of all, losing the game. Upon losing a game, some of the children would run to a corner of the room, bury their heads in their arms, and sob uncontrollably. Others would end up screaming, yelling, crying, hitting. An observer would probably consider their behavior as overreacting — after all, it was nothing but a game. But to the children involved, it was the game of life. Being accused of cheating was just another example of the constant accusations they faced. Their defense in the game was a matter of life and death to each of them. When the bedlam ceased, we would continue playing.

Play Therapy

The way any particular child played games was a good barometer of how he was coping in his life. As the year went by, we continued to play games in spite of any carrying-on over them, and each child made discernible, sometimes remarkable, progress in learning to cope with game-playing. The games helped the child learn about relating to others in life, and as he grew stronger in his life, his game-playing attitudes improved.

In spite of the frequent strong negative reactions of these disturbed children during the course of their games, they wanted to play and loved to play. This is not unexpected; most children love to play games. But these children rarely had an opportunity to play at home because of their intense reactions. Many of the children brought games from home to the group, where they could share and fight over them with abandon.

The games I use in the therapeutic setting serve multiple purposes. I sometimes use a game to round out the rest of a session when the child is finished with a piece of work. Children know when they need to stop. After divulging and talking through important situations and feelings, they sometimes say abruptly and sensibly, "Let's play a game." This is the child's way of saying, "Let's stop now. I feel finished for now. I need to assimilate what happened, allow for integration, mull this over."

Games are not only fun and relaxing; they help the therapist know the child, often get past the initial resistance, and promote mutual trust and confidence. Games are particularly good with children who have trouble communicating, and with those who need some focusing activity. They are valuable for improving contact skills right in the therapy setting. As I play with a child, much of his process, his stance in life, comes through.

Psychoanalytical therapists often use games as a method of promoting the "transference" state between child and therapist. As the child begins to react to the therapist as if he were an important other adult in his life, such as his mother or father, the therapist makes use of this "as if" behavior in the therapy process. Although this kind of reaction to me may be important, I am not interested in promoting this fantasy. I am not the child's mother, I am me. I will relate to the child as me, exploring the differences with him.

I don't like to use complicated games, games that require intense concentration, involvement, and time, such as Monopoly or chess. Rather, I use simple games, like Chinese checkers, three-dimensional tic-tac-toe (a favorite of many children), Blockhead (my favorite), jacks, pick-up-sticks (another favorite of children), Memory, Perfection, Connect 4, a marble roll game, Don't Break The Ice, dominoes, some card games, and checkers. Children often bring in their own games to play.

I avoid suggesting games I don't like too well, such as checkers, although I will play the game if the child wants to very much, making sure he knows my feelings.

An excellent activity for a group situation is to divide the group into pairs or threes and have each small group play a different game. After a time the groups each switch to a different game, and later the groups can change players.

There are some commercial board and card games on the market today that deal with feelings. Typical of such games are The Ungame and the Talking, Feeling, and Doing Game, which I have used often. I find with these games that children often enjoy the mechanical aspects of the game-playing-markers, the game board, tokens, spinners while answering questions and sharing feelings and content related to their lives. Such games can be invented, and for these, blank boards, cards that wipe off, markers, spinners, and tokens are all available at educational supply stores.

Construction sets such as Lego, Tinker Toys, Lincoln Logs, and others, are excellent materials for use in the therapy situation. They often help ease children's initial resistance and help them relax. Some children need to have something to do with their hands as they talk with the therapist. These sets provide creative outlets as well, and can be used as materials in the sand tray or other play situations. The child's process is evident in his approach to building tasks.

Some children enjoy working with puzzles. Simple jigsaw puzzles and other more advanced three-dimensional kinds of puzzle games appeal to children. Often a child and I will work on these together, and sometimes the child uses them as a form of relaxation. Sometimes the challenge of these puzzles is akin to the child's process in the game playing, and in his life.

I have used some magic tricks in my work with children. Richard Gardner is one of the few therapists who has ever written about the use of magic with children. He writes in *Psychotherapeutic Approaches to the Resistant Child*:

One of the most predictable ways to make oneself attractive to a child is to show him a few magic tricks. It is a rare child who is so recalcitrant, uncooperative, distractible, etc. who will not respond affirmatively to the therapist's question: "Would you like to see a magic trick?" Although not generally useful as primary, high-efficiency therapeutic tools, magic tricks can be extremely useful in facilitating the child's involvement with the therapist. Only five minutes spent in such activities can make a significant session. The anxious child will generally be made less tense and will then be freer to engage in higher-order therapeutic activities. The child who is very resistant often becomes less so after such an "ice breaker." The uninvolved or distractible child will usually become quite interested in them and will then be more readily shifted into more efficient therapeutic activities. In short, they facilitate attention and involvement. In addition, because they make the therapist more fun to be with and more attractive to the child, they contribute to a deepening of the therapeutic relationship which, as already emphasized, is the mainstay of the therapeutic process. (pp. 56-57)

In an article called "The Sorcerer's Apprentice, or the Use of Magic in Child Psychotherapy," Joel Moskowitz outlines in detail his use of magic with children from ages three to fifteen years. He found that magic tricks serve to establish relationship and trust, substituted as a kind of universal language for a child who spoke little English, and provided security and self-confidence for a boy who had a reputation of being careless and clumsy. There are magic shops in any metropolitan area that sell inexpensive, easy-to-learn magic tricks.

Projective Tests as Therapeutic Technique

Although designed as diagnostic tools, many projective tests and inventories lend themselves to therapeutic use. And although the diagnostic accuracy of the test is questionable, there is no question about their usefulness as an *expressive* medium. I work with the test material just as I would use any other story, drawing, dream or sand tray scene.

Reading aloud the interpretive notes in the test manuals is also a very helpful technique. The child is encouraged to make some response about how he sees himself. His ability to say, "Yes, that's how I am, all right," or "No, I'm not like that at all," or "Well, sometimes that's true," or "I'm like that with certain people, but not others," lends itself not only to further discussion, but gives the child the kind of added strength and self-support that comes from making specific, definite statements about himself. Learning how to spit out statements that don't fit for him is a crucial part of this process.

Children's Apperception Test: I ask children to tell me a story about a picture and then I work with it as I would any other story.

Thematic Apperception Test: This test is particularly useful with teenagers. I ask the child to tell something about what he thinks is happening in the picture and we may work with it as above. Sometimes I write down his responses to several pictures, and then take out my manual and read to him what the manual says his responses mean. I ask if he thinks the manual is right or wrong (explaining that it definitely can be wrong). For example, I may say, "The manual says that according to your response to this picture, you are sexually attracted to older men, or you have death wishes toward your mother." The young person to whom this may be nonsense, generally enters into a lively discussion with me (to whom the manual's statement also may be nonsense) about his or her feelings relating to this interpretation.

Draw-A-Person Test and the House-Tree-Person Test: Again, I often bring out the manual and read to the child the manual's interpretation of the drawing for his agreement or disagreement. If necessary, I translate the words into those the child can understand.

Make A Picture Story: I use this test only in a therapeutic sense, asking the child to tell her story.

Actions, Styles And Symbols in Kinetic Family Drawings: In this test the child is asked to draw his family doing something. I have used this as I might any drawing, or I read the manual's interpretation to the child for his or her agreement.

Rorschach Cards (ink-blots): I have asked children to tell me what they see, and I have worked with what they tell me as I would with any fantasy. I might have them make up a story, be whatever they see, dialogue between parts, and so forth.

An easy way to make your own ink-blot designs is with food colors. Small squeeze bottles of different colors can be purchased for about a dollar. Squeeze, dot, or streak some colors on a sheet of paper, fold the paper, and gently press down: Then open it and you will have your own colorful ink-blot in which you can see all kinds of things.

The Luscher Color Test: This is a favorite with teenagers. They pick their most-favorite to least-favorite colors, and again I read to them what the interpretive notes say about their response.

The Hand Test: This test presents a number of pictures with hands in different positions — reaching, clenching, etc. The person suggests what she thinks the hand is doing. This test is a good one for inviting stories, impressions and so forth. We might go with the story or impression, expanding it, or we might see what the manual has to say about the person's response.

Sentence Completion Tests: Working with the responses in a therapeutic way is very productive.

The Taylor Johnson Temperament Analysis: This test indicates how a person feels about himself in terms of a number of polarities: nervous/composed; depressive/lighthearted; and so forth. The test is designed for working with the results as indicated on a profile. Often I will go back to the initial testing questions for further reaction.

The Mooney Problem Check List: This is one of my most valuable tools for working with older children and young teenagers. The list includes 210 statements related to junior high or high school children. (There is also one for college level.) I will read the statements, asking the child to respond with true or false, or yes or no. Statements range from "Often I have headaches" to "I'm feeling ashamed of something I've done." Children never fall to respond to the internal nature of the statements as presented, telling me many things about themselves they never have before. After the test is given, we go back and pursue some of the responses.

WINDOWS TO OUR CHILDREN

The Despert Fable Test: Each fable was originally devised to aim at some conflict or crucial situation. Example:

> A Daddy and Mommy bird, and their little birdie, are asleep in the nest on a branch. But all of a sudden a big wind blows; it shakes the tree and the nest falls on the ground. The three birds awaken all of a sudden. The Daddy flies quickly to a pine tree, the mother to another pine tree. What is the little bird going to do? He knows how to fly a little, already.

There are many other tests available that I haven't mentioned, and you can easily see how any such test could be put to therapeutic use.

When these tests are used diagnostically, we have to be *very* cautious about accepting the results. Ordinarily the child has no chance to respond to what is stated about him, no chance to disagree with the conclusions of the expert. Testing results can have a depersonalized finality about them that is difficult to counter once they are filed. Sometimes this can be very harmful to the child.

In one case a child was diagnosed as schizophrenic by a psychologist who had administered a series of formal tests to him. This diagnosis was on permanent file in the records of a social agency. Later I happened to see this boy in therapy and received copies of all the testing results. After five minutes with this child I knew that he was not schizophrenic. He was, however, quite frightened of the psychologist who had tested him (as he later told me), and as a result he had withdrawn into a silent shell. The psychologist did not intentionally do anything to frighten the child, but the child was nevertheless put off for some reason. What matters here is that although the psychologist probably did his best, and with goodwill, the results were erroneous. After the tests, everyone treated this child as if he were very severely disturbed.

Recently a child was referred to me who had been "tested" by the school system and diagnosed as mentally retarded. I could tell from our initial contact that he wasn't. He was an American Indian who had lived on a reservation all seven years of his life, and he was simply overwhelmed by his new school situation.

Play Therapy

For an interesting view of some of the psychological interpretations made on children's drawings, I suggest *Children's Drawings as Diagnostic Aids*, by Joseph H. Di Leo. He suggests what a child's drawing may be saying within the context of what he knows about the particular child's life situation. Drawings, like dreams, tend to make accurate statements about what's going on in one's life at the moment. Only the child can verify this, however, and unless he does verify it in some way (if only to himself as he expresses through the drawing) there is really no value in my making diagnoses. I can only use my diagnostic guesses to help me guide the therapy process, and if I am on the wrong road the child will somehow let me know. I need to be able to recognize when he does let me know.

A good example of a misinterpretation can be found in the book, *Human Figure Drawings in Adolescence*. A child, age thirteen, is diagnosed as exhibiting pseudo retarded childhood schizophrenia, and the following comment is made about his drawings:

> The diagnosis is clarified by these startling productions. The patient sees himself as depersonalized, a kind of grandfather . . . clock with numbers reversed and antennae reaching out. The detached pendulum disc suggests an umbilicus. (p. 109)

It is clear to me — and I'm pretty certain that the child, had he been asked, would have verified the fact — that this is a very good picture of a TV set! The "detached pendulum disc" is the on-off switch knob. The "clock with numbers reversed" is the channel selector. Anyone who has carefully looked at a TV set, as this child has obviously done, will see that the numbers on the channel selector are always counterclockwise.

It is extremely important for anyone studying children's pictures to have a knowledge of the normal development of children's art. There are many good books available that describe typical drawings at various stages of a child's development. Ruth Kellogg has done extensive study in this area and her book, *Analyzing Children's Art*, is an excellent and comprehensive work.

WINDOWS TO OUR CHILDREN

When I was a student teacher in a kindergarten class a number of years ago I witnessed an incident that was repeated over and over, and left me in tears of helplessness and frustration. The teacher to whom I was assigned was considered to be a "master teacher," but in my opinion she knew nothing about children. A child was happily painting at an easel one day when suddenly the teacher abruptly tore the picture off the easel, ripped it into shreds, and shouted, "Do your arms come out of your head?" Later when I questioned her about this, she insisted that it was her job to teach these children how to do things right! I could not make her understand that nearly every child goes through a stage in which the arms and legs are typically drawn coming out of the head. By demanding that the children do exactly as she instructed, she stifled growth, creativity, expression, and learning. When we visited the harbor and they were asked to represent their view of the harbor in block play, each child's building had to look exactly like everyone else's, with so many blocks on this side, and so on. She told me that she was teaching them how to see things accurately! This teacher was highly praised because of her quiet, orderly, well-behaved class.

Although I don't stress testing in my work with children, I find that parents, schools, and social agencies are eager for me to administer them to the children and are overly influenced and impressed by the results. They seem to want confirmation of their own observations of the child through specific tests. So the adults are delighted if I do give several approved tests, and then indicate a specific conclusion in a report, such as, "This child shows, according to the results of the above tests, tendencies toward antisocial behavior. He is restrictive and fearful and has much hidden anger which has been directed against himself and now occasionally at others." We all already knew these things about the child anyway, but the tests have made them true. So, with a sigh of relief that we now know what the problem is, we can get down to the business of therapy.

9

The Therapy Process

The Child Comes into Therapy

What is it that motivates a parent to bring a child into therapy? Many children manifest the kinds of behaviors that indicate something is awry. Yet most parents hesitate before getting help. I think most parents would rather not believe that their child has the kind of problems that might need professional help. They tell themselves, "It's just a stage; the child will grow out of it." Who wants to admit that they have been less than a perfect parent? And for most people the cost of therapy is not easily dismissed, not to mention the time involved in bringing the child in for the sessions. There's a risk, too, in regard to what might come out of taking the child to a therapist. Some parents secretly feel that they are the ones that may need help, and this fact is not easily faced.

My daughter developed a tic when she was about eleven years old. She would throw her head back as if stretching her neck muscles. She did this often until it became an annoying mannerism. We took her to a medical doctor who dismissed it as nothing to be concerned about. Yet she did not stop. Her father and I, both psychotherapists, did not rush to take her to someone who might help her uncover what was behind this tic. We ourselves were not paying attention to what her body was trying to tell us. Fortunately, after a time, she did stop doing it. In retrospect we realized that we, like many other parents, may tend to wait too long before seeking psychological help. Had she continued, perhaps to the point of damage to her neck muscles, we belatedly would have taken her for help.

By the time the parents make that first phone call seeking help, the situation generally has become very difficult, if not unbearable, for either the child or the parents. Even if the parents aren't directly affected by the child's behavior, they have reached such a point of discomfort, anxiety, or concern that they feel driven to take action.

Sometimes parents bring children into therapy because something unusual has happened and they want to be sure that the child expresses and finishes any overwhelming feelings resulting from the incident. Examples of such happenings might be death or illness of a loved one, abuse, molestation, or a deeply frightening experience such as an accident or an earthquake.

Occasionally a child will directly ask to see someone. Many teenagers have initiated therapy. Children I have previously worked with sometimes request help. A nine-year-old girl I had once seen for about three months in ongoing treatment will every now and then say to her mother, "I need for you to make an appointment for me with Violet."

If asked for some general statement about the right time to bring a child in for therapy, in truth I don't know what I would say. How can one determine the "right time" or whether the problem will resolve itself of its own accord? Certainly it would be ridiculous to run to a therapist for every conflict and every problem. I feel strongly that parents need to learn how to be, in a sense, "therapists in residence." Although children will not always share with parents what's going on inside of themselves, there are ways that parents can learn to deal with many situations that come up in everyday life. Most of the techniques described in this book are useful for parents. Helping parents learn how to communicate with their children through such programs as Parent Effectiveness Training is often all that is needed to remedy many situations. Sometimes when I see a child I know that with some guidance the parents can do everything themselves: a couple of sessions with parents who are eager to cooperate is all that is needed.

Diana, age nine, and her family had befriended a young man at a campground. One day Diana's parents asked him to stay with Diana while they drove into town for supplies. While they were gone, the young man, about twenty-years-old, held Diana on his lap, kissed her lips, and fondled her. Later Diana told her mother what had happened, whereupon the mother became quite upset and admonished Diana not to tell her father. Diana (who had not been hurt physically and had admitted that she enjoyed the young man's attentions) reacted by remaining inside the tent for the rest of the week, claiming she was ill. When they got home, the mother brought her in to see me. Diana was having nightmares and stomachaches, and she refused to go to school.

When Diana and I met alone she expressed a great deal of curiosity about her mother's reaction. "Why was she so upset? Why didn't she want me to tell my father?" As it turned out, Diana herself had the answers to these questions. Diana had a very lively interest in sexual information, a fact that her parents chose to ignore. After two sessions with Diana and her parents in which sex was freely discussed, as well as the impropriety of a twenty-year-old's fondling of a nine-year-old, Diana again became her former self. Her parents found a new way to discuss previously taboo subjects openly and frankly with Diana. The last thing Diana said to me as she left my office was, "If that guy should have been hugging and kissing girls his own age instead of me, he must be afraid of them but not of me. I guess he needs to grow up more. Maybe his mother didn't give him enough hugs and kisses when he was little."

It's not a simple matter to judge the proper moment for bringing a child into therapy. The child himself often sees to it that something is done — by fighting harder and harder in some way until someone notices. The schools are often the first to notice and yet will not recommend help until the situation is severe. After one boy had spent weeks sitting in the principal's office each recess and lunchtime for disruptive behavior on the playground, the parents were finally contacted and told that if they did not get help, the boy would be placed in a class for disturbed children.

Many of my referrals have come from the courts. Many of these children have shown disturbing behavior long before being arrested. A sixteen-year-old boy, referred to counseling by court order, had been "causing trouble," as his mother put it, since he started first grade. He had had much trouble learning to read and sitting still in school, she said, and that seemed to be the beginning of all the trouble. Yet this was his first experience in getting any psychological counseling.

WINDOWS TO OUR CHILDREN

Physicians see children with physical symptoms which they will diagnose as psychogenic, and some have been known to dismiss the child without seriously recommending and urging psychological help. A ten-year-old girl suffered from severe stomach pains. After intensive testing, doctors concluded that there were no physical causes for the pains; they were caused by anxiety and tension. They prescribed tranquilizing drugs, but made no mention of seeking psychological help. When the pains persisted, the parents finally brought her in for therapy.

I think another big reason that parents hesitate to seek help is that they think of therapy as a continuing process that involves a long period of time, perhaps years (I discuss this further in the section on termination). Certainly, there are children who require long-term treatment. In general, however, I find that many problems can be dealt with in three to six months of once-weekly sessions.

Before I start working with a child I sometimes receive stacks of papers relating to the child; test results, diagnostic reports, court proceedings, school records. They make interesting reading, but when it comes right down to it I can only deal with the child as she presents herself to me. If I rely on the information given me about the child to form my basis of working with her, I would be dealing with what's written on a piece of paper, rather than with the child. Written on these papers are someone else's perceptions, findings, and often unfair judgments.

A fifteen-year-old girl said to me, "I want my mother to send me away to a school I heard about in Arizona because no one will know anything about me there and I can start all over." She was stuck in the mire of negative expectations from others (expectations that were carefully documented in administrative files) and she felt defeat.

So I must begin with the child from where she is with me, regardless of anything else I hear, read, or even diagnose about her myself.

She is making contact with someone who is willing to accept her as she is at the moment, without an overlay of preconceived biases and judgments about her. She can show another side of herself, perhaps a gentle, responsive side, a part of herself she may have difficulty expressing to her parents and teachers. If a child is docile and receptive with me, even though reports describe her as aggressively loud, or my own tests show her to be defensively hostile, I can still actually only relate to her in the way that she is at the moment with me, the way she now chooses to be. She is a many-faceted individual who is capable of many ways of being.

Prior to my first encounter with Jennifer, age thirteen, I received a thick folder containing a variety of records: school records, psychiatric evaluations, psychological test results, a probation officer summary. She was described as hostile, resistant to help or suggestions of any kind, having very little conscience related to her acts of truancy, running away, shoplifting, sexual promiscuity, and having no interest in school or future. The prognosis given her was that she would probably get pregnant or continue in her antisocial ways until she landed in prison. I felt a great deal of anxiety about my coming meeting with Jennifer and wondered how I could even begin to help her on the face of her prior experience with counseling. I imagined a tough, sneering, sophisticated girl. I wondered, though, about her documented refusal to see another "shrink" unless it was a woman, and I reminded myself about my own principle of withholding judgment until I make my own personal contact with a client.

Jennifer was brought to my office by her father, who told me in her presence that he had given up all hope that anything could be done for her.

The first thing I did when Jennifer and I were alone was to tell her how anxious I was on the basis of what I had heard about her. Jennifer, a thin, frail, pale child, looked at me in amazement. I told her how I had imagined her, even standing up and acting out the part, and we both laughed. She wanted to know how I saw her now, so I got up and pulled myself in, hunched my shoulders, put my head down and walked around the room in small, hesitant steps. "When I walk this way," I said, "I feel like a frightened little mouse." Jennifer's answer: "You guessed it." I asked her about her request to see a woman therapist. "I hate the way men talk to me," she said. How could Jennifer even begin to talk to anyone about herself and her deeper feelings, if she hated the way she was talked to?

The First Session

Generally parents call me and attempt to explain the problem over the phone as they make the first appointment. I will explain that when they come in to see me with their child I want them to tell me again what the problem is, with the child present. I feel that it is important for the child to be present in order to alleviate his worst fantasies about what is wrong. The child always knows that something is wrong, and often imagines it to be much worse than it is.

I will never have a child wait in a waiting room while his parents are in my office. Whatever they need to say must be said in front of the child. In this way I can observe the child's reactions, the dynamics between parent and child, and hear all sides. This is also the beginning of my establishing a trusting relationship with the child. He will see that I am a fair and impartial participant, interested in everyone — especially the child.

So when the family comes into my office, I ask someone to begin to tell me what has prompted the parents to come in to see me with their child. Usually the mother begins. After the first few sentences I will stop and ask the child if he agrees with what the parent has said. Often the parent will use big words, attempting to talk to me over the child's head. I am very wary of this, and do not allow it to happen. If the parent says "His behavior has been extremely disruptive in school," I will ask the child if he knows what his mother is talking about. Even if he says yes to this, I will ask the mother to tell me what she means, specifically. One child's response to the parent's use of the word "disruptive" was "I don't have that!" — as if it were the measles. Another child had that exact same reaction to the word "withdrawn."

I'm generally not too concerned if the child is unwilling to talk or give his view at this time. I'm interested in having him be there to hear what his parents say, and to get a good look at me. He discovers that I am interested in him, see him, hear him, treat him with respect. I don't talk down to him, ignore him, disregard him, or act as if he were an object to be discussed. I attempt to include him in every way, if only by checking things out with him and by making eye contact with him. He soon knows that I am taking him very seriously.

I am interested in making it very clear that I hear that the parent or teacher is concerned about some of the child's behavior, but it also becomes clear that I don't necessarily accept what is said as hard fact. I will pinpoint, too, *whose* problem it is. If the child agrees that there is a problem, I want to know this. If he doesn't agree, I make it clear that I am aware of this too, and that the problem is the school's or the parents', and not his. This is very relieving to the child.

The Therapy Process

For example, a mother brought her six-year-old daughter into my office and told me that the teacher had recommended counseling for the child because the child had been biting and hitting other children, and didn't have any friends. First we needed to make sure the child understood as much as possible what counseling was. Then when I asked her if she agreed that she was biting and hitting other children, and didn't have any friends, she said "I *do too* have friends!" I said, "I guess your teacher is worried — it's *her* problem. Somehow she, the teacher, is getting the idea you don't have friends and is worried about it, and also thinks you're hitting and biting." I asked the mother if she thought her daughter didn't have friends. Her mother said, "Well, she spends a lot of time in the house, but she does have a little friend up the street she plays with." So I said, "Then *you* don't consider it much of a problem." "No," the mother responded, "I never thought of it as a problem." So it came down to being the teacher's problem. This pleased the child very much, and she obviously became much more relaxed.

I don't use an intake form in my initial interview. My "intake" consists of the process of the first session, in which the parents and child meet with me to talk about why they have come to see me. A therapist friend of mine devised a fairly simple intake questionnaire that she has used with children and teenagers which she feels helps break the ice. It requests the name, address, birthday, hobby, children in the family, own room or share, school and grade, and the like. But I'm not particularly comfortable with doing a formal intake. I imagine that the child or parents will subsequently assume that I've obtained everything I need to know about the child, and that I will keep this information in my memory bank to be brought forth and used as needed. My preference is to learn about the child as I go along, as the information seems to come up within a meaningful context during the sessions. I suppose intake is used by others in much the same way as I might use a picture drawing at an initial session. We all need to find some way to begin the relationship — it is often awkward and uneasy at first.

After the problem is brought up and assigned, I will often ask the parents to wait outside while I talk with the child. I may say something about doing what I can do to make things better, that I'll be doing some things with him that will be fun, that I'll be finding out about him and hope he will too, and something about confidentiality. The child generally has already looked over the office and seen the games and toys, paint table, and sand tray — it looks intriguing, and he is beginning to feel interested. If there is time, I may invite the child to look around more closely, to check out what I have. Or, I will ask the child to draw a person and a house, or some picture. I explain that we will be using some of the things in the office and will be doing some talking. I say that we will talk about feelings sometimes, and we will paint feelings sometimes.

Even though I have many doubts about the value of testing, I do some of it. I sometimes give tests as a way of relating to the child in the beginning of our relationship, though tests can also create and maintain distance. Or I use them as a delaying pretext when I don't know what else to do. The *Draw-A-Person Test* and the *House-Tree-Person Test* are simple tasks for most children to complete. The actual evaluation process needs to be an ongoing one, since nothing ever stays the same. We and the children we work with are in a continuous flow of change, influenced by the changing events around us. I learn quite a bit about the child as she draws her person. I learn more about her by paying attention to her process than I do by reading the interpretive remarks in the testing manual after she has finished. How the child approaches the task is illuminating. She may hesitate, repeatedly state her inadequacy in drawing, ask for a pencil and ruler; these are signs of feelings of insecurity. The drawings may appear disorganized, even bizarre. They may be colorful, creative, full of humor. The child may work in great sweeping strokes, laugh as she works, hum, talk to me, or be very still and silent, hardly moving her hand. She may work very diligently, precisely, carefully. Or she may do a slapdash drawing. She may use lots of detail and a variety of colors, or draw a picture that is merely a shadow or an outline. The maturity of the drawing may be inconsistent with the age of the child. *How* she does the drawing may be indicative of how she is in life, or how she feels at this moment with me in my office.

The child reveals many things in the drawings, but I suspend judgement. Interpretation is of little value unless I use it as a clue for further exploration. The child may leave out hands in a drawing for a variety of reasons; in the final analysis only the child knows. If a child draws tiny figures on one small corner of a large piece of paper he may indeed be frightened and insecure. But his apparent fear and insecurity may be evident only in this one situation — his meeting with me. At home he may draw with abandon.

One child, age eight, after my request that she draw a person, asked "Why?" I said it would help me find out some things about her. When she finished she wanted to know what I had found out. I looked at her picture and said, "Well, I see you like the color red, and your person is smiling, so maybe you feel pretty good right now. You drew a very small picture, so I guess you don't feel like making big pictures today (gesturing with my arm), but feel like staying in one little area. And you like flowers, because there are quite a few of them there. Is any of that right?" She smiled broadly and nodded, agreeing with my guesses.

Sometimes the whole initial session is used up in dealing with the presented problem-first with the parents, and then with the child alone. I believe strongly in openly confronting the problem. After all, we all know by this time why we are here together, so why not deal with it? This may seem obvious, but in the experience of some families the problem is often avoided in counseling, or kept hidden until the magic moment, or "We don't need to mention it; it will work out by itself."

A thirteen-year-old boy came in with his parents because of chronic bed-wetting. After the preliminaries I said, "OK, we all agree that the bed-wetting is the reason for Jimmy's being here, and now I want to know how each of you feels about this bed-wetting." The father, with tears in his eyes, said, "It is such a relief to be open about what I'm feeling about this. The last therapist we took him to never spoke about it after we explained the situation on the phone making the appointment, advised us not to talk about it, and never saw the three of us together." Jimmy, at the second session, as he was painting a very large ocean to depict what it felt like to wake up in his wet bed, confirmed the fact that he and his previous therapist had never talked about the bed-wetting specifically.

I realize that the "presenting problem" is just that — a presenting symptom. I know there is usually (though not always!) much deeper stuff to be worked through. But I believe we must begin with what we have — look at it, experience it, explore it, before we can know how to go deeper. I must deal with what *is* before I can go further.

Nine-year-old Jeff said very little as his mother spoke of her reasons for bringing him in. When she left the room I said to him, "Jeff, I get the feeling from looking at you that you are afraid of me. Are you afraid of me?" Jeff shrugged, looking down at his feet, face appearing paler and even more pinched than during the first part of the session. "Is it the kind of fear you have when you go to the principal's office at school?" Slight nod. "Or the doctor's office? Does going to the doctor scare you?" He looked straight at me: "Yes." "Tell me about that."

Jeff tells me a little of his fear and begins to loosen up, his voice becoming stronger. "Want to see a trick I learned today?" We have finally made some contact. Jeff shows me his magic trick, the time is up, and he looks pleased as I make the next appointment with his mother.

Lucy was an eight-year-old girl whose mother brought her in because she was concerned about her daughter's reaction following her separation from her husband. Lucy seemed to her unusually withdrawn and quiet, was not eating much, and generally seemed "different from her usual self." As Lucy's mother talked, Lucy sat huddled in a corner of the couch. I asked the mother to direct her remarks concerning her worries to her daughter. When she did so, Lucy merely shrugged in response. Her mother turned to me. "See? That's what I mean. She just won't talk to me. I know she needs to get her feelings out, but she won't say anything." Lucy then spoke, "I can't talk. It doesn't do any good." The mother began to weep. She spoke then about her own feelings of sorrow about the separation. Lucy listened but made no comment. The mother said, "I know it helps me a lot when I talk about how I feel."

During our time alone in this first session, I asked Lucy to draw a picture of her family. She drew a picture of each person, including her father, each standing leaning against the other. Each face bore a rigid smile, all were dressed in identical colors, and all held their hands behind their backs. She would not discuss the picture, but it spoke loudly for her.

Lucy's statement about her present place in life was clear: she would not talk — what good would it do? I guessed from her picture that she was afraid of letting go. She wanted and needed the support of her family leaning against each other or her whole world would crumble. Her world had already crumbled, but she could not yet deal with it. This first session had great impact; it set the course of the therapy and charted the way for future work.

The Therapy Process

After every first session, I jot down a few notes about what we did, what happened, my feelings, reactions, observations. I used to dislike record-keeping intensely, but my attitude has changed lately. Sometimes I will jot down something as I sit with a child, as a reminder of something we might want to continue at the next session, or make a note that I have given him some kind of homework. (An example of homework: "Do one nice thing for yourself each day, something you might not ordinarily do, to see how you feel about being nurturing to yourself.") I find that it is important for me to make notes following each session. After each session I make some notation about what we did and what happened. These notes are generally quite short but sometimes I am so excited by a particular session I will type up a description of the whole session. Occasionally I will tape-record a session, though I find this difficult to do with children unless we are using the tape recorder as an integral part of the session. Many children become quite self-conscious when they know the tape recorder is on.

These notes are an important part of the therapeutic process for me. I can see what's been happening; I can make determinations about what appears to be needed in terms of activity for our next session. If I feel that I have pushed too hard, I will remind myself to go easier the next time. I write down my own feelings and reactions, to be used only as temporary guidelines.

I do not share these notes with parents (except for very general summaries regarding the progress of work), but I often read them to the children. I have discovered that children are fascinated by what is in their "folders." Their fascination probably stems from the cumulative files kept on each child all through school. Children know that these school records exist and want to know what is said in them. I think that children have a right to know what's said or written about them if they want to know.

They love to hear what I have written. One thirteen-year-old asked me if I could get her records from her probation officer so she could find out what was written in that file about her. She worried terribly about what they might have said. I called the probation officer. He could not send me a copy of the records but was very willing to tell me over the phone the essence of what was written, as an aid to my work with the child. I told the probation officer that the girl was quite worried about the officer's impressions of her. I told her what I had heard, reading verbatim from my notes during the phone conversation. She asked me several times, "Are you sure that's all he said?" I read them again. We talked about her anxieties and fears about her "file." She was extremely relieved, she told me, that the name of the boy she was with when she was picked up by the police as a runaway was not in the records. "I've been so worried he'd get into trouble on account of me," she said.

What My Office Is Like

People often ask me what my office is like, perhaps imagining a vast playground or playroom with magnificent toys. As a matter of fact my office is very small, about 10' x 14'. It includes a small couch, two chairs, a couple of end tables. These items are used mostly by the adults I see. There is also an old heavy coffee table which I use as a painting table. There is a shelf under this table on which I keep cans and jars of paint, some newspaper, paper towels, brushes. There is a good-sized cabinet with doors in which I keep other art supplies: paper, crayons, pastels, felt pens, finger paints, clay, wood and woodworking tools and so forth. There is a sand tray, and next to this is a large bookcase containing mostly toys, baskets of items for the sand tray, games, and some books.

The toys that seem generally the most valuable are the miniature wooden blocks, the dollhouse, dollhouse furniture and assorted doll figures, all kinds of transportation toys (cars, planes, boats, trucks, police cars, fire engines, ambulances), Lego blocks, a doctor set, two toy telephones, army men, army tanks and jeeps, puppets, small toy animals (particularly wild animals), a couple of large rubber snakes, a sea monster, dinosaurs, a shark.

I have a chalkboard, a dart board and cork board to shoot at, and a Puncho (a large inflated figure weighted at the bottom, so that it always returns to an upright position after being punched or hit). A few large stuffed animals have also been useful.

My office room is carpeted, there are some large pillows on the floor, and colorful posters on the wall. It is not an ideal room for working. I would certainly like to have a larger room and an outdoor area. I find that even though I am not too satisfied with my working space, children don't mind at all. They generally seem fascinated by the room and take to it easily and happily. We sit on the floor most of the time as we work and/ or talk.

It is informal and cheerful, and lends itself to the kind of work I do with children.

The Process of Therapy

Children do not come into my office announcing, "This is what I want to work on today." If they know me and trust me, they will come in with pleasant expectations of what we might be doing today. Sometimes they come in knowing what media they want to use, what they want to play with, sometimes with something they want to tell me about what has happened to them since they saw me last. They do not know what they want to explore, or work through, or discover about themselves. Most of the time they don't even acknowledge that this is something they could do, or might even want to do.

Teenagers often have situations they want to discuss with me, but here again they generally want simply to share what has happened in their lives, or complaints about school or family members. They, too, invariably stop short of delving deeper on their own.

So it is up to me to provide the means by which we will open doors and windows to their inner worlds. I need to provide methods for children to express their feelings, to get what they are keeping guarded inside out into the open, so that together we can deal with this material. In this way a child can make closure, make choices, and lighten the burdens which get heavier and heavier the longer they are carried.

Most of the techniques I use with children encourage projection. The child draws a picture or tells a story, and at first glance it may appear to have nothing to do with the child herself or her life. It's "out there," safe, and fun too. We know that projection is often called a "defense mechanism," a defense against hurt to the inner self. People may project onto somebody else what they are feeling, unable to face the fact that these feelings are within themselves. Or some people see themselves only through the eyes of others and are forever worried about how others see them.

But projection is also the basis for all artistic and scientific creativity. In therapy it is a very valuable tool. Since our projections come from inside us, from our own experiences, from what we know and care about, they tell a lot about our sense of self. I find that what the child expresses "out there" can display her own fantasies, anxieties, fears, avoidances, frustrations, attitudes, patterns, manipulations, impulses, resistances, resentments, guilts, wishes, wants, needs, and feelings. The stuff she puts out there is powerful material to be handled with care. How I, as the therapist, handle this material is extremely important. Often projection will be the only way that the child will be willing to disclose herself. She may say things as a puppet or to a puppet that she would never say directly to me. Projections are useful for children who don't talk because what comes out in a drawing, for example, can be very expressive and serves to "speak" for the child. Projections are also useful for children who talk a lot because they serve to focus on what's underneath all the talk.

In general I do not make interpretations of the material the child sets forth through projections, although I do attempt to translate what I see and hear in order to guide my interactions with the child. I believe that any interpretations I might make would be useless as therapy for the child. Interpretations at best may give me guidelines for direction, but they are my own ideas, based on my feelings and experiences, and I keep them tentative. If I do lead the child in directions guided by my own interpretations I must be doubly careful.

What I do mostly is to very gently and softly help the child open the doors to self-awareness and self-ownership. Most children can readily move into accepting and acknowledging their projections for themselves. How I help the child begin to "own" what he has safely put "out there" is evident to a degree. But I cannot guarantee that if you follow my directions, step by step, you will be assured results all the time. Each therapist must find her or his own way. Therapy is an art; unless one can combine skill and knowledge and experience with an inner intuitive, creative, flowing sense, probably not too much will happen. It seems fairly obvious to me, too, that one must truly like and appreciate children in order to work with them. That is not to say that a child cannot annoy you, rub you the wrong way, irritate you. However, when this happens with me, it is a glaring red light; I stop and examine what the child is doing, how I am reacting, and where my own reactions are coming from. These deliberations can serve as rich material for the therapeutic process. And because I care about the child I may say, "Hey, I can't stand what's happening here!" And then we talk about what is happening.

The Therapy Process

I find that some children, especially very young ones, do not necessarily need to verbalize their discoveries, insights, and awarenesses of the what and how of their behaviors. Often it seems that it is enough to bring out into the open the behaviors or blocked feelings that have interfered with their emotional growth process. Then they can become integrated, responsible, happy human beings, better able to cope with the many frustrations of growing up in their worlds. They can begin to relate more positively with their peers and with the adults in their lives. They can begin to experience a feeling of calmness, joy and self-worth.

The techniques are numerous. I am constantly finding new ways to work with children. There is a limitless supply of resources all around us in our world which can be brought into the process of doing therapy with children. But techniques are never just gimmicks, or recipes for aimless activity. The technique selected for use is never regarded as a means to an end in itself (as, for example, so many teacher's "lesson plans" are). One must keep in mind that each child is a unique individual. No matter what particular technique is used, a good therapist stays with the process evolving with the child. The procedure or technique is merely a catalyst. Depending on the children and situation, each session is unpredictable. One idea leads to another, and new techniques for creative expression are constantly evolving: the creative process is open-ended.

I don't always know *why* I'm doing what I do at the moment. Sometimes we do things because I'm experimenting, or because it seems that it might be fun, or because the child wants to do it. Some of my best therapy sessions have happened this way. A colleague of mine recently told me about a ten-year-old boy she is working with who came in and wanted to talk about how our country is divided into states, something he is studying in school. He drew a picture for her of the United States with lines to show divisions of states. He seemed fascinated with the concept of our country's dividedness. She then, after a while, asked him if he ever felt divided. He drew a picture of himself and his divisions: happy, sad, angry, and so on.

I don't want to give the impression that something wonderful happens at each session. Often nothing that is outwardly exciting and important seems to happen. But at each session the child and I are together. He soon learns to know me as someone who accepts him, who is honest with him. Sometimes the child doesn't feel like doing anything, so we just talk or listen to music. Usually, though, he is willing — often eager — to try one of my suggestions. Occasionally he knows exactly what he wants to do. Nothing that appears therapeutically significant may come out of these activities, but I know that something is happening all the time.

None of the techniques that I'm writing about were invented by me. Most are in the public domain — things I've known about all along. Some things are just out there in the environment to be used. Some ideas I learned from other people, and some of their ideas I took and adapted in my own way. Some techniques I have used very, very often. There are many techniques I haven't tried or thought of, and others that I know of, but may never use. Wherever possible I have referred to my source, and at the end of this book is a fairly comprehensive list of books and other resources which you can use for ideas and techniques — which you can adapt in your own way for your needs and those of the children with whom you work.

Resistance

Children are often wary about doing some of the things I ask them to do. A boy of ten, asked to be the red color in his picture, said, "Are you crazy?" Children are sometimes embarrassed, especially in a group, to do "crazy" things, or they are so closed and tight and protective that they are unable to let go freely into the realms of imagination. When this happens I deal with the particular child in the manner I think most appropriate for him or her. I may say gently, "I know this is hard" (or silly, or crazy — for certainly it is); "Do it anyway." While I want to go past the resistance, I respect it. I may only slightly nod at the protestation and go right on with my instructions. I usually don't smile during this interaction. I take the resistance seriously. I acknowledge it and I want to very delicately move past it, over it, under it, around it. Children will giggle, make disgusting type noises, and make sure that the other children and I know for sure that they do not think what I'm asking them to do is a good idea or very clever. I have had children fall over on the floor in mock faint. I am not bothered by these demonstrations; I expect them and accept them, and go on with my business. As soon as children are sure that the group and I are not taking the activity seriously, they generally get right into it. After the first time or two, this kind of resistance disappears.

Some children are not consciously resistant, but are so inhibited or tight that they may need to first experience some safe activities that may help free their imaginative processes. I know that some children are quite fearful about letting go of themselves in some of the ways I suggest, and I may deal directly with the fear behind the resistance. Or I may just allow a child to decide for himself when he is ready to risk something that is difficult for him. He will become more open as his trust builds; he will begin to risk as his sense of self strengthens.

When the children begin to express themselves easily through the fantasy material and the varied types of expressive projections, I attempt to guide them back gently into the reality of their lives — by having them own or accept the parts of themselves they have exposed so that they can begin to feel a new sense of self-identity, responsibility, and self-support. This is difficult for many children. I continually attempt to guide the child from his symbolic expressions and fantasy material to reality and his own life experiences. I approach this task with much gentleness, though there are times when I am firm and other times when I find it best to give no guidance at all, and be patient.

One of the most effective techniques for helping children through their blocks is what has been termed modeling. In either a session with an individual child or a group, if *I* do what I ask the children to do, they will do it too. If a child cannot find a picture in his scribble after two or three attempts, I will do one of my own. The child is fascinated, now knows what I'm asking of him, and feels better about doing it once I do it. I usually take my turn at games, puppet shows, charades, fantasy and drawing exercises. I do this as honestly as I can, and I am not afraid to expose my own weaknesses, problems, and history. (One boy was very interested when he found out that I was divorced, and wanted very much to know how my children reacted.) If children are afraid to get started I often say, "Pretend you are only four years old and draw as if you were that age." I sometimes show children how to make stick figures and stick animals to give them more confidence in getting started.

WINDOWS TO OUR CHILDREN

The way a child approaches drawing is often the same as his process in approaching life. Perhaps he is tentative about most things, new things especially. If a child is extremely anxious about drawing, I certainly won't press him to draw. We might talk about his anxiety about drawing, or we might move on to something less threatening. I might ask him to use a chalk board or a magic slate — that has a plastic cover which, when lifted, causes the markings to disappear. Both of these have value for children who are worried about the permanence of their drawings; they feel secure in the knowledge that their creations can be quickly erased. Like adults, children must be accepted where they *are*. From there — the point of their existence, their edge, their boundary — they can begin to gradually move on to viewing themselves with more security and worthiness. Usually if I approach the child in a gentle, very nonthreatening way, he will make some attempt. Sometimes asking the child to tell *me* what to draw is helpful, or I may draw a picture of the child as he watches me (in fascination). My own drawing ability is not very good and is rather childlike, and this gives the child greater confidence in his own ability.

Besides the child's unwillingness to participate in the techniques of therapy, there is also an initial resistance during the first meetings between you and the child. Getting through this kind of resistance is a very subtle process, difficult to put into words. It involves your own intuitive sense, which you must feel and pay attention to before approaching the child directly, and it involves the child's own sense of knowing that you are someone she can trust.

What happens in the first session between you, the parents, and the child is crucial. The child watches you, hears you, sizes you up. Children have a finely tuned way of quickly evaluating adults and their ways with children.

During your time alone with the child you have another chance for him to know if you are open, honest, authentic, straight, nonjudgmental, accepting, amiable. He can find this out as you briefly talk, as you ask him questions for a simple intake form, as you stand by while he looks the room and equipment over, as you play a simple game with him, as you introduce a nonthreatening activity. The child may decide in one session that you are a person to relate to and trust, or he may need three or four to be sure.

The Therapy Process

When it happens, you will know immediately. If it never happens, you will know this too, and you may wish to take time to acknowledge this, and examine what is going on between you and the child.

Above all, realize that children are resistant and defensive for good reason. As I have said over and over, they do what they have to do to survive, to protect themselves. They have learned — from the chaotic worlds in which they are involved and from the schools which are so often harsh and uncaring and unseeing — that they must do what they can to take care of themselves, to remain protected against intrusion. As a child begins to trust me she will begin to allow herself to open, to be a little more vulnerable. I must move in easily, gently, softly.

In a group I was supervising as a consultant, a participant brought up her frustration at meeting resistance in a child. I found myself giving her all kinds of suggestions for getting through the resistance, when I suddenly realized what I was doing: I was siding with her against the child. Making her stronger by my alliance to battle the child's resistance would only serve to *increase* his resistance. "Hey," I said to myself, "Wait a minute. Do you think the child ought not to be resistant?" Why shouldn't a child be resistant? He has reason to be. We must learn to accept resistance, not defensively or offensively but just matter-of-factly.

We will meet resistance in some children over and over. The child will move along after his initial wariness, but time and time again we will bump up against his resistance. He is in effect saying "STOP! I must stop right here. This is too much! This is too hard! This is too dangerous. I don't want to see what's on the other side of my protective wall. I don't want to face it." Every time we reach this place with a child we are making progress. In every wall of resistance there is a new door that opens into new areas of growth. This is a fearful place; the child protects himself well, and why not? I sometimes see this place as similar to what Fritz Perls called the impasse. When we come to an impasse we are witnessing a person in the process of giving up his old strategies, and feeling as if he has no support. He often does what he can to avoid this — to run away from it, or bring in confusion to cloud the situation. When we can recognize this impasse for what it is, we can anticipate that the child is on the verge of a new way of being, a new discovery. So each time the resistance shows itself we can know that we are not encountering a rigid boundary, but a place that has just beyond it a stretching, a growing edge.

Termination

I believe an important reason that parents hesitate to seek psychological help for a child is the notion that it is the beginning of a prolonged time in therapy, perhaps years. This has been the image of therapy, and of course a few children do require long-term treatment. I believe as a general rule, though, that children should not be in therapy for a long time.

Children don't have the many layers of unfinished business and the "old tapes" that adults accumulate over the years. I have seen dramatic results with children in as few as three or four sessions. If I knew of a child in therapy with someone for a very long time, say over a year, and there were no very unusual circumstances in the child's life, I would want to take a hard look at what was going on in that therapeutic relationship.

Usually there is enough progress in three to six months to warrant termination. Children reach a plateau in therapy, and this can be a good stopping place. The child needs an opportunity to integrate, and assimilate with his own natural maturation and growth, the changes taking place as the result of the therapy. Sometimes this plateau is a sign of resistance that needs to be respected. It's as if the child knows he cannot handle breaking through this particular wall at this time. He needs more time, more strength; he may need to open up to this particular place when he is older. Children seem to have an inner sense of this fact, and the therapist needs to recognize the difference between this stopping place and previous stumbling blocks.

There are clues for knowing when it's time to stop. The child's behavior has changed, as reported by the school and his parents. Suddenly he becomes involved in outside activities — baseball, clubs, friends. Therapy begins to get in the way of his life. After the initial wariness, and until such a plateau is reached, the child generally looks forward to coming to the sessions. If he doesn't, one needs to take a close look at what's happening.

Improved behavior alone may not be reason enough to stop the therapy. Changed behavior can be due to the child's opening up and expressing a deeper self to the therapist. So we look for clues in the work itself as well. The material that comes through in the sessions can be good indicators of stopping places.

A five-year-old boy, labeled as an "impossible" child by both his kindergarten teacher and his mother, had for quite a while changed his behavior so that he was now a "possible" child. But his work with me continued to uncover feelings that I helped him express and deal with. After about three months, however, I perceived a shift. He began to "play" with me — and the sessions no longer seemed to have the aura of "therapy work." One day I showed him some pictures I sometimes used for story telling. One picture (from the *Children's Apperception Test*) shows a rabbit sitting up in bed in a darkened room, the door to the room half open. Generally this picture elicits fear, or the feeling of being left out, or lonely responses. This child said, "The little boy, I mean rabbit, woke up and he's sitting in his room, but it's too early to get up, so he's waiting for it to be real morning." I said, "It looks kind of dark. Do you think he's scared?" His response: "No, he's not scared. Why should he be scared? His mother and father are in the next room." I said, "I wonder why that door is open." He looked at me incredulously and said, "So he can get in and out." I knew he was OK now.

This same boy told a story about another picture showing a mother kangaroo with a baby kangaroo in her pocket and a little kangaroo riding behind on a tricycle. The mother kangaroo has a basket of groceries on her arm. The baby holds a balloon.

Billy: They have just come from the store and are going on a picnic. The baby will play with his balloon and the boy will ride his tricycle.

What will the mother do?

Billy: She'll eat. (Billy's mother is overly fond of eating.)

Do you think the boy would like to be riding in the pocket where the baby is? (There was a new baby in his house.)

Billy: (He looks at the picture for a very long time.) No. You see, he had his turn to ride there when he was a baby. Now he's big enough to ride a tricycle, but the baby can't even walk.

Just like you had your chance to be a baby and now it's your brother's turn?

Billy: That's right!! (big smile)

WINDOWS TO OUR CHILDREN

Often the child has done enough work so that he can continue on his own. This is especially true if the parents have been involved and continue the therapy on their own with the child — if they have learned new ways of being with their child. Sometimes the child stops coming, and one or both parents decide to explore and work through some of their own conflicts and feelings. The experience of having brought their child into therapy often paves the way and helps the parents feel comfortable, and sometimes eager, to enter into a therapeutic relationship themselves.

As the child is involved in his therapy, the parents are relieved and begin to feel better and the atmosphere at home becomes more relaxed. This helps the child get more out of the therapy and he begins to show some very positive behavior changes. The teachers sometimes notice and they begin to feel better about the situation. All this time the child is getting older and wiser. Growing up and maturing are on the side of the child as well. All these variables work together as adjuncts to his therapy; there is a snowballing effect, an accumulation of good things, a synergism.

It is possible, of course, to end the therapy prematurely. A seven-year-old girl seemed to show all the signs of termination time. She was doing well in school, at home, and with friends, and our sessions seemed to be less and less productive in terms of "work." I had been seeing her for six months. At one session I mentioned to her and to her mother that we might begin to think about a good stopping time since everything was going so well. When the child went home that day she began reverting to some of her old behaviors — setting fires, stealing, destroying property. When her mother distraughtly brought the matter up at our next session, the child said, "If I'm good I won't get to come and see Violet any more." I realized then that either I had not done a good job of preparing her for terminating, or that I had misjudged her readiness for stopping. Children tell us what we need to know.

Preparing a child for termination is important. Though we help kids gain as much independence and self-support as we can, we certainly do form caring attachments with each other. We need to deal with the feelings involved in saying good-bye to anyone we like and care about.

Termination need not have the finality that the name implies. Termination is merely a coming to a stopping place, an ending at this time. Some children need reassurance that they will be able to come back if they

The Therapy Process

need to (if indeed it is possible). I usually have a session with the parents present when we are exploring the possibility of stopping, and discuss this openly. Sometimes it's not possible. I received the note on the following page from an eight-year-old girl after my leaving an agency where I had been an intern.

I don't like to stop seeing a child abruptly. I will suggest that we meet a couple of times or more, on alternate weeks. We begin to talk about our times together and what has happened — a sort of evaluation time. Sometimes we look through the child's folder at all the drawings, remembering some of the things we talked about. One child, an eight-year-old girl, said to me, "I'd like to make you a good-bye card." I said OK and got out the materials. She made me a very flowery valentine-like card. She handed it to me and said, "I'm going to miss you," and I said, "I'm going to miss you too," and she began to weep. She sat on my lap and I hugged her and talked about how hard it was sometimes to say good-bye. She nodded and cried, and I cried a little too, and then finally she stood up and said, "I think I'll make you another card." She smiled and winked mischievously. She made a very funny card, like a contemporary cartoon card. We laughed and I gave her my address and phone number and asked her to call me or write me if she ever wanted to.

When I worked in the schools I gave my phone number to those children who were moving on to the regular classroom. Occasionally I would get a phone call from one of them. The calls were generally very short, a brief touching over the telephone wires. I felt good about these calls and never for a moment felt I was encouraging dependency ties. They were social calls between people who had spent some very close times together. I rarely get such calls from the children I see in private therapy, but I do get letters in a similar vein. I will return a brief note card and I notice that those children who have had the need to reach out to me in this way taper off after one or two exchanges.

WINDOWS TO OUR CHILDREN

The Therapy Process

I think a typical mistake teachers make in the last days of school is to handle termination by asking children to draw pictures of what they're going to do during the summer. (And in the fall the teachers ask them to draw pictures of what they did during the summer.) Thinking about something the kids probably aren't too sure about prevents full awareness of what's happening right now. Why not a picture, in colors, lines and shapes, of what it feels like now to be leaving this classroom?

A social worker in a school, who had been conducting two ongoing groups, told me that at the end of the school year she felt sad that the year was at an end because she was changing jobs and would not see the children again, but that she was really glad to be leaving too. She was puzzled about how to handle her own ambivalence and her own feelings about the impending separation. She didn't want to make the children feel bad, she said, by telling them about her sadness about leaving and then confusing them by telling them about her gladness about leaving! It seemed to me that this was a perfect opportunity to share mixed feelings with the children — to express both of her feelings truthfully. Kids often have mixed feelings too, and get quite confused because of them. She said, "Yeah, I think it's true — it's really important to express your feelings to them. Separation is really hard. I wish in other situations, when people had cared, they would have expressed it to me more."

We always have some unfinished business about separation and good-byes that makes termination that much more difficult. We need to be in touch with our own feelings at such times and not be afraid to express them honestly. There's nothing wrong with being sad (or for that matter, glad) over a leave-taking!

10

Specific Problem Behaviors

In this chapter I discuss some of the particular behaviors that children present that bring them into therapy. I do not view a child's behavior, displeasing as it may sometimes be, as sickness. I view it as the child's evidence of strength and survival. A child will do what he can in any way to survive in this world. He will do what he thinks is the best thing to do to get through the job of growing up.

Childhood is a difficult time, contrary to popular myth. In his book *Escape from Childhood*, John Holt discusses in detail the fallacy of the myth:

> Most people who believe in the institution of childhood as we know it see it as a kind of walled garden in which children, being small and weak, are protected from the harshness of the world outside until they become strong and clever enough to cope with it. Some children experience childhood in just that way. I do not want to destroy their garden or kick them out of it. If they like it, by all means let them stay in it. But I believe that most young people, and at earlier and earlier ages, begin to experience not as a garden but as a prison.
>
> I am not saying that childhood is bad for all children all the time. But Childhood, as in Happy, Safe, Protected, Innocent Childhood, does not exist for many children. For many other

children, however good it may be, childhood goes on far too long, and there is no gradual, sensible, painless way to grow out of it or leave it. (p. 9)

I agree with Holt. I see many children who go to extreme measures to survive the best way they can in the "prison" of childhood. They seem to be doing all they can to hold out until they attain the magic state of adulthood, where they can take full responsibility for themselves, be respected, and, they hope, be treated with entitlement. Adulthood is often a long time coming.

Aggression

Adults often view children who indulge in direct, spontaneous behavior as aggressive. These children are described as "acting out," implying a striking out at the environment, the world, as opposed to holding in. "Acting out" is, to me, just another inappropriate label. Children who are passive, withdrawn, subdued, perhaps even catatonic, are also "acting out" something in their own way. Indeed, we are all generally in the process of acting something out in our own unique ways.

The child who acts up and is labeled as acting out in the classroom gets noticed first. He is often extremely restless, acts impulsively, strikes out at other children sometimes for no apparent reason (but often with good reason), is disobedient (and therefore called rebellious), talks loudly, often interrupts, teases and provokes others, elicits similar behaviors from other children, and attempts to be domineering. Adults don't like these kinds of behaviors in children. They tend to destroy the social situation we're most comfortable with in our culture. These behaviors must be viewed in perspective, for they occur in a system with a double standard between children and grownups. For example, an adult is seldom chastised for interrupting a child. Children's behaviors are often annoying to adults and children alike. But when a child is called "aggressive" or "rebellious" or "acting out" or "rude" or "disobedient" one must be aware that these are judgmental labels. I often use such phrases myself, and I want the reader to understand that I know that these are someone's labels, someone's descriptions, someone's judgements.

Specific Problem Behaviors

Sometimes a child is viewed as being aggressive when he is simply expressing anger. He may break a dish or punch another child in a pure expression of anger. Generally I feel, though, that the aggressive acts are not the true expression of anger, but deflections of the real feelings. Aggressive acts, often also called antisocial acts, can include destructive behaviors, such as destroying property, stealing, setting fires. I perceive the child who engages in hostile, intrusive, destructive behaviors as one who has deep angry feelings, feelings of rejection, feelings of insecurity and anxiety, hurt feelings, and often a diffused sense of selfhood. He has, too, a very low opinion of the self he knows. He is unable or unwilling and fearful about expressing what he is feeling, for if he does he may lose what strength he musters to engage in aggressive behaviors. He feels he needs to do what he does as his method of survival.

Clark Moustakas, in *Psychotherapy with Children*, describes a disturbed child as often motivated by undifferentiated and unfocused feelings of anger and fear. His behavior may show hostility toward almost everyone and everything. Parents and teachers often assume that a disturbance in the child comes from a specific internal source that something definite inside the child makes him act this way.

On the contrary, it is the environment that disturbs the child. The child is provoked by the environment, rather than by his internal difficulties. What he lacks internally is the ability to cope with an environment that makes him angry and fearful. He does not know how to handle the feelings that are generated inside him by this unfriendly environment. And so when he strikes out in some way, he does so because he doesn't know what else to do. In fact, the environment often actually provokes antisocial behaviors on the part of the child. A child does not usually become aggressive suddenly. He is not a sweet natured child one minute, and the next minute one who abruptly, suddenly, begins to set fires or spray parked cars with paint. The process is usually gradual. He has surely expressed his needs in more subtle ways previously, but adults usually don't pay attention until he exaggerates his behaviors. These behaviors, which are perceived by adults as antisocial, are often actually a desperate attempt to reestablish a social connection. The child is unable to communicate his true feelings in any other way but by what he is now doing. It's as if he is doing the only thing he knows, in order to go on with the struggle of living in his world.

WINDOWS TO OUR CHILDREN

Such a child is rarely aggressive in my office. As he begins to trust me, aggressiveness emerges in his play, stories, paintings, the way he handles clay. I begin with him as he presents himself; I cannot deal with aggressiveness that isn't expressed. During our first session, when the parents are present, I will hear a long list of complaints about the child as he sullenly sits in a corner of the couch pretending he doesn't hear or doesn't care, sometimes venturing to add an "I do not!" or "That's not so!" I may guess from working with many children and families that the problem here lies more with the parents and their feelings and reactions to the child. I will wait, however, before suggesting family therapy or "parent therapy" (working with one or both parents alone) until I have more concrete evidence rather than merely rule-of-thumb generalizations. I need to know the child better; I need to have a clearer sense of what's going on with this particular child and his family.

So I'll begin with this child not by talking about his aggressiveness, which would probably alienate him from me, but by presenting some very non threatening type of activity, in order to first establish some trust and relationship between us. He knows that I know why he has been brought in, and I am willing to say, "Look, I know about all those complaints about you. I hear them, and my job is to help everybody feel better. And now I'm willing to get to know you on my own and find out what's really going on." Sometimes I may say this not in actual words but through implication, by my manner and actions.

Children who are aggressive and acting out are easier for me to work with than children who are inhibited and withdrawn. The aggressive child will very quickly show me what's going on with him. I will often begin by just inviting him to do whatever he wants to. He may choose a game to play with me, or paints, or clay, or sand, or army men. If he says, "I don't know," I will suggest something. Generally I don't do any specific diagnostic work at this time. This child is generally very suspicious, on guard. In a sense I am trying to draw him into wanting to come back by giving him an enjoyable experience. He is usually so starved for the kind of attention I give him that I find it is not difficult to relate to him at all.

So in the first sessions I don't generally talk to the child confrontively or deal with his problems directly. I don't say, "I hear you're aggressive; I hear you're hitting Tommy." I deal with what comes up as he brings it up in his art or play. We do things he likes to do. Gradually I move to more directed activities as feelings begin to emerge. Usually the anger comes through first. Beneath the anger there may be hurt, but it's the anger, the rage, that seems to emerge first.

Anger

Anger is an honest, normal feeling. Everyone gets angry. I get angry. You get angry. It's what we do with these feelings, whether we can accept them, how we express them, that causes all the trouble. Not the least important influence on the way we handle anger is our cultural attitude toward it: it's not nice to get angry. Children get double messages here. They experience the wrath of anger from adults either very directly or in the indirect form of icy disapproval, but it is not usually acceptable for children to express their own anger. At a very early age they learn to suppress these feelings, experiencing instead either shame as the result of their mothers' wrath ("I must be very bad") or guilt for the angry, resentful feelings that overwhelm them at times. Children observe anger in the form of violence on TV and in the movies and in the form of military or police authority. They hear about violent crimes and war. As a result they become very frightened and often quite fascinated when they themselves feel angry. It is no wonder that anger is like some awful lurking monster continually having to be pushed down, suppressed, deflected, and avoided.

I recognize four phases in working with children's anger:

1) Giving children practical methods for expressing their angry feelings.

2) Helping children move toward the actual feeling of anger they may be holding and encouraging them to give emotional expression to this anger right there with me in my office.

3) Giving children the experience of being verbally direct with their angry feelings: saying what they need to say to the person they need to say it to.

4) Talking with them about anger: what it is, what makes them angry, how they show it, what they do when they feel it.

Children have much trouble expressing anger. Antisocial behaviors (behaviors considered to be irritating to our established social order) are not direct expressions of angry feelings but rather the avoidance of true feelings. Since hurt feelings are so commonly buried under a layer of angry feelings, it is very threatening and difficult for children, and for adults, too, for that matter, to get through the angry surface feelings to allow full expression of the authentic subsurface feelings. It is easier to just dissipate the energy through hitting out, engaging in rebellious acts, or by being sarcastic and indirect in any possible way.

All our feelings involve the use of physical energy expressed through muscle and bodily functions. If we don't express our anger in some way in a direct manner, it will express itself in some other way that is generally harmful to ourselves. When I sense that a child's anger is being held in and suppressed, I know I need to help that child learn about "appropriate" (acceptable to the adult world) ways of dealing with angry, feelings. I do this in a variety of ways.

Kevin, age six, was referred for therapy because he was literally tearing at himself. He scratched himself in any way that he could. When not hurting himself, he was destroying something of his own. When he began tearing up his mattress, the adults in his life became most concerned and brought him in. It became evident to me that Kevin had great feelings of rage and anger and was terrified about expressing these feelings. He lived in a foster home, probably the fourth or fifth home in his young life.

As Kevin was playing with clay, he made reference to another boy at school. He began to attack the clay vigorously as he talked about this boy. I asked some very gentle questions about his relationship with this boy, such as "What did you play together?" (At these moments the child is like a turtle who has tentatively poked his head out of his shell. I must tread softly, carefully, so as not to overwhelm the child into taking cover again.) Kevin's voice became tight as he talked. At one point I said, "Does he make you mad sometimes?" Kevin nodded and told me how this boy teased him. I set up a pillow and asked Kevin to tell the boy on the pillow how he felt. I showed Kevin how to do this by talking to this boy myself. Soon Kevin was saying many things to the boy expressing angry feelings. I then asked Kevin to punch the pillow, and again, I did it first. Kevin did this very hesitantly at first, but soon got into the spirit of it while talking to the boy. I told Kevin to do this at home on his pillow or bed whenever he felt mad at this boy or anyone else. His foster mother reported that he did this every day after school for hours during the first week and then gradually tapered off, and that he stopped scratching at himself and his mattress. Of course we did some other work too, eventually dealing with some deeper feelings Kevin had about his real mother and about what was happening to him in his life. But we needed to begin with those events which lay at the surface, and Kevin needed some tools for dealing with feelings that frightened him. He needed to gain some strength for himself.

I have suggested many other ways of expressing anger besides punching a pillow: tearing newspaper, wadding paper, kicking a pillow, kicking a can, running around the block, hitting a bed with a tennis racket, yelling in the shower, writing all the bad words they can think of on a piece of paper, writing about the anger, drawing the angry feelings. I talk to children about the physical-body feelings of anger that must come out in some way. We talk about muscles contracting it the head, in the stomach, in the chest, causing headaches, stomachaches, and chest pains. Children readily understand this.

Children are very concerned about the reactions of the adults around them. A twelve-year-old boy made me a scream box, and one for himself. He put wads of newspaper into a box, made a hole on top in which he inserted a paper towel roll, and showed me that when he screamed into this box the sound was so dulled that his mother wouldn't become alarmed at the noises. A thirteen-year-old boy said to me, "If I told the principal what I really wanted to tell him, I'd get thrown out of school!" So instead of directly dealing with his angry feelings, he made a pest out of himself on the playground and was "hyperactive" in his classroom. If I, an adult, am terribly angry I do the same kind of thing: I feel better if I shake and move and tap my foot and bite my nails and chew gum hard. I also know that if I am holding in a lot of unexpressed feelings, I have trouble concentrating on anything else.

What do I mean by the phrase "direct expression of anger?" If the boy dealt directly with his anger at his principal, he would stand in front of him, look him straight in the eye, and state, or perhaps shout, his mad feelings directly to the principal. What seems to be necessary is to allow the child to be *conscious* of the anger, to know the anger. This is the first step in helping children feel strong and whole instead of fearfully running from and avoiding angry feelings, or discharging them in indirect ways which might harm themselves or alienate others. Next the child needs to learn to assess the situation, and to make a choice about whether to express the anger directly to the person or to express it privately in some other way.

Sometimes we talk about what anger is. I asked a group of children I worked with to tell me all the words they used or thought of when they were angry. I wrote these words without judgement on a large chalk board. One boy, age twelve, lay on the floor laughing hysterically with glee and utter amazement that I would write forbidden words so calmly for all to see. After we had a long list we looked at them. I noticed that some of the words were attacking, striking-out words, while others were inside-feeling words. We talked about this a while. We then discussed individual ways of handling anger, inside or outside. I asked "What kinds of things make you angry?" "What happens?" "What do you do?" "What can you do to avoid getting into trouble when you feel angry?"

I asked the children to draw their angry feelings, or something that makes them angry, or what they do when they are angry. The pictures were very moving and expressive. Each child's anger process was clearly depicted. One boy, age ten, drew a maze with several stick figures at the upper right-hand corner and one at the lower left-hand corner with the words "Which way to go" next to it; at the top of his picture he wrote "Lonesomeness."

When sharing his picture he talked about his lonely feelings when he got angry at his friends. He didn't know how to get back to them: he felt separate and lonely with his feelings.

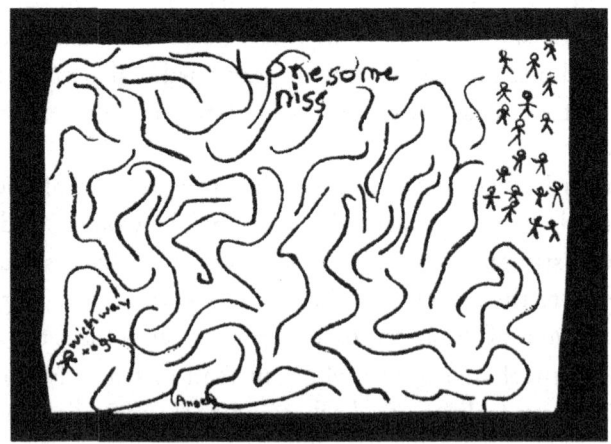

A similar sentiment was expressed to me in an individual session with a nine-year-old boy who, after scribbling on his paper to show his angry feelings, said "I feel lonely when I get mad. Being mad makes me feel very lonely."

Sometimes in a session with a child, feelings of anger emerge that need to be experienced and expressed right then and there. Sometimes children express this anger indirectly through play or art work when they find it too threatening to "own" these feelings for themselves. To identify and admit one's own feelings is the most self-supporting, but even expressing anger through symbolic form is helpful.

Jimmy, age six, in time became engrossed in enacting a scenario with the doll house, furniture, and doll house figures. He had one figure commit a robbery, for which he had the other dolls express a great deal of anger. Jimmy obviously was totally involved in enacting the scene, and he expressed authentic angry feelings through the doll figures. Jimmy resisted my early attempts to relate this play to his own life. This is to be expected, especially with younger children. It took Jimmy a long time to even get to the point of expressing himself through dollplay, and this new play became very meaningful and important to him. Before this, Jimmy would often remark "Girls play with doll houses," "You ought to fix your doll house," "I don't want to play with the doll house," or "What a weird doll house."

It was as if Jimmy were acting out his own robbery — his feelings of being intruded upon, having something stolen from him. He, as an angry doll figure, protested this violation. I did not pursue my hunch, my interpretation of his play, for somehow I felt that he was doing his own work, as many young children do as they play. If I had wanted to engage Jimmy in some discussion with me to promote some explicit awareness (perhaps to make *me* feel good about my hunch), I might have said, "Do you ever feel that something or someone was taken away from you?" or "What do you wish you had in your life now that's missing?" or "Have you lost something in your life?" I knew that Jimmy did not have a family of his own and that he had lived in several foster homes. Had I interrupted his play with these questions at this time he may or may not have responded. Later, as our relationship became stronger, I was able to ask him directly about his feelings about not living with his own mother, and yet not being "free" for adoption.

Other children are much more direct with their anger. A five-year-old boy asked me to draw a picture of a face and put it up on the bulletin board I use for the rubber dart guns. He said the face was his father (he had never known his father), and he proceeded to shoot darts at it. I encouraged him to say words as he aimed the darts, and he shouted "I'm mad at you!" "You're a poop!" etc. He took great glee in making direct hits. After a while he asked me to draw tears on the face (perhaps projections of his own) and finally asked me to draw another face with a smile. "It's OK now," he said.

In another situation, seven-year-old Laura had been to another therapist for about three months prior to my seeing her. For some reason the experience had been unpleasant for her; she was very antagonistic toward going for her visits and later toward coming to see me. Laura was having a difficult time in her life, and her feelings were expressed through stealing, cutting up car upholstery, spray-painting cars as she walked along the street, and setting fires. It seemed impossible for us to establish a relationship. I knew that we would have to deal with her feelings about her previous psychologist before I could make any progress at all with her. I had brought the subject up once or twice before and had been met with closed eyes and tight mouth. Now I ventured to bring it up again. This time Laura murmured something and I noticed that her leg was swinging back and forth in almost a kicking motion. I said, "You look as if you would like to kick with your leg."

"Yeah! I'd like to really kick him!"

I suggested that she kick the chair as if he were sitting in it. She got up and did this. I encouraged her to continue and to tell him something with each kick.

"I hate you! You made me feel bad!"

She kept at it for quite some time as I held the chair in place. She suddenly stopped, sat down, smiled at me, and changed the subject. Her body was now relaxed and her manner towards me was open and friendly. That was the beginning of a very rewarding and successful therapeutic relationship with Laura.

Other useful items to help children express angry feelings during a therapy session are the Bataca (a foam-covered bat-like object with a handle), rubber knife, dart gun, and a Puncho inflated doll. Fashioning a real or symbolic figure out of clay and then smashing it with one's fist or a rubber mallet feels good. One young boy vented his feelings by disfiguring a clay face of his brother. I asked him to talk to the clay face as he scarred it. Much more material came forth this way than if he had merely told me or complained to me about his brother. When he finished, Danny smoothed the clay and made a new face to represent his brother. "He's had enough for now," he said to me. Clay's flexibility is valuable because it allows children to undo any damage done.

Sometimes I will ask people to draw their anger, and sometimes they will do this spontaneously. Billy, age nine, was referred to me by the public school for extremely rebellious behavior in the classroom and on the playground. His parents were advised to get help for him before steps were taken to put him in a special class. Billy's family had moved considerably during his nine years of life due to his father's service career, and he had not reacted to these moves well. At the first session Billy sat huddled in a corner of the couch, refusing to speak, as his parents rattled off a list of complaints. When I saw Billy alone he still refused to talk or play. At this first session I had noticed Billy often glancing over at the paint table. At the next session I told him that I would like him to paint a picture — anything he wanted to — and he reluctantly agreed. He painted with great absorption as I sat and watched.

Billy: This is a volcano.

Tell me about it.

Billy: We studied it in school. This is not an active volcano, it's a dormant volcano. This is the hot lava (red lines inside a brown volcano with thick walls) that hasn't erupted yet. And this is the smoke coming out of the volcano. It has to let off a little steam.

Billy, I would like you to tell me about your volcano again, and this time I'd like to imagine that the volcano has a voice. It can talk, but you will be the voice, like a puppet's voice. So tell me about your volcano again. Start with "I am a volcano."

Billy: OK. I'm a volcano. I have hot lava inside of me. I'm a dormant volcano. I haven't erupted yet. But I will. I have gray smoke coming out of me.

Billy, if you really were a volcano, if your body were the volcano, where would the hot lava be?

Billy: (very thoughtful — finally placing his hand on his abdomen) Right here.

Billy, what would that hot lava be for you, a boy, instead of a volcano?

Billy: (eyes very bright) Anger!

I then asked Billy to paint me a picture of what he thought his anger looked like, just using shapes, colors, and lines. He painted a large, thick red circle with colors inside. I wrote on his painting as he dictated: "This is Billy's anger inside his stomach. It's yellow, red and gray and orange. Smoke is coming out." I then listed some of the things that he said made him angry: "Sister messing room, when I get in fights, when I fell down off my bike, when I broke my lock, when I fell down at the skating rink."

At this point Billy realized how much he had revealed, and he would not talk about his anger further. We finished the session with a game of checkers.

Billy was not ready to give expression to his anger at this point except through painting. He knew that his rage was churning around inside him. In later sessions he gradually was able to reveal more, and as he did so his unacceptable behavior began to diminish. He made friends, joined a baseball team, and generally allowed his friendly, cheerful outgoing self to emerge. Evidence of his change that was most significant to me was that three months later when I called to find out what was happening at school with Billy, the school counselor did not remember who Billy was!

Again and again I find that energy spent in withholding feelings of anger leads to inappropriate behavior. With children the changes can be rapid since they do not have the layers and layers of suppressed anger that adults often have. And yet it always amazes me to see a child work his way through the muck to emerge as a healthier, whole being. It seems as though the process of getting to the healthy place should be a difficult one, yet it is usually very simple and obvious. A twelve-year-old girl who was classified as "predelinquent" by law-enforcement authorities drew her angry feelings: yellow and orange and gray scribbles surrounded by a thick black border. Her statement about her picture was "The anger surrounds me and squeezes in the good feelings and they can't get out." This put it quite succinctly. When Debby began to get help in letting go of her angry feelings, her good feelings poured out and her rebellious behavior dramatically decreased.

Bobby, age nine, came in for his session announcing that he had a headache, a usual complaint at home and at school. I asked him to draw his headache: "Close your eyes and look at your headache. See what shape it is and what colors it has. Then draw it." Here is Bobby's description of his headache, dictated directly to me: The spot in the middle hurts the most. The sides of the head hurt a lot too. The parts around the middle don't hurt too much. My headache is in my forehead, the orange part. Sometimes it's in the back. Green, red, gray and black-brown hurt most. Blue, orange, purple, yellow, yellow-ocher don't hurt so much. I'd like to kill my headache so it wouldn't hurt. I get them when I'm running around a lot, in the hot sun. I sometimes wake up with them. And when I get mad. And at supper time. I have a little one now.

He then drew a picture of a face with the larger headache now drawn in miniature. Just allowing himself to experience his headache markedly decreased the pain. However, my interest was in Bobby's statements, "I'd like to kill my headaches," and "I get them when . . . I get mad, and at supper time."

I asked Bobby to talk to his headache on the paper about how he'd like to kill it. With encouragement he did this for a while. I then suggested that maybe there was someone in his life he would like to "kill." He immediately responded, "Yeah! My brother!" I asked him to draw his brother's face and tell his brother how mad he was at him. He drew a large, ugly face and then proceeded to mark it up with pencil jabs as he expelled some of his anger. Bobby needed some tools for coping with his angry feelings in healthier ways than turning them into himself in the form of headaches.

One of the hardest things for children to learn is how to be straightforward with their angry feelings. They need to learn how to directly ask for what they want, and to say what they like and don't like. I think children are encouraged to be manipulative, devious, and indirect by the reaction of adults to their pointed and direct remarks. Children, especially adolescents, often tell me how the adults in their lives criticize and punish them if they are direct with their feelings. Since they learn about these negative reactions at an early age, they do not develop practice in straightforward communication that they can carry into their adult lives.

In the families that I see, I find that all the members, including the adults, have trouble communicating with each other. As simple an exercise as having each member of the family say one thing liked and one thing disliked about each person often brings powerful results. One boy said with tears of happiness to his older brother after such an exercise, "I didn't think there was *anything* you liked about me!" I have also done this exercise with groups of unrelated children, and I find that it is good practice in learning to be direct.

An eight-year-old boy was complaining to me that his father never spent any time with him. I knew this to be true — though concerned and caring about his son, his father was a busy professional — and I felt that rather than bring the father in for a family session, I could provide an opportunity for this boy to learn to communicate his needs directly instead of in the manipulative, whiny manner he generally used. I asked him to talk to his father as if his father were sitting in the empty chair (I might have used a doll figure, a puppet, a drawing on paper, or the chalk board instead) and to state his resentments and his wants. He did so; then I suggested that he go home and repeat these statements to his father. At the next session he reported that his father had really listened, and that they had worked out an arrangement for doing some things together. The boy was elated and had gained considerable self-esteem from this experience.

Specific Problem Behaviors

A mother brought her five-year-old son in for therapy because he was engaging in terrible temper tantrums which left both of them drained. As she was describing his behavior, Jeff fidgeted and squirmed, pretending not to listen. I wanted to involve him so I stopped his mother and asked her to draw a picture of one thing that bugged her about Jeff, and I asked Jeff to do the same about his mother. Jeff said he didn't want to, but watched intently as his mother drew a picture of a boy lying on the floor, arms outspread, mouth wide open with red wavy lines emanating from all around his body. This was Jeff having one of his temper tantrums. Jeff then began to draw. He drew a figure lying on the floor and a much larger one standing over the smaller figure. He said, "This is my mother screaming at me when I have a temper tantrum."

I asked Jeff's mother to talk to the boy in her picture about her feelings when he had a tantrum, and I asked Jeff to talk to the mother in his picture about his feelings. Soon they were having a dialogue through the pictures, and Jeff's attention never waned.

Jeff said that his mother treated him as if he should be able to do everything and she let his three-year-old brother get away with everything. I asked him to be more specific — "What is one thing she wants you to do? Tell her what that is."

WINDOWS TO OUR CHILDREN

His answer: "One thing you always want me to do is pick up all of the toys he throws around just because they're my toys. And when I try to tell you, you never listen and it makes me have a temper tantrum."

I asked Jeff to suggest some possible solutions to the problems and he came up with some very good ones. They discussed each solution, finally came to an agreement on that issue, and went on to another one of Jeff's specific complaints. I saw Jeff for only three sessions. When he and his mother began to listen to each other, the tantrums stopped. Not all problems are so easily solved, but this is a good example of the power a child can exert — a power that can overwhelm parents even though the underlying cause may be simple, obvious, and easily dealt with.

Linda, age ten, was molested by a man, refused to speak about it to anyone, and in fact hardly spoke about anything.

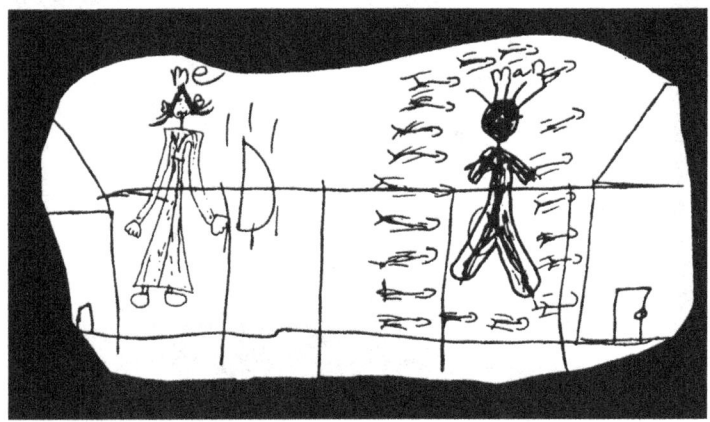

I could guess that she had many feelings — anger, fear, shame, perhaps guilt — and I knew we would have to sort out each of these feelings and deal separately with them. I directly brought up the molestation incident with Linda and asked her to draw a picture of how she felt. Without a word she picked up felt pens and drew a girl which she labeled "Me" and at the far end of the page she drew a figure all in black which she labeled "Man." She drew herself holding a bow and drew many arrows surrounding the man. They stood on a sidewalk outside of a house. Linda described what she was doing in the picture with much body expression and emotion in her voice. Had she refused to draw the picture, I would have suggested

Specific Problem Behaviors

that she do something less threatening, such as perhaps just painting anything or building a scene in the sand. If her feelings did not come through, I would continue to bring the subject up periodically, knowing that at some point she would be ready to express herself.

I asked Debby, age nine, to paint how she felt when she was happy and then how she felt when she was mad. She drew a line down the middle of her paper, wrote "mad" on one side and "happy" on the other. The "mad" side was a tight little dab of color; the "happy" side was larger, with bright colors. Debby had difficulty accepting her mad feelings; giving her the opportunity to paint her good feelings eased her tension somewhat and allowed her to begin to face her not-so-pleasant feelings. We talked about her "happy" side. In answer to "What makes you happy?" we listed on her picture "Going places, my Daddy, talking to you." Then we talked about the "mad" side. For that side she commented, "My brother's teasing me; his butting in; small things. Also school — my teacher made me feel so bad when I asked a question. I'll never ask a question again! It's lots of little things inside of me." and then she looked at me and said, "I feel like screaming." I asked her to paint how she felt when she felt like screaming. She painted with large flowing motions as she spoke, "I hate it when my mother nags me to do my homework and to practice the piano! She nags, nags, nags me. I hate it! I wish my mother's head would fall off when I'm mad at her!" then very quickly, *"No I don't!"* Often when children are angry they will have mutilation and death fantasies which frighten them terribly — another reason for keeping anger locked tightly inside. Debby and I were now able to talk about her scary fantasies.

A nine-year-old boy drew his angry feelings in a bold black and purple and red scribble. We wrote on the back of his paper, "These are Jon's mad feelings — and also some hurt. I'm mad at my brother calling me names; at my parents not treating me or acting as if I'm in the world; they ignore me. They don't answer my questions. I can't play the guitar. I wish I could take guitar lessons and they won't let me."

Susan, age eleven, talked openly and freely about her experience. A man had broken into her house, gone into her room, beat her until she was black and blue and bleeding, set fire to the house, and left. She told about this unbelievable experience, which had made the newspaper headlines, in a feelingless monotone. We sat on the floor with clay and talked about her experience as she molded the clay. I asked her to express what she felt toward this man as if the clay were he. She was unwilling at first, but with some urging she began to make some small stabs at the clay. The clay was soft and gave easily to her motions. As she allowed some of her feelings to creep through, the crack in her armor widened and she began to pound the clay with much energy. I asked her to tell the clay man what she wanted to say to him. She said quite a few things to him, and then suddenly she stopped and I could see tears forming in her eyes. She stared at me.

"What are you thinking right now, Susan?" I very gently asked her.

She whispered, "I'm so mad at my mother! I'm so mad at her!"

Susan could not tell her mother that she resented the fact that her mother had not heard her screams and had only awakened when she smelled smoke. She told me that she couldn't tell her, because her mother was so upset about what had happened. I felt that it was necessary for Susan to be straight with her feelings with her mother, that telling me about them would not help her to heal. I asked her mother to come in at the next session, and we dealt with these and other feelings that Susan had toward her mother that related to this experience. At the end of the session they held each other and wept. Her mother reported that this was the first time she had seen Susan cry since the experience. For Susan, it was an important lesson that people, including her mother, need to express their feelings. Many children will keep feelings inside in order not to further upset or burden a grieving parent. I have written at length about anger — this most feared, resisted, suppressed, threatening emotion — because it is so often the most important and the deepest hidden block to one's sense of wholeness and well-being.

The Hyperactive Child

There is a lot of controversy today about the cause and treatment of hyperactive behavior. Everyone is certainly in agreement about the manifest behavior of a hyperactive child. He may have trouble sitting still, fidgets, has to move around a great deal, sometimes talks excessively, may have annoying mannerisms, hits out at other children, often causing many kinds of conflicts and arguments, has trouble controlling urges, is impulsive, often has poor coordination or poor muscle control, is clumsy, drops things, breaks things, spills milk. He has trouble focusing his attention, is easily distracted. Sometimes he asks lots of questions but seldom waits for the answers.

I have worked with quite a few hyperactive children. They are difficult people to live with, and the first to be identified by the teacher in the classroom for special class placement. Often a hyperactive child will have severe learning disabilities caused by impairment of perceptual abilities — visual, auditory, and sometimes tactile. His motor difficulties cause poor eye-hand coordination and affect his ability to write easily and clearly. He is confused and irritated by the many stimuli in his environment. There are many secondary effects that contribute to the child's difficulties. Adults are impatient with him, do not trust him, yell at him, sometimes can't stand him. He has few friends, since he has poor interpersonal relationship skills. He is humiliated by the labels placed on him. Other children tease him and call him names. He feels bad about his learning impairments; his self-image is usually very poor. But he does fight for survival in a world that appears to him to be harsh and unjust.

Physicians prescribe drugs readily to pacify the hyperactive child. Occasionally I have seen children who, because of their daily pill intake, have been able to sit still long enough to be taught some reading or who have been made so docile that they appear to undergo a personality reversal from aggressive and obnoxious to pleasant and easygoing. However, as with behavior modification techniques, which deals only with the symptomatic behavior, the child so treated gains no inner strength of his own to deal with his world. He uses his pills as a crutch and sometimes as a manipulative tool. "Give me my pills so I can be good," is commonly heard.

It is also frightening to speculate on the physiological damage that may result from such drugs. I tend to be biased toward the advocates of good nutrition and megavitamin treatment. I know that hyperactive children often have poor diets. Large amounts of sugar and other kinds of junk food are often freely given to these children, either as rewards for doing something right or to keep them quiet and shut them up.

Children who show any or all of the various hyperactive symptoms are sometimes simply avoiding feelings that are painful. A child who is unable or unwilling to express held-in feelings certainly may have trouble sitting still, paying attention, focusing — and *not* have any neurologically-based perceptual or motor disabilities. Often anxious children will have a fear of getting involved in any kind of activity. They will constantly move from one thing to another, and appear to be unable to stay with anything and give their full attention to it. Children who are fearful, angry, or anxious may behave in this way and appear to be "hyperactive children" with all the implications of that label.

Jody, age five, was a typical example of this type of child. He was diagnosed as hyperactive and was taking ten milligrams of Ritalin per day. His mother reported that although he had been on this medication for a year, his hyperactivity had not decreased. In my office he flitted from one thing to another, unable to settle down to any one thing. He would pick something up, begin to play with it, then suddenly change his mind. He would begin to work on some project that I suggested, such as clay or a drawing, then suddenly say, "I don't want to do this anymore." Each time, I would respond by saying "OK" and would help him clean up what he had been doing. At the fourth session, Jody reported to me that he had dreamed about a monster that might kill him. I asked him to paint the monster. He worked steadily and with great absorption. When he sat back and announced he was through, I asked him to talk to his monster and tell him what he thought of him.

Jody: You scare me! You're gonna kill me!

How might he kill you, Jody?

Jody: He could eat me up.

Tell him that.

Jody: You could eat me up! (He hunches his shoulders.) Oooooo. I'm afraid of you.

Be the monster's voice and talk back to you.

Jody: Be his voice?

Yes. Pretend you're him. What does he say to you?

Jody: He says, "Watch out for me. I'm going to eat you!" (in a deep, growly voice)

We continued in this vein a while, and finally I said, "Jody, how does it feel when you're the monster?"

Jody: Good!

At this point, time was up and we had to stop. Jody's attention had never veered during the session. In subsequent sessions Jody became more and more willing to stay with an activity on his own. His play became focused on violent situations. He would carefully set up the dollhouse with furniture and family and say, "A bomb drops and everyone is killed." He would line up small cars, and then knock them all down with one of the trucks. He would set up army men in the sand and shoot at them one by one, making each fall as he did so. Whenever possible I would encourage Jody to "be" the bomb, to "be" the truck that knocked the cars down, and so forth. I wanted Jody to experience his own power. Once he felt free to do this within the safe confines of my office, he began to take this feeling of power home with him. He began to express much more directly to me and to his mother some of the things that were making him angry or afraid. His mother reported that he was at last becoming calmer and easier to get along with.

    I find it interesting that when I work with a child who is considered hyperactive, he is very rarely hyperactive in my office. I have read the school reports about his hyperactivity and even sometimes observed him myself in the classroom. I have listened to his parents and I've seen him be hyperactive in the waiting room, jumping up and down, climbing, running around. There may be some fidgeting and restlessness when he is in my office, but it's very interesting to me that there's very little of what's commonly thought of as hyperactivity in a one-to-one situation. When these children have someone's attention, are listened to so that they feel heard, and are taken seriously, they are able somehow to minimize their "hyperactive" symptoms.

    Working with these children is not very different from working with children who are aggressive and angry. I start with where the child is, and attempt to focus on the specific problems that have been presented to me, or that emerge. If hyperactive symptoms are evident I use one of two opposite approaches: 1) I may give the child what I know are very soothing, calming materials such as clay, sand, water, or finger paint. 2) I may follow the child's quick focusing and refocusing of attention, and call his attention to what he is doing to help him experience it more fully.

    I think that any tactile experience for these children helps them to focus and become more aware of themselves — their bodies and their feelings. When I worked with emotionally disturbed ("hyperactive" and "anti-social") children in the schools I often used finger paints with excellent results. I would borrow lunch trays from the lunch room, put liquid starch in each tray, and sprinkle one or two colors of powdered poster paint on the starch. The children would work (generally standing up at tables) side by side with great joy. In the six years that I worked with this program, I used this activity often with many different age groups and combinations of children, as well as with my own therapy groups of children and in individual therapy. Never once did a child smear another child or the walls. They would work with absorption, making beautiful designs and experimenting with mixing colors, talking with each other and with me as they worked. When it was time to stop we would take a large piece of paper, lay it over a final design on the tray, press down on the paper, and come away with a marvelous print which they would allow to dry and later trim and frame on a contrasting color of construction paper. Each child would clean his area of work and wash his tray.

The value of this activity was extensive. The prints they made were truly beautiful, and of course they were quite proud of them and themselves. They had engaged in a good hour of focused and joyful activity, and the camaraderie provided an experience they sorely needed. Because of the tactile and kinesthetic nature of this activity, the children experienced a heightened sense of their own bodies. Because these children are so easily distracted and sometimes confused by stimuli, they have a great need to experience coming back to feeling a sense of themselves. I believe that any tactile and kinesthetic experience promotes a new and stronger awareness of one's own body and self. With increased of self comes new awareness of feelings, thoughts, and ideas.

During these sessions the children would talk about many things, often engaging in complicated discussions involving logical thought processes. Sometimes they would talk about themselves and reveal feelings previously unexpressed. Discussions about religion, death, family problems, common experiences, drugs, and other such topics were quite common. I know that what I write here is especially meaningful to the reader who has experienced working with emotionally disturbed children in a public school setting. I often felt in awe of these children as I listened to them, and I was terribly saddened to know that the richness and depth that they held inside rarely had an opportunity to come through.

Specific Problem Behaviors

Sometimes I would play music, generally classical, as the children finger-painted. During the music there was very little conversation, allowing each child to have an enhanced experience of being fully with himself in a new way. Clay, water, and sand provide other kinds of tactile experiences. When I worked in the public school, where playground equipment was available, I could take the children out to the sandbox when no one else was using the playground. Each of the eight to twelve children would have his own space in which to work.

Water play has its own unique benefits. It is the most soothing of all the media. When I had a sink available in the classroom I would sometimes encourage a child to play at it with a variety of plastic items available for this purpose. Many of these children had never had the opportunity to play with sand and mud and water when they were very young — vital experiences for healthful development. In individual sessions with young hyperactive children I will often have a basin of water available (since there is no sink in my office) with things for pouring into and out of. One six-year-old boy began to express some of his feelings to me only after he had absorbed himself with the water for a while.

Since touching and muscle movement appear to be helpful in augmenting the child's sense of self and have a calming effect as well, it seems natural to me that massage can greatly benefit a hyperactive child. I remember that when I tried to teach some reading or arithmetic to a child in the emotionally disturbed class, I would often lightly run my hand back and forth over the child's back as he sat by me. The children loved it when I did this, often requesting it, and I know that it helped them to sit still and concentrate. I have since suggested to parents that they massage their children. There are many books available with easy instructions for the layman. Massage is also effective for children who have experienced trauma; fear and anxiety cause muscles to tighten, and massage can relax them.

My other approach to working with hyperactive children is just the opposite of providing calming, soothing, focused activities. If a child is fidgeting, going from one thing to another, etc., I may observe him do this for a while, then actually encourage this behavior — encourage him to look at this, look at that. I will call his attention to what he is doing, in a nonjudgmental way. I want to focus on what he is doing, to help him become aware of and perhaps acknowledge what he does. When children appear to be very distracted by objects, sounds, pictures, and lights, ask many questions without waiting for answers, or talk incessantly without waiting for comment from me or from other children in a group, they are not actually involved with, or making contact with, anything or anyone. They will look at something without really taking it all in before moving to something else. So as I observe this behavior, I will make some comment about each item or ask one or two questions about the item, and then I'll encourage him to look at something else. This allows the child to continue doing what he is doing, and at the same time encourages him to experience more. I may say as he goes to a candle and picks it up: "Look at that candle. What do you see? Feel the wax. Do you notice the orange part?" Then I move directly to something else as I see his attention change. "What is that noise? It sounds like a fire engine going by outside." I would like this child to make at least some acknowledgment of each thing that he experiences. "How does it feel in your leg when you shake it back and forth like that?" Or "I guess you don't want to hear the answer to your question."

In schools if children are doing something and hear noises outside they are often very distracted, sometimes going to the window. The teacher will usually say, "Get back to work. Never mind that." In my opinion, that's about the worst thing one can do. It makes much more sense to me to say, "OK, let's all go over to the window and see what's happening," to look at whatever it is, stay with it, finish with it, then to go back to the previous work.

One theory in working with distractible children is that it is best to keep the environment bland, providing as few stimuli as possible. Since I myself have never been able to feel comfortable in such an atmosphere, my working and living spaces never did fit this suggestion. I like a lot of color and things to look at and work with around me. I have never found this to be a problem with either groups or individual children, provided that I encourage children to attend to each distraction, and finish with it. I think children need to learn to deal with life around them in reality. Children learn quickly to deal with stimuli when they learn how to focus on them. Children become more observant of new sights and new sounds; their perceptual skills sharpen, and this can strengthen the child's ability to deal with his world.

To avoid stimuli by removing them or ignoring them is weakening to the child and may even worsen his posture in life. A child who has trouble catching a ball will often avoid being in any position of catching a ball. But if he is gently encouraged to catch a ball as much as possible, his eye-hand coordination can become strengthened. (I have a great resentment of teachers and coaches who choose the best pitcher, for example, to pitch in a baseball game over and over, sending the others out to the field to deteriorate.) When a child notices a new piece of jewelry I'm wearing, or a new picture in the room, or a sound that wasn't there before, I want to encourage and enhance his awareness, not criticize or discourage it.

I place great importance on methods for providing hyperactive children with a means for focusing in on themselves. As their sense of self becomes sharper, they can begin to exert the inner control that so often seems to be missing. In general I like a progression from simple sensory and tactile activities (sand, water, clay, finger paint) to activities involving more movement. Breathing and relaxation exercises can be a prelude to larger scale body movement. There's much talk about giving these children structure and limits to their activity, but very little discussion about giving them ways to create and develop their own inner structures. Children need the opportunity to make their own choices, to create their own control.

I'm not advocating complete permissiveness. I believe it is necessary to establish rules for a child's safety and my own comfort. I will quickly establish the limits I need — such as that clay is to be used on the board provided and not to be thrown across the room. Actually I rarely need to state such rules to children in my office. Children are much more aware of what is appropriate to do in a setting than we usually give them credit for. Perhaps when they choose to exceed limits it's because that's what's usually expected of them by the adults in their lives.

I have used a lot of woodworking with children. This is an excellent activity for even the most hyperactive children, most of whom have never been given the chance even to hold a saw or hammer, much less to build things with them. We talk a little about how to handle the tools — how to use them and how not to get hurt with them. The children are given pieces of wood, hammers, nails, saws, drills, and other potentially dangerous items. They will make wonderful things, experiment with new ways of making boats, boxes, airplanes, etc., solve problems, ask for help sometimes, help each other, and share the tools. I am uncomfortable with having children make arrows, rifles, and guns, so I ask them not to, making it clear to them that it is because of my own discomfort. They easily comply with my requests and pursue their work with great appreciation and happiness. Once a faculty member from California State University at Long Beach walked into the room unexpectedly to observe a student teacher in the classroom when we were "building" (the children's word for this activity) and remarked, "These look just like ordinary, normal children!" Indeed, they were just like the rest of us.

I use examples of things I have done in the schools because I want to show that these methods are effective under even the most difficult situations. Children who are in special classes in the schools have experienced so much defeat, failure, shame, and anger in schools that they hate just being in the atmosphere of the school building. They cower in the shadow of school rules, and though they may truly like their class and their teacher, the stigma of being marked and separated is ever-present.

As I write this I am reminded of several little things I have done with hyperactive children to relieve tension or enhance self-support. At school if we were invited to a program in the auditorium (and we were not always invited), I would instruct the children to run as fast as they could and wait for me at a designated spot. Off they would go (to the envy of all the other children marching in orderly lines) and then they would wait very nicely until I arrived. After sitting in a classroom, running released some of their energy and enabled them to sit again for a while in the auditorium.

I don't like making children stand or walk in a militaristic line, often without speaking as well. When we would go for a walk, I would encourage the children to walk in any kind of grouping they chose — in two's or three's or even one's. While waiting outside the door to our classroom, they would clump together in groups, holding interesting conversations. Telling them to wait in straight lines, boys on one side, girls on the other, allowing no talking, seems ridiculous to me and only increases agitation, frustration, and friction. I don't like standing in line silently waiting, and I have never seen a line of adults where conversation was prohibited. When it was necessary to stand in line in order to wait one's turn, as in the cafeteria, the children did so easily because it made sense to them.

Specific Problem Behaviors

In the classroom we had periods of time when we expected everyone to be quiet, since people were studying or concentrating, and at other times talking was part of the natural course of events. Children like to talk to each other during types of activities where quiet concentration is not essential, and these children needed all the opportunity for social interaction they could get. Some of the most creative stories were written by children in groups — talking, laughing, sharing what they had written with each other, calling out for help when they needed it. I think that teachers and others working with groups tend to discourage noise because it bothers the adults, because they fear they have lost control of the children, or because they will be judged as not having the competence to maintain control and "discipline" over the children. If the noise becomes bothersome to the adults, or to any of the children, this concern should be shared within the group. The children can then quiet down for a legitimate reason, "This noise is giving me a headache," rather than for wrong reasons "You are bad, rotten kids for making noise," or "Making noise is bad." Many signals to get the group's attention can be agreed upon in advance by the children. A gavel, a bell, a drum roll, chimes, a flicking of the light — any of these will work. Often the children will come up with some very creative ideas for signals.

Let us not forget that children, including those considered to be hyperactive, are people like the rest of us. We all have our own internal rhythms for doing things. Some of us are quick, some of us are slow. We move from one task to another in different ways, finishing one thing in our own manner before we are ready to move on to something else. In working with any group we need to know that there will be a variety of processes functioning; children are not robots moving in synchronized patterns.

Finally, I want to emphasize the profound importance of choice. All children need to experience making choices; hyperactive children especially need opportunity for exercising their will and judgement in a positive way. Making choices requires a sense of self; one must tune into one's thinking and feeling functions in order to make a decision. Taking responsibility for one's choice is a learning experience. In our zeal to create limits and structure and routine and order in the lives of hyperactive children (and I know that they require all of these things) we often neglect to give them enough experience with the strengthening process of making choices. I have watched the most fidgety, restless child stand endlessly in front of construction paper of a variety of colors, making his choice of the three colors he has been told he can choose. Often he is very worried that he will be sorry for his choice, and would rather I just hand him the three colors so that he can blame me if they turn out to be the wrong ones. One can almost see the brain moving and churning within this child's head as he contemplates the piles of paper, becoming stronger through this exercise. Seemingly simple choices are often not easy for this child to make, but I believe it is essential he be given many opportunities for decision making. I can think of no better way for reinforcing a child's selfhood.

The Withdrawn Child

What is a withdrawn child? I hear this phrase so often from parents, teachers. My dictionary says: "Withdrawn, adj. shy, reserved, etc." The verb "withdraw" is interesting. Again, my dictionary gives the following definitions: "verb, transitive. 1. to take back; remove. 2. to retract or recall (a statement, etc.). verb, intransitive. to move back; go away; retreat." So the child who is withdrawn has perhaps needed to retreat from a world which is too painful.

Generally I don't see, in therapy, children who are quiet or shy. Adults are generally pleased with such children, because they make so little trouble. The problem only becomes apparent when the child begins to exaggerate his shy behavior. He may talk as little as possible, or he may never talk. He may not speak above a whisper. He may stay on the outskirts of everything, fearful of joining in or trying new things. He is often a loner, with no friends, or at least very few.

In spite of attempts to eliminate sex-role stereotypes, many girls are accepted as shy, reserved, quiet, withdrawn. Boys are much more encouraged to contact their aggressive nature. It's considered cute when girls are quiet and shy. I find it interesting that the girls I have seen in therapy who are considered withdrawn are older, but shy boys are brought in quickly. Few parents want to see their *son* quiet and shy. Girls make use of this behavior since they have received approval for it, and by the time a girl is noticed with concern, much time has gone by.

Withdrawn children are children who hold in. The definition "to retract or recall (a statement, etc.)" is fitting. Somewhere along the line they learned to keep their mouths shut — too much was said by someone and they got the message. Children readily "clam up," tightly holding feelings and experiences inside the clamshell. Have you ever tried to talk to a child who has "clammed up"? *You* can talk, but the child will not.

I have to approach the withdrawn child delicately. This child, so powerful in the withdrawn state, is not about to give up that power easily. One mother said to me, "She never says anything! It drives me crazy!" Not talking is this child's only weapon against her mother's demands. She does well in school, completes her chores, follows the rules, does not whine or beg for anything or cry or hit or fight or yell. But she speaks only when necessary — "Please pass the salt."

This child is not using that weapon intentionally. She learned at one point in her life that it was something she had to do, and even though the circumstances may have changed, she is still doing it. Or she is doing it because she feels it too dangerous to open up and talk. It is not important for me to know why she does it. What is important is that I help her find other areas of strength so that she can freely choose to talk or not to talk. In keeping herself so tightly checked she closes off many parts of herself and her life. She is not letting herself freely experiment, explore, develop, and grow in the many areas that she needs to.

So I am delicate — force will break the clam shell rather than pry it open. I meet the child where she is, speaking very little myself. At our first session she has heard the complaints of her parents. She says nothing. When we are together she obeys me to the letter. She communicates with me by shrugs, grimaces, and soft phrases, especially, "I don't know." I am well aware of this child's power. I sometimes feel overly loud, overly talkative, overly pushy, even when attempting to hold myself in check.

This child can certainly hear, even if she doesn't talk. So I tell her that her mother is worried that she doesn't say much. I imagine that the child does not completely understand her mother's concern, for I know that generally children who don't say much are not aware of it as a problem. They just feel that they have nothing to say. I tell her this and she nods. I tell her that in our sessions, through the things we use, she may find herself having more things to say.

Expressive techniques are especially useful for the nonverbal, withdrawn child. It is through these techniques that the child will begin to communicate, without having to give up her silence.

Angie, age ten, spoke not one word during the first session. Her parents were at a loss as to what to do. Her teacher had made strong comments on her report card about her lack of expression, although her grades were good. She would not tell her parents why she wouldn't talk; she would not tell them *anything*. They hadn't worried up to now because she had always been quiet, and good, and well-behaved, and did well on her report cards. But eventually they began to see that all was not well.

As her parents waited in the other room I asked Angie to draw a person, which she did obediently and thoroughly. Her picture had vacant eyes, a smile on the face, arms stretched out. I asked her if she could make up something about the girl — her name, her age, anything. She shrugged, frowned, and shook her head. I asked if it were a picture of herself. She shook her head. I thanked her for the picture; our time was up.

At the next session I asked her to make a scene in the sand. She shrugged as if to say, "Sure, if that's what you want." She worked with great absorption as I sat next to her and watched. She examined every basket on the shelf, carefully selecting animals, fences, trees, people, a house, a rock. She arranged the scene as a zoo, with each animal fenced off and lots of people watching. She rearranged, switched, patiently picked up pieces that fell, worked very hard creating a very crowded zoo. She never spoke during this time; even her breathing was stilled. It dawned on me that this was not the first time I had noticed that withdrawn children do not breathe fully. At one end of her zoo she had placed a small bridge and on the bridge a little duck.

She looked up and sat back, indicating she was through. I asked her which animal was her favorite. She shrugged; no answer. I asked with some emphasis, "If you could be one of those animals, which one would it be?" She looked at her zoo and pointed to the duck on the bridge. I said, "Your zoo is crowded. The animals are crowded into their areas — all except this duck. Do you ever feel crowded like these animals?" She shrugged. "I see you picked the one animal that has some room to herself. Do you have a room to yourself at home?" "No." (loudly, clearly) Who do you share it with? "My sister." Do you wish you had your own room? "Yes I do! And so does she! We don't like being in the same room together." Silence after that. She stared and stared at her scene. I did not interrupt. Finally I asked what she was thinking as she looked at her zoo. Shrug. Time was up.

I was happy with this session. I felt that much more had happened than I might have expected in a second session. At each subsequent session Angie spoke more and more — through a drawing, a fantasy, a sand tray scene. I encouraged her to write in her notebook (she wrote well). She recorded dreams, thoughts, feelings. We used clay and began to carry on conversations while working with the clay. Through pictures she told stories eventually. In one session she made a collage. She loved doing this and talked much more following that session. Through these activities more and more information came out — feelings she had, things she liked to do, her favorite colors, songs. I never really found out why she did not talk for such a long period. (I knew her family history and could make some guesses, but what would be the purpose? Sometimes parents beg for my guesses and I tell them what I think, but assure them that they are only guesses.) Angie began to talk to me and to her parents, her sister, her teachers, and her friends. She found out she had something to say.

I worked with another child who did speak, but only in whispers. She was eleven, the oldest of five children. She was competent, and took care of her brothers and sisters. She did well in school and was well-behaved. Her mother was divorced and worked. I had worked previously with one of her younger brothers, who was having temper tantrums. As his behavior improved, the mother asked me if I would see the eleven-year-old. We had had some family sessions, I had seen the mother several times individually, and this woman began to view behavior in a much different way than ever before. She became concerned at her daughter's quietness. "We never know what she's feeling about anything, and I know that this is not good for her," she said.

We did many things and the daughter did begin to communicate feelings with me but only through whispers. I had a children's group at that time and decided to try putting her into it. She retreated into silence, but I noticed something interesting. Every child in the group commented on Jill's lovely bright red hair and freckles. At a private session I asked her to draw me a picture of what it was like to have red hair. She drew a figure of a girl with bright red hair and a deep black frown, and she labeled the figure ME.

WINDOWS TO OUR CHILDREN

Around this figure she drew five other people, labeling each one and drawing a word balloon from each mouth. One figure labeled A BOY was saying "Ha, you Fireball!" Another labeled A MAN was saying, "Where did you get that red hair and freckles?" A LADY was saying, "I've always wanted red hair!" LITTLE BOY was saying, "Ha freckle face strawberry." And one other boy was saying "Ha Red Flame." When she finished drawing she described this picture to me, getting up and imitating each person's comment loudly with sarcastic voice inflection!

This was the first time I had ever heard Jill speak above a whisper. I wrote on her paper as she dictated, "This is what it's like to have red hair. I get comments everywhere. Maybe if I didn't have so many comments said to me I might not be feeling bad very much." I asked Jill what color hair she preferred. "Black," she said, loud and clear. We discussed the possibility of her dyeing her hair when she was older. She told me too that she could not ever remember a time when someone didn't say something about her hair or her freckles.

Jill had many feelings of anger, sadness, and resentment which she had kept hidden for a long time. She felt abandoned by her father, resented taking care of the younger children, and was anxious about her distraught, overworked mother. All of these deeper feelings began to come out as her voice became unlocked. She told me one day that she might keep her hair red after all. "Sometimes," she said, "it's fun to get all that attention over my dumb hair. I still don't like the freckles though."

Sandra, age nine, communicated only in whispers and often had stomachaches. We spent a lot of time drawing pictures of her stomachaches. I drew the first one, since she was puzzled when I asked her to do this. One day she worked for a long time placing figures on the flannel board. The main character seemed to be a girl figure. I asked her to tell me about her.

Sandra whispered: She has no one to play with.

She looks nice. How come no one will play with her?

Sandra: She's in trouble. She was so mad at her family that she chopped their heads off.

She would say no more about the girl. Finally I asked, Are *you* mad?

Sandra: No. (she scarcely breathed)

Specific Problem Behaviors

In the sand tray she played out a story with a very bossy deer ordering other animals around. In a rosebush fantasy she said as a rosebush, speaking as the flower, "I go in when people come around. The grass and hills are my friends. I talk to them." It seemed to me that she was whispering less with me.

One day she came in and said to me in a barely audible whisper, "My father was with us this weekend while my mother went away." I asked her how that was. "I'm not used to him. I like my mother better." Her voice, face, manner, body posture seemed more withholding than when I first saw her. We sat down on the floor together, and I asked her to tell me what she was not used to with her father. Sandra turned her head away. I gently moved her head toward me and looked into her eyes. "He touches me," she said, and began to cry. The story of a long history of molestation came pouring out in a normal voice. Sandra had never told anyone before.

The withdrawn child is often in a state of isolation because he is unable to participate in free and safe interpersonal communication. He has trouble expressing feelings of affection as well as anger. He typically keeps himself in a safe place, avoiding risk of rejection or hurt. Spontaneity is unfamiliar and frightening to him, although he may admire it in others and desire to be more casual, open, flowing. Sometimes people see him as meek, fearful, shy, inhibited. Sometimes he is seen as snobbish, wanting to be alone, setting himself apart. Because he is uncommunicative, he appears to be inarticulate, perhaps unintelligent and dull, though he may do quite well in his grades at school. He may even be labeled as schizoid.

The older a person is, the more difficult it is to get through the years and years of his protective wall. But the adult may with conscious effort counteract this by his will, his determination to be different. The young child, however, is immersed in his need to protect himself and is often completely unaware of his withdrawn state, though he may know that something isn't right. It is common for teenagers to seek out therapy because they want so much to break through the hardened shell that has kept them from the fun and joy they see around them among their peers. Their shell has outworn its purpose of shielding them from pain and hurt; they realize they need help in finding a not too-uncomfortable way of breaking through it to experience good feelings.

WINDOWS TO OUR CHILDREN

A seventeen-year-old youth came to see me because he felt "different." He had few friends and was unable to enjoy the give and take of social contact that he noticed all around him at school. He said that he had always been this way, but it had never bothered him when he was younger. He enjoyed many hobbies that kept him occupied: stamp collecting, coin collecting, all kinds of collections. He felt that his home life had been very stable and he couldn't think of any reason for being so uncommunicative. These statements (in response to my questions) were the most he said for a long while. He literally had nothing to say. I felt often as if I were pulling teeth, and I was drained at the end of the sessions. I imagine that I experienced exactly what others did who came in contact with him in his life. When I asked him to do some drawings, he was so restrictive that he found this to be quite difficult, almost impossible. He was unable to describe his feelings to me, even when I told him my own reactions to his difficulty in communicating with me. During the next four months John began to undergo a transformation. Here are some notations from my records:

First Session: Told me about not liking being shy. Unable to make friends. Would like to have a girl friend. Never has had a date. Sometimes goes out with a group but they usually don't ask him again. Does well in school. Plans to go to college. Except for not being at ease with girls, not having friends, he doesn't think there's anything wrong with him. Doesn't know why he has no friends. Felt like pulling teeth to get him to tell me the above. Has no worries or problems, except for wanting to make friends. Home life fine. Childhood fine.

Next Session: Asked him to draw a picture in color, line, and shape showing his weak side and his strong side. Made an attempt. Had much trouble. Gave up. Asked about what he was feeling. Unable to respond. Found myself talking a lot.

Next Few Sessions: Pretty much the same as above. Told me something about what had happened during the week. Said he liked coming to see me — I was someone to talk to. I told him my feelings — that talking with him was like pulling teeth. No reaction. Shrugged, smiled. Said he agreed it was probably what other people felt.

Next Session: Gave him paper and asked him to do an 'I am' exercise — write sentences after the words I am — He wrote: I am a boy; I am a person; I am a student; I am a son; I am not sure about this; I am myself; I am not perfect; I am sensible; I am a realist and an idealist; I am independent within; I am not so certain; I am free; I am...

Next Session: Brought out clay. Did an exercise with him asking him to make an image of himself with his eyes closed. He was uncomfortable with the clay, but did it upon my urging. Very moving session. Said he was not defined because he had no confidence. Afraid he will be foolish and silly and get hurt if he says things, etc.

Next Sessions: John began to remember his dreams. He brought in dreams to work on. One was a dream of a near drowning, where he struggles in the water, but manages to swim to safety.

Next Session: Did an awareness continuum exercise to help him be more aware of what is going on in his body, mind, feelings. Played it as a game with me. We each took turns saying what we were aware of, what we saw, heard, felt in our bodies, our thoughts (labeling them as such), and so forth. Very successful!

Next Sessions: Realized that John was talking more and more, taking the lead about what he wanted to work on. Worked on his fears of ridicule. Drew picture of it. No problem drawing this time! Able to go back to feelings of ridicule in childhood. Began to express some anger! Suddenly he realized that a lot of things made him angry.

John entered college with new strengths. He reported making friends, feeling happy, talking up a storm. John was very intelligent and had many ideas and much to say; he had kept it all locked inside for many years. He said that sometimes his old feelings came back but that he knew what to do when they came. He stopped therapy because his life was just too full. This may sound like a corny success story; I can only say that real life is sometimes almost too corny to believe.

Fears

Children fear more than we realize. For every fear that children express openly there are many that they keep to themselves. In our society, being afraid is akin to cowardliness. Parents spend much energy in explaining children's fears away, rather than accepting their children's feelings of fear. Children learn to push their fears deep down in order to please their parents, or so as not to frighten them with their fears.

WINDOWS TO OUR CHILDREN

When I see children for aggressive behavior, withdrawn behavior, or physical symptoms, many fears that they've kept hidden away often surface during the course of our sessions. Children need to talk about these fears. Some of their fears are the result of false ideas; others are based on real situations. Many are a result of the child's unequal place in our society. All of his fears need to be acknowledged, accepted, respected. Only when they can be looked at openly can a child gain the strength to deal with a sometimes frightening world.

Some children's fears turn into phobias: their fears grow to such proportions that their efforts to avoid the things they fear greatly interfere with their lives. A ten-year-old boy had such a fear of heights that he could not tolerate being more than two stories up in a building. Hiking in the mountains was out of the question.

Although I may know that such a fear is a displacement of the actual cause of fear or anxiety — the fear is assigned to a generality such as heights rather than to its actual source — I must work with what is presented. I am usually quite directive and confrontive; I plunge right into the fear situation by asking the child to draw the fear or to reenact through doll figures or dramatic play a situation which will help the child get closer to the fear.

I asked this boy to choose whatever he wanted to do; I could sense that we needed more time to get to know each other first. In the sandbox he built a street, with houses and trees, and in the center of the sand he diligently created a *skyscraper* from Lego blocks! Following his lead, I asked him to place a doll figure on his tall building, then to be this figure and describe his feelings. He responded readily and described the sensation of feeling as if he would lose his balance and fall off. His body became rigid, tight, his breathing constricted. A person's body and breathing give obvious clues to tuning in to fear. Fear is very explicitly revealed through the body.

Getting in touch with unexpressed feelings related to the specific fear is a beginning step in the therapy. I found with this boy that one source of the fear was a feeling of having no control — he would have absolutely no choice about getting close to the edge and about what would happen next. We spent some time doing various exercises involving body control and body balance, including walking up and down a small ladder, balancing on a rope, and then walking a board. As he gained confidence and mastery, he began to experiment with trying higher and higher places. I assured him that he would feel fear since it was an old response, but that he could choose to do what he wanted to in spite of it. During the course of our work together he shared many feelings with me that on the surface seemed not to be related to his phobia. When he let go of his feelings and hidden thoughts and ideas, he began to let go of his fear. Any restriction of any kind, any holding in, seems to have a great deal to do with every aspect of our lives. Apparently the more we can let go and give up, the more control, balance, and centeredness we feel. Again, we never knew if we had hit on the "specific cause" of his fear.

Another child that I worked with was deathly afraid of water. We discovered the source of her fear through a guided fantasy. She suddenly remembered being pushed under water and held down by her older brother when she was much younger. She had been terrified and thought that she would drown. This memory was verified by her mother, and we did a lot of work on it, including getting in touch with angry feelings at her brother, doing body exercises, and homework that involved trying out water gradually, in small steps. We did not completely eliminate her fear, but we did lessen it to the point that it was not all-controlling. She felt she had come a long way in contrast to her previous complete avoidance of water, even though swimming probably will never become one of her favorite activities. This child was much older than the ten-year-old who feared heights, and her fear had been reinforced by many incidents.

Fear of burglars and intruders is very common among children. One nine-year-old girl was fearful that a burglar would climb into her window at night, and she had trouble sleeping. It was not the dark she feared, for she felt a light would only serve to guide the burglar in. I asked her to draw a picture of exactly how the burglar would get in. She drew her house, the window of her room, and a large tree next to her window that the burglar would climb to get to the window. She described her imaginary scene in great detail, even to all the things he would take. We found as we examined her fear very specifically that she was not fearful of bodily harm; rather she simply did not like the idea of a strange man coming into the house and taking things. She got the idea of hanging bells on the branch of the tree closest to her window, which she was sure would wake her up in time to scare a burglar off. This discussion and exploration diminished her fear enough to give her more peaceful sleep, and we were then able to move on to other issues in her therapy.

In a similar situation a mother reported to me that her five-year-old son was fearful of burglars coming in. He would not discuss it with me when I brought it up. I read him a little book called *Some Things Are Scary*, and after reading the story, I asked him to make up his own story about the boy in the book and what this boy would be scared of. Billy was somewhat resistant until I set up the tape recorder, which I often use in story-telling sessions. Then he immediately told a story about a boy who was afraid of a burglar coming into his house and taking various items which he listed. I made no attempt to interpret this story, even though it was quite complicated and I could have made many guesses about its meaning in view of my knowledge about Billy and his family situation. When he was finished I asked Billy to be the burglar in his story. He did this with great gusto and much body movement, crouching down and moving as stealthily as any burglar. I then asked him to be the boy in his story and pretend he could talk to the burglar. He stated that he was not afraid of this burglar and that he would beat him up, which he then proceeded to do using a pillow for the intruder. It was obvious that something important happened for him, that this was a kind of turning point. His subsequent behavior at school and at home improved markedly. I don't know what conflicts Billy may have resolved in this particular session. It seems to me that interpretation or conjecture about what happened would serve no function other than to make possibly interesting but superfluous conversation. What is important is the quality of the child's therapeutic *experience*, not anyone's analysis of the situation.

Andrew, age ten, felt afraid most of the time. He needed the light on at night, checked often to see if his mother was in bed during the night, was afraid to walk to school by himself, suffered from nightmares several nights in a row after witnessing an accident or seeing a scary TV show. We worked on some of these specific fears, but easing any one of them would not dispel many others that kept surfacing.

At one session we used the *Make a Picture Story* cards, and he created some very scary stories of his own. One story involved a graveyard where a man hid behind a tree to avoid a ghost and a monster. In another, a man was bleeding in a cave with no one to help him. In another, an injured man, an old lady, and a girl were in the middle of the ocean on a raft with no help in sight. Andrew admitted to feeling weak, helpless, and powerless most of the time. Finally, using the street scene card, he told this story:

At first there's a car coming down the road and a big giant snake came out of the sewer drain. A man standing on the street who has a broken leg saw him and he called for help. A policeman came by and started shooting at the snake but it didn't hurt the snake. Then there was a boy on the street. The man in the car was his father and his father wanted him to come home. His father was so scared he didn't want to mess with the snake. The boy called for Superman and Superman came and took the snake out of the world. The end.

I asked Andrew who he was in this story and he said he was really the boy but that he wished he were Superman so he could take care of everything in his life. I asked him what he would like to take care of.

Andrew: I'd like to get a motorcycle and I'd like to be able to read better and I'd like to never have to go to school.

OK. And what else would you like to take care of?

Andrew: I'd like to take care of my mother. She's always worried about stuff, like money and us kids.

Andrew's parents were divorced when he was five years old. His mother told me that he had made a good adjustment to the divorce and had a good relationship with his father, seeing him regularly. I then asked Andrew to be the boy in his story and talk to each story character. As the boy character he said to the father: "You should have taken care of the snake. Superman can't always be around when we need him!"

I felt that we were getting closer to the source of Andrew's fears. Once Andrew could begin to express his great fear of being responsible for his mother and his resentment about the divorce, we could then begin to help him gain the strength he needed to cope with his world.

Cindy, age ten, also suffered terribly from vague feelings of fear. At one session when I asked her to imagine that her fear was sitting in a chair in the room, she described an ugly monster with horns and green pointed teeth. I asked her to talk to her monster.

Cindy: You're ugly. Uggh. I hate you. Go away. (turning her head) I can't look at it.

WINDOWS TO OUR CHILDREN

Ask your monster why it's there, why it hangs around you.

Cindy: Why are you here?

Now be the monster. Sit over here and be the monster and answer Cindy.

Cindy: No! I can't be that ugly monster.

Cindy, you made the monster up — it's not really there. Sit over here and pretend you're the monster. (Cindy reluctantly moved to the other chair.) Monster, tell Cindy why you hang around her.

Cindy: (as monster, to me) I want her ...

No, don't tell me. Tell her (pointing to the chair Cindy just left).

Cindy: (as monster) I have to make sure you are always afraid.

Monster, tell her why you want her to be afraid all the time.

Cindy: (as monster) I want you to be afraid or you might get raped.

Sit over here again, Cindy. Cindy, are you afraid of being raped? (I ask this very gently.)

Cindy: (in low voice) Yes.

Were you ever raped?

Cindy: I don't know.

You look as if you're remembering something. Tell me what you are remembering.

And Cindy tells me of an incident when she was six years old and two boys pulled her into a garage and made her pull down her pants and touched her. She said she never told her parents because the boys said they'd kill her if she did. And she had always heard about girls being raped and killed.

Cindy's rape fears were magnified by her confused sexual knowledge. She had been frightened by the older boys when she was younger, but she had not been raped. Hearing people talk about rape and murder compounded her terror. She equated touching and exposure to the violence of rape. We talked openly and frankly about bodies, sexual activity, making babies, the fun of sex, and so on, dispelling many of her crippling fears.

Sometimes children express fear in some way but cannot specifically point to any one feared thing. The feeling is prevalent, vague and undifferentiated. Drawings are an excellent medium for getting into the fear. I have asked them to close their eyes, imagine how they would show the fear in colors, lines, shapes, or symbols. One child drew a black round ball next to a door labeled "closed door." Another showed a black square hovering over a blue rectangle labeled happiness in turn standing above a yellow triangle labeled sadness. I may ask the child to be the black thing and describe the fear symbol fully: "I am round and black and dark," etc. The symbol can "talk" to the other parts of the picture or to the child, and the child can talk to the symbol. During this process I watch closely for clues in the body and voice changes, as well as the meaning of what is said. Flashes of memory about life situations that are important sometimes come through during this activity.

Sometimes I want a child to express her fear fully. Susan, an eleven-year-old girl who had been attacked by an intruder who came into her house, talked to me about feeling afraid. But the way she talked about it seemed superficial to me — she seemed to be unable to fully vent her feelings in words. So I asked her to paint her fear. This helped her express her fear, as well as other feelings. When she finished painting her fear, she wove in other kinds of lines. The painting looked like a meaningless scribble, but it was far from meaningless to Susan. She described the fear parts when she was finished, and I asked her what the other lines were. She looked at them thoughtfully, then whispered, "anger." This was the beginning of a mobilization of angry energy that she had kept suppressed through her fear.

Fears based on fantasy are nevertheless real feelings of fear. One child could not tolerate being away from her mother. She suffered in worry and anxiety when she did not know where her mother was. Her mother had to walk her to and from school and rarely had babysitters. Long ago someone had dropped some laundry coming back from a Laundromat and it had blown into the school yard. The laundry, which included some woman's clothing, was retrieved, but not before some children gleefully made up a story of a gory murder. Debby, at that time a first grader, heard the story and became terrified. Since the clothing belonged to a woman, she imagined her mother as the victim. She was told many times that such an episode had never happened and was just a made-up story, but she was nevertheless terrified. Her mother, not wanting to further traumatize the child, catered to her fear and rarely left her. Finally, after a full year of this, her mother brought her into therapy.

My approach in this kind of situation is very direct. I talked seriously to Debby about the "murder," asked her to draw pictures of her impressions of the scene, had her act out the scene with doll figures, and examined every detail of it. It soon became a kind of joke between us, and finally one day Debby, sick and tired of talking about the murder, said to me, "Violet, there was no murder — it was just somebody's laundry that fell out of the car! Let's stop talking about it!" Debby did let go of this particular fear, and her mother felt free to leave her at times. But other fears came to take its place — a not unusual happening. She was afraid her mother would crash in an airplane on a trip she was taking, afraid her mother would be in an automobile accident, etc. We acted out each of these fears in turn, not denying the actual possibility of such occurrences. Finally, while doing a painting of her own anger over something, Debby announced that she was so mad at her mother she wished her head would fall off. She immediately went pale, clasped her hand over her mouth, and whispered, "No I don't!" Now we could begin to deal with the power and normalcy of her own angry death wishes.

I think children often get stuck in fears and don't know how to get out of them. Candy, a ten-year-old girl, was brought in to see me because she was afraid to sleep at any house other than her own. It was never much of a problem until she reached the age at which girls like to stay at friends' houses at times. She felt she was missing out on a lot of fun. On her parents' urging she had tried, but she never made it through the night. At some point in the evening they would have to go pick her up. They were at their wits' end in trying to get through this dilemma.

Candy was not sure why she was afraid. I asked her to draw a picture of what she imagined it would be like to sleep over at her friend's house. She drew a picture of her friend's family watching TV and her friend in bed in her bedroom. "Where are you?"

Candy: I'm not there where you can see me. I'm in the bathroom.
What are you doing there?
Candy: Crying. I want to go home.
It sounds like that's what happened.
Candy: Yes.
OK. Be you in the bathroom. Say what you're feeling.
Candy: (pretending to cry) I want to go home. I wonder what my mother and father are doing. I wonder what my brothers are doing. I miss them. I want my own bed.

What happened?

Candy: My friend's father took me home. Everybody was home at my house.

Did you think they wouldn't be?

Candy: I don't know. I don't like not knowing what's happening at home when I'm not there.

Now draw a picture of what it would be like not to cry and have to go home.

Candy drew a picture of her friend's bedroom, her friend and she both on the floor in sleeping bags. I asked her to be the girl in the sleeping bag that was her.

Candy: I'm in the sleeping bag in my friend's room.

Do you like being there?

Candy: Yes! It's fun. My friend and I are talking and laughing.

What's happening in the other room?

Candy: Her parents are watching TV.

What's happening at your house?

Candy: My brothers are asleep. My parents are watching TV, I think. Or maybe there's a sitter and they went to a movie.

What would you be doing if you were home — imagine it.

Candy: Probably in bed asleep. It's late.

Ask the girl in the sleeping bag if she's afraid.

Candy: Candy, are you afraid?

Candy: (in bag) No! Why should I be afraid? This is fun. We're going to make breakfast in the morning — pancakes.

Ask Candy if she is worried about what's going on at home.

Candy: OK. She said no.

Candy continued with some dialogue with herself, enjoying this process. She said she was going to try sleeping over. I reminded her that since she was used to being afraid, she probably would be a little, and that she could still choose to sleep over. I saw Candy for three sessions. Then she slept overnight at her friend's house and that was that.

Sometimes I am not successful in helping a child eliminate fears. John, ten years old, was terribly afraid of the dark. His first words to me were, "You can't help me with my problem." According to his mother during the initial family session, he had many other problems: "Hates changes, afraid to try new things, very negative, doesn't like to be touched, hugged, or kissed, doesn't have friends, doesn't like to go to people's houses, afraid to make a move, watches TV a lot."

John's retorts to his mother's comments were, typically, "People will beat me up," and "I do too have friends — at school." When I asked his mother to tell me about his good points, John looked surprised when she said he was a giving person, had a good heart, was nice to his two younger brothers, and put on good puppet shows for them.

In our first session alone, John confided to me his worry about getting mugged, beaten up. He discussed how he would fight back. He began to tell me horror stories from TV that scared him, and said he was afraid of werewolves and witches at night. I asked him to draw something that frightened him. He drew a picture of a "very scary thing that sucks people to death," which he called a "succibus." The picture was of a monster-like large figure with a black robe and white hair that stood straight up. He obviously enjoyed talking about it, but would not be it.

Then he noticed the puppets, and put on a show for me with the finger puppets that was entertaining and creative. After the show I asked him to draw a house and a person and a tree. He drew a very brightly colored picture with much detail, a smiling sun and smiling clouds, and a smiling pretty girl. Next to the house was a long road with a large sign at the side bearing the words ONE WAY. His only comment about the picture was that he had gone up the one-way road.

That was the last time I saw John. His mother cancelled the next appointment, saying she would call me for a new one after vacation. I never heard from her.

Now and then I will see a child who has a fear of growing up, who seems to have a vague, unfocused feeling of anxiety about the future. Recently I saw a ten-year-old boy who was brought in to see me because he had voiced to his parents a fear of growing up — not angrily, as in an argumentative retort to an adult, but in low, serious tones. A six-year-old girl I saw had similar fears. I found that the parents of both of these children placed great emphasis on the future, telling them that whatever is done now is done in preparation for the years to come. To the ten-year-old the parents said things like, "Do your homework — don't you want to be somebody when you grow up?" and "Some day you will thank me for making you practice." The six-year-old was told things like, "If you don't learn to behave now, how will you hold a job when you grow up?" Variations on such statements are quite common; we have all either heard them or said them at one time or another. Many of us still conduct our adult lives by these kinds of injunctions, heard as children. Some children imagine that they will never measure up to what seems to be expected of them in their coming adulthood. How can they possibly measure up, they feel, if they can't measure up now?

When I work with children who have such fears, I use exercises like the following:

Close your eyes and imagine what it will be like when you are grown up. How do you feel? What are you doing? What's the world like for you?

Close your eyes and see yourself at the age you are now, living your life in exactly the way you want. What are you doing?

Such fantasies become the starting point for further expression and clarification through whatever medium seems appropriate. I also try to help the parents see that they must allow their children to live in the present, as children. If the parents cannot see this, I can at least help the children understand this. My experience is that if a child can begin to see things for himself in better perspective — even if his parents can't — he begins to feel calmer, happier, and less fearful and anxious and does a much better job of living his childhood. If he can accept himself for who he is *now*, his stance in the world becomes more focused and productive.

Children often see the adults around them living in a state of worry and anxiety. They see a world of chaos and contradictions and uncertainty. Though some can't wait to grow up in order to experience independence and self-determination, often these children also secretly (and many others more openly) have a great fear of what may lie ahead.

Specific Stress Situations or Traumatic Experiences

Sometimes children will have a specific bad experience that needs therapeutic help. Either the child lets the parents know in some way that help is needed, or the parents are alert to the fact that some children need special support to help them cope with a difficult situation. Divorce, serious illness, death, molestation, or an earthquake are the types of events that cause emotional trauma in children. Help is often needed to work through consequent feelings that are overwhelming, or that may get buried and cause indirect problems. Sometimes the situation affects the child deeply even though it may seem to be a relatively minor one such as witnessing an accident, moving to a new city or school, the arrival of a new baby, or the death of a pet. Sometimes a child is brought in for therapy because of some kind of worrisome behavior that does not seem directly connected to any particular experience. But after some work with the child, I find that there has indeed been some experience that, when uncovered and dealt with, leaves the child no longer troubled. Sometimes the experience occurred some time ago, and everyone has since "protected" the child by not openly talking with him about it. And sometimes the child himself, because he is not ready to face it at the time, will push the experience away, only to have it emerge later.

Often a child is unable to express what he is feeling to his parents because the parents, too, may be upset by whatever happened, and the child feels protective toward them; he doesn't want to cause them any more grief and unhappiness. If the parents can face their own feelings openly, the child can more easily be open with his own feelings and confusions.

I approach these situations directly. I know that the incident needs to be brought out into the open, talked about, perhaps reenacted symbolically. Often a kind of desensitization takes place in reexamining and talking about the experience. I remember Dr. Wilbur telling *Sybil* in the TV adaptation of the book Sybil (about a woman who had sixteen separate personalities) that since she survived the actual experience she could certainly survive the *memory* of the experience.

A twelve-year-old girl was brought into therapy for behavior that was annoying her father and stepmother. Although the behavioral problem was nothing serious, it was so irritating to them that they decided to seek therapeutic help for the child. On the phone the child's stepmother explained to me that she was not the child's natural mother, that the real mother had been killed by her stepfather in a murder-suicide, and that the child had discovered their bodies some four years ago when she was about eight. The adults hadn't talked much about the incident with her because they didn't want to further upset the child.

Specific Problem Behaviors

Each time I brought the incident up, Patricia merely shrugged, offering nothing of her feelings. We had many sessions with paint and clay and stories, through which many of her then-current complaints and troubles came through and were explored. Then one day Patricia announced that she had dreamt about her mother. She proceeded to talk about this dream, then deluged me with long stored-up feelings related to her traumatic discovery. She drew pictures of the murder, pictures of the house, pictures of the police station, even pictures of her old neighborhood, which she never saw again after being taken away the day it happened. She remembered and talked about actual conversations that took place that day. She even remembered being afraid of the police when they came, somehow feeling that she had done something wrong. She began to dream a great deal about her old friends, her old house, and especially about her mother. As she worked through her grief, she became much calmer and enjoyed a marked improvement in her family relationships.

Sometimes the death of a pet causes grief and mixed emotions. Janet, an eight-year-old, had a guinea pig who died. The child felt very guilty — a guilt that emerged only after I pursued the subject of the guinea pig's death. She had played with it quite a bit and her mother had mentioned that perhaps this was the cause of its death. I told her that when I worked in the schools we had guinea pigs in our class and the children always played with them. They fed them, changed the paper, held them, petted them, loved them. Possibly they died a little sooner than they would have if they'd never been touched; but the guinea pigs enjoyed the touching, and the children gained more by loving them than by merely observing them in a sterile cage. Janet began to cry and asked if she could draw a picture of her pet to show me what it looked like. Under the picture she wrote, "Squeaky, my love." We talked about her feelings and she said good-bye to the pet depicted in her drawing, telling it "I'm sorry I didn't get to take you to school like I promised you." When the session was over she gave me the picture to keep — she didn't need it any more.

A ten-year-old boy named Brad came into a session one day, obviously upset. He had witnessed an accident, and since it was uppermost in his mind, we spent the session dealing with it. He drew an elaborate picture of the accident, complete with ambulance, police car, and fire trucks. He labeled each detail, even showing the hospital where he imagined the in-

WINDOWS TO OUR CHILDREN

jured were taken. I wrote on his picture as he dictated, "There was a big accident one day in San Pedro, California. A fire engine and police car and an ambulance from Hoover Hospital. There was a big accident. Four cars rolled over. One almost fell off a cliff. The police helped the ones who were not so much injured, but the firemen and doctors helped the very badly injured ones. One person was killed in car number two. The rest were just injured." He labeled his picture "An Upsetting Accident."

Through this picture we began to talk about some of his fears and anxieties about accidents and death. He said that after he had seen this accident he worried a lot about riding in a car. Brad needed to talk about the accident and his feelings. His parents, who were with him at the time, were upset too, but they hushed him up and would never let him talk about it. I could sense his relief at getting his feelings out to someone who would listen.

A boy named Greg, age nine, came in saying he needed to draw something. He drew a scene involving a train and a moving van. This was his story, which he dictated to me:

"Once I was walking on the sidewalk. It was a sunny day and I saw a train go by on a bridge and I said, "I wish I was on that train." I'd like to go to England (my whole family) on an airplane. There are a lot of cars on the train. I counted each one and the train went very fast. It seemed like all the cars were going slow as I was watching them. Then I saw a police car go by and I saw a moving van truck and the light was green and they had giant fat poles holding up the railroad tracks. There are people on the train moving to Michigan and the Allied Van truck is bringing the furniture there. The boy's name is John and he was glad he was moving. The police car is going to the station."

I found out then that Greg was moving, but unlike "John" in his story, he was not glad. He was frightened and anxious. His mother was from England and often talked about moving back there; this was another source of anxiety for him.

Another boy, age ten, was brought in because his mother was terminally ill. The parents had talked openly with their children about the illness, but this child refused to participate in the discussions. He would generally make up some excuse to leave the room. The mother felt very sad about this; she wanted and needed to say many things to her son. In my usual direct, though low-keyed, manner, I brought up the mother's illness. It took a couple of sessions before he responded. One day, as we worked with clay, his feelings poured out.

Divorce is a common stress experience for children. Usually children are aware of problems between their parents long before the actual separation. Though parents find it difficult to level with their children when they are having marital problems, the children are extremely sensitive to the strained relationship.

I think it's impossible to protect children from the trauma of divorce. They become very frightened about impending split-ups: Where will they live? What will happen? Will things change? Is it their fault? They imagine terrors far beyond the actual situation. Richard Gardner's book, *The Boys' and Girls' Book About Divorce*, helps dispel some of the confusion that children may have. I recommend it as an excellent guide to give parents some insight into the kinds of feelings their children may be having. In his book, *Psychotherapy with Children of Divorce*, Gardner offers a good summary of the kind of advice a therapist might need to give parents who are anxious about how to protect their children from unnecessary trauma.

I think parents need to recognize that their children will be sharing some of the intense feelings surrounding a divorce. Often children keep their feelings well hidden because they don't want to cause their parents any more grief and pain. There is no way to protect children from these feelings any more than from feelings in response to anything else. They are entitled to have feelings, and their feelings need to be expected, acknowledged, accepted, and respected.

Kelly's mother was concerned because her seven-year-old daughter was displaying worrisome behaviors since her parents' separation. She was having nightmares and waking at night, giving her teachers trouble at school, fighting with her sister more than usual, acting whiny, and crying often over little things. Much of Kelly's work with me involved her father in some way. When I asked her to draw her family, she said, "I don't want to make my dad because it reminds me of when my mom and dad were together." This statement opened the way for us to talk about what it was like when they lived together.

At the next session she placed a girl in the dollhouse after carefully setting up the furniture. She said, "This girl lives alone. Her mother and dad were killed in the war." Then we talked about her feelings of loneliness for her dad.

Another time she built a house in the sand tray, put people in it, then had dinosaurs attack and kill all the people. At this point Kelly was able to express some of her own anger at what had happened.

A little five-year-old girl whose parents had just separated made a scene in the sand involving family figures and wild animals. The lion attacked the father figure and Janie buried him in the sand, remarking, "The father was killed and now all they had was Mommy."

What was that like for them?

Janie: Sad. Everyone cried.

Did you cry when your daddy moved to another house?

Janie: Yes.

You miss him a lot.

Janie: Yes . . . But I get to see him and he takes me places.

Another child, age eight, was able to express her feelings about her parents' divorce when I asked her to draw, in scribbly colors, one thing that she felt was bad about the divorce, one thing that was good, one thing that was somewhere in between, and one thing that was of her own choosing. She divided the paper into four sections and asked me to label the sections, "Bad, Good, All Right, and In Between." Under "Bad" she scribbled in black and dictated, "Not having dinner and being together when we go to bed." Under "Good" she scribbled in pink and dictated, "We see him more often and do things." Under "In Between" she scribbled in blue and dictated, "Sometimes I feel it's all right and sometimes I don't," and finally, under "All Right" she scribbled in turquoise and dictated, "Divorce is OK because they weren't happy together."

Later, when I asked this same child to draw a picture of the worst thing in her life and the nicest thing in her life, she drew a large picture of a building and wrote, "The worst thing in my life is having to go to school," and for the nicest she drew a picture of herself standing next to her friend and on the other side of the paper her mother and father. She wrote, "The nicest thing in my life is having friends to play with and having parents." At this point she looked up at me, smiled, and said, "Even if they are divorced!"

Physical Symptoms

An example of the child taking care of himself is the bed-wetter. I tell this child and his parents that his wetting the bed is a sign of health! Some time ago this child was unable to express what he needed to in one way, so he began to do it another way. Perhaps if he had not found a way to express himself by wetting the bed, he would have done it by getting asthma or developing eczema. I don't think it's merely coincidental that many of the bed-welters I have worked with are very easygoing, amiable children who don't express much anger.

The mother of a child I had been working with complained to me that her son was expressing much verbal anger since he had been seeing me, and so he certainly was not getting better. She felt that since he was angry, he must be unhappy. I asked her if he was still wetting his bed, walking in his sleep, and having nightmares that woke the whole — the actions that prompted her to bring him into therapy. She seemed puzzled, then said, "Oh, those! He hasn't been doing those things for some time!"

I approach bed-wetting, as well as other physical manifestations, in several ways. For one, I want the parents — and sometimes the whole family — to share their feelings about the situation. Also, I attempt to give the responsibility of the body back to its owner: the child is responsible for the bed-wetting. Furthermore, I want to help the child experience the physical symptom as much as possible. Finally, I want to help the child learn a more suitable way to express whatever it is he needs to express. I do not attempt to establish the original cause of the bed-wetting. I'm not interested in his toilet training experience. I'm much more interested in his present process — his way of being in his life today.

Of utmost importance is a first session with parents and child. Later, if I feel that others in the family are involved, a family session is important. Everyone has lots of feelings about the bed-wetter that may or may not have anything to do with the bed-wetting itself. It is necessary that these feelings come out and be shared. Most parents have run the gamut in trying to solve the bed-wetting dilemma: from being kind and understanding to yelling and screaming, from making the kid wash his own sheets to ignoring the whole thing. There are many, many feelings churning around in everyone — worry, shame, guilt, anxiety, resentment, fear, anger, sadness. Most of these feelings are not shared directly, they come out in a great many other ways. It is no wonder that the child, who generally cannot express feelings directly anyway, has to keep on wetting his bed. No child wants to wet the bed. Sometimes parents actually imagine that the child purposely wants to wake up in a wet, cold, smelly, uncomfortable bed to get back at them.

The next step is giving the child responsibility for his own bed-wetting. This is a very important prerequisite for stopping. I tell him that he is doing this to take care of himself: he is doing it, not anyone else. It becomes openly clear that he does not want to continue, even if he *has* yelled defiantly, "I don't care," or has taken on a casually unconcerned stance. Furthermore, it is important for the parents to understand that it is the child who is responsible, not they. He wakes up in the wet bed; they do not. He can learn to change his own bed, wash his own sheets. If they want to do this for him, they must take responsibility for that choice. If he is too young (though most children are brought in for this problem at a fairly competent age) he can ask for the help he needs. The parents must learn that bed-wetting is not an area for reward or punishment, approval or disapproval. Praise is not helpful if he does not wet his bed; neither are recriminations if he does. (We generally don't praise a child for not having a headache nor do we call him a stupid idiot if he does.)

Once it is clear who is responsible for the bed-wetting, the next step is working toward helping the child *experience* his body and his bed-wet-

Specific Problem Behaviors

ting. I first give the child a notebook to record his bed-wetting. This helps the child to become more conscious and aware of what he is doing. A curious thing happens when one records any undesired behavior: it automatically reduces itself. If you use a golf counter to record each time you notice yourself biting your nails, you will bite your nails less. As soon as the child begins to keep a record of his bed-wetting instances, they reduce dramatically. If a child is adept at writing I may ask him to record in his notebook words and phrases that describe the feeling of waking up in his wet bed. I often ask children to paint the feeling of being in a wet bed: As we work on these pictures, feelings begin to emerge. George von Hilsheimer in *How to Live with Your Special Child*, writes about an interesting method of helping kids become aware of their bodies while urinating in their sleep. He offered the bed-wetters money for wetting the bed, thus getting the kids to consciously attempt to wet their beds.

Helping bed-wetting children become aware of their bodies is an important part of the therapeutic procedure for them. We do many kinds of body exercises including breathing, meditation, movement, games. Knowing their bodies and learning mastery and control is satisfying, exciting, and essential.

Sometimes the bed-wetting *increases* for a brief period during some phase of the therapy. One boy wet his bed much more often for a while as his parents withdrew from involving themselves in the bed-wetting drama. Perhaps he was testing his parents to see if they would keep their bargain to let him have responsibility for the situation (they did), or perhaps he was giving himself permission to fully experience his bed-wetting.

The last, and most important, step is to help the child express his feelings about bed-wetting and other relevant aspects of his living. It is interesting to note that the child often continues the bed-wetting behavior even if the original event or events, real or imagined, that led to bed-wetting are no longer present. The body once received a message to wet the bed, and since then the right circuits have not been located for receiving a new message. The child's bed-wetting will stop as he begins to take control of himself, and as he finds new ways of expressing his feelings. He will always have feelings to express, even if everything is now wonderful in his family.

I have discussed the issue of bed-wetting in some detail here because it is such a common problem. I consider working with bed-wetters not

WINDOWS TO OUR CHILDREN

much different from working with children with other physical manifestations of psychological problems, though of course I do use some variations depending on the particular problem.

Some children defecate in their pants during the day, and this is a special kind of problem. Everyone around them is aware of the problem because of the smell. Often these children suffer from constipation, holding in their bowel movements for days at a time and suffering from abdominal pains as a result. They will mess their pants at odd times and often hide their underwear from their parents. I am never sure what exactly causes a child to be encropetic. But I do explain to the child that it is some expression of his body's quest for health. The feces drop because the body is aware of the toxicity of the waste products, and the initial withholding is a substitute for expression of some kind.

The procedure for working with children who are struggling with this problem is much the same as that for bed-wetters. Often I will guide the sessions to give maximum opportunity for expression of withheld feelings of anger. Many of the children I have seen who have this problem are hostile, sarcastic, highly verbal, argumentative. But they never seem to get all of their angry feelings out.

I have sometimes been incorrect pursuing this premise of withheld anger, however. I worked with a ten-year-old girl for quite some time, offering her many experiences with clay, the Bataca, puppets. Much anger did emerge; but the problem persisted. There began to be times of improvement, but any stress situation immediately brought on the problem full force. In one session through a story-telling clue, I sensed that she was feeling fearful. This was the first time that fear had come through. I found subsequently that she had some very deep fears which she kept carefully hidden. One was a fear of drowning, even though she knew how to swim and showed no outward fear of going swimming. No one, not even her parents, knew of this fear! We thoroughly explored all aspects of this fear area. She had no memory at all of ever experiencing a problem in water or of knowing anyone close to her that did.

One day, on a hunch, I did a fantasy with her, asking her to imagine being a two-year-old sitting on a toilet. We did this lightly, with laughter and humor. She was smiling with her eyes closed listening to my voice while I guided the fantasy. Suddenly she sat upright, eyes wide open, and said she was afraid she would fall into the toilet and be flushed away along with her bowel movement. She was extremely excited by this discovery, feeling certain that this was the original cause of her problem. We explored the fears of a little two-year-old faced with a huge toilet and the mysteries of plumbing. I drew a quick sketch of a little child on a big toilet, and she reassured the picture-child as a mother might.

This may or may not have been the original cause of her problem. Perhaps this child simply needed some way to give herself final permission to move on to new growth. Her fear of drowning, a secret she kept well hidden, was real, and she experienced great relief in sharing this fear with, me and, when she felt ready, with her parents. She began to take responsibility for a program of toilet-sitting and found that she could have her bowel movements with almost precise regularity.

Other kinds of physical symptoms that might bring a child into therapy include headaches, stomachaches, tics, allergies, asthma. Sometimes such physical problems come up during the course of the work even when they were not the original reason for entering therapy.

A sixteen-year-old young woman complained of a big knot at the back of her neck. I asked her to draw a picture of this knot on paper. She drew her neck with a large round black spot on it. I asked her to unravel the black knot on another piece of paper. She grabbed the crayon and began to scribble furiously. I stopped her, and asked her to do it very slowly, concentrating on the knot and her feelings as she did it. She began to draw her unraveling very deliberately. When she finished the drawing, the knot in her neck was gone.

Although we didn't focus on any particular content during this process, my client learned something about paying attention to pain, and about the results of experiencing it rather than avoiding it. She learned that she controlled the muscles that gave her the pain, and that she could take the pain away as well.

An eleven-year-old boy came into a group announcing that he couldn't stay because he had a bad stomachache. I asked him to tell me a little bit about his pain, and asked where it hurt.

Ken: Here. I don't know.

Tell me what it feels like.

WINDOWS TO OUR CHILDREN

Ken: It feels like a knot and it's squeezing me, and it really hurts. (His voice was sad and tearful, as he said this.)

You sound very sad to me.

Ken: I am. What's happening to me is sad.

I'd like to hear about it.

Ken: It's my father. He hasn't been drinking, but he's so nervous! He takes everything out on me — yells at me when I haven't done anything, throws things at me, hits me. It's just as bad as if he were drinking. He takes it out on me because I'm the oldest kid. It happened again today.

By then Ken was sobbing freely. After a while he said, "Maybe I'll stay a little longer." He stayed the whole session, stomachache forgotten. I'd like to add here that Ken was having stomachaches frequently. His mother would give him much attention because of them — take him to the doctor often, give him special food, and worry about his getting an ulcer. What she didn't do was listen to him and tune in to his feelings. Eventually Ken needed to learn to take care of himself in other ways besides giving himself stomachaches. He came to realize that this was one way — but not the only way — he could get lots of attention from his mother.

Carl, age thirteen, came into the session too tired to do anything. I asked him to draw a picture of his tiredness. Using brown, black, and dark purple, he drew a design representing his tiredness, "especially my shoulders." I then asked him to draw a picture of how he would feel if he were the opposite of tired. He drew two cylinders opposite each other, both very brightly colored, separated by a brown line resembling a mountain range. I asked him to conduct a dialogue between these two forms, which, he said, represented his hands and feet. His dialogue led to a desire to do something, go somewhere, mobilize his tired "old" body. He began to talk about his restlessness, his wish to be where he wasn't, his frustration with his life at home and at school. (Usually, Carl, a bed-wetter, announced everything was fine.)

Tammy, now fifteen, had begun to have mild seizures when she was twelve years old. She was referred to me by a neurologist who felt that her seizures were psychologically based. She seemed to behave in ways that eventually provoked her mother into rage. Her mother said, "If I talk to her she gets worse. She seems to force me into spanking her. She's done this for years. Almost like she likes to be hit! When I spank her she becomes calm, happy. When I don't, she keeps going until she has a seizure."

Tammy and I worked together for several weeks. One day, as she talked to me while fooling with clay, she began to tell me about something that happened between her mother and her that made her angry. Since she was already using the clay, I asked her to express her mad feeling through the clay. She looked down at the clay and then said she couldn't do that. I suggested that she draw a picture for me that would express her angry feelings. She agreed to this and drew a circle in the middle with the letters YEEEKE printed in it. This was a scream, she told me. She drew two red triangles. "These are devil ears. I feel like hitting someone super hard, like my brother." She drew two eyes with red and yellow zigzag lines coming out of them. "This is fire out of my eyes. My eyes get squinty and bother me." She drew some red, yellow, and blue lines. "This is fire in my throat. It hurts when I scream." She drew a black shape. "This is black smoke coming out of my ears. My ears get hot and clogged up." Tammy was consumed with angry feelings — violent feelings that filled her with guilt and fear. Gradually as we worked with her intense anger, first expressed so vividly through her picture, her need for punishment to the point of giving herself a seizure began to dissipate.

While I was working with a young woman one day, she slumped over and complained of intense menstrual cramps. I gave her a piece of modeling clay and asked her to fashion her uterus as she imagined it. When she finished I asked her to describe her uterus as if it could talk, to be the uterus and say what was happening. She said something like, "I am Cathy's uterus. I'm squeezing and squeezing until she can't stand it." She continued with this for a while, with my encouragement. When she finished she announced in amazement that the pain was gone. We talked about how tensing muscles to try to avoid pain often causes further pain. Being her uterus helped Cathy experience how she did this to herself.

Ellen, age sixteen, talked about a pain she experienced often, just below her chest. She had been to a doctor who could find no physical cause. She was having the pain at the moment. I asked her to close her eyes, go into the pain, and describe it to me.

Ellen: It feels like a hole just below my chest, like a deep empty hole. Like a slinky. It goes very deep. It's hard to describe.

WINDOWS TO OUR CHILDREN

Would you be willing to draw it?

Ellen: I can't draw.

Pretend you're only three years old and draw it. You can explain it to me as you go along.

Ellen: (Draws a spiral, circular, tunnel) I'll use black. Of course my tunnel is black. It's very deep, black, dark. It's endless. I don't know what's down there. This is me (tiny stick figure at edge of tunnel). I'm sitting on the edge feeling very small.

What does it feel like now — the pain?

Ellen: Well it's smaller, but that's how it is — it gets bigger and smaller. It can do that at any time.

Be the little figure and tell about yourself.

Ellen: Well, I'm sitting here on the edge of this tunnel. My knees are hunched up.

Sit on the floor and do that. Be the figure.

Ellen: (Sitting on floor with knees up, hugging knees, head down.) I'm hunched up, very small, sitting on the edge of a tunnel.

Can you see beyond the tunnel on the other side?

Ellen: No. But I know there's something out there. There's a lot out there but I can't get to it. (She begins to cry.)

What do you see if you look down the tunnel?

Ellen: I can't see much. It's very dark. I don't know what's down there but I imagine it's very scary things.

Close your eyes and imagine going down into the tunnel. (She closes her eyes.) What's happening?

Ellen: I didn't go down. I can't go down there. It's too scary. I'm still sitting here on the edge.

OK. You don't have to go down there. I'd like you to be the tunnel now. Describe yourself.

Ellen: I'm a tunnel inside of Ellen. I make her hurt. I am deep and endless and powerful and strong.

What are you feeling now, Ellen?

Ellen: I feel strong and powerful. I'm still with the tunnel.

We have to stop today. Next time maybe you'd like to explore your fears about going into the tunnel so we can see what's in there. Remember, it's your tunnel and the tunnel feelings are yours too.

Ellen: Yeah. Oops. Now I feel like that little figure again!

There was still more to do, but this was a good beginning.

Sixteen-year-old Beth had suffered from severe lassitude for several months. She had no energy. She had been given a clean bill of health from her physician but somehow was too tired for anything more than to go to school, do a few household chores, and collapse. She had no energy left for things she formerly enjoyed doing: sports, art projects, going out with friends. I used many expressive techniques to give Beth an opportunity to emerge from beneath her shell of inertness. As we worked, many tightly held-in feelings emerged. It takes a lot of energy to close off feelings, hold feelings in.

Probably the most revealing exercise was the *I Am* — list. Beth spent a whole session working on *I Am* — sentences: I am a daughter. I am a student. I am tall. I am tired a lot. I am afraid of being lonely. I am afraid of my feelings . . . .

Beth read her *I Am* — list to me at the next session and wept. Three months after our first session, Beth worked with clay, making an object with her eyes closed. She made an animal that she said could not see and could not move, but that felt happy and peaceful. I asked her how she could help the animal to see. She made holes in the animals, "to let the light through. These are good holes that let light through me, and let new awareness come through." I asked her about helping the animal to move. "Well, I need Beth to pick me up and make me go," she said as she moved the animal along the table. She smiled and looked at me. "Hey, I think I'll go home and make a kite." And she did — flew it, too.

Insecurity; Hanging On; Excessive Pleasing

The term "insecure" is widely used in describing children who behave in many different ways. The dictionary defines this word as "not safe from danger, feeling more anxiety than seems warranted, unprotected." I view most of the children I see in therapy as insecure, though they express this in many different ways.

Sometimes I see children who literally hang on to people, thus driving them away. As people move away, they try to hang on all the more.

WINDOWS TO OUR CHILDREN

These children physically grab people as if to ease their insecure feelings and make themselves feel safer.

I first saw Melissa when she was five years old. She was a classic hanger-on, clinging to everyone she could, to the point where she drove people away. Even her mother could no longer tolerate her hanging on. Children her own age were uncomfortable with her excessive touching and hugging of them, and withdrew from her.

Melissa could not draw a picture without asking me continually "Is this good? What color should I use? Do you like this circle?" and so forth. With each question I would smile and she would resume working, seemingly content with my reaction. When she used the sand tray, she would take almost all the baskets of objects down, placing them on her lap and on the floor near her feet. She would do the same thing with the toys when she played, seeming to need the security of as many things close at hand as possible. When she first heard her own voice on the tape recorder she did not recognize it. "Who is that?" she asked, and when I told her it was her own voice, that she had just recorded it, she seemed truly amazed and wanted to hear it over and over. She was captivated by a large drawing that I did of her one day. She looked in the mirror when I asked, "What color is your hair," and then watched with delight as I drew in her straight brown hair.

After about five sessions a change began to take place. She seemed to begin to see herself as a person separate from the others in her life. She began to express feelings, thoughts, and ideas of her own. When asked to paint her family, she now painted with absorption without her former need for constant reassurance. She talked about each member: "My mom plays and gets silly . . . My dad is mean to my mom and they fight . . . Me, I always stare when they fight. I don't like it. I get afraid."

When asked to paint something that made her sad, she painted herself sitting in her room, and dictated, "I don't like to sit in my room. I feel bad when I have to sit in my room sometimes." When we talked about what happened to cause her mother to send her to her room, she said, "My mom gets mad because she said I won't do what she said, that I always want to tell her what to do." I asked her if she liked to tell people what to do. "Yeah! But my friends don't like it." We then played a game where we took turns telling each other what to do, much to her delight.

Specific Problem Behaviors

Later when asked to paint anything she wanted, she painted a boy and dictated, "This is David. He is mean. I don't like David. He hits me a lot." Then she painted a picture of herself and dictated, "I'm very mad here. I'm very, very mad when my mommy doesn't let me do what I want to do. I hate when my mother calls me in. I hate it. The end."

As Melissa began to talk about herself, her feelings, her likes and dislikes, as she began to make clear statements about herself and her life, her hanging-on behavior markedly decreased. It seemed that as she began to know herself better, to have a sense of herself, to feel conscious of herself, she did not need to clutch at other people to verify her existence.

The child, (or adult) who must physically hold on to others has such a vague sense of self that she feels OK only if she can merge with someone else. She exists only in a state of confluence with another person. Being separate is a frightening and strange concept to her. She doesn't know where she begins and ends. She confuses herself with others, in her intense need for identity.

Working with such children involves progressive experiences of strengthening the self. We need to bring the child back to herself, introduce her to herself, give her an identity she can recognize. We may begin with sensory activities; move on to body exercises and games that involve becoming familiar with feelings, self-image, and body image, and finally integrate all of this with experiences in making choices, expressing opinions, determining her needs, wants, likes, and dislikes, and learning how to verbally make her needs, wants, and opinions known.

As we work, material emerges to be dealt with, for this child is not a nonentity; she is a real, live, important and unique human being who for the time being has lost herself. Once she begins to find herself, her contact skills improve until she no longer feels the need to hang on to other people. The hanging on was her former way of surviving; she now has other options, other ways of being.

Children who go to great lengths to please adults, and who are seemingly overly obedient have similar insecure feelings. They seek approval in a way that is often highly reinforced by the adults in their lives. It is not unusual to see adults who are still living according to these childhood patterns, who can never say "No" to anything, who never seem to have an opinion or thought of their own, who are so compulsively obedient and "good" that we may find them dull and boring to be with.

What we are dealing with here is an overbalance on the "good" side of one's personality. All children want approval; they all have it within their capacity to be "good" and follow instructions and to do the "right thing." They also have it within their capacity to be angry, to rebel, to disagree, to stand on their own feet and express their views when they disagree. We need to help the kids who are "too good" to find themselves, to find those other sides of themselves that seem scary and frightening to them. Then they can freely choose to express themselves in whatever way they want to, rather than being locked into one mode of expression. The child who is intent on pleasing uses up much of her energy in this way. She is constantly directing energy outward rather than meeting her own needs.

It is up to the therapist to provide the child with experiences for self-expression, for this child modestly and unobtrusively waits for you to tell her what to do. Activities that will be effective involve those in which the self can be identified, enhanced, and appreciated. "Draw something you like or want, a place you enjoy." Giving them the opportunity to make choices — "Here are two games; which one shall we play?" — is important. Gradually we move in to help them express their assertiveness.

Fourteen-year-old Frank was an "over pleaser." He had lived with a variety of relatives since his mother and father died in an accident when he was seven. Now his sister, about eight years older, had married and wanted very much to have Frank live with her. Her husband was agreeable, and they made every effort to make his life comfortable. His sister came in for counseling with him because she felt that her brother was just too good. There was no natural give-and-take at home. He did everything that was asked of him, never spoke unless spoken to, never complained about anything. She said that she and her husband had assured him that no matter what happened, their home was his home too. His overly pleasing manner was causing a strain in the household.

Frank was very noncommunicative with me as well. I could feel my own frustration at his complete acquiescence. But making use of expressive techniques made all the difference in my work with Frank. As a rosebush he said, "I'm in front of a house . . . it might be abandoned. I haven't seen the people. Maybe I'm wild. Maybe someone once took care of me. I'm in the middle of nowhere. I don't know about my roots. I have thorns. I don't know if I'm growing. There are weeds around me. I'm not lonely... I don't feel lonely. The weeds keep me company." I could almost feel his reluctance to own any of these statements for himself. I very gently repeated each statement as I had written them from his dictation. " 'It might be abandoned.' Do you ever feel that you were abandoned?" Hesitantly, haltingly, he finally answered, "Well, yes. I used to feel that way when I was little. After my parents were killed."

Frank told this story, using the raft card in the *Make a Picture Story* set: "There's a raft. On it is a man who's dying, a priest, a boy, a lady, a dog. They've been shipwrecked. They're floating in the ocean, but they'll find land after a long time. The dying man's relatives are crying."

Frank, which one are you? Be one of those characters.

Frank: (after looking at the picture with figures placed on it, for a long time) I'm the dog.

Tell me about what's going on with you as the dog.

Frank: Well, I'm watching and waiting to see what will happen. There's nothing I can do. I'm afraid. I'm very afraid.

Does any of that remind you of anything in your life?

Frank: (looking at me, sighing) Yes. There wasn't anything I could do when my parents died. I was so afraid. I just had to drift along wherever I was sent.

Eventually Frank could express his grief, his anger, and his fear about "being sent away." He began to risk being himself, not only with me, but in his world.

Occasionally I will see a child who appears to be so fragile that I think she might break. This child is a mere shadow of herself. She needs all the skills at my command to help her regain and strengthen herself. I begin with safe, nonthreatening experiences. At first she may need to be able to take back what she does — erase the chalk board picture, smear the finger paint design, wipe clear the sand tray. Gradually she will begin to allow more permanence in her expressions. As she can allow her expressions to begin to come through, she will often appear to become physically sturdier. Tara was such a child. As Tara, thin, fragile, fearful, began to express herself through painting and stories and clay and sand, she seemed to grow physically sturdier and stronger as well. Games involving body movement were an important aspect of her therapy. She seemed to take delight in discovering her body and all that it could do. She began to take delight in herself, in living.

The Loner

Some children who are loners are resourceful enough to keep themselves busy, and to find their own way. They may spend long hours sorting stamp collections or pursuing any number of other hobbies. Some children lose themselves in books (though this is becoming a rarity) and others watch TV a lot. The resourceful loners are not the ones I usually see. Though feeling comfortable when alone shows a healthy self-assurance, we all need a balance in our lives — times for being alone and times for being with other people.

Most children who spend most of their leisure alone out of choice (in contrast to those who have no playmates available) do so because they fear being rejected by others. Children who are brought into therapy generally have some kind of presenting problem other than their aloneness. These are the not-so-resourceful ones who pester their parents, are sullen and argumentative, are hyperactive, engage in aggressive or antisocial behavior, hate to go to school or do poorly in school, or are unusually withdrawn. In the course of the therapy we often find not only that they spend much time alone but that they have no close friends and are quite lonely.

Children who are loners often remain so into adulthood. Many children deny vehemently that they have a problem relating to their peers, and it is certainly true that the last thing they need is a parent who nags them to "get out and make friends." They need to have an atmosphere where they can be accepted for who they are; this alone can sometimes give them the strength and courage to begin to seek out others and experiment with making relationships on their own.

Many of the problem loners secretly feel different from everyone else. Sometimes they feel so different that they do the opposite, trying to act as much like everyone else as humanly possible. Of course at some period most children go to great lengths to conform, to be like each other or like what they imagine each other to be. Even those that go against the "norm" usually do so in clusters. Wanting to be like others indicates a search for

Specific Problem Behaviors

self-identity as a member of some desired community. But because the loners feel that everyone else is so very different from them, they face a dilemma.

One of the main tasks in working with these children and their families is to emphasize that uniqueness is to be treasured. Too often parents want all their children to be alike, emphasizing conformity. Parents need to respect the uniqueness of each child.

Most children experiment with a variety of ways of being, until they come into their own. But some children need help, and these usually misbehave in ways that signal this need. Unfortunately, there may be no one around at the time who can read the signals. As we work with these children to enhance their self-esteem, strengthen their self-identify, and promote self-support, they begin to learn how to relate to other children.

One of the most exciting exercises I have done with children, to dramatize the fascination and desirability of uniqueness, is the orange experience. I first read about this in George Brown's book, *Human Teaching for Human Learning*. In one group of eleven and twelve-year-olds that I tried it with, the kids talked about it for months. I brought in a bag of oranges, one for each child. We looked at our oranges, smelled them, compared their shapes and markings, held them, tossed them back and forth in our hands, and did whatever else we could think of to do with an orange short of eating it. Then we peeled them. Each of us tasted the rind, inside and outside, and explored the texture of the inside surface with our fingertips. Then we carefully peeled the remnants of the white part of the skin from the fruit, talking about what this felt like to us. We broke our oranges into sections, then felt one section, smelled it, licked it, and finally ate it. The most exciting, interesting part of the exercise came next — trading sections with each other. We discovered that no two sections tasted the same! I think my own excitement over this discovery was the highest in the group. One section was sweeter, one was juicier, one was tarter, one was somewhat dry, and so forth; but they were all enjoyable, and all the more delicious! We had a lot of fun with this experiment and easily slid into a discussion of the children in our group — their differences and similarities, each wonderful.

In working with children who are loners, I do many of the same things that I do for the children who need to regain a sense and appreciation of self. Further than this, I need to encourage these children to experiment with reaching out to others. They would like to reach out and join in but they are fearful and do not know how to. So I need to deal with the fear, and I need to help them experiment with new ways of being.

Adam, age eleven, was a child with no friends. He was bright and arrogant and seemed not to care that he spent most of his time alone. His mother sought help for him because she considered him to be a "discipline problem." He never did what she asked, he was sullen and rude to her, and he argued and fought constantly with his younger brother. When I asked her if he had friends, she said, "No, he doesn't seem to have any friends and he doesn't seem to want any."

Adam was quite resistant to coming in for therapy. In our first session alone together he complained of a headache and said he thought it was dumb for his mother to spend money for him to see me. I asked him to draw a picture of his headache. With great amusement he drew a scribbly picture with a variety of colors. I asked him what his biggest problem was with his mother. "She never believes anything I say," he answered immediately. "How about your father?" I asked. (His parents were divorced.) "He's OK, but he's always thinking about his own troubles."

Adam participated, with an air of amusement, in the projective techniques I suggested. Each time he did so, he revealed more and more of himself. As we worked together it became clear that he felt rejected, unworthy. At one session he said to me, "I'm like a turtle with a hard shell. If I talk about things inside of me, people yell at me. So I just keep inside my shell." As Adam came more and more out of his shell with me, he began to feel better about himself and stronger about reaching out to other children. We had some joint sessions with each of his parents, and as his communication with them improved, Adam's disposition and family interaction improved markedly.

Seth's father was in the Navy, and they moved a lot. Each time he made friends, he soon had to say good-bye to them. By the time he was nine years old he had stopped making the effort to get to know the kids in a new neighborhood, and he would reject any overtures other children made toward him. He was referred for counseling by his school for his sullenness and refusal to participate in anything.

Seth eagerly responded to our sessions. He enjoyed painting, working with clay, making sand tray scenes, telling stories, participating vigorously. Out of this activity came his deep feelings of loneliness. His father was often away at sea for months at a time, and his mother had difficulties herself in adjusting to these separations and uprootings. We talked a lot about the pain of making friends and then leaving them. As Seth began to feel his own self-support through self-expression, he presented this idea to me: "I'm lucky that I can get to meet so many people and see so many different places." Six months later the family moved to Japan, and I subsequently received a letter from Seth telling me excitedly about his new school, the new things he was doing, and the new friends he was making.

Loneliness

Loneliness comes up over and over in my work with children. Who among us can look back into our childhoods and not recognize this feeling? Yet I have found that in their initial defensiveness, children will rarely admit feeling lonely.

Children who are considered poorly adjusted in their environments are especially lonely. The therapeutic process seems blocked until this feeling is expressed openly in some way, either verbally or through expressive techniques. Clark Moustakas says in the preface to his book, *Loneliness*:

> . . . . loneliness is a condition of human life, an experience of being human which enables the individual to sustain, extend, and deepen his humanity. Man is ultimately and forever lonely whether living in isolation or illness, the sense of absence caused by a loved one's death, or the piercing joy experienced in triumphant creation. I believe it is necessary for every person to recognize his loneliness, to become intensely aware that, ultimately, in every fibre of his being, man is alone — terribly, utterly alone. Efforts to overcome or escape the existential experience of loneliness can result only in self-alienation. When man is removed from a fundamental truth of life, when he successfully evades and denies the terrible loneliness of

individual existence, he shuts himself off from one significant avenue of his own self growth.

Moustakas believes we are inevitably lonely — that we all have a basic existential loneliness to contend with. Most of us find loneliness difficult to accept, and go to great lengths to escape the pain of our lonely feelings. We, as adults, are adept at finding ways to submerge our loneliness, such as with incessant activity. I agree with Moustakas that when we do this, we often alienate or lose our selves. Some of us are not comfortable with the self that we are and would rather not know it, face it, look at it, be with it, so we frantically avoid being with it in any way we can.

Children, groping for self-identity, certainly do not know how to cope with their existential loneliness. I believe that children feel especially lonely because deep down they feel different, and they are not comfortable with, accepting of, or appreciative of, their own specialness. Children have their own ways of covering up their feelings of terrifying loneliness. The methods they choose are often highly contradictory to our society's concept of nice, normal, conforming behavior. To make matters worse, their antisocial behavior usually serves to further alienate and isolate them, thereby causing them to increase their defensive, protective cover. This in turn promotes further isolation, and so the cycle perpetuates itself.

Suzanne Gordon, in her book *Lonely in America*, sums up her study of the loneliness of children and adolescents this way:

> For these children loneliness comes as an overwhelming awareness that there is no support anywhere — that people upon whom they depend for survival, warmth, affection and interest, can provide only the most meager attention to their needs. In this situation children also feel helpless. They have nowhere else to go, there is no one else to turn to, and no one, including themselves can meet their needs. The child's response to this overwhelming sense of loneliness is anxiety. In the case of small children, anxiety and fear cause them to cling to the mothering figure. (p. 48)

Specific Problem Behaviors

I think that children often feel helpless and anxious because they have trouble expressing their empty and lonely feelings to anyone. Those children who come into therapy can be looked upon as the lucky ones — for here they have an opportunity to surface these feelings. I have had children express lonely feelings in a variety of ways, not necessarily using the word "lonely." Even very young children have confessed the feeling of wanting to die or to kill themselves. I hear this as an expression not only of a deep inner despair, but of loneliness as well.

Loneliness is often an ally of the generally futile quest for happiness. Fairy tales all end with, "and they lived happily ever after." Many of us spend a lifetime searching for some vague state called happiness, as if when that's found we will have crossed some border into a new state in life where we will never again feel sorrow or pain or hurt. We have told ourselves that to feel "unhappy" is sick. We talk about disturbed children as "unhappy," equating this with disease, something that needs to be cured.

An incident out of my own life had a lasting impact on me. When our mother was suddenly killed in an accident, my brother and I flew separately to a sorrowful meeting at my mother's house. I was in the depths of depression, for this was the third very close person in my life to die, and my own son was at this time terminally ill. As my brother and I went through the motions of taking care of everything, going through my mother's belongings, making necessary arrangements, at one point I tearfully said to him, "This is it. I can't take another thing. If anything else happens to me I will give up." My brother, who had gone through the same sorrows as I, and more, looked at me in surprise and said, "Violet! What a ridiculous thing to say! The longer you live, the more things you'll experience, including the painful things. Something's *always* going to happen!" And with that he ended the conversation. I have never forgotten what he said, though he probably has.

If the happiness experienced in looking forward to things becomes the dominant form of happiness in a person's life, she has set a cruel trap for herself. As I learned to concentrate my life experiences in the present, rather than dwelling on past memories and elegant fantasies of the future, I have learned that I *can* take it.

The younger a child is, the more she still has the capacity to live in the here and now. So when I work with children who express feelings of loneliness, I want to help them regain that skill of fully experiencing themselves rather than clinging to feelings of helplessness. I think that through self-acceptance and self-strengthening, children can learn to mobilize their energies, their life forces, to meet some of their own needs.

Holding in feelings results in loneliness. The less one is able to express what is going on inside, the more isolated and alienated one feels. Each time feelings go unexpressed, the protective wall or shell gets thicker and the feeling of loneliness swells behind the barrier.

Children whose feelings aren't listened to and acknowledged feel lonely. Their feelings are their very core, their very being, and if their feelings are rejected, the child feels rejected. So when a child says, "I feel lonely when I get mad — being mad makes me feel very lonely," it is because he faces a world of people who will not remain in contact with him as he expresses his angry feelings. He is admonished, renounced, punished, avoided, and all this thrusts him into isolation.

When I, as a therapist, provide means for a child to express his feelings openly, to hear them and accept them, he feels less lonely and begins to see the world as a friendlier place. He can begin to reach out again and make connections with others.

I think that one of the reasons children seek each other out and need each other so much is that they feel that perhaps other children will have some understanding of what they go through and feel like. In groups of children with whom I work, I am privileged to hear some of the things they talk about with each other. Usually we don't realize the scope and depth of what children think and feel because they are so very careful to censor what they say in front of the adults in their world.

The Child Who Is In and Out of Reality

I have had some experience with children who at times are lucid and contactful but who at other times just don't seem to make sense, have gone off into some world of their own.

Chris, age eleven, was such a boy. For a long time in our work together I had trouble making sense of what he said. I tried very hard to stay on his plane. Any one thing I might say would set him off into places I had difficulty going. He enjoyed working with clay, paints (especially finger paints), and the sand tray. He liked to tell stories, too. And his stories and sand tray creations and art work reflected a place I had difficulty understanding. Yet Chris' work appeared to have intent and purpose for him. Everything he did seemed to have some meaning for him.

Chris talked to me even though I didn't follow him. He smiled at me and greeted me warmly when he came for his sessions. Sometimes he would begin to tell me about something in his life that really made sense to me, then suddenly he would be off into another realm. He might say, "My older brother came home from college yesterday." Responding to the light in his eye I would say, "You seem to be glad." He would answer, "Yes, I am and when I was walking on my street I saw a big fire and light that shot up into the sky so big if you could get in it you could go across the ocean and it would make a big blast and then a lion came jumping in and I don't know where he came from and three kids at school shared lunches with me and did you ever see big fireworks that reached across the moon and light and my house is bigger than anything like that, and my brother came in with a swoosh...."

For a long time I didn't pull him back — I just went along with him, or stopped trying so hard and just listened. And then one day I said firmly, "Chris, you didn't answer my question. You are saying something that has nothing to do with my question." And he looked at me and answered it.

I know that Chris was very much afraid of his world. He had to leave it to feel safe. As he learned to know me and trust me, he was more and more able to stay on my earthly plane. Through many of our exercises he gained a strong sense of what he could do. It was important that I go with him, be with him where he wanted to be, needed to be. As he would paint his enigmatic paintings he would talk an equally enigmatic language, and I would listen to the sound of his voice, would watch his body and his face. I was able to respond to him on the basis of those observations. I could say to the sadness in his tone, "What you are telling me sounds sad." I could say to the vividness of his painting, "This place you made looks colorful and happy." I could say, the day he came in with shoulders hunched, "Something you didn't like must have happened to you today — you are not standing tall and straight." Chris gave immediate response to these remarks, casting sudden, swift glances of surprise, nodding in assent.

WINDOWS TO OUR CHILDREN

At this time I had a group of children about his age. I thought it would be good for him to come into the group now. He had no friends at home, and did not relate to kids his own age. He was in a special class at school and had no friends there, either.

Chris came into the group fearfully. He regressed into more and more "out of reality" behaviors. The children were astonished but took their cues from me and my co-therapist. When we made rounds he would say things no one could understand. We listened attentively and thanked him, sometimes having to remind him gently that we needed to move on. When we drew pictures, his were incomprehensible. He would show them and sometimes share them, though we could not follow. He made an effort to participate in everything in his way.

He developed a crush on one of the girls and wanted to sit by her, touch her, and hold her hand. This was most annoying to her and she would avoid him and move away. We knew that this had to be talked about openly. We asked the children to draw pictures of something that bugged them and something they liked about some person in the group. Sally drew a picture of Chris acting silly over her, as she described it. When she shared, with our encouragement, tears came into Chris' eyes. We had a good opportunity to accept her annoyance, accept his sadness, and talk about the reality of what was going on. The atmosphere was much more relaxed after this. Later we did an oral exercise similar to the picture exercise, and Sally said to Chris, "I like the fact that you don't bother me any more . . . I don't like it when you talk about things I don't understand." Many of the children shared that latter sentiment with him. They told him gently, kindly, caringly. He looked at them when they spoke to him, delighted that they saw him back.

Soon we noticed that when we drew pictures he drew two — one that was scribbly, puzzling to us, and one that was clearly in response to the directions.

One day we played a game in which each child was asked to be an animal. Chris said he was an alley cat with asthma. He crawled around the room purring and wanting to be petted. The children responded, to his delight. We asked him if he knew what asthma was. He said, "Yes! I've got a big block here (pointing to chest) and he can't breathe too good!" (He often said "he" when he meant "I.") We knew that he didn't have asthma, but we believed that he had a block in his chest. We knew we were getting closer to his expression of this block.

We began to notice that Chris was able to make more and more contact with us, and I began to insist on it. I felt that we had allowed him to ramble on meaninglessly (from our viewpoint) for along time. And so now when he did, I would firmly say, "I don't understand what you're saying, Chris. Say it again so I know what you're saying." Or, when he would begin and then go off into his own safe place, "Tell me what you are angry about or who you are angry at." (Anything to do with anger frightened him terribly and was sure to send him spinning.) I knew it was time to patiently, purposefully bring Chris back into the group with us whenever he "took off." I knew he could take it now.

At the end of each group session we would encourage final comments, reactions to the session, anything anyone wanted to say. One boy said one day, "I'm glad Chris is one of us now!" Asked to say this *to* Chris, he said, "I'm glad you're part of our group now. I'm glad you don't talk crazy the way you used to." Chris glowed, and the two of them walked out together, arms around each other.

Autism

I'm not going to write much about working with autistic children. This is certainly a subject that needs the attention of a whole book in itself. I have worked with autistic children only briefly, but I would like to share some interesting observations of some colleagues of mine who have had extensive experiences with severely autistic children.

Cathy Saliba found, after working with such children for some time, that they made their needs known readily but in ways that were easily overlooked: Needs were indicated in rather subtle ways that interfered with the prepared structure of a program. Saliba discovered that if she tuned in to what the child wanted to do, rather than forcing him to do what she had planned, some exciting things happened. For example, one boy, age five, stood in front of the full length wall mirror, ignoring her call to work on a puzzle with her. Instead of insisting that he come to her, she went to him, sat by the mirror without a word, and watched as he looked at himself and felt parts of his face. She realized that he was actually seeing himself. Suddenly he noticed that her reflection was in the mirror as well, and he was so delighted and excited that he settled right down into her lap. Twenty minutes had gone by and the teacher had said not one word, issued not one command. Saliba began naming the parts of his face, as he continued to point to them, looking in the mirror. But when he came to his mouth, she did not respond. He looked at her expectantly through the mirror and shouted, "mouth!" Saliba describes this process, which became a regular one with highly positive results, as follows:

> Up until that first day when Sean showed an interest in the mirror, I had planned what each student would do during my hours of contact with them. I knew exactly what puzzle would be done by which student at what time, and for how long. I believed that autistic children needed a lot of structure, and in essence, I was demanding them to perform what, when, how, where, and to what extent, I thought they needed all day long. When I allowed Sean that time in front of the mirror, I was taking a cue from him, which was, "Hey, I want to study my reflection, and I *like* doing it." From that time on, I was able to open myself up enough to see that Sean could make other needs and desires known. As a matter of fact, I just needed to let myself see and respond to those cues instead of always imposing my own demands on him.

And so Saliba began to experiment with *staying with* the children and found, through this method, that much learning took place. She also discovered to her great astonishment that each child knew much more than anyone realized. For example, one child could read the ads in many magazines. She began to use this as a base for teaching him to read other things. This kind of attention is difficult unless there are enough adults assigned to the class to allow one teacher to go with a child as the need arises.

Another friend of mine told me about using finger paint in a unique way with autistic children. The children often would get paint all over themselves. One day she "went" with this and painted parts of each child's face in front of the mirror, naming the parts as she did. The children were delighted, and after a while were able to do this to themselves as they looked in the mirror. Then they did it to the teacher. They not only were gaining a new sense of self, which they so sorely needed, but they were engaging in contactful, companionable behavior.

Ariel Malek experimented with an approach similar to Saliba's. She also found that staying with the child's process rather than with prescribed activities reaped far greater rewards. She says, "I may set up a lesson to teach the child the color red, but then become more focused on overcoming her resistance to participating." A balance between following the plans of the teacher/therapist and following the cues of the child must be carefully maintained. ". . . I am usually willing to drop the planned lesson in order to follow an important cue the child is giving me. I also believe that creating the opportunities for the child to have the upper hand in directing our interactions has great value."

It seems that the guidelines I use with more normal children also apply to autistic children. Begin where the child is. Stay with him. Take cues from him. Be alert to his process and *his* interests (rather than yours). Bring him back to his self-awareness over and over by providing many sensory activities such as water play, finger painting, sand play, and clay work. Saliba describes taking the children to the beach where they could smell the ocean, could see, feel, sit in, and roll in water and sand, and could feel the sun and air. Body work is essential — using mats, giving them massages, "wrestling" with them and encouraging them to wrestle with each other, using a trampoline and other playground equipment. These children need lots of opportunities to have controlled use of their bodies.

Although this kind of working is at a far less verbal level, feelings are there nonetheless. By watching the child's body language and facial expressions, the teacher/therapist can guess what the child is feeling and begin to reflect verbally to the child what she imagines those feelings are. (Often the child's sounds and body movements are very explicit expressions of his feelings.) Language is interspersed throughout all activities so the child can begin to see the relationship between verbal communication and everything he does. Through language he will learn that he can have some control over his life, make his needs known clearly, and so forth.

The most important aspect of this is acquainting the child with himself, a necessary step before increased contact can be made with his peers, parents, teachers, and environment. Both Saliba and Malek have found that the more the children came in contact with themselves — their senses, their bodies — and the more self-discovery that took place, the calmer these children became. The frantic movements subsided and the aimless self-stimulation lessened. (Saliba tells about visitors to the classroom who claimed that the children were not truly autistic since the "autistic behavior" had so markedly decreased.) These children were beginning to learn; they were relating to each other and to their teachers far more than ever before.

Guilt

Guilt is generally retroflected anger or resentment — anger turned against oneself rather than directed at the target of the anger. A child is yelled at for spilling milk. Being yelled at makes him angry, but since he is unable to express his anger, he pushes it in and feels guilty for spilling his milk. If the anger is expressed directly, the guilt may leave, or the child may feel guilty for getting angry, depending on the response of the parent.

Resentment accompanies all guilt. If the child cannot express the anger and feels guilty, he becomes resentful at the adult (or perhaps another child) for this unpleasant feeling. Along with the resentment there is usually an unexpressed demand. The child may resent the parent for yelling at him, and the demand may be for the parent to be more tolerant of his milk-spilling.

The child is also confused about who is at fault for a precipitating situation such as spilling milk, and he readily takes on the blame, being continually yelled at for something he knows he did not intentionally do. He blames himself and feels that he is bad. So anger, guilt, resentment, and self-blame become diffused and mixed up with the child's self-image. Some children are made to feel ashamed for being milk-spillers, and everything else they do, and before long they begin to feel ashamed of being alive.

To lessen his feelings of guilt, the child who feels very guilty may go around doing what he thinks others want him to do, but he feels resentful all the while. He is confused and unsure about what is expected of him, but he knows for sure that he must bury the anger and rage festering inside himself. He tries hard to please and becomes confluent with everyone around him. He ceases to feel differentiated from the people in his life, completely losing his sense of self and entitlement.

Understanding some of the elements that go into the process of guiltmaking helps the therapist guide the child in sorting things out. A child who has developed a pattern of avoiding guilt by trying never to do anything wrong needs help in separating himself from the people in his life. He needs help in discovering who he is, what his needs are, what he wants. He needs help in learning to verbalize his wants, opinions, thoughts. He needs help in making clear choices and in taking responsibility for his choices.

The child needs to experiment with expressing his anger, his resentments and demands. The more direct the child can be with his angry feelings, the less guilt will remain to weaken and immobilize him.

Ralph, age seven, was a fire-setter.

When his mother brought him in, she told me that he had been a battered child — a child who had been severely beaten and injured from the time he was 2 until the age of about five, when she had received much needed help. Though she no longer abused him, she felt very guilty and blamed herself for his present behavior of setting fires and his generally hostile and belligerent attitude.

At one session I asked Ralph to draw a picture of himself setting a fire. He drew a large red fire and a child lighting a match to it, saying, "You do it too" in a balloon to another child who said, "OK." (Ralph explained that he set fires because another child always told him to.) Taking up half the picture was a drawing of a huge sun crying and frowning. I asked Ralph to be the boy in the picture and say how it feels to set the fire.

Ralph: It's a big fire. I like doing it.

Now be the fire. Pretend you can talk as a fire. Say what you're like.

WINDOWS TO OUR CHILDREN

Ralph: I'm a big fire. A *very* big fire. You can see me all around.
What does it feel like to be a fire?
Ralph: Strong!

Now be the sun. What does the sun say.
Ralph: (as sun) I'm sad. I'm crying. Ralph will get into trouble.
Tell that to Ralph, sun.
Ralph: (as the sun talking to the fire-setting boy in the picture) You'll get into lots of trouble. You are very bad.
Sun, tell Ralph how he'll get into trouble.
Ralph: (as sun) Oh, your mother will kill you, she'll be so mad. (then to me) Do you know that I'm adopted?
No, I didn't know that.
Ralph: Yes. My real mom was only sixteen when she had me and she couldn't take care of me so my mom got me. If I say "real mom" to my mom, she cries.
Are you ever afraid your mother will hurt you again like she did when you were little?
Ralph: Yes, but I was bad. I'm still bad but she doesn't hurt me now.
Ralph carried around feelings of guilt — he still blamed himself for his previous abuse. He continually tested his mother to see if she would hurt him, and eventually give him away like his real mom did. Setting fires

made him feel strong and powerful. As he began to express his resentment, anger, and grief, as he could feel his own entitlement and worth and power, his hostile behavior began to diminish.

James, a nine-year-old boy who messed his pants, expressed his feelings of guilt one day when he made a figure of himself and of his brother in clay and then smashed himself, leaving his brother intact. James' brother, two years older, teased him about everything. James never got mad but told me that he believed he deserved teasing because he always messed his pants like a baby. "I'd tease him too, if he did it." His inability to focus his anger on his brother was typical of his general behavior. He secretly admitted to me that he thought something was wrong with him "since I was born." He felt guilty for being alive. As James began to express his feelings through many of the expressive techniques, he began to be more direct with his feelings at home. His mother stopped his therapy one day, saying, "He's only getting worse. He used to be so easygoing. Now he acts mad and hits his brother and even talks back to me and his father." I was unable to convince her that it was far healthier for him to be direct with his angry feelings than to express them through withholding his bowels and messing his pants, and that his assertion represented his new feelings of self-worth.

Many of the adults I work with have a lot of guilt left over from their childhood. Feelings of guilt that crept in long ago permeated all areas of their lives, causing much heartache. Childhood feelings and messages can stay with us a long time, and can even affect us for life.

A man came to see me who was unable to enjoy a sexual relationship with his wife. Robert suffered from pain in his groin whenever he had an erection. He had tried to ignore this all of his sexually mature life, but now his marriage was deteriorating as a result of it. He had visited doctors, none of whom had found any reason for the pain.

In one of our sessions I asked him to close his eyes and fantasize this pain, to stay with it, and to report to me if he had any thoughts, ideas, sensations, or flashes as he did so. As he sat with his eyes closed he suddenly remembered something he had completely forgotten long ago: "When I was eight years old I remember waking up one night needing to go to the bathroom. I thought it was the middle of the night, but it must not have been so late, for my mother was in the living room entertaining some guests. I sleepily wandered out of my bedroom into the living room. I had on pajamas. When I came into the room my mother stared directly at my groin and gasped. She screamed, "Robert! What's the matter with you? What are you doing?" She grabbed me and dragged me out of the room. I don't remember what happened after that except that I guess I must have had an erection. God! I can remember how confused and terrible I felt."

Robert's memory may not have recapitulated the exact scene (memories never can), and this may not have been the only incident that caused his present pain. What is important is that during therapy he contacted some feelings that he had buried when he was a kid. We were able to work on this memory as we might a dream, and he had an opportunity to deal with some long forgotten (but still incapacitating) feelings and conflicts. Such feelings of guilt are often devastating. The memory above may have been interwoven with a fantasy; Robert may have imagined that his mother was upset over his erection when, in fact, she may merely have been annoyed at his coming out of his room. She may not actually have looked at his groin even though he remembers that she did. Enough had happened before that incident and certainly after it to reinforce the guilty feelings he had about his erect penis. Shame, guilt, and a great deal of buried, forgotten, unexpressed anger and resentment needed to come out in order for Robert to have a sense of self-worth, self-support and well-being in his life.

Self-esteem; Self-concept; Self-image

I have always been a little disturbed by words like self-esteem, self-concept, self-image. Esteem refers to how highly we value something; a concept is — an idea, a notion, what we think. An image is a representation of something, not the real thing. The definitions in the literature relating to children are vague and elusive, and they differ by individual interpretation. Many writers avoid defining self-concept but readily discuss the manifestations of a negative self-concept and the need to improve the child's self-concept.

A baby is not born with bad feelings about himself. All babies think they are wonderful. How a child feels about himself after a time, however, is certainly determined to a great extent by the early messages he gets about himself from his parents. In the final analysis though, it is the child himself who translates those message to himself. The child will select from the environment anything that will reinforce parental messages.

Haim Ginott in *Between Parent and Child* and *Between Parent and Teenager* says that when a child maintains that he is stupid or ugly or bad, there is nothing we can say or do to change his self-image immediately. "A person's ingrained opinion of himself resists direct attempts at alteration. As one child said to his father, 'I know you mean well, Dad, but I am not that stupid to take your word that I am bright.'" Ginnot cautions parents to distinguish between generalized praise and descriptive praise. If a parent says, "Thank you for washing my car. I like the way it looks," the child will translate this message to himself as perhaps, "I can do a good job at car washing." if the parent says, "What a wonderful child you are! You are the best car washer in the world!" the child may translate, "I know I'm not all that wonderful, so she must be fooling."

It is not always easy to find the source of a child's low self-opinion. Sometimes the messages he has received are very vague and subtle. Sometimes the child embellishes them with his own fantasy material. Sometimes they result from, or are reinforced by, situations and events which the parents had no control over, or never even knew about. If nothing else, our society's general lack of respect for children as entitled human beings serves to deteriorate every child's sense of self-worth.

Most of the children I work with in therapy, and most of the children I have had in classes for the emotionally disturbed, have low self-esteem. This is not unexpected since how we perceive and value ourselves determines to a great extent how we behave, how we cope with life, how we manage ourselves.

Children manifest their low self-esteem in many different ways. They may not even be *aware* that they don't feel too good about themselves, though they know something is wrong. Some common signs are: whining, needing to win, cheating in games, perfectionism, exaggerated bragging, giving away candy, money, or toys, resorting to numerous attention-getting devices such as clowning, acting very silly, teasing, antisocial behavior, being self-critical, withdrawn or shy, blaming others for everything, making excuses for everything, constantly apologizing, being fearful of trying new things, distrusting people, wanting many things, behaving defensively, overeating, ever pleasing, feeling unable to make fears and decisions, never saying, "No."

This list includes nearly every kind of behavior that is likely to bring a child into therapy. Since our society values the swift and the agile, children who are clumsy and awkward often have a low self-esteem. And so the society in general can be the source of a lessened sense of self-value. Those that are looked upon with great favor in our culture — slim people, attractive people, rich people, white people — may not feel better about themselves than fatter, less attractive, poorer, and people of minorities, but people who find themselves in the latter categories can be adversely affected by the values of our society.

When I see a child in therapy, I have the opportunity to give her self back to her, for in a sense a poor self-concept is a lost sense of self. I have a chance to bring her in touch with her own potency, to help her feel at home in the world. I can help her give up negative messages and reform positive ones. In regaining her sense of self, she can then throw herself fully into the process of exploring and discovering all the things in her world.

Here are some basic guidelines for parents for enhancing a child's feelings of self.

Listen to, acknowledge, and accept the child's feelings.
Treat her with respect. Accept her as she is.
Give her specific praise, to the point.
Be honest with her.
Use "I" messages rather than "you" messages: "I am bugged by the noise of your record player," rather than "You are so noisy."
Be specific in criticism, rather than: "You always . . ." or "You never . . ."

Though she needs consistency, rules and controls, she needs even more urgently some space in her life to learn how to manage her own life. Give her responsibilities, independence, and the freedom to make choices.

Involve her in problem-solving and decision-making relative to her own life. Respect her feelings, needs, wants, suggestions, wisdom.

Allow her to experiment, pursue her own interests, be creative or not creative.

Remember the uniqueness principle: She is wonderful and amazing in her own uniqueness even though it may be a far different uniqueness from yours.

Be a good model — think well of yourself, do things for yourself.

Realize that it is good to appreciate oneself. It is fine to feel satisfied with accomplishments. It is good to find pleasure for oneself.

Avoid being judgmental, giving lots of "shoulds" and needless advice.

Take her seriously. Accept her judgment; she knows when she's not hungry.

If the child expresses negative self-feelings, the parent or therapist must be careful not to contradict the child. For example, if the child says, "I'm so ugly!" one might be tempted to say, "Oh no! You're so pretty!" To do this would serve only to increase her bad self-feelings, not to change them, because the implicit message is "You're wrong to think you're ugly." The change must come from within the child herself, and this can be accomplished only by allowing and accepting her bad feelings.

Once bad feelings are expressed openly, they can be fully explored. If a child talks about what a rotten ball player she is, I might ask her to tell me more about how bad a player she really is. What generally happens is that somewhere along the way the child stops and says, "Well, I'm not really that bad," or perhaps, "Well, I'm not good at ball playing but I'm not bad at swimming." This is a good example of Arnold Beisser's "paradoxical theory of change." In his article in *Gestalt Therapy Now* he says:

> *Change occurs when one becomes what he is, not when he tries to become what he is not.*
>
> Change does not take place through a coercive attempt by the individual or by another person to change him but it does take place if one takes the time and effort to be where he is — to be fully invested in his current positions. By rejecting the

> role of change agent, we make meaningful and orderly change possible.(p. 77)

A seven-year-old girl I was seeing constantly talked about how popular she was with other children, how smart she was, how she could do anything better than anyone else, etc. One day I began to tell her a story that started, "Once there was a little girl who never did anything right." She interrupted to ask me the little girl's name. I said I wasn't sure and asked her to give me a name for her. She thought for a moment, then pointed to herself, nodding her head vigorously, mouth set. "It's you?" Much nodding this time, mouth downcast. This was the beginning of dealing with her real feelings of self — and the beginning of change. Young children often use the phrase "I never do anything right" as an expression of bad feelings about themselves.

Children with low self-esteem need many activities involving experiences with the senses focusing on similarities and differences between themselves and objects, animals, people, fruits and vegetables. Through an awareness of differences they can begin to view themselves with new appreciation and begin to see and approach and contact others in the same light.

Body awareness is basic to a strong sense of self. Relaxation and breathing exercises are helpful, as well as body movement experiences. Body-image is an important aspect of self-acceptance. Most children with low self-concepts are not only unfamiliar with their bodies — how they feel, what they can do, but they generally don't like how they look (or how they *think* they look). And so I do many activities involving drawing self-portraits, looking in the mirror, talking to the image in the mirror, looking at old baby photographs, looking at new photographs that I take, drawing an outline of the body on a large sheet of paper, going inside the body in fantasy, and so forth. Sometimes I will draw a picture of the child on a large sheet of paper and we will discuss each feature, each article of clothing, each part of the body as I draw. Young children are quite delighted with this technique.

To help a child feel better about herself, we need to bring her back to herself. The first, and essential, step in this process is to accept her present feelings — the rotten, blank, nothing, despairing ones she has now. As she accepts these feelings, she can become reacquainted with her senses and her body and all she can do with it. She can learn about herself and her uniqueness from the inside, instead of through the judgements and opinions of others, and begin to feel a sense of well-being — that it is OK to be who she is.

11

Other Considerations

Some activities and approaches are better suited for certain ages than others; some are more appropriate for group settings while others work best in individual sessions. Most of the techniques can be *adapted* to just about anybody and any kind of situation. I summarize here some of my thoughts and opinions about particularly effective ways of dealing with various age levels, groupings, settings, etc.

Groups

Groups have the advantage of being a kind of insulated little world in which present behavior can be experienced and new behaviors tried out. Group work is an ideal setting for children who need to practice contact skills. It is natural for most children to seek out other children. Providing an arena for those who have difficulties relating to their peers can help them to discover and work through whatever has blocked this natural process.

I think each therapist needs to decide on the size and kind of group that she finds most productive; there cannot be one general rule for all. I have enjoyed a variety of group situations in my practice, and I have discovered my own preferences. I like working with another therapist, and I like the group to be fairly small — from three to six children — when the children are under eight. When the children are older, I like the group to be larger — from six to ten children. Generally my groups meet for 90 minutes, though sometimes that does not seem to be enough time.

WINDOWS TO OUR CHILDREN

Certain procedures and techniques are particularly effective in group settings. I usually begin each group session by having the children make rounds, each child having a turn to report his present feelings and awareness, and to say something, if he wants to, about anything that has happened to him since our last meeting. This technique is especially useful for giving each child an opportunity to participate. Sometimes I request that the rounds be focused on the present setting only, that each child report his awareness at the moment: what he feels now, what he senses in his body, what he sees, what he is thinking right now. I make it clear to the children, however, that if something that happened during the week is still with the child, and he doesn't have to search his memory for it, then that is certainly part of his present awareness. Often a child comes into the group angry, hurt, or excited about something that happened just before coming to the group, and he needs to express this in order to bring his full attention to the group.

Generally group sessions with children are structured; that is, I have a pretty good idea what we will be doing in that session. However, it is important to be open, flexible, and creative. After rounds, I may ask the group if anyone would like to share something, talk about something, express something that may be on his mind or in his feelings. Sometimes a child presents a problem that involves a great deal of participation from the others in the group. On the other hand, the problem may be something that requires individual attention, in which case the child and I will work together while the others watch. Groups that have met for some time become more sophisticated about what they can get from a group. Such children have done "work," have asked for sharing of experience from other children, have brought in dreams to work on, and so forth. If, in the course of a group session, I interrupt the group activity to work with one child, I do so with the realization that the other children will, at the same time, get a lot of vicarious benefit out of the other's work. Ruth Cohn, in an article "Therapy in Groups: Psychoanalytic, Experiential and Gestalt" in *Gestalt Therapy Now* writes:

> I have taught workshops on "Five Models of Group Interaction," which have included the experiential, analytic, and gestalt therapy models together with the T-group and my own

theme-centered interactional approach. In these workshops the students were led to experience each demonstrated model by participation. Invariably, the groups reacted with the greatest personal involvement in the Gestalt therapy workshop, in spite of the fact that they were spectators rather than interacting participants most of the time. Observing the dramatic therapeutic dialogue was of greater impact than personal interactional exchange. The patient's vertical plunge into previously avoided emotions seemed to touch the group of observers in the truest sense of identification and purification of a Greek drama. The members of the Greek chorus seem indeed to experience the tragic and joyful feelings of the patient's responses within themselves. (p. 138)

I also find this to be true with children's groups of any age: what I do with an individual has impact and meaning for the observers as well.

Themes are especially suitable for group settings. Children have often suggested their own themes after getting the idea. A good example of a theme is "Ridicule" or "Being Laughed At." At one session we talked about what it meant to each of us, whether we ever experienced it, what we did when we experienced it, how we felt, and the difference between our feelings and our actions. We talked about doing it to others. Next, they all closed their eyes and I asked them to get in touch with a time that they remember feeling laughed at, jeered at, ridiculed. I asked them to make one up if they couldn't remember, or if it had never happened to them. I prompted their memories with such questions and suggestions as, "What's happening — what is the situation? Who's involved — who's around? Are others watching? What are you feeling? Try to get into the feelings you are having as you are being laughed at." The children then drew pictures of their feelings, or of the incident, and we shared and talked about our drawings. The children spoke quietly, shared deeply, and listened intently.

Sometimes we only have time to allow each child to share his expressive creations (never forcing those that don't wish to) or to share feelings and experiences brought about by a particular exercise. At other times we allow time to work more in depth with one or more of the children. If necessary, we continue the work at the next meeting. I may say, "Next time we might want to work with the feeling of loneliness you expressed as you talked about your clay piece." But no preplanned activity takes precedence over whatever important may be happening now within the group or with a particular child.

The group process is the most valuable aspect of group work with children. How they experience each other and how they react and relate to each other in the therapy group openly displays their interpersonal relations in general.

The group is a place for the child to become aware of how he interacts with other children, to learn to take responsibility for what he does, and to experiment with new behaviors. In addition, every child needs connection with other children, to know that others have similar feelings and similar problems.

Giving children the opportunity to play games with each other gives them fundamental experiences in interrelating. Sometimes the group as a whole can play these games, and sometimes the group can be divided into pairs and trios. In one of my group sessions I brought in a number of simple games including jacks, three-dimensional tic-tac-toe, Blockhead, pick up sticks, dominoes. The children, ages ten to twelve, divided into pairs and each pair was given a game. We set a kitchen timer for ten minutes. When the timer sounded, games and partners were rotated. After game-playing time, we talked about the experience. Here are some of the comments:

This is the first time I ever played jacks with a boy. I had to teach him how to do it. It was great!

I'm the first boy to know how to play jacks!

I lost and felt bad and was glad when the timer rang.

Chris cheated, but stopped when I told him I didn't like it.

He didn't cheat at all with me. He was really cooperative.

I had trouble with the jacks and Susan helped me.

The general tone of the children was gentle and tolerant. An air of contentment and calmness permeated the room during and after the game period. There was a lot of noise, too — the kind of noise one hears when people talk with each other.

We can use the group to deal with the child's projections. If he says, "I don't like the way he's looking at me!" I will ask him to describe what he imagines that look is saying to him, and then to say it to himself so that he can see if he projected another child's facial expression to support his own self-criticism. Here's how such an exchange might go:

Phillip: I don't like the way Allen's looking at me!

What do you imagine he's saying to you with that look?

Phillip: He's saying, "You're stupid!"

Phillip, pretend you're sitting on that pillow and say those words to yourself. Say, "You're stupid" to yourself.

Phillip: (to pillow) You're stupid!

Do you have a voice inside of you that says that to yourself sometimes?

Phillip: Yeah.

Children need to learn that seeing a facial grimace is not the same as knowing the person's thoughts. The other child might have a stomachache. Sometimes, however, the other child is actually feeling what the first child imagined, and this also needs to be checked out with the other child.

We can examine the child's introjects, helping him to give up what is not fitting. We might play a game in which each person in the group plays his own mother or father and have him be his parents in a mock group session and role-play them or tell us about his "child." This activity is greatly enhanced if the leader enters in wholeheartedly.

John Enright describes his use of the following techniques in group therapy to enhance awareness, responsibility, and listening skills in his paper "An Introduction to Gestalt Techniques" in *Gestalt Therapy Now*. All of these techniques can be effectively applied to children.

1) Telling children to speak directly to each other rather than telling the therapist about another child. "He poked me!" becomes "I don't like having you poke me!" Power and strength are evident in the latter statement; complaining and weakness are characteristic of the first.

2) A good exercise in helping children practice directness is to have each child go around the room making statements to each person, such as "Something I like about you is . . . .; something that bugs me about you is . . . ." Or, "Something I'd like you to know about me is . . . .; something I don't want you to know about me is . . . ."

3) Directing children to substitute statements for questions. Many questions are masks for implied statements. For example, "Why did you poke me?" really means "I don't like it when you poke me." This is not only

strengthening for the poked child, who has made a clear statement, but also for the poker, since he must then find some other means of communicating besides indirect, devious poking. The therapist can direct the poking child to make a statement of his own to substitute for the original masked communication.

4) Paying attention to how children listen to each other. This is vital in a children's group in which children often interrupt, withdraw into day dreaming, or are disruptive through other means: talking to other children, hitting, making noises, walking around. It may be helpful to focus on the interrupter. Interrupting or other ways of not listening are devious, indirect messages that need to be translated into direct statements, such as, "I am bored," "I need some attention," etc. There are times when I have requested that an interrupter leave the room until he feels ready to return. Interruptions can be annoying to the children as well as to me.

Usually we establish group rules, such as allowing one person to finish talking without being interrupted. Often the group itself monitors and enforces these rules, telling a child if he continually interrupts. If the whole group is disruptive, it would seem clear that the therapist must take a good look at what *she* is doing. The therapist's role is an important one in group settings. It is she who must set the tone of the group as a place where the children can feel safe and accepted. A certain amount of modeling must take place; children take their cues from the therapist.

It's important, too, that the therapist join in many of the activities with the children. When we play games, act out characters, or tell stories, I take my turn. If I am not inclined to participate in some particular exercise, I will make a positive statement to this effect. I find that much more happens when I involve myself in activities, share of myself, and share my present awareness and feelings.

The therapist must be continuously alert to, and aware of, each child. If a child is visibly upset or hurt, the therapist needs to be able to sense it. It is essential that the group be a place that children can trust, and in which nothing hurtful to any child will be passed over by the therapist.

Group sessions ought to be enjoyable experiences. A satisfactory group session is one in which each child feels interested, interesting, safe, and accepted. As the child feels freer to reveal himself and his emotions, thoughts, and opinions, as he knows that he will find support and connection with the therapist and the other children, he will grow stronger within himself.

I generally allow a finishing time for every group meeting. This is a time when the children can make some comment about the activity or the session, say something they need to say to anyone in the room, report on how they feel at the moment, and voice any appreciations, resentments, or wants. Typically in the beginning sessions, children will say very little during finishing time, but as time progresses and the children begin to feel comfortable with themselves and with each other, this time becomes an important and integral part of the therapeutic group process.

Adolescents

Many therapists feel that the troubled adolescent is a victim of the family scenario and that unless the family undergoes therapeutic change, not much can be done for the unlucky child. But my feelings about this age group are no different than they are for other age groups. All children can benefit from the kind of experience in self-support that a therapist can provide. The older the child, the more maturity and knowledge he brings to the therapeutic process.

Family sessions, when possible, are in order, but these sessions should not preclude working with the young person apart from the family. The family session is a place for bringing out into the open the interaction and communication dynamics that take place within the family. However, the troubled adolescent can do much for himself. Like the adult he almost is, he has introjected many faulty messages that affect his feelings about himself. He has many feelings, memories, and fantasies from his past that interrupt his natural flow. He has a depth of feeling that he finds difficult to share with his family. He needs assistance in expressing his feelings of anxiety, loneliness, frustration, self-disparagement, sexual confusion, and fear. He needs to see how he can take responsibility for his own life as much as possible, and how he interrupts his own organismic flow.

Many adolescents are reluctant to receive therapeutic intervention (though others request it). Parents bring them in because things have gotten so bad in the family that they feel they have reached a dead end. Or sometimes a court order requires that they get counseling. In the first session, I can usually see that the child's perceptions about life and those of the parents are so different that they are unable to talk to one another. It is particularly important for children who resist therapy to know that I'm hearing both these divergent life views. Only when each can begin to hear what the other has to say, when the family members can begin at least to talk to each other and share feelings congruently, can anything constructive begin to happen in the family.

I am very direct in these situations. If a family member has been so intent on getting his own point across that he has not even heard what someone else has to say, I am just as quick to point this out to a parent as to a child. I also want to make sure that the underlying messages and feelings are brought into everyone's awareness. If a father says to his daughter, "I don't like the way you dress," he and she both need to know if what he means is: "I don't like the way you flaunt your budding breasts," or "I would like to keep you my little girl." Underneath that message might be "I worry about your safety and losing you to that world out there." This father also needs to know if his message is received by his daughter as "I don't like you or trust you."

I think that most parents of adolescents are reluctant to have their children grow up. Loving parents are afraid to give their children up to the world, yet they must. Again and again I find myself taking a stand on this issue with parents. They cannot take responsibility for their children's school work, friends, or future plans. They cannot follow them around to make sure they are not engaging in sex, smoking pot, drinking, etc. What they can do is to state their positions about these matters. They can also expect their children to participate in the running of a household in which they live, they can negotiate on certain limits they feel are important, and they can be available for love and support. But they must also begin to let go, and see their son or daughter as a separate, entitled human being.

To the reluctant adolescent, I sometimes say, "As long as you're going to be coming here to see me for a while, let's use this time to find out about yourself." I often use psychological projective tests to give these young people a chance to accept or reject statements made as interpretations about them. Linda Goodman's *Sun Signs*, an astrology book, is a fun starting place for talking about the self. I read a paragraph written in this book about an individual's birth sign and then discuss with her whether, in her opinion, it fits for her or not.

Once I was invited to come and do some work at a residential home for "delinquent teenagers." I was met by a mixed bag of young people who exhibited either hostility or lassitude. I forged ahead, telling them that I could feel their rejection and distrust, but that since I was asked to come and do a job, I would do the best I could. I explained a little bit about the use of fantasy and drawings to help them know themselves better, and then presented an exercise which started by having them close their eyes and visualize themselves as very weak in terms of colors, lines, shapes. Here is how I instructed them:

See yourself feeling very weak. Weakness can mean different things to different people. Just go with what it means for you. If you had to put yourself down as weak on paper, what colors would you use, what shapes might you see, what kinds of lines. Would you cover the whole paper or just part of it? Would you bear down heavily or lightly on the paper? Does a symbol of your weakness come to your mind? If nothing comes to you, just pick a color while you think weak and let your hand move over the paper. As you begin, something will come. Feel free to add anything as you go along. Whenever you're ready, you can begin.

After a few moments I did a similar exercise, asking them to draw themselves very strong. Many of the people walked away, disinterested. Several stayed and did it. When we were through we shared our pictures, and I worked further with several volunteers. As we worked, those who were disinterested began to filter back, perhaps out of curiosity. They listened to us quietly, attentively. When we were through, one boy who did not participate said to me, "I hope you get to come back . . . I wish I had done that drawing."

In an individual session, a seventeen-year-old young man talked about his suicidal wishes only after he had done the rosebush fantasy and drawn his branches as dead. A fifteen-year-old girl told about her deep feelings of hurt over her father's rejection of her; she opened up to me only after she had lightly told a story, while looking at a picture from the *Thematic Apperception Test*, about a man who wouldn't listen to his wife. This kind of experience is not unusual; it is typical of the openings that come about through the use of projective/expressive techniques.

WINDOWS TO OUR CHILDREN

Many adolescents come for therapy willingly, and many continue willingly even though they have resisted at first. Young people have many concerns that are difficult to share with others. A sixteen-year-old girl said:

"I can talk to anybody, like I can tell them about myself, what I do, about a lot of things. But when it comes to talking about some things, it's not so easy. Like, if I'm feeling insecure, like if I feel as if I don't really have any friends, I can't tell those people that I can talk to about anything, or I can't tell my friends or my Mom and Dad. I can't tell people things like that, I can't tell what I'm feeling, what really is *me*, what's *really* inside of me. I especially can't tell my parents. I can't even tell them things I can tell my friends."

What this young woman said is typical of what many young people have told me. I talked with another young woman in a group of mine concerning her feelings about the value of the group. She said:

"The group's good for a lot of reasons. I can talk about things there it's hard to talk about in other places. And the self-discovery — I can begin to discover myself. I don't think *I* even know myself. I don't know how to get things I feel to come out — to express them. It's hard. Like what I'm thinking about myself. What I feel about myself. Like if I feel really raunchy. I know if I can feel really good about myself then I can be a much better person. But I don't think I feel really good about myself. Everybody thinks I have lots of friends, but I feel really insecure about friends. It always seems as if everybody else has lots of friends — they're always doing something, always getting together, things like that. I look at other friends that have that, and I feel envious. I don't think I have that. Maybe I don't fit in with one or the other kinds of groups, like one kind has people who are kind of phony, people who put on a big act for everybody and the other are people who are so open they don't care what people are thinking and they act weird sometimes. I'm somewhere in the middle. The group is a nice place to be, I feel really comfortable and look forward to it. You know that people really care about what you have to say and about your feelings."

When I work with adolescents I find that they appreciate it if I explain to them what therapy is all about. They want to know how I will go about helping them find out about themselves, and what good it will do. Here's a sample conversation I had with a young client of mine:

Other Considerations

Rachel: What do you do when you go about discovering yourself, your inner self? How would you go about doing that?

Well, it's a matter of being clear about the things that you think, and the things you like, and what you feel, and how you are in the world — how you are with your friends, your parents, your teachers. It's also being clear about what's going on with you, what makes you do the things you do. For example, remember in our group when Chris talked about her boyfriend — how he made her feel bad and yet she didn't want to break up with him? As I worked with her she discovered that even though she didn't like what was happening, she didn't want to give up the relationship because it made her feel secure just to have it.

Rachel: Yeah, she was complaining about it, and then found out it was her own choice to be with him.

Right. As we explored her feelings we found that out. She opened herself just by telling us how she felt. No one knew that she didn't like going with him! We were the first to know.

Rachel: It seemed like a big relief to her to tell us. That's how I feel, sometimes.

You know how that feels. Also her opening herself like that keeps her from being blocked. When we keep too many things inside, we get blocked, tied up in knots, and it's hard to grow fully and feel strong within ourselves. Now we can begin to look at what it is about herself and her life that makes her stay in a painful relationship just for security. We can look at that so she can maybe begin to find ways to feel secure that are better than the way she's doing it, or she can perhaps decide to take a risk and just let herself feel insecure.

Rachel: Maybe she felt insecure when she was little and is afraid of how it feels.

Right. You found out you do some things now because of what you felt or what happened to you when you were younger. And every time you find out something new about yourself, or get really clear about what you're doing and how you are, you open yourself up to new growth and new choices. We never stand still; the more we know about ourselves, the more there is open to us. And we can begin to feel stronger, calmer, centered.

Rachel: Sometimes we do things like drawings and I find out things about myself I thought I already knew but it seems different when I do it that way. Like when we drew about anger. I thought I knew how I was when I was angry. I drew it because I knew it. But more came out, things I never thought of when I did it.

Can you remember what?

Rachel: Well, I remember I drew a big explosion because that's what happens when I get mad. I really explode, especially with my mother. I think I get destructive . . . . nothing good comes out of it. When I talked about it I remember I felt like I was a little mouse or a hamster and that my parents were poking and jabbing at me when they were mad at me or criticizing me or making a speech at me or something. They don't really poke me, but it feels that way. And I feel like I can't defend myself. I know what I feel, but I can't say it so it will make sense, so I end up being totally out of control. It's like they're coming at me and I'm a mouse and have to go back further and further and then there's no place to go, so I just explode! I yell and cry and scream. I wish I could stay in control of the situation, be calm. I want to work on some more of that.

Sure, we'll do that if you want to.

School, friends, parents, feeling different, anger, feeling dumb, not meeting expectations of themselves as well as of their parents — these are just a few of the issues that concern young people. The body and sexuality are important concerns, too. One of the things I discovered was that the adolescents I worked with did not bring up the subject of sex or body image feelings unless I did.

I did an all-day workshop with another therapist with a group of eighteen young women, ages fourteen through seventeen, on the topic of sexuality. The workshop was organized by a community agency and was open to the public at no charge to participants. The girls arrived in singles, pairs, trios. They were of various religious, economic, and cultural backgrounds. Most of them did not know each other and did not know us. They sat waiting for us to begin.

After we introduced ourselves we started off with a series of fantasy experiences involving getting in touch with first events: first memory, first memory of being female, first time of menstruation, etc. The first sharing was to the whole group, the others were in small groups of four and five. After a very open discussion of feelings about menstruation, we presented the next first memory: "Close your eyes again and go back to the time you

Other Considerations

remember first masturbating. Can you remember when you first touched yourself, what the sensations were like, how you felt about it, what happened? If you can't remember, get in touch with the first time you ever heard about it and what you felt."

At the word "masturbation" every girl sat up and opened her eyes. The reactions were embarrassment, giggling, discomfort, fears, horror, denial. I told them that each one of them had masturbated as babies; that all babies discover the sensual pleasures of their own bodies. If they no longer masturbated, or forgot, or were embarrassed or ashamed, it was because they had received some kind of message that it was wrong to touch and know one's own body and feel pleasure sensations.

What followed was one of the most moving, open, honest discussions about sexuality that I have ever experienced. These girls had all participated in sex education classes in school, but the things they wanted to know, the questions and confusions, the deepest conflicts and feelings they felt, were not covered in these classes.

Since that time, I bring up the subject of sexuality with adolescents I see. If I wait for them to bring it up, I may wait forever. I do this with boys and girls, in individual sessions and in groups. I tell them about my workshop experience, and I do a variety of exercises to help them feel comfortable to talk and share and ask. Here are a few:

Ask members of a group to write down or call out as you write down all the words they have ever heard used to name or describe female genitals, male genitals, breasts, the sex act, masturbation, etc. Look at these words, read them off, talk about how they affect their feelings about sex and bodies.

Ask members of a group to write down on a piece of paper some secret involving sexuality: something they once did and never told about, something that once happened to them, something they would like to know about but don't have the nerve to bring up, etc. These papers are not signed. Put them in the middle of the room and have each person pick one and read it. The sharing and discussion that follows is always valuable and moving. By the rules of this "game," the person who wrote the particular statement or question is not allowed to own up to it.

Go back to first memories, as described above. Along with first memory of being female or male, and first memory of menstruation and masturbation, you might include first memory of having a wet dream, first memory of having an erection, first memory of sexual involvement with someone else.

Ask people to draw pictures of how they *feel* about their bodies in colors, lines, and shapes. Always begin these exercises with eyes closed and some kind of breathing-meditative experience.

Have them draw how they feel about their own sexuality, or where they are with their sexuality — "How do you feel as a woman? How do you feel as a man?"

Have them draw pictures of how they are with members of the opposite sex and with their own sex.

Have them draw pictures of how they imagine people of the opposite sex see them, and how people of their own sex see them.

Read a poem involving some aspect of sexuality while the person or group listens with eyes closed. Have them draw any feelings that come from the poem, or anything the poem reminds them of. The book *Male and Female Under 18* contains many good poems written by young people about their sex roles in today's world.

Body image is a large concern for adolescents, and again a subject not easily introduced by the young person. I have found that young men as well as young women worry about how they look. I sometimes ask adolescents to draw a picture of how they think they look, and one of how they would like to look. Or I ask them to draw a picture of their bodies, exaggerating the parts they don't like. I sometimes do a fantasy exercise asking them to imagine that they are in a dark room and that they begin to walk toward a lighted area, finding a large full-length mirror. They stand in front of the mirror and begin a dialogue with their own image about their bodies. These exercises help the adolescent share feelings that are not easy for them to share. We spend some time, too, talking about the influence of the media upon our feelings of how we ought to look.

The adolescent is very much affected by the realities of the world. Whereas the young child seems to put off facing the world by playing — an activity that adults accept as normal for youngsters — the adolescent knows that he will soon be thrust out into the world to make his own way. He longs for the freedom and independence of adulthood, and also is fearful and anxious for himself. Many young people make attempts to learn about dealing with the world — they try to find jobs, make decisions for themselves, and experiment with independence. But most are ignored, rebuffed, not taken seriously.

I find teenagers to be intelligent, and far wiser than society gives them credit for. They teach me a great deal about life. But many are confused and bewildered by the mixed messages they receive about themselves from their parents and society — messages that downgrade their abilities and wisdom. They sometimes become anxious, depressed, worried, and fearful about themselves and life, especially about the future. Some assume a casual, "I don't care" stance. Others rebel outright. Some fight hard to take their own stand. Those that come into therapy have an opportunity to become clear about themselves, their needs and their wants. They can gain strength to deal with the problems and conflicts of the world that they will need to face.

Adults

Many of these approaches and techniques are useful with adults as presented here, or can be easily used with adults with slight changes or modifications.

Since adults generally come in to work with a set program, I usually don't need to introduce many projective techniques. If, however, someone appears blank about where to go next in their work, I can present a technique as a method for bringing unfinished material to the foreground for work. This works well, too, for a group in which everyone is just sitting and no one seems to want to begin.

Just as I may determine that a particular child needs more experience with body work or tactile sensation or exercises and games that involve making specific statements of choice, so I might make such a determination with an adult. An adult who talks incessantly and has trouble staying in touch with his body sensations will derive much value from working with clay, for example.

Often in the course of work, I know that using a particular technique will enhance and clarify the work. One woman had trouble describing the sensations in her chest. When she drew it in colors, lines, and shapes, then the work flowed smoothly. Many therapists find the use of fantasy images helpful. A man who had trouble dialoguing with the part of him that caused him to overeat found it easier when he created a visual image of a very fat pig to talk to. Someone working on a headache saw the headache as an image of a heavy hammer, and this image helped the work to take on new clarity.

Much of what we deal with in therapy relates to childhood memories, experiences, introjections. Many of us are still doing the things we did as children — those things we needed to do to survive, to get through. They were the only things we knew to do at the time. We may still be doing those things, although they may now be inappropriate and may greatly interfere with our living. A client of mine was working on the part of her that kept her from doing the kinds of physical activities she wanted to do. She wanted to ski, for example, but was fearful. In the course of the work, she discovered a very fearful little girl part of herself. She talked to this little girl part, and then I talked to this little girl part. The little girl part had difficulty expressing herself, so I asked her to draw a picture of what it was like to feel afraid. Out of this drawing came much material that directly related to her need to keep herself protected. When we brought this out in the open, my client could begin to see the separation of her then and now experience of self.

The Older Adult

I don't like to differentiate the older adult in a special category. However, I know that we need to do this now in a different way — not to set older people apart, but to begin to understand something about old age and all the myths that surround it. For a long time therapists have worked with older people hesitantly, as if it were too late to do anything. We now recognize that this idea is another misconception and another form of subtle oppression, and we are seeing the process of aging in a new light.

I think it's true that many old people close in their real feelings to protect themselves from a harsh world. Lately, with the new realization that older people play an important part in our society (and in fact will soon outnumber young people), there has been a lot of attention given to them. Programs are being developed for the benefit of older adults, and some of these programs include psychological counseling. All of us, including the aged themselves, have swallowed the many myths surrounding aging. The aged, like the rest of us, need help in throwing off faulty introjected material and regaining the power and self-determination that is rightly theirs.

Gerontology studies are increasing in the colleges — programs to assist people in the study of what getting older is all about. The students in these programs are also involving themselves directly in a variety of different kinds of work with older people. Several people who had taken my training class have told me that they have used many of these techniques in helping older people express their deep feelings about themselves and about life.

Siblings

Occasionally I have had the opportunity to work with siblings who are having relationship problems. Often I find that brothers and sisters do their mutual hitting, poking, biting, kicking, and screaming within hearing or viewing distance of their parents. It is usually obvious that this behavior is more of a communication to the parents than to each other.

I find, however, that it can be very valuable and illuminating to see these children without their parents. I work with them as I might any group, introducing the kinds of activities that are fun and conducive to greater self-expression. I find that as the children begin to know each other, hear each other, talk to each other, and express resentments, angry feelings, jealousies, and appreciations to each other, they begin to develop a cooperation that helps them to cope with the total family situation. It is amazing to me that these children can live under the same roof and yet know very little about each other. Sometimes parents will say, "They really are very close," having no awareness of the distance that exists between them.

I don't necessarily feel that siblings must like each other just because they are related. I do feel that they, too, need to appreciate their own differentness from each other, just as their parents need to appreciate each child's specialness. Sometimes they learn to like each other in the process of the therapy.

WINDOWS TO OUR CHILDREN

Very Young Children

Generally when I am asked to see a very young child, perhaps four to five years old, I am fairly certain that there are some particular family dynamics that the child is reacting to by behaving in a manner that causes concern. I will, nevertheless, see the child alone after the first session. I can tell a lot about the family situation by what happens as the child plays. Young children involve themselves freely in their play, and some invite me to participate.

Although many young children play out some worries and conflicts, the play therapy alone is not enough to overcome a difficult child/parent relationship. When I can begin to understand what the child tells me about his life through his play or through talking to me, I can then begin to involve the parents.

When we have a family session, young children quickly become bored and restless. But I need to make sure that the child is an involved participant. One way of doing this is to ask the parents to draw a picture of a particular problem. I try to move from generalities into specifics whenever possible; so if a parent says, "He never does what I ask him to do," I might ask her to draw a picture of one thing he never does. The child, too, is invited to draw a picture of something his mother doesn't do.

The mother of a five-year-old boy complained about his relationship with his older sister and younger brother. As she spoke, the boy sat with his hands over his ears. I asked her to draw a picture of one thing that bothered her. He watched in fascination as she drew a picture of a table at mealtime with the family sitting around eating. She described this time as particularly stressful. I asked her to speak to her five-year-old in the picture.

Mother: Paul, I wish you wouldn't tease your brother and hit your sister when we're eating dinner. It's the only time we have to be together lately. (The mother, a single parent, worked and went to school.) When you do that, they start yelling and hitting too, and I can't stand it and I start screaming at you.

Paul: (from the sidelines) Cathy always hits me first! (I instructed the mother to continue talking to the boy in the picture.)

Other Considerations

Mother: It's hard for me to tell who starts it, Paul. I just know you do it a lot, and maybe if you wouldn't do it, she wouldn't. (I continue by asking the mother to tell Paul in the picture how she would like the mealtime to be.)

Mother: I want to hear what's going on with everyone. I want to be with all of you. I hardly ever get to be with you these days. (She begins to weep.)

Tell the children in the picture about your tears.

Mother: I feel so bad that I don't have time to be with you more. I worry that it isn't good for you, Paul. I know you hit sometimes because you need me more, and I'm so tired now. (Paul's mother weeps openly. Paul goes over to his mother and she holds him.)

Paul: Mommy, when you're through with school you said you'd have more time with us.

Mother: That's right!

They sat and hugged. We talked a little while longer before the session ended. Paul's mother told me later that mealtime tension had decreased markedly. Paul became a leader in getting his little brother and older sister to adopt a more thoughtful attitude toward their hardworking mother.

Children respond amazingly well to talking through pictures. A four year-old boy drew a figure with an open mouth he labeled a "yelling mother." I asked him to be the picture and yell. He began yelling at an imaginary boy, himself. At another time, I asked him to draw his house with a person, maybe himself, standing next to it. He drew his house and a large head with a very downcast mouth. As the head, he expressed many bad feelings about what went on in that house.

I will often draw pictures on paper, the chalk board, or the magic slate as young children talk to me. I might draw a large picture of a child as she describes herself — sometimes by looking in a mirror. Or I will draw pictures to be hung on the dart board. One young boy who had made no effort to hide his anger at me and the whole idea of being in my office became my friend when I drew a picture of myself, tacked it up on the dart board, and said "Here, if you're so mad at me, why not take some shots at me." The boy thoroughly enjoyed hitting the picture of me square in the mouth with the rubber-tipped darts.

WINDOWS TO OUR CHILDREN

When I see very young children by themselves, I sometimes ask the mother (who usually brings the child) to join us at the beginning of the sessions so that we can talk about how things are going at home. I have found that many times the mother will raise an issue involving the child that he can work through later in his play.

I had been seeing Kenny, a five-year-old boy whose problem behaviors were temper tantrums, fighting with other children, and hitting everyone in sight. After three months of once-a-week sessions, some of which included one or both parents, and some of which included siblings, Kenny apparently no longer needed to hit out and call for help as before. I asked his mother to join us at the beginning of a session to discuss possible termination. Kenny listened as his mother talked about her pleasure in her son and the changes that had taken place for the whole family. She felt, though, that he was not ready to terminate because she was now beginning to be aware of some things that she had not noticed before. I asked her to tell me about one of those things. She worried about the fact that he seemed more fearful of things than she thought he ought to be, and that she had never noticed these fears previously, since he had concealed everything with his aggressive behavior. Kenny listened to all this while drawing doodles and designs on paper with felt pens. Although he said nothing, we treated him as a partner in the conversation, not as someone we were just talking about.

When his mother left the room, he immediately sat down at the wet sand tray. He made a large hill with the sand at the side of his lake and put dinosaurs on the hill and in the water. In the dry sand tray he put tanks and jeeps and army men. He proceeded to have a battle between the army men and the dinosaurs, making many sounds to express the action taking place. Finally the army men captured one very large dinosaur and surrounded him in the dry sand. He then took an Indian from a basket and had the Indian walk up close to the dinosaur. He told me that the Indian was the only one who was not afraid. I asked him to be this Indian and talk about his fearlessness. One of the things he said was, "I'm not afraid of you, even if you are so big." I said, "Does the world seem very big to you sometimes, Kenny?" He nodded, eyes big. We talked about this feeling of being small in an overwhelming world. Previously he had needed to show everyone how big he thought he was. This session paved the way for fruitful work with

Kenny about his fearfulness. In another month he was ready to begin winding down our visits together.

The Family

I am often asked how I can do therapy with children if I can't get the family to come in and do some changing. Sometimes children are referred to as if they are appendages of their parents. Certainly a child is often the scapegoat for an unhealthy family, but this does not make him less a person in his own right. At times the parents choose to point the finger at a particular child as the source of a problem because the child is making life uncomfortable in some way for them. I would never turn this child away, even when perhaps the parents are the ones that need psychological help but refuse it. He is indicating his rebellion through the behavior that motivates parents to seek help for him. This child needs to know he can find support and connection with someone who respects him as an individual with the right to his own growth.

My first contact with the family, following my initial phone conversation with one of the parents, is at the first session. Rarely does a member of the family say, "Our whole family is in trouble and we all need therapy." Most practitioners will agree that the adults in the family generally single out one person as the one with all the problems.

Since I can only begin with what is presented to me, I begin with the child who is identified as having the problems. In the first session, which generally does not include siblings unless a specific sibling relationship is the identified problem, I meet with the child and the parents. Since I see many single-parent families, often only the mother is present. This first meeting is an important one: It gives me my first experience of the child. It allows me to observe the source of worry — the presenting problem. The child can find out — sometimes for the first time — what is troubling the parents about her. The child has a chance to see me and evaluate me and what I do. Above all I can get some sense of the dynamics of the parent-child relationship. Often at this first session I can decide on the beginning procedure for the therapy. I can make some determination about the usefulness of seeing the child alone, the mother and/or father alone, or with the child, or if there are other children or family members (such as significant grandparents), the whole family.

If I make an error in my initial determination, it will soon surface. With that in mind, I go where my observations and intuition direct, feeling free to change direction at any time.

Even though it may be obvious that the child is merely a scapegoat in a chaotic or malfunctioning family, I will often begin by seeing the child alone. The very fact that he has been singled out as the problem and that he has done something that has called attention to himself indicates that this child needs an opportunity to gain some support for himself.

After a few sessions of seeing the child, the situation begins to take on a clearer perspective. At this point I may decide it is time for the family to come in. It may be clear now that unless we change the family's present system of relating, nothing much will happen to help the distressing symptom or behavior. Or I may feel that I need to gain an even clearer sense of the family's methods of interacting with each other before I do further work with the child.

When I feel that the family should be invited in for a session, I discuss this with the child. Sometimes the child objects violently, telling me even more about his family's dynamics. If he does this, we then deal with his objection, knowing that the expression and resolution of this objection is an important opportunity for growth. Sometimes a child is so fearful of a joint session with his family that we need to continue our individual work further until he is ready to deal with his fears. Often, though, the child is receptive to the idea, and sometimes quite pleased with it.

I had been seeing nine-year-old Don for about a month when I arranged a family session. On their arrival — mother, father, older brother, younger sister — Don requested that he come into the room by himself at first. He came in and immediately began straightening up the room! He bustled about, setting the shelves in order, arranging the chairs, plumping up pillows. He then announced he was ready for the others. As his family entered the room he directed each to a particular seat, introducing me to his brother and sister. (I had met the parents at the first session.) The family, unused to such directive, organized behavior from this boy, meekly followed his instructions. When we were all seated (his place next to mine) he smiled broadly at me, as if to say, "You can begin now."

Other Considerations

I don't use family sessions as forums for evaluation of a child's progress and behavior. I want to get some picture of how a family functions together. Walter Kempler in his book *Principles of Gestalt Family Therapy*, describes six procedures for therapist intervention to carry this task out: 1) Starting a family conversation, 2) The search for personal needs, 3) Refining the message, 4) The prompt, poignant delivery, 5) A time for response, 6) Monitoring the family conversation.

The family conversation makes it possible for the therapist to determine patterns of relating. I may begin by throwing out any topic or by waiting for someone else to take the lead. Generally one parent makes some remark such as, "We're wondering why you wanted us to come in" or "Don really surprised us by the way he told us where to sit" or "Don seems to be doing better at home." As soon as I can, I request that remarks be directed to the person, rather than to me.

Mother: Don, you surprised me by how you told us where to sit.

Don: Why? (I know he means more by "why," since his question represents an underlying statement. He may mean, "I can do lots of things that you don't know about because you never notice." But I don't pursue this at this early point.)

If Don makes no response, I might ask him to respond. Or I might ask his mother to say something to Don about her surprise at his competence, to clarify her response:

Mother: Well, you never did anything like that before. I liked your doing it.

And we have started a conversation with at least two members. I might intervene again here to ask the father and the other children if they were surprised. Or, taking a cue from her pleased surprise over the seating direction, I might ask the mother to tell Don what she would like from him at home. Kempler suggests requests like, "What do you want from each other that you aren't getting these days?" or "Give me one problem you all want cured today." The depths of individual wants, needs, wishes, and hopes are rarely heard in many families.

I find that families tend to be very general in their interactions. I will constantly ask for more specific data. If an adult member says "I don't like your attitude toward me," I may say "Tell her a specific example of how her attitude bothers you, or how it bothers you here." The child, too, will have many generalized complaints, like "You never take me anywhere," and I may say, "Tell her one place where you would like her to take you."

In family sessions, messages need to be spoken directly to the person they are meant for. It must be made clear that one either talks about himself or to another. "I'm feeling very sad right now" is self-expression. "Don makes me feel sad when he acts the way he does" is not only a distortion, it is an accusation thrown in the general direction of Don to which he can only respond defensively. Asking the mother to direct her remarks to Don can clarify the meaning and promote communication.

Mother: Don, I feel sad when I see you getting in trouble at school.
Please elaborate on this.
Mother: Well, it makes me feel that I haven't done a good job as a mother.

When the message is direct, the hidden feelings begin to emerge. The family members begin to see each other in new ways. Sometimes I will suggest an exercise to promote direct communication. I might, for example, ask the family members each to go around the room and say one thing they like and one thing that bothers them about each other person.

In his paper, "Experiential Family Therapy" Kempler postulates three principles as requirements for fruitful family interviews: no interruptions, no questions (instead, making the statement that is usually behind the question), and no gossip (instead, talking directly to the person, not *about* him). Kempler emphasizes the importance of prompt, direct response by family members. Interruptions are also common among family members, and the therapist needs to deal with the interruptive pattern as it emerges.

I must determine when to intervene and when to sit back and watch. I need to listen very carefully to the content and to the feelings embedded in the content. I need to watch for generalities and big words that children may not understand. I need to watch the body postures, gestures, expressions, and breathing of each member as clues for directing awareness to what is happening with each person. I need to determine patterns in the process that I see unfolding before my eyes. I need to remind people to stay with the here and now situation, and also to know when unfinished business from the past needs to be dealt with. I need to keep the communication focused, rather than scattered, diffused, and fragmented. I need to be

Other Considerations

sure that each person's message is clear and that each message is heard. I may need to ask someone to restate a message they have received, to make sure that it has been understood. I might ask for example, "Mother, what did you just hear Don saying to you?"

In the therapeutic family session, I become the extra eyes and ears for the whole family. In the heat of their involvement, or behind the wall of their isolation, the family members often cannot see and hear what I can. I need to direct attention to what I think and feel is important.

I need to pay attention to my own feelings in such a session. If I am getting a headache because of a frantic bedlam gotten out of hand, I will shout out my feelings. If I am moved by a child's response, I will tell him so. In this type of session I am part of the group, with feelings, messages, and responses of my own.

I did an all day workshop once with a group of children and their parents in which we drew pictures, worked with clay, and did some fantasies. Many of the parents were surprised at the responses of their children, and the children, too, were fascinated to hear their own parents share their experiences with the exercises. After an exercise with clay in which everyone was asked to keep their eyes closed and make some form, a father said, as his piece of clay, "I'm a rectangular form and on top of me is a large lump. The lump is pressing down on my rectangular form and I have trouble holding it up. It's heavy and not too secure. That's how I feel sometimes (voice low), like there's just too much pressing on my shoulders." His eleven-year-old son reached out to touch his father and with tears in his eyes said, "I didn't know that, Dad." The father looked at his son, and they embraced. There weren't too many dry eyes among the rest of the group as they watched and listened.

The word "communication" is much overused. Often a parent will say, "We don't know how to communicate with each other. What we want from you is to teach us how to communicate." Or, "She never talks to us." Although I know that communication is important, and there are valuable exercises available to help improve communication skills, the real trouble is usually deeper. When communication is presented as a problem, I can be sure that feelings aren't being heard, acknowledged, and accepted. When faulty communication is stated as the source of all the trouble, I can be pretty sure that someone feels manipulated, or powerless, or deadlocked in a power struggle. I can also feel sure that under those feelings that aren't being heard are some that are not even being expressed. Communication is not just talking to each other in a nice, civilized way. In the first place, talking to each other is not easy. And to maintain a good level of communication and healthy interaction one must expect and be willing to experience conflict, pain, anger, sadness, jealousy, and resentment, etc., along with the good feelings that come with sound, vigorous, intimate interchange.

The child who says, "My parents don't listen to me. They don't even know who I am!" is a child whose feelings have been bypassed. The father who says, "Why I know him! He likes to play ball, he'd rather be with his friends than with us or do his homework, he likes music, he gets mad easy . . . ." has no inkling of his son's real feelings about anything. Some parents will admit, "I just don't know her anymore." The daughter has long stopped expressing her feelings to her parents, her doubts and concerns and wonderings. She has been ignored, rebuffed, overridden too many times. When she tries to express her opinions and feelings, as she may every now and then, she can sense their disapproval and disagreement even as they attempt to listen politely. Somewhere along the line she has stopped living up to their expectations — the *image* of the daughter they thought they were raising — and so they don't know *her* anymore.

The family session provides a good arena wherein the therapist can establish the differentness and uniqueness of the various family members. Parents who truly want to relate to their children are often shocked to discover how biased and unaccepting they are of the child's separateness — her likes, dislikes, desires, present life-style, friends, opinions, future plans, and sometimes even appearance. They may have difficulty even *seeing*, much less acknowledging, that she is a separate, unique person with tastes of her own. They may continue to view her as the child of five they once knew, or the daughter they assumed would be just like them.

In *Conjoint Family Therapy*, Virginia Satir states, "Dysfunctional families have great trouble acknowledging differentness or individuality. In such families, to be different is to be bad, and invites being unloved." She goes on to say that such families tend to "overlook" or to "blur" their disagreements, whether these are disagreements over perception or opinion, and that ". . . dysfunctional families have just as much trouble communicating about pleasure as they have communicating about pain."

Other Considerations

Parents need to begin to learn to give clear messages to the child as well as to acknowledge and respect the child as a separate, unique, entitled, worthwhile individual. This will promote the child's own feelings of self-worth and self-support, and will enhance his contact skills and abilities. As parents become able to view him in all his uniqueness and separateness, he is able to sharpen his own abilities to experience his environment and cope with it.

Some of my work with parents becomes simple teaching and guiding. Many parents beg for specific advice and guidelines for working with their children, and I am willing to make suggestions to relieve family tension. However, I believe that more long-lasting results come about through giving the parents the opportunity to become aware of, and work through, their present attitudes, reactions, and interactions with their children.

In the section on self-esteem, I list many suggestions that are useful to help strengthen a child's feelings of self. Often I will refer the parents to various books I think would assist them in better parenting. Here are two additional suggestions that bring very quick positive results:

With young children, provide a regular time each day for a "mad session." This is a time the child can say all the things that made him mad that day without argument, contradiction, explanation, justification or comment from the parent. Bedtime is a good time for this — it does *not*, as some might think, leave the child in a bad mood for sleeping.

Spend a regular time each day, or every other day, with your child that is his very own special time with you. This time can be quite short, twenty to thirty minutes, and a kitchen timer can be used to mark the end of the period. The child makes the decision for the activity. Mothers will say, "I spend a lot of time with him." Most of this time, however, is not a time where the parent gives the child undivided attention doing something *he* wants to do. Bedtime rituals don't count for this time.

I sometimes point out to parents who are at their wit's end that whatever they have been doing has not been working. They need to see clearly what has been happening and to make some effort to break the vicious cycle. Trying any new behavior is often useful. Even if it is not particularly useful in itself, it can help make the existing pattern clearer. And by introducing something new, it can soften the rigidity of the present situation.

WINDOWS TO OUR CHILDREN

Over and over I must remind parents that they are not their children. Many parents become so identified with their children that they have trouble recognizing that their children are separate people. For example, one mother became enraged when her son dawdled. When this mother was a child, her own mother had screamed at her for dawdling. Now when her son dawdled, she would scream at him, even though as a child she had hated her own mother's screaming. She seemed to become, at these moments, both her own child and her own mother simultaneously. With awareness of what was happening, she was able to begin to view these scenes with new perspective and behave in a more appropriate manner.

Often parents project onto their children what they are feeling. Children are not only separate beings, they also have their own separate feelings. One mother said to me, "I know Jackie is burying his feelings about his handicap (he walked with a limp). I try to talk to him about it but he doesn't seem as concerned as I know he must be." Certainly Jackie had some feelings about his limp, but not nearly the intense ones his mother assumed he felt. She, however, had many strong feelings about the limp that she had trouble coping with.

Schools, Teachers, and Training

Since children spend most of their time in school, it seems logical to me that all people who work with children outside the school setting ought to take the time to find out what schools are like for children today. Our own school experiences, if not forgotten, may have been quite different.

It worries me that far too many of the children I see in therapy dislike school. They may have one teacher they like and they may enjoy being with friends, but on the whole they seem to view school as a kind of prison. In *Crisis in the Classroom*, Silberman presents a brilliant analysis following his four-year study of the public educational system in the United States. He argues the need for radical change, giving example after example of the failure of the schools to meet the needs of children, both intellectually and emotionally.

The negative attitude of children toward schools ought to alarm us. Yet, except for a few innovative programs here and there, I see no real

Other Considerations

changes taking place. Because I work with children who are troubled enough to have found their way into therapy, I am particularly concerned about what goes on in the schools. It would seem that a place where children need to spend so much time should be a joyful place, a place for experiencing and learning in the broadest sense. We seem to feel a need to grind out the reading and the writing and the arithmetic skills, but we pay too little attention to the fact that unless we meet the psychological and emotional needs of children, we are helping to create and maintain a society that does not value people.

I have long felt that teachers ought to be trained as therapists as well as educators. The emotional needs of children ought to be given priority in the learning situation. Many teachers today are feeling the need for more of this kind of training and are seeking help on their own if they can't find it in the colleges or in the in-service programs of the school systems.

I have taught a number of classes for teachers on the kind of work I do. I don't pretend to give any in-depth kind of training, but I do present a basic rationale and a variety of ideas and techniques for teachers to use with kids. This can help the teachers make better contact with the children, help the children feel that the classroom can be a safe, comfortable place to be, and help the children and the teacher open up to each other as human beings with human problems. I want to help teachers begin to see children in a different light. I want them to see that if kids are anxious or are suffering in some way, or are feeling that they're not worth much, they are not going to learn. Children who see the teacher as indifferent and cold to them, and who are not treated as entitled, worthy human beings will learn less. So I introduce some new attitudes and some new ways that they can help to improve the child's self-concept, some methods for expressing interest in the child's feelings and life, and ways to make it possible for the child to express himself as well.

Many teachers themselves are discouraged, frustrated, and negatively affected by the school regimen and the demands the schools place upon them. They take the brunt of the children's rejecting attitudes toward school, and sometimes out of their own frustration they turn their own negative feelings toward the children.

I am well aware that even the most dedicated, humanistic teachers face an uphill battle. Nothing much can be done until the power structure

WINDOWS TO OUR CHILDREN

is changed to better meet the needs of children. Much must be done outside the classroom. There are ways, however, to make some beginnings inside the classroom. Teachers can join with the children they teach in knowing each other better, seeing each other's tasks in the school setting in a realistic light, and helping each other feel stronger and better about themselves.

Even though teachers are not trained as therapists, they can still make use of these methods at whatever level is comfortable for them. The teachers I meet in my work have a deep interest in children and use these ideas in a responsible way. I have not yet come across a teacher who would use any of these techniques to embarrass a child, or to dig recklessly into the child's psyche, or who would break the child's confidence by reporting private information to parents or other school personnel.

Many teachers want to make schools a better place for children and they need some tools and techniques for making a start. Some of these teachers are encouraged to do what they can by the administration. Others are fearful of consequences. Some go ahead in spite of fear. One teacher wrote to me: "I'm going to be teaching a remedial math class this summer, and you can be sure that we'll be using some of these techniques every day, even if they fire me for it. I can't believe what a difference it made in my regular classroom when I started this stuff. I was happier, the kids were happier, you could just feel the good vibrations in the class. It was like a secret we all shared, and there was a feeling of caring and 'we're in this together.' It carried over into everything we did."

I'm impressed by comments like this, and also by the new suggestions that I continue to receive from teachers that I've met through my classes and consulting work.

These comments consistently tell about differences in attitudes between teachers and students, better relationships between students, and children who appear to be more relaxed and calm and who have better concentration, seem happier, and look forward to and enjoy the experiences. These methods can make a difference. They have been used by teachers of children from kindergarten through high school. Here are some other comments from teachers after they had put some of these techniques into practice:

Other Considerations

Sixth grade teacher: I felt much closer to, and happier being with, my students and they reacted more positively and warmly toward me. I think they started to care about each other.

Third grade teacher: I was really surprised at how courteous and interested in each other they became (forty kids makes a lot of listening to do without talking or being rude, and this was done without any prompting from me!)

Seventh grade English teacher: Next year I'd like to start this earlier so I could learn more about my students and they would feel more comfortable with other students and me. It is interesting that students wanted to be free and away from problems and yet also wanted to be secure and taken care of by others. I guess that is the classic dilemma for adolescents. For example, one girl wanted to be on a hill all by herself and yet wanted to be a cat because she wanted a lot of attention. (The exercise she did was "Draw your favorite animal, and the place you would want to be.")

Kindergarten teacher: One of my boys happens to be a slow learner and also a discipline problem, and the exercise gave me much insight into his thoughts. (The teacher had placed a number of objects on the floor. Each child was told to pick any item and tell how it feels to be that item.) This boy picked a large red cardboard star. He chose this because he said he would make people happy, because he would be on their paper when they did good work.

Seventh grade English: There was absolute silence through the whole rosebush fantasy experience. They all seemed to be very involved in what was taking place. When colored pencils were passed out, this was one time when there was no fighting or arguing over materials. I was surprised and overwhelmed by the honesty and personal feelings they expressed to me when I asked them — after a few shared orally — to write something about their rosebush on their papers. This is the last week of the school year, and yet after this exercise I realize that I don't really know some of the students too well. I wish I knew about this sooner. Next year I'll start right in at the beginning. I'm excited about it.

Ninth grade algebra teacher: I spent five minutes doing a fantasy where they closed their eyes and finished their unfinished thoughts and feelings before coming into this class, and then led them through a fantasy of a place they'd like to be. The time spent doing this was no more than the usual time of getting the class started, but the productivity seemed much greater. The exercise had a very calming influence and the students seemed to be able to concentrate on their studies better after the experience. They even seemed to relate much better with one another.

High school nurse: I haven't had time to do drawings and things but because of my new awareness of myself and my students, it seems that my relationship has improved with students and other faculty. The girls who have sat behind my closed door in pregnancy counseling have a new look in their eyes, a look that says to me that they see that I *really care* about them and not just about giving them information.

Fourth grade teacher: As each child talked about his drawing the child seemed to take on a different personality from his school self.

Seventh/eighth grade English teacher: Everybody listened to everybody else and I think we all got to know each other better. We found that there were things that we had in common with one another and that other people shared our interests.

First grade teacher: I never dreamed that a picture could help a person become more aware of himself or other people. When I did an exercise asking the kids to draw their families as animals I was amazed at what came out. The most interesting part to me was having the children give explanations of their pictures. If I had made my own interpretations I would have been way off base. The class loves doing these things.

Tenth grade English teacher: After applying some of the techniques that I learned and seeing the results, I've really become interested and excited about teaching again. Two boys always disrupted and never did any assignments. Now, since I've been paying attention to their feelings and to them as people through the exercises we've been doing, they have been doing all of their work, and more than that, we've become friends with each other.

The best way for me to teach therapists, teachers, and other people to use these techniques is to give them direct experience with them. One of the difficulties with reading a book is that you don't experience anything except the reading. Even the ideas I present will be understood and taken in by you through what you bring of yourself to the reading — your own experiences, ideas, views.

Other Considerations

In my classes, I find that when people *do* some of the things I talk about, when they work with me through these experiences, the integration of the techniques is far greater. Through the experience, they gain some new understanding of themselves and bring new depth to their work with children.

Role-playing is one of several projective techniques that is especially useful for training. When we role-play a particular character, we bring ourselves, our own experiences, into the playing out of that character.

For example, in one of my consulting groups we were talking about the first session, with parent and child. I sensed that people were not quite grasping the ideas I was trying to get across to them. We devised a role-playing situation of a first session, with one of the counselors playing a six-year-old girl, while another volunteered to be the mother. I acted as therapist, though someone else might have taken on this task. We did not determine in advance what the situation would be, but allowed the "six-year-old" to decide how she would act and the "mother" to present the problem and decide how she would conduct herself in the session. Each allowed herself to react freely as the session progressed, and this spontaneity greatly added to the role-playing situation.

Each of us can contact our six-year-old self if we try, and each can contact the mother (the introjected mother as well as the mother role we may have in real life). Both of these people allowed themselves to fully "be" these characters, and the ideas I had been talking about took on a living clarity as we put them into practice.

A difficulty I have encountered in training sessions is the presentation of theoretical material. Students come from many different levels of professional training, and sometimes I have a hard time finding a common ground for the presentation of theory. I myself learned most of my theoretical knowledge in the process of doing.

Lecturing on theory and recommending books on theory is certainly part of the training procedure. However, the best presentation of theory comes from integrating it with the doing. As I work with people in their experience of the techniques I present, I want to connect this work with theoretical understanding. I don't do this *as* I work, for this would interrupt the flow of the work itself, but I do this as soon as I can in a follow-up discussion and interaction. As people can connect theoretical concepts with their own work, the work of others that they observe, and the work of children that we talk about, they begin to integrate an understanding of theory as it fits with practice.

Sexism

Prejudice or discrimination based on gender has been so much a part of our culture for so long that we take it for granted. Hence, we must begin to weed it out by recognizing it in all of its subtle, insidious forms.

Sexism affects the growth of children. It suppresses many of their natural capabilities, preventing full free-flowing organismic development. Girls are often encouraged to develop only that which we label as "feminine" and boys are encouraged to only do that which is considered "masculine," thus inhibiting huge areas of inherent human capacities in each. These capacities keep pushing to break through anyway, and what happens when they do greatly affects the child's emotional health.

What we call masculine qualities and feminine qualities both ought to be considered as part of everyone's total makeup. We used to worry a lot about a child's need to identify with the parent of his own sex. We felt he needed a masculine model, and she needed a feminine model. I think we have come to realize that both men and women need *all* the qualities of being human: both feeling and acting, dependence and assertion, anger and sadness, etc. Those qualities that we once acknowledged as manly and those that we called womanly need to be realized in every human being, both man and woman. Children need to know that what we do in life can be drawn from the total of human experience, not limited and biased by cultural expectations, and can be geared to the person's individual uniqueness, interests, talents, and abilities.

Although progress has been made, our society is today still plagued by sexist attitudes, and we sometimes have to stress and exaggerate all of the possibilities available to our children. When my son was two years old, people were aghast that we gave him a doll carriage and a doll for his birthday. Today they smile acceptingly as they see him tenderly and gently care for his own young son. My daughter has been greatly influenced, I think, from watching my own struggle to be my own person at a time when this was even more difficult than it is today. I see her as having great vitality and fierce independence along with her tender loving qualities, and I think that my own intense grapplings with myself and my life gave her the permission and impetus to allow her own personal strength to be cultivated.

Many of us are still fighting the battle. Our own sexist attitudes creep up inside us often, impeding our progress toward full self-realization. As I work with young people I see the effects of sexist attitudes that have penetrated into their feelings and behaviors, and I am as amazed as I become aware of my own. I see, too, their confused struggles against their own natural needs and wants.

Parental attitudes, the media, and schools all play a large part in the formation of sexist attitudes. Even those of us who want to change these attitudes often participate in perpetuating them. I highly recommend the book *And Jill Came Tumbling After: Sexism in American Education*. This book presents a variety of writings that point out succinctly how we perpetuate attitudes of sexism from early childhood on, not only in the schools but at home and in the world, a world that includes the therapist's office.

12

Interview with Violet Oaklander

Christiane Elsbree: Violet, I first met you in 1979 shortly after *Windows to Our Children* was published. During these past thirty years, I've witnessed the expansion of your work, your prolific writing of chapters and articles. I've witnessed the demand for you to travel worldwide to speak and to teach. I've watched the production of several audiotapes and videotapes describing your work with children and adolescents. I've seen the development of your two-week training program, from the first training program to the last training program, and the publication of Peter Mortola's book based on his study of that training program. I've seen the interest in *Windows to Our Children* give rise to translations in thirteen different languages.

There's probably another translation underway as we speak. [Laughs] The number of translations is mentioned often. But, what is most telling to me about the breadth of the impact of your work are the languages in which *Windows* appears. So, I'm going to take the time to note those languages here: German, Portuguese, Spanish, Hebrew, Russian, Croatian and Serbo-Croatian, Italian, Chinese, Korean, Czech, Lithuanian, and the English language edition appears in South Africa, Australia, New Zealand, the British Isles, and of course, North America.

Now, today, I'm here with you in "The House that Martha Built," to which you have retired after writing your second book, *Hidden Treasures*, which already, in this brief time that it's been out, has been published in Spanish and Lithuanian, and is being translated into German. We're here surrounded with mementos from your travels. So, tell me how it all began.

WINDOWS TO OUR CHILDREN

Violet: [Laughs] How did it all begin? Well, it wasn't planned. I'll tell you that much. My work sort of evolved — it evolved. I started working with children, even as a teenager, when I worked in camps for several years as a counselor. And, even after I was married, my husband and I worked in camps. So, I've had quite a bit of experience working with kids. I was an arts and craft counselor. I was singing — I used to lead all the singing. I was the swimming counselor. I did a variety of things like that. I taught nursery school briefly, in Denver for the Jewish Community Centers for about a year. Of course, I've had three children of my own.

I went back to school when I had three young children after we moved to California because it was so easy to go to school here. I'd only had one year of college when I got married and I went to work so my husband could go to school. I thought I would be a teacher so I could be home with my children when they were home. After I graduated, I got a job in Long Beach, California as a teacher. It was not an easy thing for me. I didn't think I was cut out to be a teacher because, I guess, I was an alternative teacher before I knew what that meant. I used to do a lot of different things with the kids. The principal asked me why I didn't go into recreation instead of being a teacher. [Laughter] He actually did.

I could write a book about what I did in those days. It was really pretty interesting. But, the counselor of the school that I worked in said: "Why don't you look into teaching emotionally disturbed children, you'd be really good at that, and they're just starting these programs?" It was pretty new. This was in 1967, I mean, I started teaching in 1965, so the middle of 1967. So, I went to visit those classes, they had just started them. They didn't have teachers who would do it. But, I thought it was wonderful — you could do whatever you wanted, and there were twelve kids and an aide. So, I transferred into doing that, and it was amazing.

After I did it for about . . . Oh, I did it all together for six years with emotionally disturbed children. I won a United States Office of Education Fellowship to get my master's in special education with emotionally disturbed children. I did that at Cal State University at Long Beach. They had a big, Special Ed Department, and work with emotionally disturbed children was quite new.

Just about that time, I started training at the Gestalt Therapy Institute of Los Angeles. I thought at some point I might leave working in the school system and go into private practice. So, I trained for about three years. I became certified. While I was training, I realized they never talked about children. And we studied a lot of books. There were a couple of books, one was George Brown's *Human Teaching for Human Learning*, but it was, mostly about Gestalt awareness in education. There was another book by Janet Lederman, *Anger and the Rocking Chair*, which is almost like a lyrical poem about her work with disturbed children.

But, there really wasn't anything about doing psychotherapy with children. So, I started doing a lot of thinking about applying Gestalt therapy to children, the theory, and the philosophy. It really seemed to fit for me. I brought that into my classroom with emotionally disturbed children. I did a lot of experimenting with some of the practices and techniques with the theoretical foundation in my mind of what I was doing. It was so successful.

For example, I used to have different groups. At one point, I had a group of boys who were eleven, twelve, and thirteen — very disturbed boys. I had them finger painting, because I felt that they needed that sensory experience. They had very little sensory experience because they were so disturbed they weren't allowed to do many kinds of things. Their lives were so structured. In fact, they weren't in school until these classes opened up. There weren't that many of those classes either.

So they would stand around, we would put the tables together. I had these trays that I took from the cafeteria and I would put colors on the trays, and they experimented. They realized that if you put red, yellow, and blue, it became brown. [Laughs] So they learned that by experimenting. But, they would finger paint and talk to each other, and make contact in ways that they had never done before. [Before that] mostly, they would hit each other. So that was an amazing experience.

Plus, they felt so good about what they did, because we used to make block prints. They would finally make a design and then I would put the paper over the finger paint, over the tray and out would come this beautiful block print. They could never get over it.

WINDOWS TO OUR CHILDREN

The other thing we used to do that was so amazing was work with wood — and the same thing. They had never been allowed to touch saws and hammers, and we had all that. I saw the other classes order a toolkit, like a cart with all these tools. I thought, "Why not us?" So, I sort of put in my order and in came this wood and the cart with all these saws and all that and sawhorses. They used to have to share a sawhorse, and we had strict boundaries, strict rules. If they swung the saw, they had to sit down that day. So they never did. They loved this.

The head of the Special Ed Department at the university, I had a student teacher who was assigned to me, came in to see his student and watched them working with wood and he said, "You shouldn't be doing this now. You should do this at the end of the day for a reward." They looked like ordinary kids. "Obviously, you are wasting your time having them do this now." Which I felt was ridiculous, because they learned math, they were measuring, they made boxes, and they made birds. They made all kinds of things, except guns. I wouldn't let them make guns. They talked to each other. They shared. There was so much mastery in this activity, and good feeling and contact. We did it every day in the morning. [Laughs] I never used it as a reward, because if I did they would never get to do it.

Anyway, we also had two empty chairs in the room, as one of the things that were always set up. They would have a fight with a teacher or another kid on the playground, and they'd come running, "I need to use the empty chairs." They would put the other kid in the empty chair, that old empty chair technique. I sort of guided, and after they finished they would feel so calm and relaxed. It was something that was always there for them to use.

So that kind of thing, I would try out various things and began to even write some of this stuff down . . . what I was doing. So that was like you might say the beginnings of my ideas, of thinking about using things with children, getting them to express themselves.

Chris: I want to underscore something here. I think that for a lot of teachers to do that and make it successful the way you did, to have a classroom of twelve emotionally disturbed children, who usually were hitting each other but in your classroom didn't, and to have one assistant, and to give them saws and things like that, I imagine that it was your — I don't need to be imagining what it was — I think that the effort that you put into your presence and your contactfulness, to put out the extra effort that it takes to make boundaries, well, to be clearly active and present is what makes that successful in a way that other people don't often do.

Violet: Well, that makes me think of one of the things that happened during this time. I took a leave for about six months because one of my children became very ill. He was in the hospital for a long time, and then he died. Soon after he died, he was almost fifteen, the district called me. They begged me to come back, because a teacher had walked out. She couldn't control the group, and I came back. These were kids around early adolescence. I came back, and they were so wild. I could see why the teacher had walked out. I mean they were running around. They were knocking chairs over, throwing books. They were totally wild.

I sat there watching them. I couldn't believe what I was seeing. The aide kept saying, "Should I call the principal?" And I said, "No, no." I just watched, until one of the boys came over and he said, "How come you're not mad?" [Laughs] I said, "Listen, I just lost my son. Why should this upset me?" "What do you mean?" And they wanted to hear. They gradually all came over and I told them what happened. They asked me lots of questions, and I talked about it, and this brought up a lot of their own issues with loss and grief, and it was amazing. I never had any trouble with them after that, never.

I also had ideas — and I don't know really where I got these ideas. The traditional idea at the time was when you worked with kids like this you had to have to have an environment that had no stimulation. In fact, some classes had cubicles so the kids would not be stimulated. Well, my room was just the opposite. It had all kinds of interesting things in it, all kinds of stuff, a lot like this. [Indicating her artwork and mementos]

Chris: Like your home — colorful? [Laughter]

Violet: Yes. I felt that if you didn't provide these things, they tried to make it on their own. If you put a kid in a cubicle and there is no stimulation, he makes his own stimulation and distraction. So what we would do is, when I would bring something in and I would hang it up or whatever, we'd all look at it. If a plane would go by outside and a kid would run to the window, I would invite everybody to run to the window and look at the plane. We would kind of focus on whatever was foreground at that time. And after a while it was there, and it didn't disturb them or distract them whatever it was. We always did that. We sort of made the distraction foreground.

I did a number of things. For example, we occasionally were invited to an assembly in the school, we didn't often get invited. I would say to the kids, "See that tree?" which would be near the auditorium. "I want you to run as fast as you can to that tree." They would be running to the tree, while all the other classes were marching in order to the auditorium. Of course, the teachers hated me and my class. But I felt like if they were going to sit in the auditorium, they needed to run first. [Laughs] They certainly didn't have that opportunity before in the classroom, so they would run to the tree and wait for me. Then we'd go into the [Laughs] auditorium.

Another thing is I let them chew gum in my classroom. And of course they weren't supposed to chew gum. We had a talk about if they got in trouble, like when it was recess. Always they'd be running around. There'd be another teacher who might yell at them or punish them. But they could chew gum in the classroom because my theory was [Laughs] that they needed to do that. It made them feel better. And now I've read research that gum chewing is really good for the brain. [Laughter]

Chris: I haven't heard that.

Violet: Yes, I read that. In fact, I cut it out somewhere. [Laughs] I did some off-the-wall things like that. The principal I had at that school appreciated it because of what I had done with those kids who were so wild. Then he thought I was a miracle worker. All I was was genuine. All I was was contactful with them.

But I did set boundaries, and they believed me because I followed through. I heard from those kids for years. Some of them would call me. The aim was to get them into a regular mainstream class. Some of them did eventually.

But that was the beginning. What happened was also I had a group. I don't remember whether it was during that time or right after. A Gestalt therapist was working with men in the Navy. Long Beach, where I lived, had a big naval base, and they had a drug and alcohol rehabilitation center, and she was working with mostly men.

They had children. These Navy families used to move together. They had Navy housing. She said, "There are a lot of kids who are children of these men, and I would like to start a group but I don't know anything about kids." So she was in my training program, I guess, when I was training at the Gestalt Therapy Institute of Los Angeles, and knew that I was doing this work.

So she said, "Would you be willing to lead the group?" And I said, "Sure." [Laughs] So I had this group of actually twelve, again, of all ages. I broke all the rules of groups. I think I'm a rule breaker. They were from eight years old to sixteen, and there were some siblings in the group. Some of them would come and go because they'd move. [Laughs] And others would move in. They met in my living room, right in my living room. For two years I had that group. You would think, if you walked into that group after a few sessions when we got really going, that you were walking into an adult Gestalt therapy group. We worked on dreams. [Laughs] We worked with clay right in my living room. We drew pictures. We did all the things I actually eventually wrote about.

Here's one story. We worked on dreams, and this girl was about thirteen. She said, "Oh, I had this dream last night." That was something we sometimes did, so she tells the dream: She was lying in a coffin, and everybody thought she was dead. They were crying, and they were grieving over her. She said, "But I wasn't dead. I kept saying, 'I'm not dead! I'm not dead!' But they didn't hear me. [Laughs] So that was my dream. It was so frustrating because they didn't hear me or see me!"

So I said, "OK. Well, we'll act out the dream. So you lie on the rug. Make believe you're in the coffin, and we'll be the mourners." All the kids got up and surrounded her. [Laughs] I sort of acted it out, and they followed me. We grieved and we cried. And she's yelling, "I'm not dead! I'm not dead!" [Laughter]

And I'm saying, "We don't hear her. We'll ignore her." And that's what we did. And then we talked about what does that tell you? She said, "Sometimes nobody does hear me. They don't pay any attention to what I'm saying. They're not listening to me." And all the kids, of course, could connect with that. And we had the most incredible discussion about how

WINDOWS TO OUR CHILDREN

they don't get heard, and what could we do about it? How can we get ourselves heard?

I didn't work with their families at all. I never even met their fathers or their mothers actually. [Laughs] Well, that's not true. I actually met a couple of them who came in later as a family unit. But this was later when I was in private practice.

That's the kind of thing we did. Or we did clay and had them make something with their eyes closed, and then be that thing they made.

I remember one girl said, "Well, I'm the sun." She made a happy sun. We dialogued a little bit, and I said, "What do you do?" "Well, I warm people and I make people feel good. People like me." I said, "You look happy." The kids could give their comments. It was all really done in a very nice way. Then I said, "How does that fit for you in your life?" She was not a happy kid, and she said, "I don't let myself be like that sun. I'm not like that sun." I said, "How come?" She said, "Well, if I am, people will think that everything is good and it isn't. And I don't want them to think everything is good, so I don't smile and be like that sun." That was exactly her process. That's the kind of thing that we would get out of these activities, and right in my living room. [Laughs]

Chris: And this was while you were in the Gestalt Therapy Institute of Los Angeles training program?

Violet: Yes. I think it was during that time. It was during that time because that woman was one of the people — I wasn't licensed yet, and I was working sort of under her.

Finally, I left the school system. My marriage broke up, and I decided I didn't want to stay working for the school system; I'd be there forever. I had good pay and good benefits [laughs] and I'd be stuck. I hated the bureaucracy of the school district. They wanted accountability and lots of paperwork.

I left and went back to school because the Board of Behavior Sciences accepted my Masters in Special Education, but I needed more. I needed three classes and five-hundred more hours. I actually had done a few workshops as sort of a co-therapist with my husband who was a Gestalt trainer. He had trained with Fritz Perls himself. But they wouldn't give me credit for that because he was my husband. At the time they just wouldn't do that. I think they later did, but that was at that time. And I didn't protest it. I went back to school; got another Masters, in Marriage, Family, Child Counseling, did an internship at the American Institute of Family Relations, and got a lot of the hours.

And in that internship we got a lot of kids, not just me but also the other students. Nobody knew what to do with them except me [Laughs] because I already had had tons of experience. So they asked me to teach a class on working with kids. "Counseling with Children" they called it, and for two years I did that. That was through Chapman University, this program. So I wrote a very long paper about my ideas, and I gave it out to all the students. It turned out to be somewhat of an outline of *Windows to Our Children*. I didn't know it at the time.

Because I was so naive, I didn't even have my address on the paper. One of the Gestalt people heard about this paper. He was teaching psychology at Cal State Los Angeles. He gave that paper out to all his students. Then the paper kind of spread around. Somebody said to me, "You know, I'm a social worker, I work for the L.A. Social Services and we were all given your paper as an orientation." I didn't even have my phone number on there. [Laughs] Nothing. That was so interesting. I realized at that time, too, that there's a tremendous need for how to work with kids. Nobody seemed to know how to work with kids.

Chris: What was popular and what was available at the time would be things like Virginia Axline, with *Dibs in Search of Self*, Anna Freud — all of the psychoanalytically oriented child psychotherapies.

Violet: Of course, I have read all of that stuff. One of the things that happened in my Masters in Special Ed. program, there were four of us who won this United States Office of Education Fellowship, three guys from L.A., and me, from Long Beach. It was at Long Beach State. We didn't like the program and we fought to get a better program. We had already worked in the field and we already knew what we needed. They fought us, because it was the United States Office of Education Fellowship, they paid us a stipend to go while we're getting this degree, they finally gave in.

One of the things that I wanted very much that I finally got — two things — one was to visit all kinds of mental health programs for children all over Los Angeles County. They let me do that and I met with one of my

WINDOWS TO OUR CHILDREN

professors to talk about it or write it up. Another was to read all the books about child therapy — which wasn't part of their program. I would meet with the professor and talk. So I read all of those things.

What I realized later is that they don't really tell you how to work with kids. They're fascinating, especially like Dibs, or Clark Moustakas' work, it's fascinating. I love it. Play therapy, the old play therapy, which is what Clark Moustakas and Virginia Axline did, where the child plays and soon they're going to play out what they need. It takes a long time. I decided, the kids I worked with, I didn't have that much time. I had to be more directive, as I've often said, "A kid doesn't come in and say, 'I have to work on my stepfather who molested me.'" Never will a kid do that. So, you have to become more directive in terms of what you provide in an interesting way.

I started giving workshops through the Gestalt Therapy Institute of Los Angeles. There was a period when they offered a lot of workshops in Los Angeles for the public. I started doing some of that — then I worked for the Los Angeles school system as a consultant with psychologists and school counselors and I gave workshops. People would come up to me and they would say, "I have a Ph.D. in child psychology — in clinical psychology, I'm a child psychologist — what do you do with the kid?" That became such a phrase that I was going to call *Windows to Our Children, What Do You Do with the Kid?* But, the publishers thought people would misunderstand the title. I heard that over and over, "What do you do with the kid?"

So I would give these workshops about my ideas about actually what you do, and I gradually developed the therapeutic process, which in the beginning I really hadn't thought through. It took me a while before I — in fact it isn't even written about in *Windows to Our Children* — the therapeutic process. Which I'll talk about a little bit later. In a sense, I was doing it, but I hadn't articulated it theoretically. People were so excited about doing.

Here's a story: I actually consulted for a while at Camarillo State Hospital, which no longer exists. They had a children's unit and an adolescent unit for incorrigible adolescents and very disturbed children. I would go and I did a series of things in each unit. The therapist, in the adolescent

Interview with Violet Oaklander

unit, one of the therapists, said, "I want you to come into one of my groups, because I don't know what to do with those kids."

It's the same phrase, "I don't know what to do with the kids." So, I went into this group and there's this group of adolescents and they're wandering in and out and they're not paying any attention. They're no doing anything. I brought with me, I don't know, I just thought, I'll just bring some sand tray toys with me — I brought drawing paper, I brought sand trays, I brought whatever you could do.

I put these toys out, in the middle of the room, there were very interested, they all came over to see what there was. I said — this one particular group had mostly boys, actually, and young adolescents — and I said, "Everybody take a toy. You can't keep it, but take one for now." They all took a toy.

I modeled, I don't remember which toy I took, "I just want you to go around and say, 'I'm this dump truck and I carry a lot of junk in me and I don't know what to do with it.'" It was amazing. They all really listened. I remember one kid picked this snake and he said, "I'm a snake, and everybody's afraid of me." He got really into it.

I said, "Well, now you have to say one thing about what you said, that fits about you." He said, "I can't think of anything." All of the other kids said, "What do you mean? Everybody's afraid of you." Here was a great big kid and they said, "You scare everybody." They started having this discussion . . . each kid would say something and they all would chime in about what they thought about what he said. The therapist couldn't get over it. He said, "I've never had them have a discussion. They never will have a discussion about anything; they will never even stay in the room."

We did that a lot. I started bringing in different things; drawings we did, drawings they did, your strong side and your weak side, we did that. It never occurred to him to do that kind of thing with the group. It seemed to me logical.

Chris: There's something about your face, Violet, even as you relate this event that happened so long ago with this boy and the snake, where your face lights up and softens and your eyes are very clear and I can just see you looking at him directly. This gentle smile on your face, and I think that's an element that people, as they know about your work, as they hear about the various modalities, may or may not have experienced or seen, that is, I think, one of the very essential pieces of your work. I think of it as the "I-Thou" that your work is infused with, that is an essential piece of Gestalt therapy.

[Laughter]

Violet: Thank you. So I started to say, I wrote this paper and I taught this class for two years, actually, when I had already gotten my masters and I was out. That was the beginning of actually writing, you might say.

What happened was, that after that I got my license, the marriage family therapy license, and I went into practice, and worked with a psychologist. He was in Long Beach. I worked with him because at that time if you were on Medi-Cal, which was for poor kids, and poor families, you could see a [marriage and family] therapist if a licensed psychologist supervised [the work]. I know that they wouldn't allow that anymore. The psychologist has to see the kid.

So I worked with a psychologist who had an office and I rented a room, and he hated working with kids. He'd get all these Medi-Cal referrals and he just sent them over to me. Of course, I was, at the time, so broke that I would see anyone for like a dollar [jokingly]. I was very happy. He didn't like doing it . . . besides he didn't know how to work with kids and they paid so little.

I saw many kids under that Medi-Cal thing. Which was wonderful because I had such a variety of children that I worked with. I was very compulsive; I had to take notes a lot, because you had to have the paperwork. I had all these files, and I kept everything for a long time. I was still giving workshops. I had adults, about half my clients were adults, and half were kids, children, teenagers, from even three all the way through eighteen. I loved the work, and I did a lot of it.

In fact, that's where Ariel came into my life. She, at that time, was Marilyn Malek. She was going and getting her degree, and she found out about me through Harold. She came to ask me if she could work with me and learn from me. That was when I started taking apprentices, who would work right with me; she was one of the first. I started doing that a lot later, in a more organized way.

Interview with Violet Oaklander

I still remember this one case — here's another wonderful, great story.

Chris: OK.

Violet: This kid, who was a Navy family kid, was acting out, very acting out. The school wanted to put him in a special class, and the parents were very much against that. They came in for therapy, thinking that would help. The father was in the Navy, and he left, he was shipped away. So there is the mother, she has two kids, new in this town, and now he's gone. There she is, she was very depressed herself, very religious, that was her one support, and very depressed.

This kid, meanwhile, is acting out a lot. I asked him if he wanted to paint, because he kept looking at these paints that I had on a shelf, and his eyes lit up. We put the paper, and newspaper on the table, and put the paints out. Ariel is watching all of this, she's not really intervening, she's just observing. He paints with great absorption. When he's done, I said, "Tell me about it." He said, "It's a volcano." He was a kid who had never been in a classroom. They told me he mostly sat in the principal's office because he was so disruptive, but he knew a lot about volcanoes. [Laughter]

He said, "We're studying volcanoes," and he describes this. I said, "OK, what I want you to do is be the volcano." "How do I do that?" I said, "Just stand over there, and close your eyes, and imagine you're a volcano, and I'm going to stand in front of you." I stood in front of him and he closed his eyes. He was nine years old. I said, "OK, volcano, tell me about yourself. Where's your hot lava?" He went like this [pointing], "Inside of me — here — hot lava." After that, he had steam, and he said, "There's the steam." It was coming out of him, he hadn't erupted yet, he's in Hawaii, he said. Anyway, I said, "What would hot lava be for a boy?" He had his eyes closed. He was the volcano. He opened his eyes, he said, "Anger!" It was stunning.

[Laughter]

I kept my cool. I said, "OK, I'd like you to paint your anger." So, he sat down and he painted a round thing with different colors. I said, "Tell me about your anger, I'm going to make a list here of what you're angry about." He started dictating. He didn't say I'm angry because my father left. "I'm angry because I fell off my bike, because my sister messes with my stuff." He doesn't say I'm angry because my mother's depressed. He's angry. First, we're dealing with the surface angers before we can get into anything deeper. Not to mention the fact that part of that was grief. He's angry that he falls off his bike and with his sister, but he's also grieving that his father's gone. He's also grieving that his mother doesn't pay any attention and is so depressed.

Ariel said, "You planted him." [Laughter] So then, little by little, we were able to talk about his deeper angers, that kind of thing. We had to start with what was safe for him. That was the first session with him alone. Pretty amazing. This work is very powerful. Of course, there is the contact and the relationship . . . I know that you can't really do anything without having a relationship. It can just be the thread of a relationship, but it has to be something, and there has to be some contact between us . . . that's what leads to the millions of experiences I've had like that.

Chris: So there you were, practicing with your Marriage and Family Therapist license and you don't yet have your doctorate.

Violet: No, not yet.

Chris: How did that come about?

Violet: I was also giving workshops around Los Angeles, Long Beach, Orange County, and people would always say to me, "Do you have any more information?" "This is great! Do you have anything else?" [Laughs] "Do you have anything written?" [Laughs] "Something I could take with me?"

So, I got this idea that maybe I should write a book. Of course, I had that paper I had written, and my cousin Ruth, who had done a lot of writing said, "You know, Violet, that's an outline of a book." I looked at it and thought, "Well, yeah, that could be." I didn't think of myself as a writer. I decided I would write this stuff up, but I wouldn't tell anybody because I'm not really a writer. [Laughter]

I secretly worked on it for a year. I had all these files and stuff. I started writing, and I really didn't know how to write a book. I didn't know where to begin, where to end. I know now that there are so many books you can buy about writing, but at the time or maybe because I didn't share it, I kept it all to myself. I worked on it for about a year.

Interview with Violet Oaklander

What happened was, I was supervising some students who were at Goddard College, there's a branch that used to be, I don't know if it's still here, in Los Angeles. I would go down to their office to sign some papers, and I used to write "Violet Oaklander, M.S., M.A." because I have a Master of Science in Special Education and a Master of Arts in Counseling, so I would write "M.S., M.A." They'd kid me and they'd tease me and they'd say, "You know you should trade that in for a Ph.D., all those letters." I'd say, "I don't want go back to school. I just can't go back to school."

I was writing this book, and I got this idea that if I could find a school that would let me write this book for a dissertation, that would be good, so I started asking around, especially at Goddard. I kept hearing about this one place — a lot of people mentioned it to me — called International College.

It was started by some guys at UCLA who wanted to start a graduate program equivalent to the European tutorial system. In Europe, when you're working on your Ph.D., you work with tutors. So they started this school, called International College and it was a graduate program. They had, not just psychology, but you could get a degree in music from Yehudi Menuhin. Anais Nin was on their staff; you could get a degree in English. The tutor had to approve you, accept you, not just the school, but the tutor, too.

I went down to talk to them and they had all these cards, or a book of all the different tutors and what the requirements were. I discovered there were two tutors who did an interdisciplinary group. The group met once a week on a Saturday, for the day, and their requirements were, for your eventual dissertation: that it be part of the work you are doing, not something different; that it never had been done before, that it make a contribution; that it would be not an experimental, but a qualitative work.

Whatever the requirements were, it fit exactly what I was trying to do. It had never been done before. I knew that because I kept looking around for a book like that to help me and I never could find one, and I thought, "I'll have to write it." It was part of my work, and I felt it would make a contribution. It had to be a creative work, that was the fourth thing.

I talked to them and I decided to enroll, and I did. It took three years. I didn't have to take a lot of courses because I had two traditional

WINDOWS TO OUR CHILDREN

Masters' degrees, with statistics and all the stuff you have to take. They had a curriculum that matched the Board of Behavioral Science requirements for clinical psychologists. You could sit for the exam, if you took all these things, which I did. I was already working in the field for quite a while. I entered that program and that's how I wrote *Windows to Our Children*. Although, the dissertation is much bigger, you do the review of literature and a lot of other stuff. It's two big, fat volumes.

What happened was, while I was working on my dissertation, there were ten people in our group and only two finished. They were so hard on us because — they were so unusual, such an unusual school — that they were especially hard on everybody. They were a wonderful group: people in different disciplines, anthropology, sociology and various disciplines, psychology. I maybe had another year to go — I don't remember exactly the time frame — except it took another three full years. I had two tutors; they were John Sealy and Peter Marin. They're not famous or anything, but some people knew who they were.

Peter Marin, especially, had written a number of books, so he was very helpful to me in terms of writing. John Sealy was the one that would say, he'd look at my writing and he'd say, "What do you mean by this?" "What do you mean when you say this word?" "What do you mean by that?" "This looks like bullshit to me." [Laughter] He was the one that really got me paying attention to my writing, so that I wouldn't write to impress.

Chris: It should be noted that you just put your glasses on to demonstrate how he looked at your paper. You're holding the paper in your hands, examining it very carefully.

Violet: He taught me not to write to impress, but, to write from my heart, really is what he taught me. Peter was very supportive, Peter Marin, in terms of getting me . . . At one point, I said to Peter Marin, "I don't know what to do; I could be doing this forever because John Sealy is always saying something." "You have to tell him when you feel done. When you feel done, tell him that." That's exactly what happened. I said, "I think I'm done, John." And he said, "OK."

Chris: What was it that made you feel done?

Interview with Violet Oaklander

Violet: Well, I felt like I had written, at that point, as much as I wanted to. It felt like this is enough right now. They gave me a lot of suggestions, especially Peter, about what I should include and that kind of thing. They were really wonderful, when I'm thinking back. At the time, I was under a lot of stress.

What happened was, before I was done, I got a call from a publisher, Real People Press. John Stevens called me. It turned out I had given a workshop in Berkeley, a Gestalt Therapy Workshop. I had committed myself way before I knew that I was writing a dissertation, and I didn't have time to go to Berkeley. It was a conference. I wasn't getting paid or anything. But, I had committed myself, so I went up there, and in my workshop was John Stevens' girlfriend, who he later married and took her name, Connie Andreas. He's known as Steve . . . because everybody used to call him Steve . . . Steve Andreas, he took his wife's name.

He was the editor, he still is, of Real People Press that had published some Fritz Perls' books and others. Barry Stevens was his mother; he published a couple of her books. Anyway, he said, "I heard you're writing a book on Gestalt therapy with children, and I'm interested in publishing it." I said, "I'm just writing my dissertation." He said, "Well, when you finish the first draft, could you send it to me?"

We had a first draft, and the second draft. Anyway, I sent him the first draft and he sent it back and he said, "I'd like to publish this, if you would . . . ," and there were pages and pages of yellow legal pad stuff, "On page 63, add more examples; on page 82, take out that Ph.D. window-dressing, I don't want any Ph.D. window-dressing."

It was a lot of work, really, pages and pages of stuff. How can you not do it? I didn't care about the Ph.D., I was really interested in the book, and people said, "Oh, you can't get a book published; it's too hard to get a book published." Here this publisher calls me. I agreed to do it. I went and met him in San Diego, he was going to be giving a workshop there, and signed the contract. I remember I had a headache for two days. I met them at a hotel and signed the contract.

Chris: What year was that?

Violet: You know, it, actually, was published in October of 1978, near 1979. It was several months before that, I guess, because it took me four months or so. He said, "I want it done by . . ." you know, he gave me a deadline. So, I had to put my dissertation aside, and work on what he wanted. It was very hard work. I did it, and, I mean, I had to work to support myself and help Sara, who was still in college, and even help Mha Atma. He was in chiropractic school, and they had a baby.

But, I borrowed money left and right. I had to stop working. I stopped working because I could not do this while I was working. And I, somehow, had faith, and I didn't know it was going to be like that. But, it was so important to me. It was like the most important thing in my life. I can honestly say that.

At that time, I was living in Hermosa Beach. That's all I really did was write, and I'd go for walks on the beach.

Chris: How long did you not work? How long of a hiatus did you take?

Violet: Maybe nine months or something, a long time. I had three adult clients who came to my office. So, I wrote this book on a little Hermes portable typewriter. That should be in here, because now . . . I wrote *Hidden Treasure* on a computer. That took me a long time because it wasn't the most important thing in my life.

There were two theoretical chapters or three that John Stevens — at that time, Steve — took out, because he wanted the book to be something that people would use. He said, "We have enough books where people get bogged down in theory, and then they get tired. They're working hard." I didn't know he was right. He was absolutely right because that's one of the things that made the book so popular. It was almost like a handbook, you might say. In fact that used to bother me, that people thought it was more like a cookbook or a handbook.

Chris: And sometimes they say, "the Bible."

Violet: Well, that's something else. They didn't say it then, at that time.

Chris: Say more about how they spoke of it as a cookbook.

Violet: I only heard this occasionally. I don't know if that was prevalent. I do know that it became very popular underground. It was not like a big bestseller, but I got hundreds and hundreds of letters. I have scrapbooks with these letters. They were all from therapists or students, occasionally from parents. It wasn't in the public domain. It became this underground, cult book, you might say. It spread underground. I don't even know, because there wasn't a lot of publicity for it or anything.

It was before I was traveling. I mean, I started traveling, and then that helped the book in terms of giving many, many, many workshops. But, it, totally, changed my life, totally. You hear that, and it changed my life because I started traveling. I mean I was on a plane every month somewhere in the United States or Canada or Mexico. Then, at least once a year, if not twice, to Australia or Europe. I started going to Germany every single year, and other countries in Europe and Israel.

I was traveling a lot, plus maintaining my practice. Plus, I started doing the two-week training program. I had a group at night of adults . . . I was still working with adults as a Gestalt therapist, you know. I love doing that. I was doing a tremendous amount. Then, I started the Center for Child and Adolescent Therapy, when I met you (After the book was published). I went back into practice in Manhattan Beach . . . I would have so many referrals. I don't know why, I didn't even have business cards yet for my new address. I don't know how that happened. I started getting a lot of referrals, and I knew I needed people I could refer to. So, at that point, I met you. I was looking for this group of people.

Chris: I think, you were talking with Judith Wygal, Judith Coreman. She asked you, I think, also to bring in Janet Graham Ross. You invited me to come in.

Violet: Yes, and Ariel and Ivan.

Chris: Ivan Diamond and Helen Sherry.

Violet: Yes, and we rented this office together, which was so wonderful. That was a wonderful experience, too.

Chris: That began in 1980.

Violet: Yes, about that, yes.

Chris: So, the book had been published in October of '78.

Chris: We opened the Center, I think, in June of '80.

Violet: Yes. So, I went back to work because I was in terrible debt. I had to just work to . . . I was getting a lot of referrals, which I took. I was working really hard. But, it was all worth it. So, the book was out, there was this book! Now, of course, since that time — I mean, it's been 1979, it came out, '89, '99, 30 years, 2009 — it's been out thirty years, and it's still there. It's in thirteen languages.

They call it "the Bible," I'll say something about that. I first heard that expression in Brazil. I worked in Brazil, in Sao Paolo. People told me they call the book "the Bible." They said, "Did you bring 'the Bible'?" It's not like a cookbook, which describes what they do, but it's a book they carry around with them. It's a book they need at all times. It's a book, without the book, they say, they don't know what to do.

I began to be self-conscious about the fact that I wanted more theory in the book. So, when I started doing all these workshops, I was traveling and doing workshops, I began to include a lot of theory stuff about what the book represented. I mean, if you were a Gestalt therapist you recognized it. When you looked at the book, you recognized the Gestalt therapy behind the book, but it's never, specifically, talked about. So, that's when I started doing the tapes on my book.

My brother, Sidney Solomon, came to California to work in Radio Shack. He actually worked at the headquarters of Radio Shack, Chicago. But, he wanted to live in California, so he became a Radio Shack manager. Anyway, my nephew, Max Solomon, had a sound studio. So, my brother, who was very supportive of my work, got this idea that I could make tapes with Max's sound studio.

The first tape was about Gestalt therapy with children. We did it as a question-and-answer format. My sister-in-law, Phyllis, who had been married before my brother, her daughter, Ellen, was the questioner. She has a very nice voice. So, we made that tape. That first tape I just wrote over and over. I kept writing and changing it and writing and changing it. Then I finally did it.

But, I realized I really hadn't thought of writing another book because I was working so much. I just couldn't even conceive of it. But, it seemed like I could write a tape even though that first one took a lot of work. After that, I relaxed, and I didn't actually work as hard on the next tapes. But, it was my brother who decided to start this tape company and other people got involved in making tapes, too, for him. Most of them were about working with children. We even put out a whole catalog. You, Chris, put out a tape.

Interview with Violet Oaklander

Chris: Sidney asked me to do a tape and I did that one. I asked him then, "Could I do this other one as well?" I did three in all. You also did some videotapes for him?

Violet: That came a little bit later. I did the audiotapes . . . I did a tape on the therapeutic process. I had worked a lot on developing this therapeutic process. That was an important piece of work for me; it made a big difference in terms of explaining what I do. To me, that therapeutic process is the core of my work, starting with the relationship and contact and moving on from there.

Then, Sidney got the idea of my doing videotapes. So, we had to rent a studio. Max had a sound studio, but it wasn't a video studio. We didn't rent the studio at first. We came to my office. That's right. I'm remembering now. We came to my office. There was a lot of traffic noise. But, we did that tape with Abram who at the time was twelve years old.

He hadn't actually been in therapy with me, but he'd been in therapy with somebody who had worked with me. I forget her name now, but she had also come and been an apprentice with me. He was in therapy with her, so he was familiar with the process. He had a lot of problems at that time, and that was the first tape on anger.

Then we did a second tape. By that time . . . now let's see . . . when we did the second tape, I'd already moved to Santa Barbara. But they rented the studio in Long Beach, and we decided to do a tape on the sand tray.

I remember I had to pack everything up. I bought these Lucite storage containers that you use in closets. I packed up all my sand tray toys and things and even a couple of sand trays, drove down to Long Beach. He, Abram, had done sand tray in his therapy, but he didn't want to do a sand tray. Here we rented this studio and we had decided it was going to be on sand tray. That's why I called it "An Atypical Sand Tray Session." I think it's an interesting video. He, finally, at the end, did a sand tray. [The video] opens with a beautiful sand tray; the camera crew did that sand tray. They were so intrigued. [Laughs] Anyway that was good.

Then, I was invited to come down to San Diego at a child abuse agency to work with a child. They would watch through a two-way mirror. I don't quite believe in two-way mirrors, frankly. I've had lots of people observe my work, but the child knows they're observing. I think it's kind of sneaky to get behind a two-way mirror and do it. I worked with this boy and I told him right away there were people watching us.

Anyway, that's the Carlos tape.

I like that tape a lot. We got permission to use it as a video, and he gets a royalty for every tape that's sold. So does Abram, still, to this day, get the royalty for every tape that's sold.

Chris: Then, there's another tape done as well.

Violet: Well, the other tape was not through Maxsound Tapes. That tape was part of a series called "Child Therapy with the Experts." This company, Allyn and Bacon Publishers — they're in Boston, actually — have put out other "Therapy with the Experts" tapes.

They asked me to do one of the "Child Therapy with the Experts." They had seven people, and I was the Gestalt person. That was interesting and they did it in Chicago. I had to postpone it because I got breast cancer, and I had to go through radiation treatment — seven weeks. They couldn't postpone it much further than that. They had to get it then or were not going to do it.

So, I agreed. After I finished the treatment, maybe a few days later, I flew to Chicago. I was totally wiped out. I was totally exhausted. But, they had me work with four children. They wanted me to work with five, but I ended up working with four. Then, we watched them all to decide which one we would use for this "Child Therapy with the Experts" tape. The one I chose, I felt — the others were really wonderful — but I felt that this one fit Gestalt. It was easier to see the therapeutic process and the Gestalt process with that tape.

So, we chose that tape and they put it in the format of a talk show of asking me a lot of questions and then showing the tape, and then they had an audience. More recently, the tapes are available through a company called Psychotherapy.net online and they're not in a VHS format now. They're in a DVD format. It's one of my favorite tapes. It's a really good tape, but I'm not involved in it, in terms of the tape company.

Chris: I could ask you about your therapeutic process, the therapeutic process, but actually I won't because that you've written about it and it's in your book.

Violet: It's in my new book. A whole chapter of it is in my new book.

Chris: So, people will find that there, but I want to talk more about your family. I mean, all of these tapes, this was a family that was supportive of your work.

Violet: Yeah.

Chris: So, tell me more about how your family has influenced your work.

Violet: Well, I mean, you can't say, I don't know about influencing my work. I didn't know I was going to do this work when I was growing up [laughs] but I had a wonderful family. I had wonderful parents. They were extremely nurturing and loving. They were Russian Jewish immigrants and they were, I think, pretty unusual.

My mother, for example, when I was doing this work, when I was grown up, I couldn't think of, I still can't think of one thing she ever did that was wrong in raising me. I thought everybody had parents like that until I talked to my friends and I realized … my husband, my friends … they didn't have parents like that. And it was, I guess, pretty unusual.

My father was a tailor. My father was a feminist before they ever heard the expression. He always told me I could do anything I wanted to do. I think I disappointed him when I quit school after a year and got married when I was very young and went to work so my husband could go to school. But he did live to see me finish when I went back to school and I became a teacher. He was very happy he saw me do that.

He didn't know that I went further and that I've written books, but I think of him. I hear his voice often in my head telling me I can do anything I want to do. He was, both my parents were, very supportive of me, and loving and wonderful, and they were very involved in social action.

They believed in peace and justice and equality and that's how I grew up with those values and they were very involved with that kind of work. They were not religious Jews, but very much cultural Jews. So, I grew up knowing a lot about Jewish culture. What else would you want to know?

Oh, and I had two older brothers. My brother, I was the younger one, my brother Sidney, who I mentioned, was nine years older than me, eight and half years older, and my other brother was seven years older than me. I loved … that brother's name was Arthur Solomon. As a kid he spent a lot of time with me, especially, did things with me, took me places. I just adored him and he was killed at the end of World War II as a soldier, in Germany. That was heartbreaking for my whole family and for me, and had a great effect on me to this day.

And, so that's something about my family. I really had a wonderful childhood, in that way. I had some trauma. I was badly burned when I was five years old, just turned five. Boiling water fell on me at a neighbor, at a relative's house we were visiting and it was a terrible experience. I was in the hospital a long time with skin grafts and that had a big effect, maybe, on my work.

I've often thought what it would be like if I'd had a therapist come in and talk to me when I was a little girl. I still remember the doctors and nurses saying to me, "Be a good girl. Stop that crying." I still hear that voice and because it was before penicillin and they used to have to clean me every day, and it was so painful, you know, the burn areas. It was really a bad experience.

I often say that we blame everything on the family and the parents when we work with children. The fact is there are other systems that affect children, the medical system being one. The school system, the court system, the religious system, many systems affect children.

I had other traumas. When I was seven my ears became badly infected and, again, it was before penicillin. I had to have surgery on both my ears. It was due to the measles actually. They became infected and they removed the bones in the back of the ears and the canals collapsed, so I'm hearing impaired. I gradually have become more and more hearing impaired. I have to wear very powerful hearing aids. It's a difficult thing to go through, but it's OK. [Laughs]

Chris: I'm stumbling and feeling like I'm not replying, responding to that piece. I want to pick up the piece you said about your parents being social activists and very involved and interested in social justice. I'm thinking about the fact that your book is a global phenomenon. It's impacting children's lives globally. I'm curious about what you've seen, what you've noticed that children need worldwide. What are some of the global concerns for children? What are the therapists saying to you about what children need in their countries?

Interview with Violet Oaklander

Violet: It seems like the problems are the same all over the world. I hear the same things everywhere I've been. There are certain cultural phenomena that we really do need to understand and pay attention to.

For example, in South Africa we learned that children are taught not to ever look at the adult. In my training program I've had people tell about how they think it's very important that the child look at you when you talk to them, to make contact. I've even had them talk about how they move the child's face. "Look at me," they say, "Look at me."

Well, in South Africa they don't do that, they're taught not to do that. So, it would be kind of ridiculous to, you know, make an issue of it. Although, I find that here, too. I've had, when I've had a family come in, I've had parents to do that in this country, want the child to look at them or look at me when we're talking. I always say, "I know he's listening," because I know how hard it is for children to do that sometimes. Even adults, if I look at you, and we look at each other, it can be a little bit scary. [Laughter] We talk a lot about that in Gestalt therapy, how, when we make contact, it's important to withdraw. If we have fixed contact, it's not real contact anyway. So the withdrawal is very important in making contact. With children, they tend to need to withdraw a lot, in order to feel comfortable.

In some cultures, it's very difficult for children to express their feelings because they're taught not to express feeling. A lot of that's true here, too. I mean, actually, here the issue of anger and what children do about anger, about their feelings about anger, if they even know they're angry. It's all over the world; it's the same problem, same situation. I always feel that the development of the child is the same everywhere in the world. It's what you do with it that becomes different. That's what I have found and that's why I think the work, the book and the work, appeals all over the world.

And, again, I worked in South Africa in three cities, and there were five-hundred therapists that came to these workshops, and they were two-day workshops each. They told me a lot about the effect of the work and why the work is so important. One had to do with the fact that there are so many problems with children in South Africa. AIDS is rampant, and a lot of kids are orphaned. If they're not sick themselves, they're orphaned because their parents have been sick and died. They just don't have enough therapists to deal with all the children, so they find that the work is powerful enough that they find they achieve results much faster than any other kind of therapy they've tried.

I think the work we do, using a lot of creative, expressive techniques, is very powerful. It's important to remember that cultures all over the world have used expressive techniques to express themselves, whether it be drawing, movement or singing or clay. Clay has been very important, storytelling; all of this has been used by cultures all over the world, so it appeals to many different cultures, in their own way. They pick what fits best for them.

Chris: While we're talking about those kinds of creative, expressive techniques, I'd like you to say something about music and your use of music with children, and how you developed that. I know you have a collection of wonderful instruments.

Violet: The particular process that I used came about a certain way. I mean, I've been involved in music. My parents sang in a chorus and I played the guitar for many years. I've been very interested in folk music particularly for many, many, many years. I went to a workshop at Esalen Institute one time with Paul Winter.

Paul Winter is a new-age musician. He plays the saxophone. He is incredible; he writes music to nature and to animals and different cultures, really incredible music. I was so impressed with what he does, I went to his music village in Connecticut one summer, and learned how he does that. And his philosophy is: "There's no such thing as a wrong note." I've always found music to be so important because it comes from a place away from your head, from your whole body. We talk a lot about that in Gestalt therapy, being a holistic kind of therapy, involving the body. What Winter does is use all kinds of instruments, percussion mostly, although he actually uses even others — and you don't have to know how to play any of these instruments, you can just make sounds, because he says that's what the birds and animals and the wolves do, they make sounds.

And so, I developed a way of using it with children. He was doing another workshop at Esalen, he had to leave, so he asked me, if I'd come up and take it over being that I'd been to the Music Village and I did that. So, anyway, I developed this process with children, a way of making music, and you can do it with a group or one on one, where they each have instruments. I have tons of percussion instruments, and they pick one, some are melodic instruments, like a xylophone. I just figured it all out, and some of the kids I worked with helped me figure out new things, new ways of using it.

It's just wonderful, absolutely wonderful. Whenever I would do it in the two-week training program, it was amazing. The adults that did it really loved it, most people. There's always a couple that might not, but most people were very enthusiastic. I have no idea if they're using it with their kids. It's a wonderful experience.

Chris: I'm hearing from everything you've said that Gestalt therapy has been very congruent with whom you are and fit with your upbringing, your philosophies, your values. But how was it you got to be involved in Gestalt therapy instead of some other therapy?

Violet: All this time I was working in the schools, I wasn't — this was before I was training in the Gestalt Institute — so I wasn't really experimenting with that yet, but I think that innately, I was. As I said before, I was teaching emotionally disturbed children and I was in a regular classroom for two and a half years. I did some pretty amazing things, I should write a book about that. It was probably part of my nature, to be a Gestalt therapist.

But really, what happened was, my husband, my late ex-husband, he died, actually it's been twenty years, I think now, that he died, of a brain tumor, suddenly at the age of sixty-two. We stayed very close for many years, even after we separated.

I mentioned earlier that one of our children became very ill, Michael had systemic lupus, and it attacked his kidneys. He was given a year to eighteen months to live, which is kind of a horrible sentence for any parent to hear. My way of dealing with it was to attempt to save his life, and Harold went into grief, so that had an effect on our marriage, actually. What happened is that the last six months of Michael's life, he became very ill. He was in the hospital, and I began to see that he was failing. As Harold would point out to me, "He's dying." I had a lot of trouble dealing with that of course, and I became very depressed.

This was maybe two months before he died. At the urging of some of my friends and Harold, I decided I needed to see somebody. I went to a couple of different therapists, and it was useless. They cried. There was no help whatsoever from them.

A friend of mine was going up to Esalen to do a workshop with Jim Simkin, and he encouraged me to go, so I did. My mother-in-law came to take care of the kids, and I went up to Esalen to work with Jim Simkin. Fritz Perls was there that weekend, but I never got to work with him. I did observe him, but I was in this group with Jim Simkin for a week, and it totally changed my life. When people say that, you wonder, "What does that mean? It changed your life?" But I can say, honestly, that that week with Jim Simkin changed my life.

He got me working on my grief, on my anger, on my avoidance, on everything, my denial of what was happening, everything, but at the same time he was always with me. Talk about an "I-Thou" relationship. He was with me.

Outside the group, he and his wife, Anne, were very compassionate and I really enjoyed their company. In the group, I did a lot of work. He really got me working. When I say it changed my life, I mean it somehow transformed me.

When I left Esalen and returned to Long Beach, my son is in the hospital, he's dying, and as an example I went to a grocery store to get some groceries. I saw a neighbor I hadn't seen in quite a while, and she said to me, "You look so wonderful. What's happening in your life?" I had to tell her about Michael, and she backed away. She couldn't even talk to me.

It was a very strange thing. When I went to the hospital, Michael started to get better. He actually responded to me. We were pretty close, we were very close, and he responded to me, to the point where he was sent home. The doctors could not understand it, because there's never been a remission with what he had. This lupus attacks all of your organs, which it was doing.

Up until now, he couldn't even sit up anymore; he couldn't eat. He was eating. He was walking. He came home for six weeks. We went to the movies. We went to Japanese Deer Park which had all these animals. He loved animals. We went to all these different places. We went to my cousin's for Thanksgiving dinner. It was unbelievable. It was a real gift. He even started school. He was starting high school, and he was going to be fifteen in just a couple of weeks. They sent a cab for him because he was pretty weak still.

It seemed like he was gaining his strength, and then he started coughing one night. We went to the doctor, and he cried all the way. He said "I don't want to go," and the doctor wanted him to go to the hospital. He had pneumonia. He said, "Oh, it's not serious. It's just a light case, but to be safe, let's put him in the hospital." Michael cried all the way to the hospital. He said, "I don't think I'm ever going to come out." And, of course, I couldn't hear that, and he died the next day. So, it was pretty bad.

It was after he died — I was in literally terrible grief — that the school district called me and said you've got to come. This teacher walked out, and we've got this class. It was that time I went in and told the kids I had just lost my son. He died December 12, his birthday was December 20, and I went back January 4 or 5.

Chris: Oh, my goodness, it was right on the heels of his death.

Violet: Yeah. I was impressed with what had happened. We had that gift for six weeks of Michael being home and I have those memories. They're so wonderful. I was impressed with Gestalt Therapy and Jim Simkin. So I decided, they had just started this training program in Los Angeles; I decided I would, with the encouragement of my husband, Harold, enter the program. That's how I got into Gestalt therapy. Even though Harold had been in it, it was his thing, it wasn't my thing. It became my thing.

Chris: Did you continue training with Jim Simkin at that time?

Violet: I did go to a couple of workshops with him, and in fact my whole training group went up to his house for a week.

Chris: He was in Esalen then?

Violet: No, he was next door to Esalen. He built the house next door to Esalen. So, I had training with him.

Chris: And you observed Fritz Perls?

Violet: Yes, but I never actually worked with him, even though Harold had actually trained with him.

Chris: And what about Laura?

Violet: Well, I went to a couple of workshops; one of them was with you in New Orleans. I was impressed with her because, especially, because she seemed so human. I still remember, there would be this group, and maybe there would be a person in the corner who never said a word, and after a while she'd say, "How are you? Are you OK? You haven't said anything."

Fritz Perls would never have done that. You were responsible for yourself, and that was it. I admired that about her.

I had that same experience with another one of my trainers, Allen Darbonne. He was like that, too, very loving. I found out you could be loving and be a Gestalt therapist. [Laughter]

Chris: Which you are!

Violet: Thank you. I also learned from another trainer, Bob Martin, that you could be creative, because Bob was very creative in the groups. I learned that you could do that, and it was a good thing. You could say I was greatly influenced by Jim Simkin, Allen Darbonne and Bob Martin. Period. I mean, I had some other good trainers, too, but they [are the ones who] really influenced me.

The Los Angeles Gestalt Therapy Institute was what it was called then. We had twelve trainers. Every two months, we went to a different trainer. After a year I was put into an advanced group. Then we could choose our trainers, and we'd go from Allen Darbonne, Bob Martin to Bob Resnick, Allen Darbonne, and we all went to Jim Simkin's, the whole group, for a week. It was a wonderful training, I felt like I, I don't know what it's like now, but I felt like it was a wonderful, wonderful training experience.

I trained there for three years, I went through the certification which a lot of people wouldn't do because it's kind of scary, but I wanted to do it and I did it. Some of the trainers today were not there when I was there, and I didn't experience them, but I had great trainers.

Chris: We haven't talked about how you came to be in Santa Barbara.

Violet: Well, what happened was that, as I mentioned earlier, I was working so much, to repeat, I had a full practice of maybe . . . I used to see half adults, half children and, by now, it was three-quarter children and adolescents, and one-quarter adults.

Chris: And by full practice what do you mean?

Violet: Oh, for me like twenty a week. We did a study [laughs]. I always tell people this, we did a study about time and we found that if you have twenty-five clients you worked fifty hours a week. Especially when you worked with children. There's a lot of paperwork, a lot of talking to parents, going to the schools, talking to principals, writing reports, talking to the court system, going to court. I mean it's just time consuming — twenty-five is really very full. I hear of therapists now who see thirty to thirty-five and to me I don't see how they can do a good job. [Laughs]

I had an adult group once a week at night. I was traveling. Every month I was on a plane going somewhere and then rushing back to see my clients. I was going out of the country at least once a year, sometimes twice. I was doing a two-week training program, which I started in 1981 until 2007 and for six years I did two, one in July and one in August. And there's a lot of work preparing for it, administrative kind of work, and even though I had somebody helping, I had a lot of work, a lot of work. I know I'm leaving something out.

Chris: Well, what you're leaving out is that you were director for the Center for Child and Adolescent Therapy.

Violet: Right.

Chris: And we had meetings.

Violet: And we had meetings and supervision and I was going and doing. Patric remembers that I used to volunteer supervision at this child abuse agency that he worked at. I forgot about that. I was doing some writing, and I mean, I worked more than a person should work.

And I got sick, and I got sick with chronic fatigue, finally they diagnosed it as, one doctor diagnosed it, as chronic mononucleosis, actually. And then we discovered the Epstein-Barr virus is involved with mononucleosis, but anyway, finally we now know it was Chronic Fatigue Syndrome.

I was very sick, I lost 20 pounds without trying, it should only happen to me now [laughs]. But I couldn't eat. I would force some food in my mouth because I knew you had to eat and I was still working. I finally couldn't work, for about two weeks, I didn't work. But mostly I was working and flying and I still remember working at a big conference, a child abuse conference in Alaska. I did many things, and after I would do whatever I had to do . . . it'd be like six o'clock, and I'd go to my hotel room and go to bed, I wouldn't even eat dinner.

It was a little weird, but so when I got sick I realized that I had to change my life. It kind of scared me and I went to a . . . I did take . . . I guess it was in August when you don't have many clients anyway, you sort of have a little reprieve. I went to a Tai Chi retreat in Hawaii for three weeks. I knew that I would make up my mind what I was going to do. Because I either had to change my life, where I was living in Hermosa Beach or move somewhere that was more nurturing. Because Hermosa was a bedroom community really and I was driving to L.A. a lot. Traffic was getting bad already and Hermosa was getting more crowded. I felt I needed an easier life or a move.

I got it in my head I should really move and I didn't know where to move, but I knew one person in Santa Barbara, Felicia Carroll. I had gone up there. I had done some workshops up there, and also, my daughter went to college there, undergraduate, and I would visit her sometimes. But, I never quite thought of it as a community for me to live in. I thought it was tourist town, although I had done these workshops, and Felicia lived there.

In Hawaii, I made up my mind I would move, and it wasn't an easy thing. I had a little house in Hermosa. I had an office where I had a five-year lease. I had to buy a house because otherwise I would have to pay a lot of taxes. I had a practice in Hermosa; I wasn't going to have a practice up there. I would travel and do the training, although it was hard to make that shift. But I did, I made up my mind and I would deal with everything. I won't go into all the details.

It all worked out and I fell in love with Santa Barbara, what a wonderful community that was. It was a nurturing, wonderful community to live in. I've lived there for twenty-one and a half years, twenty-one years and loved every minute of it. So that's how I got to Santa Barbara. [Laughs]

Chris: And maybe I should add, how did you get here?

Violet: Here in Los Angeles, well, I've been here almost a year.

After I turned eighty, which was two years ago, my son decided that I should move near him. He tore down his garage, and he started to build, had a little cottage built. I said, "Never, I'm never moving to Los Angeles." [Laughs] But, as time went by I began to realize that I am getting older and it would be . . . I'm very close to my son and my daughter-in-law, and it would be really nice living near them. "Maybe I should do it." And so, like I've made every decision in my life, I think about it for a week or two and then I say, "OK, I'm going to do it," and deal with whatever happens when you make the decision. I've done that all my life.

So they built this lovely little cottage. Last August, after I turned eighty-one in April, I decided, "I will do it" and, I did it. I sold my condo immediately. It was unbelievable. It was like meant to be and here I am. It's a big adjustment.

Chris: And what about your gradual retirement over the years from practice? What has retirement looked like for you? I mean, I know you've just got back from Spain.

Violet: About ten years ago, when I was seventy-two, I'd decided, really with the support of my daughter, who lives in Boston, Sara, and my son, Mha Atma, who lives in Los Angeles. They encouraged me, and encouraged me, to not work so hard. I still worked hard, even when I moved to Santa Barbara. As nurturing a community as it is, I still worked my head off.

So I decided they were right, but I had built an office onto my house, a wonderful, wonderful office. And, I knew, if I still lived there I would not be able to stop seeing clients. So, I decided to move. That's the way I am. I sold my house and I bought a condominium without an office. I didn't have an office, so I stopped seeing clients. I continued to do supervision, because the people I supervised or consulted with, therapists would come to my condo, and I continued to supervise at a counseling center there, the Community Counseling Center.

I continued to do my training, and I continued to travel, but I didn't see clients, so I cut back somewhat. And, then, I decided I should be writing another book, so I started writing another book. I guess I can't . . . it's hard for me not to work.

Chris: The piece I left out is that you did indeed develop a full practice in Santa Barbara.

Violet: Oh, yeah. Yeah. That's an interesting story, but I did do that. I don't know if you want to hear that.

Chris: I'd love to.

WINDOWS TO OUR CHILDREN

Violet: You want to hear that story? You could cut it out of this. Well, soon after I moved there, I got a phone call. I worried, because the practice is my income to count on. I moved there, soon after that in the fall, I moved in June, but in the fall I got a phone call from the Family Service Agency where the child guidance clinic was housed.

They said, "We heard you moved to Santa Barbara, and we'd like to advertise, let people know more about our agency and what we do, especially, the Child Guidance Clinic, so we wondered if you would be willing to do a workshop?" And I said, "Sure." It was on anger. I decided . . . it was called "The Many Faces of Anger," how anger presents itself in many different ways.

They sent fliers home with every single child. In all the schools, from Carpentaria through Goleta, every kid got a flier about this workshop to take home. It was for parents and teachers, and they had posters all over Santa Barbara. Santa Barbara has 90,000 people within its limits, but it's like a small town, everybody knows each other. It's that way. It's wonderful. They had posters all over the city. I was on the local radio station. They sent a TV unit from the local TV station to the workshop to film it. I mean, you couldn't have asked for better publicity! After that, my phone was ringing off the wall, and I had my practice.

Chris: And that was the start of your practice.

Violet: Yeah.

Chris: So you stopped seeing clients and you moved to the condominium. What happens next? What was the next step?

Violet: I got breast cancer about two years after that, but I was still doing all of those other things I told you about, and I still continued to do all those things. I wrote, I had been writing, writing, writing. It took me a lot longer to write *Hidden Treasures* because it wasn't the most important thing in my life the way *Windows to Our Children* was. So it took several years. I used the tapes. I decided to put the six tapes into that book. I rewrote, went through them, I had written the scripts, so I went through them and that made it a lot easier, too. And the theoretical chapters, and so I . . . what happened? I was doing all this stuff, and then I realized, maybe two years ago, that I need to cut down.

Interview with Violet Oaklander

Chris: You were saying that Sara and Mha Atma were encouraging you, urging you to cut back.

Violet: So I finally did the last two-week training, which was very hard because I loved doing that, but it really needed to be. It came to an end.

Chris: That was two years ago.

Violet: Two years ago. The summer before last was my last one. I decided to move here, because I knew if I'm here I'd definitely cut back a lot. The book was done, so I came here, in this little house. I still do some supervision. I still have a couple people come here, and I do some on the phone, from Ohio and Seattle. I did more, but gradually they've cut down. I was invited to go to a big International Gestalt Therapy Conference, and I'd never been to Spain, so my daughter Sara went with me to Spain. Last year, I went to Puebla, Mexico. I did a workshop in March in Tijuana. Mha Atma, my son, went with me to both of those.

Chris: Tell me about the Violet Solomon Oaklander Foundation.

Violet: Oh, my goodness . . . I think it's been five years now since we started it. One of the people that I supervise, Sue Talley, had had the idea of starting a foundation for a long time. She talked to me about it periodically. I finally said, "Well, if you want to do it, do it." So I gave her some names, and she contacted a variety of people who had their first meeting. I don't know, were you there? It was at Taffy's.

Chris: No, I was in Seattle.

Violet: You were in Seattle. So, they had that meeting, and it was very moving. They all talked about the work and how important it is to them. That was the beginning. The decision was made. Then about three and a half years ago, almost four years ago, we had the first party to launch the foundation. That was a wonderful experience.

And so, the Foundation is supposed to be there to carry on my work. It's small, we've got nonprofit status. That took a lot of work. My daughter-in-law, Martha, did a lot of work; she worked like crazy to finally get approval for nonprofit status. A lot of people have worked hard. Lynn Stadler has put out a newsletter. She's looking for someone now to take it over, but she's put out this wonderful newsletter.

WINDOWS TO OUR CHILDREN

A lot of people have done a lot of work, and we've had a meeting about every three or four months. We met in Santa Barbara, but we've also met here in Los Angeles. We've met in Agora Hills, where Sue Talley lives. Most of the people live within the area in California, because otherwise it's hard to get to. People who live in San Luis Obispo come. A lot of people are interested that don't live here. But we've been meeting and the meetings are wonderful because the people are so dedicated and interested.

We now have a store, an online store, that sells both my books, in English and in Spanish, and, all my tapes and Peter Mortola's book, and if anybody else in the Foundation would write a book we'd sell that, too. We would put it on the website [laughs]. Anyway, it's been really nice.

Chris: People sometimes refer to your work as the "Oaklander Model." Is that a term, a phrase, that you use yourself?

Violet: You know, I think everybody has their own way of working. I developed the therapeutic process. It's not part of . . . even though it is based on . . . the theory and philosophy and practice of Gestalt therapy, it's my model. It's really connected to Gestalt therapy as well as child development theory. So I guess that is the Oaklander Model.

Chris: And then the other question is, I know, I have heard you talk about going to Cleveland to their regular Gestalt Therapy Conference. Is it the Cleveland . . .

Violet: Not exactly, I think the first one was sponsored by the Cleveland Institute. The second one was in Esalen or a third one or maybe two. I forget exactly but one of them was sponsored by Esalen and that was the more recent one. So people came from all over and they also presented their methods and ways of working with children. I was honored, so that was really nice. Gordon Wheeler, I think, organized a lot of it.

It was a wonderful experience. I appreciated the [recognition]. You know, over the years I've done my work. I didn't really know how the Gestalt community accepted my work, except for Ohio, because Norman Shub and the Gestalt Institute of Central Ohio have always been extremely supportive of my work; the Institute has sent people to the training. The Institute, his practice, has paid for it and paid for people that I have supervised, and so I knew how they felt about the work. I did many, many, many workshops over the years in Columbus, Ohio. But I didn't have a sense . . . I did a workshop in the Gestalt Therapy Institute of Philadelphia. I had some recognition, but I never really had a sense of how the work has been accepted.

So in Cleveland and then in Esalen, I felt really good because a lot of people came from different places I knew in Europe, I have worked at a Gestalt institute in Germany for many years. I worked in one in London, but I have worked in a lot of other places. I have worked for people who weren't associated with Gestalt therapy: universities, I've worked for a lot of hospitals, I have worked for agencies that have invited me, I have worked for all kinds of people, the Association for Play Therapy conferences, all kinds of people. A lot of the people that I gave workshops to weren't involved in Gestalt therapy at all. Many of them went on to get Gestalt therapy training because I always identify myself as a Gestalt therapist. The work is based on Gestalt therapy theory, practice and philosophy.

Chris: Is there anything else?

Violet: I know there was a question that I felt that work with children is not that accepted and respected by Gestalt therapists. For many years I have felt . . . maybe it isn't even just Gestalt therapists. For many years I have felt particularly in the Gestalt community that they never really gave much recognition to working with children. It was like, oh, that isn't much of anything. You're just with the kid and you play games or something. [Laughs] But I hope that is changing. I hope that is changing.

Chris: I know at one time I used to hear people say you can't do Gestalt therapy with children because their ego has not developed yet.

Violet: [laughs] Yeah.

Chris: And I know even today, now in the field of psychotherapy broadly and generally the whole field of infant mental health has opened up.

Violet: Yeah. And working with the brain. That's been a big, big, new [development]. And of course children, it starts with infancy, the brain. I strongly believe that Gestalt therapy is so organic that it stands to reason that it fits the development of children.

I talk about how you look at a baby and the baby is very sensuous and Gestalt therapy talks about coming to your . . . as Fritz Perls used to say, "Lose your mind and come to your senses." And, the baby is very sensory. And then the body movement as the baby is developing becomes a very important part of growth and development; and, then the expression of emotions and the use of the intellect and development of the child. It's all so organic and it's all basic to Gestalt therapy. So to me, how could it not be? So that's in terms of working with kids and assessing, making an assessment, if they're having difficulty expressing emotions. It's all part of their development. It begins, even with adults, it begins in childhood. You don't suddenly block your ability to express emotions as an adult. It starts way back. So, it seems to me very essential and organic and obvious that the development of the child is much akin to Gestalt therapy theory.

Chris: I'd like you to say something about doing individual therapy with children versus doing family therapy with children. I know that some therapists believe strongly that family therapy is the way to go.

Violet: Well, I've worked with many children who don't have families. I've worked with many foster care children. Others in situations where they are just being cared for, they don't really have a family. In fact, they move from place to place. And, I feel that in my practice when I could involve the parents, particularly, I would do that. Of course, I mean, it would stand to reason that you would want to do that. So, I had a practice of seeing the parents once a month while I was seeing a child individually, to kind of check in. There were times when I saw the parents with the child every other week, and the child the alternate week alone. Certainly, to me, there is no hard and fast rule.

I don't see the child as glued to the family. I mean, the child is an individual person. And if I could work with the child, if the family would not want to come in — when I say family, I mean the parents, sometimes I would see the whole family, siblings. There were times when I saw them regularly. And other times when I would only have them come in every now and then, or not at all. The siblings that is. [pauses] I'm getting a little scattered.

Chris: [laughs] Let me try not to be scattered myself here. So, it sounds like you wanted to attend and address the child's needs, whether the parents wanted to come or not.

Violet: I just feel that if the parents are willing to bring a child in, I'll work with the child. If they're not willing to come in — I've had that happen many times. One of the interesting things that sometimes happens is that when I do work with the child individually, the child becomes somewhat like the parents' therapist, or they begin to change in some way that draws the parents in. And this is not the same as you hear, which I think is a myth, that when the child begins to get better and healthier, the parents don't like it. I have never found that to happen. I have never met a parent who doesn't want their child to be happier, to do better, and to function in the world better.

And there may be such parents, but honestly, I haven't seen them. I suppose there can be, and they'd be very dysfunctional parents, abusive parents. And I have seen very dysfunctional parents. And I have even seen abusive parents — I had one case where the mother was in a program for abusive parents and the child was referred to an outside therapist. And as the child made a great attachment to me, we made a good relationship and contact, the mother pulled him out of the therapy and told me, "I can't stand it that he loves to come to your sessions." That was like the one time, with my life of my many years of working that that has happened to me.

So, you see all kinds of things. I have another situation where the parents refused to come in. The father was in the Navy and was shipped out and the mother refused to come in. Ever! Even for the first session. She would just drop him off. He was referred by the schools because he was acting out a lot. And, he began to go home and... Well, here's an example: somehow, we got into how lonely he felt. It was a Navy family. They had moved a lot. And, he had trouble; he was now in the fourth grade, making friends. They had their little cliques. And that came out of a sand tray scene that he made, which I don't want to go into the story unless you want me to. [Laughs] But, I could if you want me to! [Laughs]

Chris: [laughs] Oh dear, I hate to say no!

Violet: Anyway, he made a sand scene with two armies. He very meticulously put them in rows. And I said, "Tell me about it," when he said, "I'm done." He said, "There are two armies and they are having a war." "And I said, "What are they fighting about?" He said, "I don't know, maybe land." So I said, "Well, have them do it." He said, "What do you mean?" I said, "Well, they're just standing there. If they are having a war, have them do it!" He said, "Really?" I said, "Sure!" So he started [makes shooting noises] pretending they were shooting.

And pretty soon on one side all the soldiers were still standing in disarray. On the other side they were all buried in the sand except one. And he said, "This side won." And I said, "Well, who's that guy?" And he said,

WINDOWS TO OUR CHILDREN

"That's the leader of that side, but they lost." They were all buried in the sand [laughs]. And I said, "Well, I would like you to be him. Would you be him?" He said, "No. I'll be him." "Who's that?" "The captain of the winning team." We dialogued. I said, "Well, Captain, what happened?" "Well, we had this battle and we won." "And how does that feel?" "It feels great! We're really happy! We're having a party!"

And so, I said, "I really want you to be the captain of the losing team." I start to dialogue with the captain. I said, "Captain, what happened on your side?" So, he felt a little support from being on the winning side, so he said, "Well, we tried, but we lost." And when I'd say to him, "What did you lose?" earlier, he said, "I don't know." [Laughs] So, that didn't really matter. It was the experience of winning and losing. And so I said, "What was that like for you?" He said, "All my comrades . . ." He used that word 'comrade.' It was so interesting. He said, "All my comrades are dead." And I said, "What is that like for you?" He said, "It's very lonely."

And then he shut down. I mean it's kind of like, that's enough, you could see he was breaking contact. But before he quite broke contact, I said, "Does that ever fit for you in your life, that lonely feeling?" He said, "All the time." And then he closed. You know? So, the next time I wanted to bring up that issue of loneliness, and I think he drew what that feels like. He didn't want to talk about it, but was willing to draw what it feels like. And then I said, "I wonder if your mother feels lonely. Because, you know, you've moved a lot." And he said, "I don't know." I said, "Maybe you should ask her." He said, "Yeah, I'm going to ask her."

And he went home, and he asked her. And no one had ever asked her anything like that. And it was so moving to her that she came in the next time and she said, "You know, last week, you drew some interesting things here. Last week, we drew us . . . he made me draw a safe place." [Laughs] Because we had done that. And he kind of became her therapist. And she gradually softened, and began to talk to me a little bit more. You know, willing to talk to me. So, that's what sometimes . . . I've seen that happen with other family situations, too.

Chris: It sounds like you made room for him to have the feelings. And then he could bring those feelings into the family, and make room for his mother to have them. And then they can relate to each other.

Violet: Yeah. Yeah. Because up 'til then they really didn't relate to each other. She was only angry at him all the time, because she was always being called down to the school for his acting out, behaving . . . I should say that I saw that boy for four months, once a week for four months. And his behavior totally changed. In fact, I called the school, and the counselor said, "Well, he hasn't been sent to the office, you know, for a while." And she called me back. She said, "I spoke to teacher, and she said he was just fine." And then she said, "Maybe he was going through a stage."

[Laughter]

Violet: Which you often hear, you know.

Chris: Yeah.

Violet: And of course, that's not valid here. But what happened was that they moved again. They moved to Okinawa. I remember this. And he wrote me a letter. Because I always gave kids my card when they were leaving. And he said, "I wanted to tell you that we now moved to Okinawa." He said, "But I'm OK." He said, "I remember everything we did, and everything we talked about, and I think I'm going to have friends all over the world." He said, "And I'm really OK." I'll never forget that letter.

Chris: Yeah.

Violet: Yeah. And that's kind of what happens with this work. Kids just . . . it's like they tell you what's going on deep inside of them, and they get back to themselves, you know.

Chris: So now I'm torn, because yesterday, when we talked, you talked about how powerful this work is.

Violet: Yeah.

Chris: And you were saying that the other child therapy . . . the other play therapy techniques that were available were . . . just took too long, took a long time, often. And, that this work with these creative and expressive techniques, which are central to Gestalt therapy, is very powerful. And I wondered if you wanted to say more about that?

Violet: Yeah. Well, it is . . . In play therapy, they talk about how play is the child's language. Well, it's the same thing with these techniques. We use some play also, of course. And when we use drawings . . . These are projective techniques. They are techniques that the child is projecting something that's inside outside, so that it's safe. It's a way of talking about things that are very safe, and then gradually bringing it back to themselves, where they can own the feelings. We use all of these techniques for that purpose, or to give them experience with parts of themselves that they no longer own or experience.

So, for example, it's quite well known that children who are sexually molested will anesthetize themselves, so they don't have to feel too much. And so we might do a lot of sensory work, even with adolescents, in order to help them get back in touch with their senses — the touching, and looking, and listening, and tasting, and smelling. And feel their senses, which are such an integral part of the organism, the senses.

And so we give them experiences with parts of themselves, and we also use it as projection. And they're fun. And they're fun to do. And as I said, I think yesterday, people have used these techniques for thousands and thousands of years to express themselves.

So we use every kind of projective technique you can imagine, that fits with what the child might be interested in. We have music, and clay, and drawings, and sand tray, and storytelling, and metaphors, and movement, and sensory experiences, as I said, all of these. And children come up with some. They invent some. And, we do all of these kinds of things that the children connect to, and are interested in, and out of this will come who they are, expressions from their inner selves, that they certainly can't talk about.

I mean, I remember, I've worked with a lot of kids from divorced families — pretty typical of a lot of therapists these days. I would ask them . . . I'd say, "Make a scene in the sand about the divorce in your family." And they would make things that they couldn't possibly articulate. I mean, it would never occur to them to articulate it. But, they could somehow make it in the sand. And then out of that we could begin to talk about it. And they could then own the feelings. And that's kind of the step that isn't always possible.

If I say, "Does this ever fit with you in your life? Or does that remind you of your life? Or you of anything." And they can't own it. If they say, "No," then I might say something like, "Well, you know, in this scene that you made . . ." There was a twelve-year-old boy, and I said, "In this scene that you made, the surfer drowned. And you, the other surfer, who you said was you, could have saved his life, but he didn't. I'm wondering if there's anything in your life that you feel you're responsible for, that's not .

.." He burst into tears. His parents were in a bitter custody battle over him. And he said, "It's all my fault. It's all my fault." And this was a boy who said, "I don't care what they do. It's their problem." And was in total separation from anything that he was affected by, except his grades were falling, and he had headaches, and stomachaches — retroflected kind of behavior.

So, once he was able to own his place in this, then we could really deal with it, you know. I attempted to bring the parents in to talk to them about what they were doing. But, they were in therapy through the courts, and they wouldn't come in to see me. But, I helped this child cope with his parents, which is another part of that question about seeing children individually. Sometimes you have to help them cope with their family situation, you know, and find ways to be OK in that family. And we do that a lot too.

Chris: There's a lot of discussion in the therapy literature about bipolar disorders in children, addictions in adolescence, autism, impulse disorders, attention deficit disorder — how do Gestalt therapists who work with children think about therapeutic approaches with these children? Or I should say, how did you think about therapeutic approaches with children manifesting those kinds of symptoms?

Violet: Well, you know it doesn't matter who you work with. The main thing is to establish a relationship, make contact, and meet them where they are. I mean you could work with three-year-olds or thirty-three-year-olds or adolescents. It's the same thing; you meet them where they are. You make contact with them where they are . . . if they are unable to establish a relationship, I've worked with some autistic type kids. They weren't severely autistic but they were not present most of the time. But, the focus of the therapy was to keep them in contact and for me to be in contact with them. And in that way we began to establish a relationship, and it doesn't matter who I work with, it's the same thing. It's making contact; it's being present with them, meeting them where they are.

Chris: Thank you. One more question. So, an element within the therapy process that you've talked about a lot is self-nurturing. What do you mean by this? How did you come to include this in your therapeutic model?

Violet: This is a subject dear to my heart, the self. I've included it in the therapeutic process as a step that's very important because, as a Gestalt therapist I don't remember ever really dealing with that step in my training, or hearing too much about it, or reading too much about it. And you read books about the "inner child" and accepting the inner child and it's a little bit different from that kind of thing because it doesn't work to stand in front of a mirror and say affirmations. It really doesn't, I mean it's a whole different kind of process, and I came to it actually in an interesting way.

I took some training in body therapy with Jack Rosenberg for a couple of years, and one of the things he used to do that impressed me in my work with him was he talked about the "good mother." And after you did a whole lot of really deep emotional work — he'd bring in the "good mother." You'd be lying on the mat after doing a lot of body breathing and working and crying and all, because he combined Gestalt therapy with the body work and . . . I don't want to go into that, but anyway he'd bring in this "good mother." He had certain vocabulary that the "good mother" would say to you. "You're good," and "I'm here for you," and "I'll never leave you," and that kind of thing. It was very powerful after you had expressed a lot of emotion and dealt with the issue that you were dealing with.

Somehow I found that very meaningful, and so I thought a lot about "How can I use that in my work with kids?" And I first did it, of course, with adult clients . . . I did some body work, had them lying on the mat, and breathing, charged breathing and then talking to them as a Gestalt therapist, my dialogue is with them and that was interesting so I thought, well maybe how could I do that with kids? It's very powerful work. I don't think it would be good to do it with kids. I don't think they're developed enough to handle that kind of deep, deep, deep emotion. I tried it with some adolescents, older adolescents, and it was with some it was effective, but I didn't want to use it with younger children.

So, I thought a lot about it and I began to realize that one of the things that happens, like in my experience was that when you are dealing with these deep emotions, you are fragmented. Like there's a part of you that just admits to feeling horrible about something. There's another part of you that has functioned in the world without all of that, and I thought, "Well kids do that." I mean kids have a lot of introjects and most kids take in these negative messages at an early age. I often say we function, all of us function, on the level of a three or four or five-year-old, what we believe at those ages. And it's those ages where the child has not the cognitive ability to say, this fits for me and this doesn't. "You're stupid." "You're dumb."

Interview with Violet Oaklander

Maybe they hear this, and they don't know that maybe it doesn't fit for them at all. The other person was angry or their brother was mad at them, jealous, or who knows what, and so they take it all in.

And it's not always over. I mean, they get these from the parents and teachers. Sometimes they don't mean to give the child these negative messages, but it's kind of their reaction to certain things the child says. "I'm klutzy, I'm dumb, I'm stupid, I'm no good, I'm whatever, I'm not perfect." And they learn that in our culture, too, in the world they start comparing themselves. And they become, what I see as fragmented, because the child's job is to grow up, and they will do that no matter what.

They go for it, they develop and their bodies develop. They try to grow up. And the other part just gets pushed down. So, one of the things I realized in the self-nurturing work is that in order for child to become nurturing to the self, you have to dig out those negative messages. You can't build a house on a rotten foundation. You have to dig it up and put a nice clean foundation.

So how do we do that? We use a lot of these expressive techniques, that would be the natural way to do it. So, we have different ways, it depends on the situation. One way is to think about the parts of themselves they don't like and draw a picture of it. I had this coloring book I came across called, *Demons* and it was actually done by a French artist, Randy La Chapelle, who drew different pages of his demons and named them: my angry self, my procrastinating self . . . a whole bunch of others . . . and sometimes I'll do something like that, maybe talk about the parts of myself I don't like, that I worry, that I . . . you know that kind of thing.

So, we play a game almost like that, thinking about the parts we don't like and have a kid draw that. Or there are many other ways that we do it, or make it out of clay, make the part of yourself you don't like. And you know it's getting the message across that we all have those feelings, that we all have parts of ourselves we don't like. So, I share some of the ones that I might want to share with them. So, we do that. I'll give you an example of that process, because there are different ways of doing it.

A boy that I work with . . . he's eleven. He falls down and bumps into things all the time. He's a not well-coordinated kid. Of course, in our culture, boys have to be athletic and graceful about that kind of thing — and he's not. Even though his father — it's a divorced family — his father has spent a lot of time trying to teach him how to play baseball, and how to hold the bat, hit the ball and all that, it only makes him feel worse because he never quite does it right.

He had a lot of other parts of himself, as we all do, that he didn't particularly think were so great. But, he drew a picture of a figure like that, that was very clumsy, and he had Band-Aids all over the picture because he said that he bumps himself, he falls down, he does everything, he can't do anything right physically and we called it "Mr. Klutz."

There's a whole process. First, they talk about parts, and they pick one, and draw it. He drew it, named it "Mr. Klutz." Then I said, "I want you to be Mr. Klutz." By this time, they will learn how to do that. So he becomes this, and I dialogue with Mr. Klutz — "Yeah, I can't do — I fall off my bike all the time, I'm always bumping into things. I can't do anything right." He goes on and describes this. I'm commiserating, "Oh! That must be..."

And then I say to the kid, "What do you think of Mr. Klutz?" And the typical answer is, "I hate him. I hate him." That's what most of us who have parts of ourselves we don't like, we'd like to get rid of them. We don't feel they should be in our lives. They make our lives miserable. "Get rid of them." So, I encourage that at first. What I'm looking for, to get ahead, is integration. But, I'm encouraging him to separate and to really personify that part that he doesn't like. I encourage him to get to the anger. Most kids will say, "I don't like him" or "I hate them." Not always do they say, "He's OK." Then, I know we've got more work to do because he's not quite ready to get that anger out.

What's happening is that we retroflect that feeling into ourselves so we feel bad. We're such bad people. But, if we can say, "I hate you!" there's a lot of energy that comes out of that. So, I encourage that. I say, "Tell him!" I become a cheerleader, "Tell him how much you hate him! Good. Tell him!" They'll just [makes growling sound] tell him. He said to this part, "Get out of my life. I hate you. What's the matter with you? You make me sick."

Sometimes, when that happens, something comes in. You hear a voice. You hear their voice and you know it's not them speaking. I have said, "Who does that sound like." They'll say, "It sounds just like my father," or "my mother." Usually one or the other. [Laughs] Or maybe "my teacher." Usually, these happen at a young age. But, he just was yelling at that time. He's got a lot of this energy, and he takes that breath where right now he's finished yelling at Mr. Klutz.

So, that's when I bring in the nurturer. The nurturer is an aspect of themselves. It's a fragmented part of themselves that is capable of being a nurturer. Sometimes, it has to be an outside element. Not, "Say something nice to Mr. Klutz." They're not ready for that.

He's eleven, but I still used the puppet. I said, "We need the Fairy Godmother. You know how Fairy Godmothers are. They think you're wonderful. No matter what you do, they don't care." So, I had this Fairy Godmother puppet. So, he takes it, puts it on his hand and I say, "So, what does the Fairy Godmother say to Mr. Klutz." I say, "You know, how Fairy Godmothers are. They think you're great no matter what you do." He says, "Yeah. She says . . . and then I can see the energy breaking. He's breaking contact. It's how you know a kid is breaking contact — the energy fades. I can see. I've said it twice. So, this time I say, "Try Your Fairy Godmother, try saying, 'I like you'." He's relieved to have something to say. He says, "Yeah. I like you." Sometimes I'm using a puppet talking to the Fairy Godmother, but in this case I actually didn't. I said, "Fairy Godmother, tell Mr. Klutz why you like him." This kid says, "Yeah, you're a good kid. You try things. Yeah! You try things!"

This kid turns to me and he says, "Yeah, I try things!" It's integration before your eyes. It doesn't always happen like that, but it did with him. And there was this [breathes out]. You could see it in his face. Sometimes I have to say, "Put the Fairy Godmother away and see if you can say that to yourself. "You try things" or "You're a good kid." I feed this line, "Fairy Godmother, say to Mr. Klutz, 'I like you even when you fall down and bump yourself. It's OK with me. And you do try things and sometimes you fall down and I like you even then.'" He really liked that and had the Fairy Godmother say it.

In that case, afterwards I said, "Can you say that to yourself?" He had a little trouble saying that to himself. So, I give him homework and the homework is, "This week anytime you bump into something, or you fall down on your bike or you . . . whatever. I want you to imagine the Fairy Godmother is on your shoulder and she's saying, 'It's OK. I like you even when you bump yourself or hurt yourself because you try things.'"

WINDOWS TO OUR CHILDREN

He came back the following week. He said, "I didn't have so much trouble. It's not so bad. I don't fall all the time. I can do a lot of things." It sometimes works that way, and if it doesn't . . . I did talk to his father. I told his father not to play or teach him how to [play baseball]. "That's my job, isn't it?" "No, your job right now is to have fun with him. Take him to the park and play. Have fun. Play Frisbee, or something, not to teach him how to hold the bat."

This was a very bright kid. He probably was not going to be an athlete. His father was very athletic. But, it didn't make any difference. His father made a big effort and really did listen to me. It didn't make any difference. The child still has that negative introject. It gets pushed down because he's happy to have fun with his father. But, the message is still there. It's the child's work. It cannot be done by the parents. They could say, "You're smart" or "You're not clumsy" or "I didn't mean it" or "I don't know how you got that idea," it doesn't matter. It's the child's work. And that's where the individual work is really important.

I've actually done this work with parents present, though, to see what we're doing. I won't go into the stories but I have done that. But it's the most powerful work I know. I've always felt that it had to happen after we've done a lot of work, because you need a certain amount of strength, self-support to do it, to get in touch with that nurturer part. But, it doesn't hurt to try it earlier. It just won't work if you haven't given them enough sense of self, and we do a lot of self-work, to help children feel that sense of self and express their emotions before they get into this self-nurturing. But, I can tell you times when it's happened earlier and it's been, with some kids, very effective.

That's one way. We have other ways of doing it, but that's probably the most typical way, using a projective technique or drawing something or making it out of clay, of a part that they don't like.

OK, I'll say something about the self. I talk about how we do a lot of self-work; it's actually one of the steps of the therapeutic process, which begins with the I-Thou relationship and contact. Those are probably the two prerequisites because if there's no relationship, you might as well just go home. I mean, that becomes the focus of the therapy, if it's difficult for a child. If they've been injured at an early life, you just kind of focus on any creative way to acknowledge, I could give you stories of establishing a relationship. It could be just a thread of a relationship; it doesn't have to be a full-blown relationship. So, that develops, and then there has to be contact.

Contact goes in and out, in and out, but there has to be some contact present in the specific work you're doing, and children will close down and break contact when it becomes too much for them. And you have to go with that, and respect them. There are times when I'll say, before they even know it, because I see it in their bodies, "Why don't we stop and let's play a game. We have a few more minutes, let's play a game." The energy comes back up, you know?

Then, the next step that I talk about has to do with the self. Building the self, helping a child feel a sense of self, self-support, strength within the self, and that helps them express their emotions and do some self-nurturing work. And it sometimes goes back and forth and it's not linear the way you need the relationship and the contact present, it goes back and forth, and contact goes back and forth too. Sometimes it's present, sometimes it isn't. And the focus of the therapy might become helping that child sustain some contact, you know, if they have trouble with that. In any creative way, there are many different ways of doing it.

In any case, the self has a lot of steps to it, not linear steps. For a child, developmentally, many things help them feel strength or sense of self, starting from babyhood, infancy, and the one of them that comes to mind right now is mastery. We see babies develop, work at developing mastery as they develop into toddlers and little ones and as they grow, there are certain developmental tasks that children engage in that gives them a sense of mastery. That's a very important part of development. A lot of the kids we work with don't have those experiences because of dysfunctional families, because of trauma, all kinds of reasons that they have not developed sense of mastery. So, that becomes a focus of the work too, to help them feel mastery and to build the self. There are several other aspects to the self, that help build the self, that we can provide experiences for.

Choices would be one, helping children make choices, helping parents help their children make choices, just choosing. I have seen kids stand in front of a stack of colored paper, and I might say, "Pick two colors," and they can't commit themselves to two colors because they might make a mistake, they might pick the wrong color. They cannot make a choice. This is such a simple, obvious thing, and yet those kinds of things, that build the self, and you have to mean it, if the kid says, "I want yellow and green," you can't say "Well, no, you can't take the yellow because I'm saving it for something else." You have to mean it when you give them a choice, and I tell that to parents.

These are things that are, for children as they're growing, that they develop feelings of strength from. There are a whole list of those kinds of . . . I don't know what you'd call them but.

Chris: Those developmental tasks?

Violet: Well, yeah. And other things that are related to the self. In our work in therapy, sometimes when we're working, a child who has had a lot of difficulty, lots of trauma. I'm thinking I've had so many kids, I could think of a million examples, but there's one, for instance, a girl whose parents separated when she was two. She never knew her father, mother married again when she was four, the stepfather molested her until she was almost nine. The mother worked nights as a waitress. The stepfather was with her. He beat her and molested her, and a teacher noticed she had bruises when she was nine, all those years, and reported it. They didn't know she'd been sexually abused. They felt that the mother should have seen the bruises or maybe the mother did it; so they removed her from the home, put her in a group home while they investigated. They had her examined physically. They discovered she'd been severely sexually abused.

The stepfather ran away. They never found him. The mother would visit the girl at the group home and then she left a letter saying she was leaving, she knew where the stepfather was, and that the girl was available for adoption. This girl's already nine years old.

So then she was put into a foster home for a year and a half, and then she went to live at another foster home, an older woman who never had children, never even been married, who adopted her. And that was an incredible relationship, and she's the one who brought her into therapy, paid for it herself, because she was already adopted, you know. Otherwise, she had not had any therapy whatsoever, in all that time because they don't have the money to provide therapy for these kids, social services. So, money's being cut and they don't even have the time to investigate the cases. So that's when I saw her.

Her process or way of being was like maybe a five-year-old. She walked, she hunched over. She was tall. She was ten and a half when I saw her. And she kind of walked hunched over. She had a little, tiny girly voice and she just was a pleaser. She'd smile all the time.

And no sense of self. You could see it in her body. You could see it in her manner, no sense of self. She could not do anything. We saw her with her new mother every other week because she really wanted to have her mother there, and I saw her alone.

She made a great attachment. Almost more confluent than she might, but she needed to get back her sense of self. She got her sense of self more from her mother than from me at the beginning. So gradually we established a relationship, and we did a lot of things to help her stay in contact.

She liked to color so I brought in coloring books. We'd sit on the floor and color, and gradually I'd say, "I can't decide what color to make this. What do you think?" And she'd look and pretty soon she was able to say, "Green?" [Laughs] Or I'd say, "Oh, look at that bird in your picture. I wonder what the bird would say if it could talk." You know, and we started doing some projective work.

All of a sudden she took over the sessions and that's the part I was getting to. She'd start, "I have this game I thought of." And when her mother was there she had this idea we should throw this softball. We'd have the bataka be like a bat, and if the ball landed here it was three points and if it landed there is was ten points.

And she just controlled the game, and I immediately said, "Where should I stand?" And her mother modeled me. She might not have done that if she hadn't seen me kind of give the power to the child. And the girl conducted this whole thing.

And then with me she thought of other ways. She'd sort of developed these scenarios. She's the doctor and I'm the patient, that kind of thing. And so when I would say to her, you know, something about her stepfather, she'd lose contact.

A couple of times, she would be sitting with paper. We'd been drawing or something and I'd say, "Could draw your stepfather?" And she'd draw rainbows. [Laughs] Or she'd just totally act like she didn't hear me. So I would let it go, and we'd go back, whatever. She had all these different scenarios.

And then one day it happened, where she could stay with it. She made her stepfather out of clay and smashed him with the mallet. Little by little we began to deal with that, and she cried over her mother. She drew a picture of her mother who had left her. And we worked through that that way.

It was an amazing thing to watch how she developed, and developed her separation and her own sense of self. And with that, she began to express those emotions of anger and grief. And then to the self-nurturing. We really couldn't even do it earlier because she didn't quite understand what I was talking about.

Chris: But you helped her find herself.

Violet: The self, to me, of course, is the whole integrated person. The total organism is made up of senses, the body, the expression of emotions, the use of your intellect, your thoughts and ideas, and questions. All of that working in an integrated way is the self.

And the kids we work with or everybody, all of us really, have damaged places where we're not totally integrated. We all have, I don't know, I can't think of the word now, but "lacks" you might say of the self, "holes" in the self. And when we're doing this work, we're kind of building up those holes, replacing those aspects.

If kids are walking like this boy. You know, he walked like a puppet. He didn't have his free use of his body. He could go out there and play soccer, but in regular life, didn't have his free use of his body. So, we might spend some time doing some games involved using the body in different ways, like playing Twister or something. You know, or creative dramatics where you really have to use your body.

They begin to learn that you have to use different parts of your body to get the message across. If you see that a kid can't express emotions, you maybe have to just talk about emotions, play games around emotions until they get used to the idea, you know, and to own some of those emotions. So, it's like we're filling in the gaps, creating the whole person.

And yet we make assessments. When we work with kids we say, we make assessments about where these gaps are. But, the assessment doesn't do anything. Making an assessment and writing the notes doesn't do a thing for the kid. And of course we use all these projective, expressive techniques because that's what the children will respond to. You know, adults too, they respond to that kind of thing, too.

So that's the self. And we need to strengthen the self, have a feeling of power. And we talk about . . . I always talk about aggressive energy as . . . We do a lot of work around aggressive energy. People don't like that word, aggressive. It's not aggression.

Aggressive energy is, as I always say, it's like if you have an apple and if you licked it, you'd never get anything. You have to bite it or you have to take a knife and cut it. That's aggressive energy. And it's that kind of energy, it's an action, it's a feeling of power with an action, that a lot of kids are lacking, even aggressive kids. It doesn't matter whether they're withdrawn and timid or aggressive and acting out.

They are lacking that feeling of centered power, of knowing themselves and acting on it. So, we exaggerate that and do a lot of work to help them get in touch with that aggressive energy. I guess it's what Perl's talked about, about chewing and biting, and if it's no good, you spit it out. And if it's good, you chew it up and swallow it.

You have to be able to differentiate and you have to feel that power of "This is good, this is OK for me." It's pretty complicated; it's not that simple. The self is a complicated entity made up of a lot of things.

Chris: There's nothing in all of this that you've said that says anything about a particular curriculum, a certain way every child has to be. I hear you talking about each child's discovery of their own organism.

Violet: Yes. And it's true because through their experience in life, early years particularly, and as they move on, that's when you tend to cut certain aspects of yourself away. You don't own them, you disown. You cut away. You try to compensate with other parts of yourself. It reminds me of a book, actually, that I've sometimes read with kids. I don't know if you want to include that.

Chris: I'd love to hear what book it is.

Violet: It's called *Little Tree*, and it's by Joyce Mills, who's a wonderful therapist who uses a lot of metaphors. In fact, she wrote a book about how to create therapeutic metaphors for children and adults. She wrote this children's book; it's called *Little Tree*. It's about a tree that loses, in a storm, parts of its branches. It's a whole story of how sad this is for the tree. It was meant, originally, to be used with kids who have maybe illness, or they've lost some of their limbs, or they've lost use of parts of themselves. But, it's really effective for anybody, all kids and adults as well.

You know, a children's book is good if an adult can connect to it. That's what I've discovered. If I like it, I know it's a good children's book. So, the whole story is about how the tree learns that it can use what it has left, all of itself. It doesn't have those limbs anymore; the branches have been torn away. It's about using what you have. But, the fact is that it's really good for anybody, because what we tend to do, we don't lose arms and legs maybe unless we're in an accident, but we cut parts of ourselves off. We block parts of ourselves, and we don't fully use them.

So, that's what happens when our kids have experienced a lot of dysfunction or trauma. Life, all of us do this just in regular life. So, we provide those experiences to help the child own back what they have lost, what they had when they were born as healthy babies that they made full use of. It's like needing to give them back what they lost at that time through the dysfunctional or trauma or whatever.

Chris: Thank you. What a beautiful description and examples that you've given to illustrate all of the complexity of the development of the self and the self-nurturing, introjects, working with introjects, all of that. Thank you.

This issue of the *International Gestalt Journal* is going to be dedicated to you, this one coming up in the fall. But your work, your writing, has appeared in the *Gestalt Journal* before. You're not writing for this journal. You've been very, very generous with your time for this interview.

Violet: Yes. I should say — you know, we talked about it yesterday, about the Gestalt community, and how they work with children, and how that's been slow in coming. I know Norman Shub of the Gestalt Institute of Central Ohio has always been so supportive of the work that I do, and Gordon Wheeler, when we've had these children's conferences in Cleveland and at Esalen where I was honored, which was so wonderful. I have felt that in Europe that they really appreciate the work.

But, what I didn't say was it's through the Gestalt Journal Press, Joe Wysong, has always been supportive of this work. I remember when they had a Gestalt Conference in Manhattan Beach and he asked me to be a keynote. That was unusual.

I spoke about my work with children and what was happening with children. He really did support that. He used to have many conferences, and he always invited me to be part of those conferences. Some of my writings have been in the *Gestalt Journal*, before it was called the *International Gestalt Journal*.

And, the *Gestalt Review* has published — I wrote a whole article about the therapeutic process that was originally published there. Then, I was published in *The Heart of Development*. They asked me to write . . . I had "The Therapeutic Process" published there, too, that came out of the Cleveland Conferences. Also, another journal, the *British Gestalt Journal*, asked me to write something about my work, and it was published there. So there has been support. It isn't that there hasn't been any support for this work. It has been, quite a bit, in many areas.

Chris: Well, thank you . . .

Violet: Of course, I should mention the Gestalt Journal Press published my book *Windows to Our Children*.

Chris: Right. We talked about Real People Press and Steve Andreas. But, we didn't talk about the fact that now it's published by the Gestalt Journal Press.

Violet: Since 1988. It was originally published in 1978. Ten years later, Real People Press focused all their publishing on NLP, and Joe Wysong and the Gestalt Journal Press took over *Windows to Our Children*.

Chris: So from 1978 to 2008, so thirty-one years almost now that the book has been . . .

Violet: And still . . .

Chris: . . . is in print.

Violet: . . . out there. Yes.

Chris: Do you have any particular projects on the table right now?

Violet: Well, I should say, my daughter-in-law, Martha Oaklander, wants to help me write a book about my stories. You know, I tell a lot of stories about the kid cases. The stories, for me, are better examples of what I want to say than just saying the words.

I have millions of them, and she's really anxious to help me write a book like that, record it, and transcribe it. That's kind of on the burner. We talk about doing that. She has helped me a lot. She's come to a number of my two-week training programs to help me with them, so she's been a great source of help.

My son and my daughter want me to write my autobiography.

I actually have an envelope in my office, a thick envelope of questions that people have. When I used to give workshops, I used to ask people to send up their questions because I have trouble hearing, and it was easier for me to read the questions. So I thought it would make a great book called *The Questions People Ask Me*. I do have that envelope up there. I don't know if I'll ever get around to writing it.

Chris: I hope you get all of those things accomplished and have lots of fun.

Violet: Thank you. That's what I really want to do is have fun.

Violet: I just want to just add that the self-nurturing process is written up originally as an audio tape which is distributed by Maxsound Tapes, and then I rewrote it somewhat, and it appears in my second book *Hidden Treasure: A Map to The Child's Inner Self*. It's a chapter in that book if you're interested in learning more about it.

Chris: Thank you.

Violet: In that book, my second book, *Hidden Treasure*, appear a number of chapters that reflect some of the thoughts I've had and work I've done in all the years since the publication of *Windows to Our Children*.

Chris: And what — I just want to ask you — that book's been out a year or two?

Violet: A year or so. Two years, maybe. Yeah.

Chris: What's the response you've been getting for that book?

Violet: Well, I really don't know. I don't know.

[Laughter]

Violet: The book was published in England and it's also in Spanish, so when I was in Spain, the book was totally sold out. The Spanish edition was published in Chile by the same publishing company that published *Windows to Our Children* in Spanish.

Chris: Thank you, Violet, very much. Thank you for your time.

Violet: My pleasure.

13

A Personal Note

This book has changed and grown a great deal during the process of my writing it. I found myself opening up to new ideas as I wrote. I found myself wanting to expand and explain some of the issues I presented, but felt I needed your feedback to do this. I wanted to know what touched you, what bored you, what puzzled you, what you agreed with, what you disagreed with. I often found it difficult to write for a silent and unseen audience. I wanted to make contact with you.

I know that I wrote a lot about some things, and not enough about others. If I have left you hanging and wondering, I hope you will write me and tell me so. Every time I have taught a class, I have learned new things about my work and about myself. Writing this book also did that for me, and I want such learnings to continue, if possible, through your reactions and comments. (Write to me c/o *The Gestalt Journal Press*, P.O. Box 278, Gouldsboro, Maine 04607.)

I started out to write a down-to earth, easy-to-read, practical book. I didn't want to add another esoteric, scholarly book to the library shelves. Although I felt occasional desires to impress those (and I am one of them) who value scholarship, I kept reminding myself that I wanted to write a book about what I do, how I do it, and what I think about working with children, rather than a book to impress. I wanted to share my experience with those of you who need a handle on what to do with a child. I know that many people who work with children are struggling, floundering, needing confirmation of what they do. Others simply need some ideas about what they might do effectively to reach out to children. I hope this book helps.

Now I want to write something about how I developed my notions about childhood and working with children. I've read a lot of books about the development of children and what children are like. But when I work with kids I bring something else to my work, and my relating to them, than all the knowledge I got from books and lectures. I'm trying hard to know what it is because I know for sure that this "it" is something important and comes from a source that is so much a part of me that I no longer "think" about it. When I'm with a child, be she four or fourteen, I find that I can relate to that child from a place that's very much in tune with the child, and at the same time without losing myself. I don't see this child as a stranger. I don't mean that I presume to know everything about her, but I can easily place myself in rapport with the child, and she recognizes this.

I remember very clearly what it was like to be a child. It's not so much remembering incidents and happenings, but remembering the *being*. I remember clearly that I had deep-down feelings and knowings that I never told anyone. I knew things. I wondered about life. I philosophized. And no one really knew this side of me. I thought about death and I was in awe of the fact that life existed before I was born. I wondered at my parents having lived as long as they had, and questioned whether I would live a long time. I saw my grandparents as sages from another time and place. Since my parents often told me stories of their Russian ghetto childhoods I knew that there were places distant and different from Cambridge, Massachusetts, and I marveled and wondered. I can remember that when I was about seven I would look at houses as we drove from Cambridge to Lowell and would wonder about the families who lived on the other side of the glowing windowpanes in the towns and on the farms. I, the forty-five-year-old sociologist, wondered about those people: What were they like? How did they live? What did they do?

I remember that when I was a child I had wonderings and feelings that came from a place so deep inside me that I know I never could have put them in words if I had wanted to. I never spoke about them even to my parents, who loved me and took great interest in me. I remember too, that every moment of life's experience was very important and large to me, and that this feeling stayed with me as I took my cues from the adults around me about how to act. They worried about money and food and safety, and somehow I sensed that it was best to keep to myself those things that were most important to me but that might seem silly and inconsequential to them.

Perhaps it is my capacity to tap into these childhood memories that gives me a certain view of children that they respond to. I'm thinking now of the fun and joy and silliness and laughter of children. It is interesting that when we talk about "getting in touch with the child in us," we mostly refer to the merriment of childhood. I'm also remembering that as a child, I allowed my happy-go-lucky self its expression (it got a lot of approval) and I certainly expressed some tears of pain and sadness, and a little bit of anger. But I soon sensed that these latter expressions caused pain in the adults I loved, and I quickly learned to be careful about expressing them. I think most children get this kind of message, and at some point begin to at least tone down their expressions.

I started working with children as a camp counselor when I was a teenager. Theoretically I didn't know anything about kids; but I knew I liked kids a lot, could talk to them, could get them excited and interested in things, could teach them some things like songs, swimming, and how to put on a play. I liked listening to them and being around them. I thought then that I might like to be a social worker dealing with groups of kids. Even then I had an affinity for the kid who wasn't the successful all-American type, and who seemed to have some problems in living. I knew these kids liked talking to me and I liked that. Perhaps I felt that way because I had an image, a concept, of all-American kids — mostly white, Anglo-Saxon, slender, athletic, graceful, blonde, very calm and cool. My parents were Russian Jewish immigrants — emotional, affectionate, intellectual, vocal, revolutionary. As a child I remember sometimes feeling great envy for those cool, quiet, American, no-accent, conforming families of the kids I knew as I grew up in Massachusetts. I felt different.

I married young and had three children of my own and threw myself into parenthood with the same kind of commitment, conviction and interest that I took with me into most of my life endeavors. I became an expert about every phase that my children went through. I learned a lot, especially about early childhood development (since I seemed always to have a child at this stage), and I even taught nursery school for a couple of years. I found kids of all ages wondrous and interesting. I went back to school when my youngest was almost three, and became a teacher mostly because it was a good thing for a mother to do. I really did love children, and now that my children were in school I became interested in the education of children.

I was an "alternative" teacher before the term was invented, and ran into much difficulty in the school system. My principal told me that I was too "recreation-oriented." She knew that I had worked with numerous groups of children in Jewish Community Centers throughout the country and urged me to go back to this kind of work — where having fun was considered OK. Meanwhile all the children with problems somehow became registered in my class. After three years of "regular" teaching, I was offered a job in the district's special education program as a teacher with children specifically classified as emotionally disturbed. In the six years I worked with these children (during which time I earned my master's degree in special education), I learned the most about children.

When I was studying for my special education degree I wanted to be allowed to do independent study — to read in depth the literature and available studies on doing therapeutic work with children. Because I was one of only four people in a special program funded by a United States Office of Education grant, I was finally given permission to earn some of my credits toward the degree in the kind of study I felt I needed. I had already spent four years working with disturbed children in the public school system and I believed I *knew* what I needed in my education, and where my deficiencies lay. I knew from my experience that children do not learn how to read and write and do math when they are feeling terrible about themselves. I had already discovered in my work with children that when I took the time to do therapy with them and help them get out some of their blocked feelings, they did much better academic work. I planned to write my master's thesis on this area. I wanted to know more and learn more about doing therapy with children. But I found that classes in advanced child development, abnormal psychology, and guidance and counseling of the handicapped, as well as seminars in special education and remediation of learning disabilities, etc., *did not teach me how to do therapy with children*. I petitioned to be allowed to study on my own and to visit ongoing therapeutic programs with the sanction of the university. These petitions were finally granted after considerable struggle.

A Personal Note

And so I read many books, journals, and research studies; visited many kinds of programs, classes, clinics, schools, and agencies; talked to many people working with children to find out what they did, how they did it, and what was happening with the children. These kinds of experiences — interviewing, observing, reading — were credited to me as two full college-year classes. Thus I had quite a bit of time and leeway to do what I wanted to, and I met regularly with two of my professors to report my experiences.

This unique experience taught me a great deal, but not what I had expected and hoped for. It taught me that I probably knew as much about working with children as anyone. I realized that most of what was valuable in my training had come from the children with whom I had worked, not from courses or books. I found that one academic approach often contradicts another even when both are derived from the teachings of the same renowned "expert." I learned that everyone was groping, along with me. Many people were doing good work, but there did not seem to be a consistent rationale.

For a long time, before the vogue of behavior modification and behavioral objectives, I had complete freedom to structure my "emotionally handicapped" classes as I saw fit. I did a lot of experimenting with different methods of working with children to help them feel better about themselves and help them learn to cope with their chaotic lives, to help them express their feelings directly rather than indirectly through belligerent striking-out behavior or complete withdrawal. During this time I entered the Los Angeles Gestalt Therapy Institute training program, and my work with children took on a gestalt-oriented emphasis as I became more and more adept in Gestalt therapy theory and practice. During this part of my life I also went through much of my own therapy — a result of help I needed to cope with the eighteen-month illness and subsequent death of my fourteen-year-old son, and soon after that, the end of my marriage. I went back to school once more, earned a masters degree in marriage, family, and child counseling, got my license to practice, became a certified member of the Gestalt Therapy Institute, and launched my career as a private practitioner. In the spring of 1978 I was granted a Ph.D. in psychology from International College, and this book is an outgrowth of my dissertation.

WINDOWS TO OUR CHILDREN

As I think about my relationship to children through my life remembering what it's like to be a child, working with children in recreation centers, being a student teacher and then a teacher in my own right, working with emotionally disturbed children (openly labeled and acknowledged as having problems), and doing therapy with children in private practice, I remember many, many incidents, stories I could tell, that make me laugh and make me cry. I think of my feelings as I spent time with all the children in my life, including myself as a child.

I realize that *I learned about working with children from children, including myself as a child!* This seems so obvious to me now, almost too elementary to write. Children are our finest teachers. They already *know* how to grow, how to develop, how to learn, how to expand and discover, how to feel, laugh and cry and get mad, what is right for them and what is not right for them, what they need. They already know how to love and be joyful and to live life to its fullest, to work and to be strong and full of energy. All they (and the children within us) need is the space to do it.

About The Author

Besides having raised three children of her own, Violet Oaklander has a Ph.D. in psychology and two master's degrees: one in Marriage, Family and Child Counseling and one in Special Education of emotionally disturbed and learning disabled children. She taught emotionally disturbed children in the Long Beach Unified School District in California for six years and, since 1972, has been in fill time private practice in the South Bay area of Los Angeles, and subsequently in Santa Barbara, California. She now lives in Los Angeles. She served as the Director of the Center for Child and Adolescent Therapy in Hermosa Beach, California for eight years, and is presently the Director of the Violet Oaklander Institute specifically devoted to the supervision and training of people who work with children.

Dr. Oaklander completed three years of training with the Gestalt Therapy Institute of Los Angeles where she has been a certified member since 1973. A large portion of her work is involved with training professionals and she has given many seminars, workshops, and classes for institutions, throughout the United States, Canada, Europe, Israel and Australia. She is the author of a series of audio and video tapes related to psychotherapeutic work with children.

Dr. Oaklander's recordings are available from the Violet Oaklander Foundation (VOF) at http://www.vsof.org/store.html.

Bibliography

Actions, Styles and Symbols in Kinetic Family Drawings. Burns, R., and Kaufman, S. H. New York: Brunner/ Mazel, 1972.

A Frog and Toad are Friends. Lobel, A. New York: Harper and Row, 1970.

American Folk Songs for Children. Seeger, R. C. Garden City, NY: Doubleday, 1948.

Analyzing Children's Art. Kellog, R. Palo Alto, CA: National Press Books, 1969.

And Jill Came Tumbling After: Sexism in American Education. Stacey, J., Bereaud, S., and Daniels, J. New York: Dell, 1974.

Anger and the Rocking Chair. Lederman, J. New York: McGraw Hill, 1969.

"An Introduction to Gestalt Techniques." Enright, J. B. Chapter 8 in *Gestalt Therapy Now.* Fagan, J., and Shepherd, I. L. (Eds.) Gouldsboro ME: The Gestalt Journal Press, 2006. (Original publication: New York: Harper and Row, 1971)

Are You Listening to Your Child? Kraft, A. New York: Walker, 1973.

Art: Another Language for Learning. Cohen, E., and Gainer, R. New York: Citation Press, 1976.

Art as Therapy with Children. Kramer, E. New York: Schocken Books, 1975.

Art for the Family. D'Amico, V., Wilson, F., and Maser, M. New York: The Museum of Modern Art, 1954.

Awareness: Exploring, experimenting, experiencing. Stevens, J. Gouldsboro ME: The Gestalt Journal Press, 2007. (Original publication: Moab, Utah: Real People Press, 1971)

WINDOWS TO OUR CHILDREN

Be a Frog, a Bird, or a Tree. Carr, R. Garden City, NJ: Doubleday, 1973.
Begin Sweet World: Poetry by Children. Pearson, J. Garden City, NY: Doubleday, 1976.
Between Parent and Child. Ginott, H. New York: Macmillan, 1965.
Between Parent and Teenager. Ginott, H. New York: Macmillan, 1969.
The Boys' and Girls' Book about Divorce. Gardner, R. A. New York: Jason Aronson, 1970.
Career Awareness: Discussions and Activities to Promote Self Awareness. Williams, S., and Mitchell, R. Monterey Park, CA: Creative Teaching Press, 1976.
The Centering Book. Henricks, G., and Wills, R. Englewood Cliffs, NJ: Prentice-Hall, 1975.
Childhood and Society. Erikson, E. H. New York: Norton, 1963.
Children in Play Therapy. Moustakas, C. E. New York: Jason Aronson, 1973.
Children's Apperception Test (CAT). Bellak, L., and Bellak, S. S. Larchmont, NY: C.P.S., Inc., 1949.
Children's Drawings as Diagnostic Aids. Di Leo, J. H. New York: Brunner/Mazel, 1973.
The Children's Rights Movement: Overcoming the Oppression of Young People. Gross, B., and Gross, R. (Eds.) Garden City, NY: Anchor, 1977.
The Child's World of Make-Believe. Singer, J. New York: Academic Press, 1973.
Conjoint Family Therapy. Satir V. Palo Alto, CA: Science and Behavior Books, 1967.
"Costume Play Therapy." Marcus, I. in *Therapeutic Use of Child's Play.* Schaefer, C. (Ed.) New York: Jason Aronson, 1976.
Creative Dramatics in the Classroom. McCaslin, N. New York: David McKay, 1968.
Crisis in the Classroom. Silberman, C. New York: Random House, 1970.
Dance Therapy in the Classroom. Balazs, E. Waldwick, NJ: Hoctor Products for Education, 1977.

Bibliography

"The Despert Fable Test." Despert, J. L. in *Emotional Disorders of Children: A Case Book of Child Psychiatry.* Pearson, G. New York: Norton, 1949.

Dramakinetics in the Classroom. Complo, Sister J. M. Boston, MA: Plays Inc., 1974.

Draw A Person Test. (See Personality Projection in the Drawing of the Human Figure.)

Dr. Gardner's Fairy Tales for Today's Children. Gardner, R. A. Englewood Cliffs, NJ: Prentice-Hall, 1974.

Dr. Gardner's Modern Fairy Tales. Gardner, R. A. Philadelphia, PA: George F. Stickley, 1977.

Dr. Gardner's Stories About the Real World. Gardner, R. A. Englewood Cliffs, NJ: Prentice-Hall, 1972.

"The Emperor's New Clothes." Andersen, H. C. *Anderson's Fairy Tales.* New York: Grossett and Dunlap, 1945.

Escape from Childhood: The Needs and Rights of Children. Holt, J. New York: Ballantine, 1975.

"Experiential Family Therapy." Kempler, W. *International Journal of Group Psychotherapy,* Vol. XV, No. 1, Jan. 1965.

The Family of Man. Steichen, E. New York: The Museum of Modern Art, 1955.

Famous Folk Tales to Read Aloud. Watts, M. New York: Wonder Books, 1961.

Fantasy and Feeling in Education. Jones, R. M. New York: Harper and Row, 1968.

Fantasy Encounter Games. Otto, H. A. New York: Harper and Row, 1974.

Feelings: Inside You and Our Loud Too. Polland, B. K., and DeRoy, C. Millbrae, CA: Celestial Arts, 1975.

Fish is Fish. Lionni, L. New York: Pantheon Books, 1970.

"Four Lectures." Perls, F. Chapter 2 in in *Gestalt Therapy Now.* Fagan, J., and Shepherd, I. L. (Eds.) Gouldsboro ME: The Gestalt Journal Press, 2006. (Original publication: New York: Harper and Row, 1971)

Freedom to Learn. Rogers, C. Columbus, OH: Charles E. Merrill, 1969.

WINDOWS TO OUR CHILDREN

Free to Be . . . You and Me. Thomas, M. New York: McGraw-Hill, 1974.
The Gestalt Art Experience. Rhyne, J. Monterey, CA: Brooks/Cole, 1973.
Gestalt Therapy Integrated. Polster, E., and Polster, M. New York: Brunner/Mazel, 1973.
Go Away, Dog. Nodset, J. L. New York: Harper and Row, 1963.
Go See the Movie in Your Head. Short, J. E. New York: Popular Library, 1977.
Grownups Cry Too. Hazen, N. Chapel Hill, NC: Lollipop Power, Inc., 1973.
The Hand Test. Wagner, E. E. Los Angeles, CA: Western Psychological Services, 1969.
Have You Seen a Comet? Children's Art and Writing from Around the World. U.S. Committee for UNICEF. New York: The John Day Co., 1971.
"The House-Tree-Person Test." Buck, J. *Journal of Clinical Psychology,* 1948, 4, 151-159.
How Children Fail. Holt, J. New York: Pitman, 1964.
How Children Learn. Holt, J. New York: Pitman, 1967.
How it Feels to Be a Child. Klein, C. New York: Harper and Row, 1977.
How to Live with Your Special Child. Von Hilsheimer, G. Washington, DC: Acropolis Books, 1970.
How to Meditate. LeShan, L. New York: Bantam, 1975.
Human Figure Drawings in Adolescence. Schildkrout, M. S., Shenker, I. R., and Sonnenblick, M. New York: Brunner/Mazel, 1972.
Human Teaching for Human Learning: An Introduction to Confluent Education. Brown, G. New York: Viking Press, 1971.
If I Ran the Zoo. Geisel, T. (Dr. Seuss) New York: Random House, 1950.
I'll Build my Friend a Mountain. Katz, B. New York: Scholastic Book Services, 1972.
Improvisation for the Theater. Spolin, V. Evanston, IL: Northwestern University Press, 1963.
I Never Saw Another Butterfly. (Children's Drawings and Poems from Terezin Concentration Camp.) New York: McGraw-Hill, 1964.
I See a Child. Herbert, C. Garden City, NY: Anchor, 1974.

Is This You? Krauss, R., and Johnson, C. New York: William R. Scott, 1955.
"Just Imagine..." (Mini-Poster-Cards Book) Trend Enterprises, 1972.
Learning Time with Language Experiences for Young Children. Scott, L. B. St. Louis: McGraw-Hill, 1968.
Learning to Feel — Feeling to Learn. Lyon, H. Columbus, OH: Charles E. Merrill, 1971.
Le Centre Du Silence: Work Book. Avital, S. Boulder, CO: AlephBeith, 1975.
Left Handed Teaching: Lessons in Affective Education. Castillo, G. New York: Praeger, 1974.
Leo the Late Bloomer. Kraus, R. New York: Young Readers Press, 1971.
Let's Do Yoga. Richards, R., and Abrams, J. New York: Holt, Rhinehart and Winston, 1975.
Linda Goodman's Sun Signs. Goodman, L. New York: Bantam Books, 1971.
The Live Classroom. Brown, G., Yeomans, T., and Grizzard, G. (Eds.) New York: Viking, 1975.
The Lives of Children. Dennison, G. New York: Vintage, 1966.
Loneliness. Moustakas, C. E. Englewood Cliffs, NJ: Prentice-Hall, 1961.
Lonely in America. Gordon, S. New York: Simon and Schuster, 1976.
The Luscher Color Test. Luscher, M. New York: Pocket Books, 1971.
The Magic Hat. Chapman, K. W. Chapel Hill, NC: Lollipop Power, Inc., 1973.
Make-A-Picture Story (MAPS) Test. Schneidman, E. S. New York: The Psychological Corporation, 1949.
Making it Strange. Synectics, Inc. (Ed.) (a series of 4 books). New York: Harper and Row, 1968.
Male and Female Under 18. Larrick, N., and Merriam, E. (Eds.) New York: Avon, 1973.
Man and His Symbols. Jung, C. G. New York: Dell, 1968.
Math, Writing, and Games in the Open Classroom. Kohl, H. New York: Vintage, 1974.

Meditating with Children. Rozman, D. Boulder Creek, CA: University of the Trees Press, 1975.
Memories, Dreams, Reflections. Jung, C. G. New York: Vintage Books, 1961.
The Me Nobody Knows: Children's voices from the Ghetto. Joseph, S., (Ed.) New York: Avon, 1969.
Me the Flunkie: Yearbook of a School for Failures. Summers, A., (Ed.) New York: Fawcett, 1970.
Miracles. Collected by Richard Lewis. New York: Bantam Books, 1977.
"Moods and Emotions." Tester, S. (packet of teaching pictures and resource booklet). Elgin, IL: David C. Cook, 1970.
Mooney Problem Check List. Mooney, R. L. New York: The Psychological Corp., 1960.
Movement Games for Children of All Ages. Nelson, E. New York: Sterling, 1975.
"Music Therapy." Dreikurs, R. in *Conflict in the Classroom: The Education of Emotionally Disturbed Children.* Long, N.J., Morse, W. C., and Newman, R. G. (Eds.) Belmont, CA: Wadsworth, 1965.
My Body Feels Good. Singer, S., Olderman, S., and Maceiras, R. New York: The Feminist Press, 1974.
My Sister Looks Like a Pear: Awakening the Poetry in Young People. Anderson, D. New York: Hart Publishing Co., 1974.
The New Games Book. Fluegelman, A., (Ed.) Garden City, NY: Doubleday, 1976.
Nobody Listens to Andrew. Guilfoile, E. New York: Follet, 1957.
The Non-Coloring Book. Cazet, C. San Francisco, CA: Chandler and Sharp, 1973.
Not THIS Bear! Myers, B. New York: Scholastic Book Services, 1967.
100 Ways to Enhance Self-Concept in the Classroom. Canfield, J., and Wells, H. Englewood Cliffs, NJ: Prentice-Hall, 1976.
One Little Boy. Baruch, D. New York: Dell, 1952.
"The Paradoxical Theory of Change." Beisser, A. R. Chapter 6 in *Gestalt Therapy Now.* Fagan, J., and Shepherd, I. L. (Eds.) Gouldsboro ME:

The Gestalt Journal Press, 2006. (Original publication: New York: Harper and Row, 1971)

Personality Projection in the Drawing of the Human Figure: A Method of Personality Investigation. Machover, K. Springfield, IL: Charles C. Thomas, 1949.

P. E. T.: Parent Effectiveness Training. Gordon, T. New York: New American Library, 1975.

Play, Dreams and Imitation in Childhood. Piaget, J. New York: Norton, 1962.

Play in Childhood. Lowenfeld, M. New York: John Wiley, 1967.

Play Therapy. Axline, V. M. New York: Ballantine, 1947.

Principles of Gestalt Family Therapy. Kempler, W. The Kempler Institute (P.O. Box 1692, Costa Mesa, CA 92626), 1973.

The Psychology of Play. Millar, S. New York: Jason Aronson, 1974.

The Psychology of the Child. Piaget, J., and Inhelder, B. New York: Basic Books, 1969.

Psychosynthesis. Assagioli, R. New York: Viking, 1965.

Psychotherapeutic Approaches to the Resistant Child. Gardner, R. A. New York: Jason Aronson, 1975.

Psychotherapy with Children. Moustakas, C. E. New York: Ballantine, 1959.

Psychotherapy with Children of Divorce. Gardner, R. A. New York: Jason Aronson, 1976.

Put Your Mother on the Ceiling. De Mille, R. Gouldsboro ME: The Gestalt Journal Press, 1997. (Original publication: New York: Walker and Co., 1967).

Rainbow Activities. Seattle Public School District No. 1. South El Monte, CA: Creative Teaching Press, 1977.

Rose, Where Did You Get That Red? Teaching Great Poetry to Children. Koch, K. New York: Vintage, 1974.

The Second Centering Book. Hendricks, G. and Roberts, T. Englewood Cliffs, NJ: Prentice-Hall, 1977.

The Sensible Book: A Celebration of Your Five Senses. Polland, B. K., and Hammid, H. Millbrae, CA: Celestial Arts, 1974.

Somebody Turned on a Tap in These Kids: Poetry and Young People Today. Larrick, N., (Ed.) Delta, 1971.
Some Things Are Scary. Heide, F. P. New York: Scholastic Book Services, 1969.
Some Things You Just Can't Do by Yourself. Schiff, N., and Schiff, B. S. Stanford, CA: New Seed Press, 1973.
"The Sorcerer's Apprentice, or the Use of Magic in Child Psychotherapy." Moskowitz, J. A. *International Journal of Child Psychotherapy.* Vol. 2, No. 2, April, 1973, pp. 138-162
Spectacles. Raskin, E. New York: Atheneum, 1968.
The Story of Ferdinand. Leaf, M. New York: Viking, 1936.
"Subpersonalities." Vargiu, J. G. *Synthesis.* Vol. 1, No. 1, 1974, pp. WB 9-WB 47.
Sybil. Schreiber, F. R. Chicago: Henry Regnery, 1973.
Sylvester and the Magic Pebble. Steig, W. New York: Dutton, 1969.
The Talking, Feeling, and Doing Game; A Psychotherapeutic Game for Children. Creative Therapeutics (155 Country Road, Cresskill, NJ 07626), 1973.
Talking Time. Scott, L. B., and Thompson, J. J. St. Louis, MO: Webster, 1951.
Taylor-Johnson Temperament Analysis. Taylor, R. M. Los Angeles, CA: Psychological Publications, Inc., 1967.
Teaching Human Beings: 101 Subversive Activities for the Classroom. Schrank, J. Boston, MA, Beacon Press, 1972.
The Temper Tantrum Book. Preston, E. M. New York: Viking, 1969.
Theater in My Head. Cheifetz, Dan. Boston, MA: Little, Brown, 1971.
Thematic Apperception Test (TAT). Murray, H. A. Cambridge, MA: Harvard University Press, 1943.
Therapeutic Communication with Children: The Mutual Storytelling Technique. Gardner, R. A. New York: Science House, 1971.
Therapeutic Consultation in Child Psychiatry. Winnicott, D. W. New York: Basic Books, 1971.
Therapeutic Use of Child's Play. Schaefer, C. (Ed.) New York: Jason Aronson, 1976.

Bibliography

"Therapy in Groups: Psychoanalytic, Experiential, and Gestalt." Cohn, R. C. Chapter 10 in *Gestalt Therapy Now*. Fagan, J., and Shepherd, I. L. New York: Harper and Row, 1971.
There's a Nightmare in My Closet. Mayer, M. New York: Dial, 1968.
Toward Humanistic Education: A Curriculum of Affect. Weinstein, G., and Fantini, M. D. (Eds.) New York: Praeger, 1970.
Transpersonal Education. Hendricks, G., and Fadiman, J. (Eds.) Englewood Cliffs, NJ: Prentice-Hall, 1976.
Treasure Book of Fairy Tales. McGovern, A. New York: Crest, 1969.
The Ultimate Athlete. Leonard, G. New York: Viking, 1974.
The Un-Coloring Book: Doodles to Finish. Book II. Schumann, K. Media for Education (13208 Washington Blvd., Los Angeles, CA 90066), 1976.
The Ungame. Au-Vid, Inc. (P.O. Box 964, Garden Grove, CA 92642), 1972.
"The Use of Puppetry in Therapy." Woltmann, A. G. In *Conflict in the Classroom: The Education of Emotionally Disturbed Children*. Long, N. J., Morse, W. C., and Newman, R. G. (Eds.) Belmont, CA: Wadsworth, 1967.
The Uses of Enchantment: The Meaning and Importance of Fairy Tales. Bettelheim, B. New York: Knopf, 1976.
What Is a Boy? What is a Girl? Waxman, S. Culver City, CA: Peace Press, 1976.
What Is Your Favorite Thing to Hear? Gibson, M. T. New York: Grosset and Dunlap, 1966.
What Is Your Favorite Thing to Touch? Gibson, M. T. New York: Grosset and Dunlap, 1966.
Where the Sidewalk Ends. Silverstein, S. New York: Harper and Row, 1974.
Where the Wild Things Are. Sendak, M. New York: Harper and Row, 1963.
The Whole Word Catalogue 1. Brown, R., Hoffman, M., Kushner, K., Lopate, P., and Murphy, S., (Eds.) New York: Virgil Books, 1972.

WINDOWS TO OUR CHILDREN

The Whole Word Catalogue 2. Zavatsky, B., and Padgett, R. (Eds.) New York: McGraw-Hill, 1977.

Wishes, Lies and Dreams: Teaching Children to Write Poetry. Koch, K. New York: Vintage Books, 1970.

Yoga for Children. Diskin, E. New York: Warner Books, 1976.

Your Child's Sensory World. Liepmann, L. Baltimore, MD: Penguin, 1974.

The Zen of Seeing: Seeing/ Drawing as Meditation. Franck, F., New York: Vintage Books, 1973.

INDEX

acting out
  "role-playing" parts of self, 199, 229
  & aggression, 224
  and puppets, 116
  as an inappropriate behavioral label, 222
  working with in therapy with children, 224
adolescent
  & anger expression, 234
  & fears of growing up, 320, 337
  & issues of security vs. freedom, 337
  & loneliness, 288
  & resistance to therapy, 313, 314
  & strengthening the self, 63
  & the therapeutic use of sand tray, 184
  and therapy, 316
  goals of therapy with, 63
  individual therapy work with, 313
  parents of, 314
  therapy with, 313, 316
  work with body image, 318, 320
  work with sexuality, 318, 319
aggression
  and taking care of needs, 62
  as a judgmental label, 222
  in play behavior, 175
  understood in context, 222
aggressive
  and the hyperactive child, 239, 241
  as a behavioral "label", 222
  behavior – as communication, 223
  behavior – as means of survival, 62
  behavior – meaning of, 182, 198
  behavior & fear of rejection, 284
  behavior and fear, 256, 326
  behavior as anger, 223
  behavior in boys, 248
  behavior with therapist, 224
  in play behavior, 174
  working with in therapy, 224
anger
  & aggression, 223, 225
  & awareness continuum, 135
  & bed-wetting, 271, 272
  & body awareness, 139
  & body movement and awareness, 144
  & communication, 332
  & fear in the child, 261, 262
  & guilt, resentment, shame and self-blame, 296, 297, 299, 300
  & hyperactive child, 246
  & inappropriate behavior, 233
  & male/female qualities, 340
  & new baby in family, 32
  & physical symptoms, 271, 277
  & the child in and out of reality, 293
  & the encropetic child, 274
  & the therapeutic use of clay, 73, 78

& the therapeutic use of drawing, 45-47, 54, 228, 231, 232, 236, 237, 252, 277, 318, 325
& the therapeutic use of poetry, 108
& the therapeutic use of sand tray, 270
& the therapeutic use of sound, 125, 127
& the therapeutic use of taste, 130
& the withdrawn child, 253
against therapist – how to work with, 325
and excessive pleasing, 283
and resentment – retroflected – as guilt and shame, 296
at siblings, 158, 163
direct expression of, 227, 230
helping children identify it, 228
hidden – in child, 45
in adolescents, 318
in childhood, 225
retroflected, 139, 401
retroflected – child's fear of, 237
retroflected – experienced as guilt, 296
revealed by Psych Tests, 194
symbolic expression of, 229
therapist's comfort with, 332
unexpressed – ramification of, 234, 238
working with in therapy, 61, 225-227

animal(s)
& child in & out of reality, 292
& the therapeutic use of clay, 82
& the therapeutic use of drawing, 31, 69, 71, 337, 338
& the therapeutic use of fantasy, 16, 19, 27, 128
& the therapeutic use of play, 206
& the therapeutic use of poetry, 109
& the therapeutic use of the sand tray, 186, 270
and intuition, 131
and use of flannel boards, 99
as symbol – Assagioli, 91
Children's Apperception Test, 97
fantasy game of DeMille, 11
in books – therapeutic use, 100
in psychodrama, 157
symbols in therapy work, 279
use of in esteem building, 304
use of in therapy, 250, 253
anxiety
& breathing, 140
& destructive behavior, 223
& divorce or separation, 38, 82, 272
& dreams, 163
& excessive pleasing, 279
& fantasies, 11
& hanging on, 279
& moving to a new home, 269
& new situations, 140
& phobias, 256

& physical symptoms, 198
& separation from parent, 261
& test taking, 140
& the therapeutic use of drawing, 70
& use of massage, 243
and loneliness, 288
countering with breathing exercises, 140
excitement & breathing, 140
expression of, 313
of growing up, 264, 265
the anxious child, 134, 139, 166, 189, 212, 240, 252, 265, 269, 289, 320, 335
working with in therapy, 212

art
& child in & out of reality, 291
& collage in therapy, 89
& fairy tales, 101
& fantasy in therapy, 19
& feeling, seeing, knowing, 89
& scribble technique, 39
& sculpture in therapy, 85
& the therapeutic use of clay, 74
& use of painting in therapy, 53
& work with polarities in self, 171
anger revealed in, 229
as seeing/drawing, 123
pictures – use of in therapy, 90
attention span, 126, 180
autism, 293
awareness
& body movement, 142
& contact functions, 63
& distractible children, 245
& empty chair technique, 164
& experiencing in therapy, 64
& focus on present, 219
& low self-esteem, 304
& movement therapy, 154
& pantomiming, 152
& reowning one's ears, 124
& reowning one's eyes, 121
& restoring sensory experience, 119, 120
& the therapeutic use of drama, 151
& the therapeutic use of drawing, 58, 64
& the therapeutic use of music, 128
& the therapeutic use of poetry, 109
& the therapeutic use of taste, 130
& use of seeing exercises, 124
and tactile experiences, 242
building & the art of therapy, 208
continuum to increase body awareness, 134
directed – of emotions, 176
directed by therapist, 175, 176, 209
in family therapy, 314, 323
in young children, 209
of body in physical education, 142
of breathing, 139
of feet – in therapy, 56

of sounds – exercises for, 124
rebuilding in therapy, 63
responsibility & experiment in group therapy, 310
sensory – in infants, 61
techniques for enhancing in group therapy, 311
therapist's in group therapy, 312
use of in group therapy, 308
use of in play therapy, 175
whole body & movement, 154
work with autistic child, 295

baby
"role-playing" parts of self, 4, 5
& fantasy in therapy, 52, 97, 215
& kinesthetic perception, 139
& the therapeutic use of clay, 64, 82
& the therapeutic use of drawing, 31
costume in role playing, 156
role playing in therapy, 5
sensory development in, 61, 63
sibling reaction to new, 31, 32, 83, 127, 215, 266

baby pictures
use of in therapy, 304

bed wetting
& fantasy work in therapy, 1, 16
& the therapeutic use of storytelling, 94
as self protection, 45

body
& awareness of feelings, 63, 134
& bed-wetting, 272, 276
& centering exercises, 138
& child in and out of reality, 291, 295
& developed sense of self, 61, 304
& empty chair technique, 172
& fear in the child, 256-258
& kinesthetic perception, 138, 139
& learning disabilities, 141
& physical education in schools, 142
& relaxation exercises, 135, 136
& sense of self, 63
& the hyperkinetic child, 141
& the insecure child, 281, 283
& the therapeutic use of clay, 74, 81, 321
& the therapeutic use of drama, 150, 151
& the therapeutic use of drawing, 49, 68-70, 145, 235
& the therapeutic use of fantasy, 68
& the therapeutic use of writing, 106, 120
& use of awareness continuum, 255, 308
& work with adolescents, 318-320
and fear, 256
as issue in adolescent group, 318
awareness – & breathing, 139
awareness – & intuition, 131, 132
awareness – blocking of, 139

Index

awareness & movement, 154
awareness of & health, 64, 65, 242
breathing & anxiety, 140
cues – use of in therapy, 59, 61
drama, movement, learning, 141
image – therapeutic approaches to, 320
image issues – girl's group, 318
image issues of adolescents, 320
in normal development, 61
movement exercises for, 141
posture as clue to client, 330
sexuality – in girl's group, 318, 319
symptoms as communication, 195, 227
therapist's observations of, 157, 164, 165, 176
therapist's use of own, 182
use of in group therapy, 308
work – determining need for, 321, 330
body cues
   importance of in therapeutic process, 59
body language
   as key to feelings, 295
body movement
   & awareness, 141, 142, 304
   & awareness in therapy, 283
   & awareness of feelings, 147
   & body-awareness, 245
   & creative dramatics, 141, 152, 172, 258
   & feelings, 295

   & healthy infant development, 379
   & sensory awareness, 120
   & work with polarities in self, 172
   importance of in therapy, 138
brain
   & body awareness, 304
breath
   & bed-wetting, 273
   & body awareness, 139, 140
   & fantasy work in therapy, 1, 17
   & relaxation exercises, 245
   & sense of smell, 130
   & test taking, 140
   & the encropetic child, 292
   & the therapeutic use of clay, 76, 77
   & the therapeutic use of drawing, 59, 68, 320
   & the therapeutic use of dreams, 164
   & the withdrawn child, 250
   as cue in therapy session, 59
   as cue to fear in child, 256
   as cue to feelings, 134
   breathing & anxiety, 140
   exercises for in therapy, 136, 138
   group members' – as cue for directing awareness, 330
   therapists's use of, 330
bullying, 165
   by destructive child in schoolroom, 98
child development, 402

childhood
   & introjection – in therapy, 322
   & the therapeutic use of fantasy, 8, 69
   & the therapist's soul, 400
   as prison not garden, 222
   guilt from in adult, 299
   John Holt's discussion of, 221
   loneliness in, 287
   patterns in adulthood, 281
   reality vs. myth of, 221
   recurring dreams from, 159
   sexist attitudes formed in, 341

Children's Apperception Test (CAT)
   use of in group, 97

child's process
   & building tasks, 188
   & the therapeutic use of clay, 74, 81
   & the therapeutic use of costumes in play therapy, 157
   & the therapeutic use of fantasy, 9
   & the therapeutic use of puzzles, 188
   and therapist intervention, 65, 295
   in group storytelling, 50
   parallels – therapy & life, 50

choice
   & awareness in therapy, 64, 66, 133
   & child's inner strength, 66
   & responsibility, 247, 273, 282, 297
   & self-awareness, 63, 317
   child's awareness of, 66
   child's control of, 245, 247
   fear of making, 248, 256, 302
   importance of in therapy, 302
   realization of in therapy, 161, 167, 172
   strengthening – adult work, 321

clay
   & anger – working with, 277
   & anger expression, 179, 224, 226, 231, 238
   & anxiety, 240, 241
   & body awareness, 321
   & child with bowel issues, 74
   & enactment of body pain, 277
   & sense of mastery, 73
   & the child in and out of reality, 291
   & the hyperactive child, 245
   & the quiet child, 251
   & the therapeutic use of fantasy, 26
   & the traumatized child, 267, 269
   & work with polarities in self, 172
   advantage of in play therapy, 231
   and touch, 120
   as cue to child's process, 81
   exercises for in therapy, 75-79, 81, 82, 172
   expanding repertoire with, 75
   in work with the encropetic child, 299

occasional fear of, 74
Plasticine, 83
therapist's use of, 84
use of at home, 180
use of in family work, 331
use of in therapy sessions, 73
use of with fragile patient, 283
use of with the younger child, 82
collage
    & the quiet non-verbal child, 251
    & work with polarities in self, 172
    use of in child therapy, 87-90
color
    & the therapeutic use of drawing, 315, 320
    drawing a body sensation, 321
communication
    & the autistic child, 296
    & the therapeutic use of sound, 124, 126
    and the lonely child, 286
    and the withdrawn child, 253
    between therapist & child, 33, 49, 67
    characteristics of "good" communication, 331
    direct vs. indirect, 312
    dynamics in family, 313
    faulty communication in families, 331
    healthy – in families, 332
    indirect of sibling fights, 323
    lack of in children, 234
    speaking 'about' vs. 'to', 330

    therapeutic – of R. Gardner, 93
    working with in families, 330
computers, 123
contact
    & body awareness, 61
    & child in & out of reality, 290, 293
    & dreamwork, 158, 164
    & identification of feelings, 133
    & intuition (inner wisdom), 132
    & low self-esteem, 304
    & play-acting, 150, 151, 158
    & strong sense of self, 63, 281
    & the autistic child, 295, 296
    and re-owning of the ears, 124
    anger and loneliness, 290
    between teachers & children, 335
    between therapist & child, 67
    eye-contact in group setting, 137
    functions – loss of, 62
    functions – strengthening of, 64
    in the hyperactive child, 244
    restored – self & others, 63
    skills – parent's role in child's, 333
    skills in group therapy, 307
    skills of patient, 175
    therapist's observation of, 175, 180, 187, 198, 199
    with child in family therapy, 200, 204
    with environment, 122
    with forgotten memories, 300
    with the child within, 339

contact functions
   & child's sense of self, 63
   as common denominator of children needing therapy, 62
   impaired & need for therapy, 62
creative dramatics
   use of in therapy, 141, 149, 151, 155, 158
creativity
   & intuition (inner wisdom), 132
   & projection, 207
   in child – parental guidelines, 303
   in group therapy, 308
   play as diagnostic tool, 180
   stifled, 194
Dad
   Dad, 150
   distant – and child, 9, 150, 151, 176, 270
   in child's drawing, 29, 31, 37, 52, 59, 237
   revealed through clay work, 80, 84
   when parents fight, 280
depression
   in adolescents, 47
deprivation
   as theme of fairy tales, 102
development
   & learning disabled client, 141
   as revealed in child's art, 193
   early childhood, 401, 402
   healthy – & role of fantasy, 9
   healthy – and sexism, 340
   healthy – and water play, 243
   lags – as revealed in play, 157
   normal – restoring in therapy, 61
   play as essential to healthy, 174
distractible
   the distractible child, 189, 244
draw(ing)
   & anger expression, 227, 228, 230, 231, 233, 234, 277
   & body-awareness, 304, 309
   & deepening self-awareness, 317
   & feelings, 236
   & fire-setting child, 297
   & projection, 207
   & projection in therapy, 286
   & sense of self, 282
   & sensory experience, 120, 123, 124
   & the hanging-on child, 280
   & the hyperactive child, 240
   & the therapeutic use of music, 125, 128, 145
   & the therapeutic use of touch, 120
   & the withdrawn child, 250, 252, 254
   & therapeutic enactment, 158, 162, 163
   & therapist's modeling, 211
   & work with polarities in self, 171, 172
   and physical symptoms, 275, 276, 278
   and work with fear, 256, 257, 260, 261, 263, 264

Index

and work with trauma, 267, 268, 270
as diagnostic aid, 193, 202
Rosebush fantasy – use of, 315
strong vs. weak exercise, 315
therapist draws in session, 325
use of in children's therapy group, 292
use of in family therapy, 324
use of to reveal child's feelings about family life, 204, 325
use of with body image, 320
use of with fears, 322
use of with sexuality issues, 320

drawing
"my day, my week, my life", 48
& expression of feeling, 57
& fantasy work in therapy, 8, 11, 15, 17, 21, 23-26
& feeling, seeing, knowing, 58
& self expression, 57
& the fire-setting child, 297
& the therapeutic use of collage, 87, 88
& the therapeutic use of fantasy, 68-71
& the therapeutic use of poetry, 108, 109, 112
& the therapeutic use of puppets, 115, 118
& the therapeutic use of storytelling, 93
& therapeutic use of fantasy, 68-71
& use of color (s), 58
and painting, 52, 53

anger pictures, 45, 46
as metaphor for how child approaches life, 212
as starting place for work, 60
child's – and feelings, 8
group drawing, 50
making a statement about, 103
non specific & feelings, 49
of child's family, 29, 31, 59
Rosebush fantasy – use of, 34, 39
the Scribble – use of, 39, 43
the Squiggle – use of, 48
use of in group with delinquent teens, 315
ways of using in therapy, 71

dream
& memories, fantasies, 164
& the therapeutic use of clay, 82
& the therapeutic use of drama, 151
& the therapeutic use of drawing, 69
& the therapeutic use of poetry, 107, 113
& the therapeutic use of writing, 104
and journaling, 162
and sand tray work, 181, 184, 190
as message to child, 164
as symbol – Psychosythesis, 91
daydreaming in group, 312
function of for child, 163
in trauma work, 267
monsters in, 240

recurrent, 159
  working with in therapy, 158--160, 162-164
  working with very young children's, 163
education
  humanistic, 18
  physical – in schools, 142
empty chair technique
  therapeutic use of, 164-170, 234
enactment
  & dreamwork, 151
  and creative dramatics, 149, 151
  use of with sand tray work, 182, 185
  using with the fearful child, 177
encropesis
  the encropetic child, 274
energy
  and centering, 136
  and intuition, 132
  child's foreground and, 60
excessive pleasing, 279
fairy tales
  & the myth of happiness, 289
  therapeutic use of, 99, 101, 102
family
  "Experiential Family Therapy" of W. Kempler, 330
  & child's poor self esteem, 81, 280, 286, 287
  & the adolescent in therapy, 313
  & the foster child, 229
  & the hanging-on child, 53
  & the hyperactive child, 242
  & the therapeutic use of clay, 80, 82
  & the therapeutic use of collage, 89, 90
  & the therapeutic use of drawing, 30, 50, 69, 70
  & the therapeutic use of dreaming, 159
  & the therapeutic use of fantasy, 132
  & the therapeutic use of music, 127
  & the therapeutic use of storytelling, 101
  & the therapeutic use of the phone, 132
  & use of projective tests, 190
  advice & suggestions to vs. therapy, 333
  and child's fear of burglars, 258
  and the withdrawn child, 251, 252
  child's fear of family session, 328
  children's drawings of, 27, 29, 33, 59
  divorce and the child, 270
  dysfunctional & individuality, 332
  dysfunctional families, 332
  evaluating functioning of client's family, 329
  improving communication in, 330
  initial sessions with, 327
  interruptions, questions & gossip in dysfunctional, 330

Index

Kempler's requirements for fruitful family interviews, 330
lack of communication in, 234
members communicating in, 314
of the bedwetting child, 271--273
of the fearful child, 263, 267, 268
of the four to five-year-old client, 324
patterns of relating in, 329
seeing child as unique, 332
sessions w. young child, 324
sessions with family of child client, 328
systems – importance of, 66
talking about vs. talking to, 330
teaching members to speak directly to each other, 330
therapist as eyes/ears for, 331
therapy, 48
therapy – initial sessions, 200, 201, 204, 224
therapy of W. Kempler, 329, 330
use of drawings in session, 30
when to see family of scapegoated client, 327, 328
family drawings
   & family members as symbols or animals, 27
   as a Projective Test, 190
fantasy
   "Rosebush"– discussion of, 34
& body-awareness, 134, 304
& intuition (inner wisdom), 132
& lost feeling of aliveness, 145
& low self esteem, 301
& resitance – dealing with in therapy, 211
& specific problem behaviors, 253
& the quiet non-verbal child, 251
& the therapeutic use of drama, 151
& the therapeutic use of drawing, 1, 3, 8, 21, 54, 68, 69
& the therapeutic use of dreaming, 163
& the therapeutic use of music, 128
& the therapeutic use of puppets, 116
& therapeutic use of dreaming, 164
and group sculpture, 86
and integration of 'real life', 211
and lying as means of survival, 10
and misunderstood feelings of child, 10
and Tarot cards, 91
as a tension releaser, 136
as substitution for reality, 10
child's life process parallels fantasy process, 9
child's retreat into, 10
fear and anxiety, 261, 274

guided – to reveal source of specific problem behaviors, 257
how to accustom child to, 11, 12
images & client articulation, 321
in parent/child group, 331
in the adolescent child, 313
material for teenagers, 18, 315
materials – different kinds of, 11
therapist's use of, 1, 3, 60, 67, 211
use of w. Rorschach Cards, 191
use of with delinquent teens, 315
use of with polarities of feeling, 8
value of in the growth & development of children, 9
vs. lying, 10
work with body image, 320
work with sexuality, 318
fantasy-drawing
  use of in therapy, 3
fear
  & anger, 238
  & body-awareness, 144
  & fairy tales, 102
  & projection, 208
  & resistance – as protection, 213
  & sibling rivalry, 158
  & the hyperactive child, 240
  & the loner child, 284, 288
  & the therapeutic use of clay, 73, 74, 79
  & the therapeutic use of drama, 115, 236
  and aggression, 223
  and child's need to survive, 62
  and low self-esteem, 302
  and lying or fantasy, 10, 11
  and the withdrawn child, 248, 253, 255
  as a childhood memory, 322
  as inhibitor of choice, 64
  as revealed by body cues, 59
  breathing exercises and, 140
  child's fear of family session, 328
  in the adolescent child, 313, 320
  in the foster child, 283
  of abandonment, 53, 177, 215
  of accidents and death, 268
  of drowning, 275
  of growing up, 264, 265
  of planes, 177
  of small child in big world, 326
  of the therapist, 204
  sharing of in group therapy, 160
  types of/working with, 255-257, 259-263
  use of massage with, 243
  working with the child's, 227
feeling words
  therapeutic use of, 134
feelings
  and body awareness, 134
  helping child connect with, 133
  helping child discriminate, 133
finger painting
  finger painting, 54, 65, 67, 70, 84, 295

Index

fire
    children who set fires, 33, 216, 223, 230, 297
fire
    and trauma, 184, 237
first session
    in child and family therapy, 59, 150, 199, 201, 204, 212, 224, 231, 249, 250, 254, 264, 272, 279, 286, 313, 324, 327, 328, 339
foot painting, 55, 56
free drawing
    & the therapeutic use of drawing, 51
game
    "Animal" of deMille, 11
    "Back off", 143
    "Fantasy Encounter" – Otto, 19
    "Statues", 145
    & getting kids to write, 106
    & sensory experience, 121, 125, 127
    & strengthening the self, 281-283
    & the child in and out of reality, 292
    and physical education, 142
    and the bed-wetting child, 273
    as awareness continuum, 134
    cheating in and low self-esteem, 301
    empty chair game, 167
    how one plays parallels how one lives, 143
    improvisational, 152
    in group therapy, 310
    movement games, 144
    roleplaying parent in group, 311
    therapist's participation in, 312
    to enhance muscle control, 141
    to enhance story telling, 103
    to explore sexuality in group, 319
    to help connect w/feelings, 133
    tug of war, 154
    use of in therapy, 150, 186-188, 202, 206, 211, 212, 224, 245
    use of phone w/therapist, 133
Gestalt
    'techniques' of Enright, 311
    family therapy of W. Kepner, 329
    unfinished, 165
group
    & foot painting, 55, 56
    & the hyperactive child, 242, 244
    & the quiet child, 251, 254
    & the therapeutic use of clay, 26, 75, 76, 78
    & the therapeutic use of collage, 50, 89, 90
    & the therapeutic use of drawing, 18, 21-23, 49, 50, 70, 242
    & the therapeutic use of fantasy, 1, 3, 5, 6, 12
    & the therapeutic use of games, 187, 188, 310

& the therapeutic use of music, 126, 129
& the therapeutic use of poetry, 109
& the therapeutic use of puppets, 114
& the therapeutic use of storytelling, 17, 247
& the therapeutic use of touch, 152
& the therapeutic use of writing, 109
& therapeutic enactment, 71, 82, 117, 150, 152, 154, 155, 157
& therapeutic use of CAT, 97
advantages of group work, 307
and issue of sexuality, 319, 320
and the "orange experience" exercise of George Brown, 285
and the lonely child, 290
as useful for contact skills, 307
benefits of for children, 290
children's interaction in, 312
drawing feelings in, 109
families and communication in, 234
Gestalt therapy techniques with, 311
group drawing in therapy group, 50
hyperkinetic children in, 141
importance of group process, 310
reducing tension in, 136
resistance in, 210, 213
rigidity vs. creativity in, 246, 247
role-playing in, 339
rules of engagement in, 312
safety, interest & acceptance in, 312
sharing secrets in, 106
sibling work as, 323
techniques and situations, 308
the "in & out of reality" child in, 292, 293
therapist's attention to individual in, 312
use of in psychotherapy, 307, 308
use of massage in, 121
use of theme work in, 309
use of to explore introjects, 311
value of to client, 316
when is therapist 'part of', 331
with children & their parents, 331
work vs. individual work, 307
work with adolescent females, 318
work with children of alcoholic fathers, 159
working with anger in, 228
group drawing, 51
group process
 'finishing time' as part of, 313
groups
 and the lonely child, 289
growth
 & survival in children, 62

Index

development of symptoms for survival of child, 62
guilt
  and lying, 109
  & anger – working with, 277, 296, 299
  & child's lying/fantasies, 10
  & the death of a pet, 267
  & the fire-setting child, 297, 298
  & the therapeutic use of drawing, 71
  and bowel control problem, 75
  and resentment, 208, 225, 296, 297
  and shame – working with, 300
  and the bed-wetting child, 272
  and the molested child, 236
  as projection – working with, 208
  between mother and child, 165
  existential – for being alive, 299
  working with feeling words, 134
  working with in dreamwork, 163
hanging on, 279-281
health
  emotional – and sexism, 340
hitting
  & the therapeutic use of games, 186
  & the therapeutic use of puppets, 116
  and anger – working with, 226, 227, 277, 325
  as presenting problem, 201, 224
  between siblings, 323, 324
  in group therapy with children, 312
  in the disturbed child, 186
  parent's hitting of child, 77
  working with – in therapy with children, 94
  working with young children's, 173, 201
hostility
  & aggression, 223
  & the disturbed child, 223
  & the therapeutic use of clay, 179
  and 'delinquent teenagers', 315
humor
  humor, 18, 67, 127, 157, 202, 274
hyperactive (behavior)
  & getting attention, 6
  & importance of choice, 247
  & loneliness, 284
  & the therapeutic use of fantasy, 9, 19
  & the therapeutic use of woodworking, 87, 245
  and avoidance of feelings, 239
  and diet, 239
  and massage, 243
  and tactile experience, 241, 243
  as a substitute for anger, 227
  as means of survival, 62
  children – as a style of being, 247
  enhancing self support in, 246

increasing child's awareness of by "going with" behavior, 243
increasing self awareness in hyperactive children, 245
label – misapplied to kids, 240
symptoms disappear in therapy office, 241
therapist approach to, 241
working with in therapy, 238
identification
   (owning) & therapeutic use of fantasy, 38, 60
   group members identify with individual as in Greek drama, 309
illness
   & bodily restriction, 139
   & doctor/patient roleplay, 173
   & emotional trauma, 196, 265, 269
   & loneliness, 287
   & need for therapy, 196
imagination
   & intuition, 132
   & resistance, 210
   & the therapeutic use of collage, 89
   & the therapeutic use of drama, 11, 151
   & the therapeutic use of fantasy, 11
   & the therapeutic use of play, 180
   & the therapeutic use of song, 127
   of the therapist, 65
imaginative play, 11
improvisation
   & body movement and awareness, 141
   & the therapeutic use of body movement, 141
   & the therapeutic use of drama, 141, 150, 152, 155
   dramatics and play, 174
   in games, activities and experiences for therapy, 152, 155
insecurity
   & the therapeutic use of drawing, 202
   and breathing, 140
   and child's process in drawing, 201
   and destructive behavior, 223
   in the child client, 279
introject (introjection)
   as therapeutic issue, 311, 313, 322, 323, 339
intuition, xiv, 131, 328
isolation
   & anti-social behavior, 288
   & existential loneliness, 287
   & the withdrawn child, 253
   as theme of fairy tales, 102
   of family members, 331
   of the ignored child, 290
   of the poorly adjusted child, 287
   overcoming in group, 4
learning disabilities, 65, 66
   and body movement in therapy, 141
   and the hyperactive child, 239

Index

loneliness
  & 'poorly adjusted' child, 287
  & acting out, 183
  & fear of rejection, 284
  & sentance completion exercise, 105
  & the anti-social child, 288
  & the quest for happiness, 289
  & the Rosebush exercise, 37
  & the the therapeutic use of play, 175
  & the therapeutic use of collage, 90
  & the therapeutic use of drawing, 4, 8, 37, 69
  & the therapeutic use of fairy tales, 102
  & the therapeutic use of puppets, 117
  & use of Rosebush fantasy, 283
  & work with "feeling words", 134
  acceptance of, 287
  and parental separation, 270, 287
  and self identity, 288
  as a by-product of poor adjustment, 287
  as a condition of human life, 287
  as existential condition, 287, 288
  as result of angry feelings, 228
  as revealed in CAT(Children's Apperception Test) Rabbit, 215
  as revealed in sand tray work, 181
  escaping pain of, 288
  existential & self awareness, 288
  fear of in children, 288
  helplessness, & anxiety, 289
  importance of addressing in therapy, 287
  in books and fairy tales, 100
  of the misunderstood child, 290
  therapy as antidote, 290
  therapy with lonely children, 287
  vs. self acceptance, 290
  vs. therapist's understanding, 290
  ways of expressing, 289
  working with the child's, 287
lying
  and fantasy – intertwined, 10
  as a result of parents' behavior, 10
  as inability to cope, 10
  as means of survival to child, 10
  to parents as self-protection, 109
magic
  as part of drawing exercise, 71
  child's wish to be, 35, 36, 41, 100
  in books and fairy tales, 102
  slate – in therapy, 212, 325
  tricks in therapy, 188, 189, 204, 212
  wand in therapy, 19, 155

meditation
   & children in therapy, 137
   & the bedwetting child, 273
   and centering – bringing one back to one's self, 138
   how to, 138
   seeing & drawing as meditation (F. Franck), 123
memory
   role of in therapy, 75, 77, 158, 257, 261, 266, 274, 300, 308
   use of first memories in adolescent girl's group, 318, 319
modeling, 211
monster(s)
   in therapy, 44, 52, 69, 99, 154, 156, 163, 206, 225, 240, 258-260, 264
music
   use of in therapy, 49, 69, 77, 101, 113, 125-127, 129, 132, 137, 145, 147, 210, 243
my working model (Dr. Oaklander's), 57
pain
   & body-awareness, 275
   & guilt, resentment, shame, 299
   & loneliness, 288
   & the therapeutic use of drawing, 70, 277
   & therapeutic enactment, 151, 277
   abdominal & the encropetic child, 274
   of the adolescent, 253
   tensing muscles to avoid, 277

working with in therapy, 299
painting
   & the therapeutic use of collage, 87
   art techniques – use of in therapy, 19, 52-54, 57, 65, 68, 70, 120, 203, 206, 224, 232, 237, 261, 283, 287, 291, 295
   finger painting, 54
paradoxical theory of change of A. Beisser, 303
physical symptoms
   working with in therapy, 45, 198, 256, 271, 275
pictures
   & anger – working with, 45, 228
   & feelings, 8
   & normal development of children's art, 193
   & scribble technique, 40, 43
   & strengthening client's intuition, 132
   & the child in and out of reality, 292
   & the hyperactive child, 244
   & the scribble technique, 49
   & the therapeutic use of collage, 88
   & the therapeutic use of storytelling, 93, 97
   & the therapeutic use of TAT, 190
   & the therapeutic use of The Hand Test, 191
   & therapeutic use of CAT, 97

& work with delinquent teens, 315
and body awareness, 320
and child's fears, 261, 267
and physical symptoms, 252
and the bed-wetting child, 273
and the Squiggle Game, 49
as means of giving child a voice, 325
as projective techniques, 19
therapeutic use of, 57, 60, 90, 91
use of in children's therapy group, 309
use of in family therapy, 30, 235, 331
use of in group therapy, 320
use of to increase sensory awareness, 120

play therapy
    & family therapy, 324
    & older children, 178
    & use of costumes, 156
    play therapy, 173
    teaching parents how to use, 177
    therapist's use of, 175

poetry
    & the therapeutic use of drawing, 71
    & the therapeutic use of fantasy, 11
    & the therapeutic use of storytelling, 93
    and songs – use of in therapy, 113

how to get children to write, 107
in work with adolescents, 320
therapeutic use of, 43, 69, 93, 106-109, 111, 112, 143, 320

polarities
    & the therapeutic use of dreaming, 164
    and The Taylor Johnson Temperament Analysis, 191
    Gestalt therapy work with, 165
    helping child reconcile, 79
    in dreams – therapeutic work with, 164
    therapeutic use of, 69, 105
    working with in therapy with children, 171

pre-adolescents
    & the therapeutic use of the Scribble technique, 39

projection
    & the therapeutic use of dreaming, 159
    child's story as, 93
    therapeutic use of, 207, 208, 211, 230
    therapeutic use of in group, 310

projective technique, 286, 315, 321, 339, 383, 384, 393, 394
projective tests, 93, 189, 314

Psychosynthesis
    & work with polarities in self, 172

psychotherapy
    & child's anger and fear, 223
    & parental divorce, 269, 270

with children – use of magic, 189
punishment
  & bed-wetting, 272
  as cause of lying, 109
  self-punishment & seizures in child, 277
puppet
  therapeutic use of, 7, 93, 103, 113-118, 156, 157, 163, 170, 174, 206, 208, 211, 232, 234, 274
  use of in family work, 178
reality
  & the distractible child, 244
  & the therapeutic use of dreams, 158
  child who is in and out of, 290, 292
  orientation of child – diagnosis of, 180
  vs. lying or fantasizing, 10, 68
relaxation
  & child with bowel issues, 75
  and body movement in therapy, 245, 304
  and use of puzzles, 188
  as means to increase body awareness, 245, 304
  as sign of closure, 165
  use of in therapy, 135, 136
resistance
  & the therapeutic use of drawing, 7
  & the therapeutic use of games, 187, 188
  & the therapeutic use of play, 180
  & the therapeutic use of puppets, 114
  and fear, 211
  as cue to client's needs, 66
  as revealed by projection, 208
  in early stage of therapy, 212
  in group therapy, 211
  plateaus in therapy as sign of, 214
  to use of clay in therapy, 74
  to writing in therapy, 103
  working with in therapy with children, 210-213
role-playing
  as projective technique, 339
  enactment techniques, 70, 156, 176, 311
sand tray
  & 'pre-deliquent' child, 7
  & in & out of reality child, 291
  & projective tests, 190
  & the death of a parent, 270
  & the hanging-on child, 280, 283
  & the lonely child, 287
  & the quiet child, 251, 253
  & the therapeutic use of dreaming, 163
  & the therapeutic use of play, 174
  & the therapeutic use of storytelling, 93
  child's use of in therapy, 180, 181, 183

therapist's use of, 175, 184
toys and equipment for, 186, 188
use in initial sessions, 202
use of in trauma work, 184
schools
and the needs of children, 334
Scribble technique
& anger, 45
& movement therapy, 144
& the child with guilt feelings, 297
& the therapeutic use of drawing, 70
& the therapeutic use of poetry, 107
& therapeutic work with anger, 233, 237, 261
& therapeutic work with body pain, 275
& therapist's modeling, 211
as means to free-up client, 144
uses of, 39, 42, 43
self support
& body awareness, 143
development of in therapy, 48
self worth
development of in therapy, 26
self-concept, 300
self-esteem, 301
& communication skills, 234
in the withdrawn child, 301
signs of low self-esteem in children, 301
self-expression, 282, 287, 330

sense of self
& body awareness, 139
& tasks of therapist, 63, 64
& the clinging child, 281
& the hyperactive child, 245
& therapist's touch, 243
lost – through introjections, 63
regaining, 63
strength of, 24, 211
strength of & contact, 61, 62
strength of & use of clay, 74
senses
& body awareness in group setting, 308
& the therapeutic use of clay, 73
& the therapeutic use of play-acting, 151
and healthy sense of self, 61
and intuition, 131
body movement as, 138
in healthy development, 61
of the infant, 61
regaining – & low self-esteem, 304
regaining – in the hyperactive child, 296
regaining in therapy, 64, 119
regaining lost self awareness, 63
types – working with in therapy, 119
working with sight, 124
sensory experience
& regaining sense of self, 119, 120
& the therapeutic use of collage, 89

& the therapeutic use of dough, 84
as amalgam of senses, 131
use of in therapy, 65
sex-role stereotypes, 248
sexism
  and the growth of children, 340, 341
siblings
  working with in therapy, 79, 323, 327
sight
  sensory experience and healthy development, 119, 121, 131, 151, 152, 244
smell
  sensory experience and healthy development, 61, 62, 100, 119, 130, 131, 151, 153, 285
social interaction, 247
song
  & learning impaired children, 130
  lyrics & their impact, 127
  therapeutic use of, 113, 124
  use of with aphasic children, 126
sound
  sensory experience and healthy development, 61, 119, 124, 131, 151, 153, 244
  use of in therapy, 124, 125, 128, 129, 137, 291, 295
special education, 55, 87
specific problem behaviors, 221, 326

storytelling
  & fantasy work in therapy, 11
  & the therapeutic use of drama, 157
  & work with polarities in self, 172
  mutual storytelling technique of Gardiner, 93
  mutual storytelling using puppets, 116
  use of in therapy, 93, 96, 99, 116
stress
  & anger – working with, 274
  and divorce, 269
  child's – and the need for therapy, 265
symbols
  'visualize your world', 68
  & drawings of families, 27, 29, 31
  & strengthening intuition, 132
  & the therapeutic use of clay, 82
  & the therapeutic use of drawing, 69, 71
  Assagioli's categories of, 91
  in projective tests, 190
  use of – in empty chair work, 165
  use of – working with fear, 260
taste
  & healthy infant development, 61, 119, 123
  & sensory awareness, 130, 132, 151

& the therapeutic use of drama, 151, 153
exploring in therapy, 285
teachers
and the needs of children, 334, 335
teasing
behavior in children, 170, 237, 299
temper tantrums, 133, 235, 251, 326
termination, 214, 216, 219, 326
therapeutic process
with children, xv, 51, 57, 189, 205, 208, 287
with children and adolescents, 207
therapy process, 195, 207
& the therapeutic use of games, 187
and diagnosis, 193
touch
& healthy infant development, 61
& sibling rivalry, 77
& the hyperactive child, 243
& the therapeutic use of clay, 81
& the therapeutic use of dough, 84
& the therapeutic use of drawing, 71
and body movement, 138
as contact function, 62, 73
as sensory experience, 89, 90, 100, 119, 120, 124, 132, 151, 152

massage & concentration, 243
massage & the hyperactive child, 243
of others vs. being alone, 146
trauma
& stress, 265
& the therapeutic use of costumes in play therapy, 156
& the therapeutic use of massage, 243
& therapeutic enactment, 156
and divorce, 269
and over-protective parents, 261
therapy work with, 265, 267
very young children
& the therapeutic use of dreaming, 163
& the therapeutic use of the sand tray, 185
and suicidal thoughts, 289
and the therapeutic process, 324
special techniques for, 155, 176, 177
specific issues of working with, 324
voice
as cue for therapist, 81, 125, 164, 176, 182, 253, 261, 291
child's – as cue to child's issues, 59
giving voice to – in therapy, 4, 7, 22, 23, 114, 115, 151, 165, 232, 236, 240, 252, 311
of the Topdog, 165
of the Underdog, 166

water
    fear of, 257
withdrawn children
    & divorce, 204
    & physical holding in, 248
    & the therapeutic use of play, 150
    and hidden fears, 256
    and low self-esteem, 301
    as isolated children, 253
    as lonely children, 284
    as message to environment – "acting out", 222
    as symptom of girls vs. boys, 248
    breathing and, 250
    difficulty of working with, 224
    misdiagnosis of, 192
    parent/child interaction in, 200
    therapy with the withdrawn child, 248, 250, 253, 256, 301
    use of expressive techniques with, 250
    withdrawal as a use of power, 249
worry
    & child's fears, 264
    & the bed-wetting child, 272
    and separation anxiety, 261
    as hindrance to experiencing, 121, 122
    as revealed in dreams, 163
    as the presenting problem in child, 327
    giving voice to – in therapy, 23
    in parents – impact on the child, 265
writing
    & the bed-wetting child, 273
    & the therapeutic use of collage, 87
    & the therapeutic use of drawing, 52, 68, 71
    & the therapeutic use of poetry, 106, 107, 109, 112
    & the therapeutic use of storytelling, 93, 103
    child's reluctance to write, 104
    exercise – answering "who am I?" question, 172
    therapeutic use of, 11, 15, 103–106
    use of with anger, 227
    ways to encourage – child's personal notebook, 104
    ways to encourage – guided exercises for, 105

Made in the USA
Monee, IL
25 April 2026

48998714R00252